BASIC
ECONOMICS
SECOND EDITION

BASIC SECOND EDITION
ECONOMICS

JAMES A. DYAL · NICHOLAS KARATJAS

Indiana University of Pennsylvania

MACMILLAN PUBLISHING COMPANY
NEW YORK
COLLIER MACMILLAN PUBLISHERS
LONDON

Macmillan Publishing Company
866 Third Avenue, New York, New York 10022

Collier Macmillan Canada, Inc.

LIBRARY OF CONGRESS CATALOGING-IN-PUBLICATION DATA

Dyal, James A. (James Alan)
    Basic economics / James A. Dyal, Nicholas Karatjas. — 2nd ed.
        p.   cm.
    Includes index.
    ISBN 0-02-331211-4
    1. Economics.   I. Karatjas, Nicholas.   II. Title.
HB171.5.D88   1990
    330 — dc20   89-8032
                                                                CIP

Printing: 1 2 3 4 5 6 7 8   Year: 9 0 1 2 3 4 5 6 7 8

BOOK TEAM:
Acquisition Editor: Ken MacLeod
Production Supervisor: Jennifer Carey
Production Manager: Alan Fischer
Text Designer: Patrice Fodero
Cover Designer: Patrice Fodero
Cover 3-D illustration: Brad Lehrer
Illustrations: ECL Art Associates

This book was set in 10/12 Caslon by Progressive Typographers, Inc., printed and bound by Arcata Graphics/Halliday.
The cover was printed by Phoenix Color Corp.

Preface

The overall objectives of *Basic Economics* are to interest students in economics, to give them a foundation for a better understanding of how the economy operates, and to provide the tools for analyzing current economic issues in a systematic fashion. We designed the textbook for students who are not majoring in economics or business and who are taking a one-semester course in economics as a general education elective or are in fields just beginning to require basic economics (such as elementary and secondary education, labor relations, public administration, and social work).

The traditional core of economic theory is presented in a manner that is balanced in its coverage and written in a style that is concise, interesting, and easy for the student to comprehend. The text is up-to-date in presenting issues and applications. We made an effort to provoke the student's imagination by raising pertinent questions that continue to be controversial and by applying theory to current issues headlining the news. To give the instructor a wider choice in designing the course, we provide a broad selection of short application chapters immediately following the core chapters. The text also presents in appendices those concepts that we deem significant but secondary in importance, thereby giving the instructor an even greater ability to select the topics to be covered.

Organization of Topics

The organization of core chapters in the text follows a traditional format. Part One presents introductory concepts with an emphasis on the methodology used by economists. Basic institutions associated with the private market and mixed economy are also described. Upon completion of this introduction, the instructor may choose to proceed to either Part Two or Part Three, each of which is independent of the other.

Part Two is the microeconomic section of the text. It stresses the underlying behavior of the product and factor markets in determining prices, production, and the allocation of economic resources. The emphasis is on the polar extremes of pure competition and pure monopoly. The production and employment models of the firm, the guiding principles of profit maximization, and overall market behavior are examined at a level appropriate for a one-semester course. This section concludes with a discussion of the economic role of government in a mixed economy, public finance, benefit-cost analysis, and the problems of public choice.

Part Three covers macroeconomics, beginning with an examination of national income accounting. Keynesian demand-oriented business cycle analysis is presented, followed by a discussion of fiscal policy. Next, money and banking, including the most recent changes in banking legislation, are discussed. Monetary policy is then explored and compared in effectiveness to fiscal policy, accompanied by an introduction to monetarism. The new aggregate supply/aggregate demand model is used to analyze macroeconomic problems, with an emphasis on production problems and the current concern with stagflation.

Part Four is a special feature of the book, designed to extend applications of theories discussed in the previous sections, as well as to provide a more in-depth treatment of topics that should be especially interesting to students. This section consists of ten very brief chapters, each about half the average length of the core chapters. The following topics are covered: comparative economic systems, health, higher education, the environment, the farm problem, government regulation, poverty, international finance, unions, and the relevance of economics to nonmajors. These special topics can be integrated with the core material throughout the semester, or held back until the end of the semester to show students how economic analysis applies to many different current issues. The book concludes with an extensive glossary, a data appendix, and an index.

Special Features

Our text has many special features designed to make it easier for the student to learn, and for the instructor to teach.

Level and Approach: Both of us have taught one-semester courses in Basic Economics every semester for more than ten years. We sought to write a text that would have the flexibility to meet the needs of our students, while providing a balance both in terms of the level of difficulty and the topics covered. On several occasions we team-taught the course. The interaction we experienced in teaching the course together has helped us to gain a common perspective on the problems normally encountered in teaching the one-semester course in economics and to blend our ideas in writing the text. Students will have a reasonably easy time reading the text. Equally important, students will not feel that their intelligence is being insulted. To maintain student interest, we have provided a large number of examples that are not easily outdated and that students can readily understand in terms of their own experience. These applications are fully integrated with the main body of the text.

Flexibility: The flexibility of the text permits the instructor to emphasize a theoretical or an applications approach, using either a lecture or discussion/seminar format. The instructor may choose to emphasize theory by covering the first twelve chapters with occasional reference to the special topics chapters. Alternatively, he or she might prefer to emphasize the applications approach by assigning some of the core chapters and most of the special topics. The text is suitable for instructors who use the lecture format, with parts of the book assigned primarily as reference material. The special topics and questions at the end of each chapter make the text attractive to instructors who use the discussion format.

Self-Test Questions/Answers: At the end of each core chapter is a self-test composed of true and false questions. Solutions to these questions, with a brief explanation of the reasoning, are included. These self-test questions and answers enable students to evaluate their understanding of the material.

Problems: To reinforce analytical skills and important economic concepts, students are provided with a set of problems to solve at the end of each core chapter. Solutions to these problems are included in the instructor's manual.

Discussion Questions: Discussion questions at the end of each chapter should be helpful as a basis for stimulating class discussion and enhancing the theories presented in the text.

Inserts: Each core chapter contains a boxed insert that summarizes a news article from such sources as *Business Week, The New York Times,* and *The Wall Street Journal.* The articles we excerpted were chosen to relate real-life problems to economic theory and to maintain the highest possible level of student interest.

Key Concepts: The most important concepts are highlighted in boldface throughout the text. They are also listed at the end of each chapter to help the student review the material.

Objectives and Summaries: Each chapter begins with a list of objectives and ends with a summary to help the student gain an overview of the major topics and to reinforce essential concepts.

Appendices: Appendices at the end of six of the core chapters cover concepts that we feel are significant but only secondary in importance. We believe that this approach provides the instructor with the flexibility to better design the course to suit his or her own needs. The material in the appendices may be included in or excluded from the course content with no loss of continuity.

Supplemental Materials: In addition to the pedagogical aids presented in the text, we have developed a student study guide. This guide reviews material in a number of different ways designed to maintain student interest and to reinforce major concepts. Each chapter provides a detailed outline of topics, fill-in-the-blanks, multiple choice and true/false questions, crossword puzzles, problems, and answers. The package also includes a computerized test bank to accompany the instructor's manual — both contain 1,500 multiple choice and true/false questions.

New to this Edition

- Includes the new aggregate supply/demand model to more fully demonstrate how production problems contribute to unemployment and inflation.

- Expands the discussion of the production decision of the purely competitive firm and long-run competitive market behavior. In addition, a new appendix covers monopolistic competition and oligopoly for instructors who want to emphasize microeconomic principles.

- Includes a more in-depth discussion of public goods.

- Expands the graphic analysis of the appendix of the simplified Keynesian model to include the tables used within the main body of Chapter 9. A new appendix to Chapter 10 graphically illustrates the use of fiscal policy.

- Provides two new special topics on comparative economic systems and the relevance of economics to nonmajors.

- Expands the discussion of the impact of unemployment and inflation on the economy.

- Updates all data used within the text and reflects the most recent changes in real-world problems such as the stock market crash of 1987, an overview of the new federal tax law, and changes in the international money market.

- Provides a data appendix at the end of the text to provide easy access to statistics that complement topics discussed throughout the book. References to these data are made within the text where appropriate.

- Provides an enhanced computerized test generator.

- Expands the test bank to include 600 new items.

- Includes problem sets at the end of each core chapter with solutions provided in the instructor's manual.

- Reorganizes and simplifies material where appropriate to make the textbook more effective.

Acknowledgments

We would like to express our appreciation to Robert J. Stonebraker, a colleague at Indiana University of Pennsylvania, for providing us with many valuable suggestions that improved this text. In addition, we wish to gratefully acknowledge the advice given to us by the following reviewers: Clay Smith, Stark Technical College; John Megan, Milwaukee Area Technical College; Mark G. Johnson, Lakeland Community College; Reuben E. Slesinger, University of Pittsburgh; Roger L. Adkins, Marshall University; Fred Arnold, Madison Area

Technical College; Jeffrey P. Ryan, McHenry County College; Terry L. Riddle, Central Virginia Community College; Howard M. Wilhelm, James Madison University.

We would like to express our gratitude to our production editors, Jennifer Carey and Anna Halasz, who kept us to a tight schedule during the final phase of this project. Our list of acknowledgments would not be complete without mention of our wives, Gloria and Susan, who provided valuable editorial assistance. Without their patience, support, and understanding, this book would never have been completed. We also appreciate the feedback that we received from many of our students who used preliminary drafts of our manuscript as their textbook in Basic Economics.

J. D.
N. K.

Dedication

To my wife, Gloria, my mother, Marguerite, my children, Jeffrey and Jimmy, and the memory of my father, Tom.

J.D.

To my wife, Susan, my parents, Manuel and Katherine, and my children, Andrew and Pamela.

N.K.

Brief Contents

PART ONE

Introduction

PART TWO

Microeconomics

PART THREE

Macroeconomics

PART FOUR

Special Topics

Detailed Contents

PART THREE
MACROECONOMICS

PART
ONE
Introduction

Introduction to Economics

Objectives

Upon completion of this chapter, you should understand:

1.   Why economics is the science of choice.

2.   The role of theories and models in economic thinking.

3.   The variety of issues studied by economists.

4.   Why the study of economics is important.

5.   How to use tables and graphs.

- Should I go to college?

- When should I get married?

- Should I have children?

- How much time should I spend studying for my exam next week?

What are these questions doing in an economics text? They all involve choices, and economics is the *science of choice*. In deciding how many hours to study for an exam, a student must consider all the possible options. "Economic thinking" examines the benefits and costs of these options. For example, suppose your options for the next 2 hours are studying or sleeping. Since time is scarce, you won't be able to do both. You must *choose*. Which is the most beneficial or the least costly? If you choose to study, you lose the opportunity to sleep. (Economists refer to this as an opportunity cost.) But if you sleep, you lose the opportunity to study. The decision-making process involved here is similar to that used in determining how much the United States should spend on defense, how much new machinery a business should buy, or whether a person should go to college.

Economics is interesting because of its many applications. It will help you to understand how decisions are made through an examination of alternatives, which is accomplished by weighing the extra cost of a decision to do something against the extra benefit to be received. A careful study of economics will develop the ability to analyze questions in an orderly manner.

The purpose of this chapter is to prepare you for your study of economic theory and its many uses. We begin by describing economics and a wide variety of issues studied by economists. Next, the role of theories and models in economics is examined. Finally, we review how to read and construct graphs, since economists frequently use them to illustrate their ideas.

1.1 Economics

Economics is a social science that studies the principles governing the allocation of scarce resources among alternative uses in order to maximize the satisfaction of unlimited wants. To better understand this statement, let's break the definition of economics into its component parts.

First, economics is a *social science,* not a branch of business. Economists (like political scientists, sociologists, psychologists, and other social scientists) study the behavior of people and institutions. So in this text you will not learn the "nuts and bolts" needed to manage a business, or how to play the stock market. This is not to imply that economics is not important to persons in running their business affairs. The principles that we will study are essential to all economic decision makers, including the heads of corporations and households who are hoping to make a fortune in buying and selling stock.

Second, as a social science, the primary focus of economics is on the behavior of firms and households as they interact in the millions of markets scattered across our nation. How does our market system allocate our resources throughout the economy in order to produce those goods most valued by society? Since our resources are scarce and we have unlimited wants, we must make choices. Reread the above definition of economics, noting the phrase *the allocation of scarce resources among alternative uses.* What this phrase means is that every time we use resources to produce more of one good, these resources are not available to produce other goods. Economists call this tradeoff an *opportunity cost.* For example, the opportunity cost of allocating more resources to produce additional military goods is the amount of civilian goods that we must give up.

Third, people tend to have unlimited wants, meaning that they generally desire to have more goods and services than they currently possess. The last phrase in our definition of economics — *to maximize the satisfaction of unlimited wants* — simply means that the ultimate goal of the economy is to produce those goods that make people as happy as possible.

Economics has been dubbed the "dismal science" because the fundamental problem studied by economists is that of scarcity. ***Scarcity*** will always exist because we have *unlimited wants* and *limited economic resources* with which to produce goods for satisfying these wants. People tend to want more and more goods and services. If they live in a mobile home, they may want to move to a two-story brick house in the suburbs. If they succeed in buying this dream house, they may then want to live in a penthouse in New York City overlooking Central Park.

Microeconomics Versus Macroeconomics

The study of economics is divided into microeconomics and macroeconomics. Part II of this book deals with microeconomics. ***Microeconomics*** is the study of the behavior of buyers and sellers in the market for a particular good (such as pizza) or for a specific resource (such as electricians). It is as though we use a "microscope" to view the behavior of individual decision makers. Topics such as how individual prices are determined and how employment decisions are made by households and firms are discussed. In Part III, macroeconomics is examined. ***Macroeconomics*** is the study of how the entire economy performs. In the study of the whole economy, we will use a "telescope" to examine the actions of *all* individuals and producers. Issues such as unemployment, inflation, and the business cycle are explored.

Positive Versus Normative Economics

Positive economics deals with questions of "what was, is, and will be." Positive economics is the primary concern of economists because it involves the development of economic theory that attempts to explain causal relationships such as why a decrease in overall spending in the economy creates unemployment. Positive economics is also used to explain the policy options available to reduce unemployment. For example, unemployment could be reduced by increasing total spending either through a reduction in taxes by the federal government or through attempts to increase the amount of loans made available by banks. If people buy more goods, firms will hire more workers in order to increase production.

Note that the actual policy chosen to increase spending is a part of normative economics because the decision involves value judgments. ***Normative economics*** deals with "what ought to be," and is an area of great controversy among economists. The role of the economist is to describe what policies are available and the implications of each policy choice (positive economics), but it is up to the general public to decide what policy is most desirable (normative economics).

1.2 Economic Issues

When we examine the allocation of resources, one goal is to combine these resources in such a way that we maximize production of the goods most valued by society. Also of concern is the way in which these goods are distributed among individuals.

Efficiency

The goal of achieving *efficiency* is important because of the problem of scarcity. Since resources are scarce, it is important that they not be wasted. Therefore, efficiency deals with the question of allocating resources to the most valuable use. Another question is which method of production will a producer choose? If the goal of a producer in a competitive market were to maximize profits, the producer would use the least costly means of production. If this firm were to use inefficient means of production, it would not earn as much as it could have earned using efficient means.

In addition, society is affected. From society's perspective people are obviously better off if resources are not being used inefficiently. If resources are being used efficiently, society can produce more with the same amount of resources and be better off.

Equity

Very simply, *equity* refers to fairness. Unlike efficiency, which can be measured using objective criteria, equity is subjective. Is it fair for some families to live in 20-room houses while others live on the streets? Is it reasonable for Patrick Ewing to earn over $3,000,000 a year playing basketball for the New York Knicks while others are in poverty? These are normative questions. What may seem fair to one person may not seem fair to another.

This is one area in which there is much disagreement among economists. But this should not surprise you. Students frequently disagree over many things. For example, what is a fair way of determining who will be able to live in campus housing? Should we just let those who are able to afford the highest rents get the most housing? That may not be fair to low-income students. Or should there be a lottery in which everyone has an equal chance of getting a room? That may not be fair to upperclass students, who feel they should have an advantage over those who have not been in school as long. No matter which method is employed, one group will probably feel wronged.

The same type of problem comes up when determining poverty status. Most people agree that it is desirable to provide aid to families that are poor. The problem is to define criteria to categorize the poor. Is income an appropriate measure of well-being? If so, what is the cutoff—the amount below which a family is considered to be in poverty? In addition, how much should be provided for housing, food, medical care, clothing, and so on? As you can imagine, these are very difficult questions to answer. It is no wonder that there is disagreement over the proposed solutions.

Tradeoffs

Finally, making matters even more complex, there may be *tradeoffs* between efficiency and equity. The most efficient allocation of resources may not result in a distribution of income that is deemed fair by society. If this occurs, society may decide to redistribute income. In the United States, this redistribution is done primarily through government.

An example of a possible tradeoff between efficiency and equity occurs when a firm moves from one area to another because of the lower costs of production (e.g., lower wages, energy costs, and taxes). Not only will the firm benefit by moving, but society will benefit as well from the increased efficiency. The firm will be able to produce more goods at a lower cost, contributing to national economic growth. However, there is a possible problem of equity. The firm's move to one community will benefit it in the form of increased employment opportunities, income, and tax revenue. The community that has lost the firm bears a cost in the form of fewer job opportunities, lower income, and a lost tax base.

From the firm's perspective the move is desirable. However, what is the overall impact of this redistribution of resources on society? Since one community is benefiting and the other community is suffering, we cannot conclude that the move is equitable. If the move of the firm is deemed to be unfair, then government can cushion the damage to the community with programs such as job training, unemployment compensation, and tax relief.

1.3 Theories and Models

In order to explain the behavior of various decision makers, economists build ***models.*** These models are simplifications of reality that enable economists to predict change and to examine the structure of the economy. In this section we examine the method of reasoning behind model building.

How Economists Develop and Use Models

Economists use the ***scientific method*** to examine the behavior of households and firms. This approach, common to the physical sciences, involves the formulation of questions about the relationships between different *variables* and the collection of observations for testing. For example, a chemist might speculate about the effect of a certain chemical (e.g., dioxin) on fish. Through repeated experiments in the laboratory, the chemist might be able to find evidence that supports or refutes the hypothesis that dioxin is harmful to fish. If the data support the hypothesis, the chemist might propose a ***theory*** which states that these results tend to apply whenever fish come in contact with the chemical. A theory is a general statement of principles presented to explain phenomena.

Economists use the scientific method to construct models and to test hypotheses about the relationships between economic variables. One difference between the physical sciences and economics lies in the ability to test the performance of models. Economists do not have access to the types of laboratories that chemists, physicists, and biologists use, and therefore are unable to run controlled experiments.

For example, if we want to examine how people alter their purchases of Diet Coke when its price changes, we will have to make sure that we are able to isolate the effect of this variable on their behavior. In the lab, when a scientist wants to examine the effect of increased marijuana consumption on the ability of a rat to solve a maze, the scientist can control the items that influence the subject. On the other hand, economists cannot confine consumers, change the price of Diet Coke, and then observe how the consumers respond in the market. In addition, economists cannot control other variables (such as income, the price of other brands of diet soda, and the effect of advertising). Other ways of proving or disproving the hypothesis must be found. Imagine an economist calling up the Pepsi-Cola Company and asking it to keep its prices and advertising constant so that the economist can examine the effect of a price drop of Diet Coke on the amount of Diet Coke consumed.

The models that economists formulate and use for evaluating the performance of the economy and predicting future change aid in the decision-making process of policymakers. These models enable decision makers to cope with change, because even though these representations may not allow us to predict future behavior with certainty, they can be a reasonable gauge of future changes.

There are five basic steps in the modeling process that economists use. First, the problem to be examined must be identified and clearly described. Second, the relationship between two or more observed phenomena, called a hypothesis, is stated. Third, the technique used to test the hypothesis must be determined. Through the use of a variety of statistical procedures, economists are able to determine whether or not a particular hypothesis is valid. The fourth step is the collection of data. Data may already be available, or the researcher may have to collect new data. (See the Appendix at the end of this book for some examples of economic data and their sources.) Finally, the data are analyzed and the hypothesis is accepted, rejected, or judgment is reserved for more conclusive tests. Many of the models developed by economists require the use of computers to deal with the large volume of data and the complex mathematical operations used in the analysis. However, the difficulty in verifying theories is a major source of disagreement among economists. Before ending this section, let us examine two traps that prevent clear thinking in economics.

Traps in Economic Thinking

Ideally, people like to analyze problems in a logical manner. However, thinking logically must be *learned* — it is difficult to do without some training. People may feel that they are "thinking logically" about an issue, yet be subject to one or more flaws in their reasoning.

There are two common traps in economic thinking. The first is the ***fallacy of composition.*** It states that what is true for one person is necessarily true for everyone. For example,

Why Is the Study of Economics Important?

Many benefits can be gained from studying economics. First, economics deals with vital current problems such as inflation, unemployment, monopoly, economic growth, pollution, and poverty. Economics is a problem-oriented social science, and the problems with which it is especially concerned are among the most disturbing of our age. They fill our newspapers and pervade our politics. We like to be knowledgeable about a part of society that so many feel is important. Not only is economics relevant to the big problems of society, but it also relates to personal problems — wages, unemployment, the cost of living, taxes, and so on.

Second, the accomplishments of economics have established it as the most successful social science. For example, yours is the first generation never to have experienced a major depression. No other social science has had an equivalent success in applying reason to the shaping of humanity's destiny. Our nation has a Council of Economic Advisers; no such permanent agency exists for any other social science. In addition, in January of every year *The Economic Report of the President* is presented to Congress.

Third, economics is attractive because of its use of the scientific method for the study of people. Sometimes students view mathematics as a fascinating game or language but are frustrated by their inability to use it for really important human problems. Whereas mathematics is increasingly used by all social sciences, economics has long been in the forefront in its usage. Economists depend heavily on models (i.e., simplifying constructs) for organizing facts and for thinking about economic behavior and policy alternatives.

Fourth, a knowledge of economics and an understanding of current economic institutions and problems are essential in certain occupations. For example, business leaders are usually expected by the general public, and often by colleagues, to be knowledgeable of economic phenomena. The same is true for journalists, television commentators, editors, social studies teachers, politicians, labor leaders, bankers, lawyers, and others. Some disciplines are more easily learned on-the-job or in one's spare time than others. If you are ever to develop a basic background in economics, it will probably be in college and not later.

Finally, economics and economic issues may be your avocation. As a person knowledgeable of the subject, you may well play a leading role in the League of Women Voters, in a local or national political party, in a civic club committee on the local economy, as a bargaining agent for a union or teachers' association, or as an informed commentator on current issues at your club or at home. With the media so full of economic matters, few disciplines are as useful in preparing one to be an interested, interesting, and knowledgeable observer and interpreter of passing events.

The above is based on the *Handbook for Undergraduate Students in Economics* by Laurence Leamer issued by the Center for Economic Education and Public Policy at the State University of New York at Binghamton, 1977. For more information on the importance of economics, see *Special Topic J: Why Study Economics?*

Jill believes that she will be able to leave the parking lot faster if she leaves the basketball game ten minutes before the game ends. However, if everyone at the game acts the same way, the parking lot will be as congested as it would be if no one left until the game was over. In another example, suppose that it is easy for you to find a job. This does not mean that everyone can find a job.

The second trap is the **post hoc fallacy.** This implies that because B follows *A*, B was caused by *A*. The erroneous cause-effect conclusion can be illustrated by the following example. The vast majority of cocaine users drank milk early in their lives. Therefore, drinking milk early in one's life will lead to the use of cocaine. The absurdity of this conclusion is obvious.

1.4 Graphs

The first thing most students notice when thumbing through an economics textbook for the first time is the large number of graphs. This book is no exception. The purpose of this section is to introduce you to graphs and to show you how to use them.

Descriptive Statistics

Descriptive statistics deals with the process of data collection and presentation in order to describe economic relationships. Economists frequently attempt to draw conclusions about groups, called *populations,* on the basis of information or facts obtained from a portion of the population, called a *sample.* There are many different sources of information, including the government, which collects and publishes a wide variety of economic data. Other sources include trade associations, firms, and labor groups.

There are two basic ways of presenting statistical data. First are statistical tables, which make the presentation of large amounts of data easier. See Table 1.1. In the table, the figures are presented for the sales of the XYZ Corporation. Since sales have been listed by year, note how easy it is to compare one year's sales with another's. However, sometimes so much data

**Table 1.1
Sales of XYZ Corporation
(millions of dollars)**

Year	Dollar Sales
1989	8
1990	48
1991	117
1992	335
1993	583

are presented in a table that it becomes difficult to see trends or patterns. This leads to the second form.

The second way in which to present data is through the use of graphs. The most common types are line charts, bar charts, and pie charts. In Figure 1.1 these three types of graphs are illustrated. Figure 1.1a is a line chart illustrating the dollar sales of XYZ Corporation over the time period 1989–1993. Dollar sales are measured on the vertical axis, and time is shown on the horizontal axis. By the rising line, it is clear that XYZ's sales have increased dramatically in recent years. Figure 1.1b presents the data in the form of a bar graph. Again note how easy it is to see the huge increase in XYZ's sales. Pie charts can also simplify the presentation of data. Figure 1.1c shows the distribution of employees in different divisions for the XYZ Corporation. The largest portion of the pie chart represents the manufacturing division, which employs the largest percentage of people. Now that we have seen some uses of graphs, we will discuss how graphs are constructed.

Constructing Graphs

In order to review how graphs are constructed, let us examine a hypothetical relationship between the time students spend studying and the final grade they receive. It is assumed that the more time a student spends studying, the higher the final grade that he or she will receive. To examine this relationship, a number of assumptions must be made. It is important to note

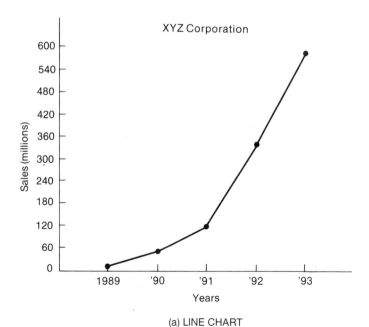

(a) LINE CHART

Figure 1.1. Three Different Types of Graphs.

11

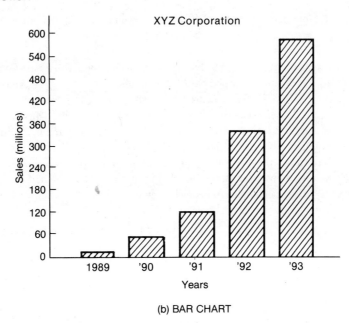

(b) BAR CHART

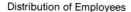

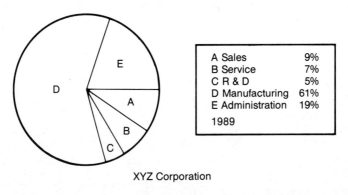

XYZ Corporation

(c) PIE CHART

Figure 1.1.   Continued

them because examining the connection between these two variables requires that we control for all factors that affect the student's grade. We will assume that the person under examination is male, a junior, 20 years old, and taking Basic Economics in the fall semester.

The relationship between time studied and final grade received is illustrated in Table 1.2. The final grade is called the *dependent variable* and the amount of study time, the *independent variable* because, in the model, the final grade depends on the amount of study time. The

Table 1.2
Relationship Between Study Time
and Final Grade

Points	Study Time per Week (hours)	Final Grade (%)
G	0	30
H	2	50
I	4	65
J	6	80
K	8	90
L	10	92

first couple of hours of study add much more to the final grade than do the last couple of hours. The model shows that even if this person does not study, he will receive a grade of 30 percent. If the student studies 2 hours, his grade will increase to a grade of 50 percent. But if the student had been studying for 8 hours and increased his study time by 2 hours (to 10 hours), his grade would only rise from 90 percent to 92 percent.

To illustrate this relationship even more clearly, we can graph the data. In Figure 1.2, the final grade is measured on the vertical axis (Y). The horizontal axis (X) indicates the hours of study time.

Each combination of values from the schedule is plotted on the graph. Points that fall on the horizontal or vertical axis are called the *X-intercept* or *Y-intercept,* respectively. For example, point G is 0 hours of study and a final grade of 30 percent. To place this point on the graph, put your pencil on 0 hours of study on the horizontal axis and vertically raise the pencil to locate the grade of 30 percent. Point G will be on the vertical axis; therefore, it is the Y-intercept. Point G picks up the effects of all other variables (not including study time) on final grade (e.g., intelligence and the health of the person). As these other influences change, the Y-intercept will change.

Let us plot one more point to make sure you have the hang of it. Combination H is a grade of 50 percent with 2 hours of study. Locate 2 hours of study on the horizontal axis and go up until you reach a grade of 50 percent. This is labeled H in Figure 1.2. Once all the combinations have been placed on the graph, the points are connected to draw a curve that illustrates the connection between hours of study and final grade. In this example, the curve is *upward* sloping, which indicates a **direct relationship** between variables. These two variables are directly related because an increase in study time will produce an increase in the final grade. In Figure 1.3 two other types of curves are illustrated.

In Figure 1.3a, an **inverse relationship** between variables X and Y is shown by a *downward*-sloping line. An increase in one of the variables is always associated with a decrease in the other. An example is the reduction in travel time that results from driving faster. As speed increases, travel time decreases. Sometimes the association between two variables is not as simple as that portrayed in Figures 1.2 and 1.3a. There may be a **complex**

13

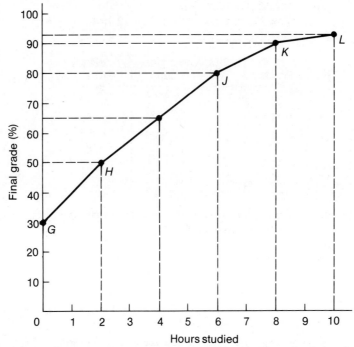

Figure 1.2. Graphing the Relationship Between Hours Studied and Final Grade in Basic Economics. An increase in the final grade received in economics is associated with an increase in the number of hours studied.

relationship between the two variables such that sometimes it is direct and on other portions of the curve it is inverse. For example, early in the day temperatures are low. As the day progresses, temperature increases. When daylight ends, temperatures typically fall until daybreak when the cycle begins again. This is illustrated in Figure 1.3b.

The power of these graphs is their ability to illustrate simply the connection between two variables. Whenever the relationship is direct, the curve is upward sloping (positively sloped). Whenever the relationship is inverse, the curve will be downward sloping (negatively sloped).

It was noted previously when examining the table that each additional 2 hours of study increases the final grade by different amounts. This is also easy to show on the graph by the changes in *slope* of the curve. Slope is defined as the change in Y divided by the change in X. With a direct (inverse) relationship the slope is positive (negative). As the value of the slope increases, the curve will appear steeper and vice versa. For example, we showed that the first 2 hours of study contribute 20 additional percentage points to the final grade, whereas the last 2 additional hours (from 8 to 10 hours) contribute only 2 percentage points. This is shown by the curve becoming flatter with additional hours of study. Therefore, the curve not only indicates

14

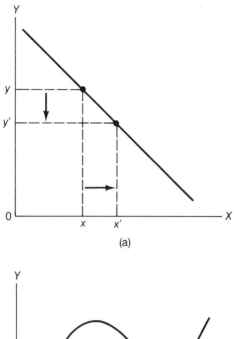

(a)

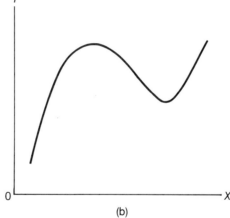

(b)

Figure 1.3. Two Additional Types of Relationships. (a) An Inverse Relationship. An increase in X is associated with a decrease in Y. (b) A complex relationship. As X increases, Y initially increases, then decreases, and finally increases again.

the direction of the relationship but also tells us something about the additional gain or loss. When we make decisions, we examine the change in expected benefits and costs resulting from different options. In this example, when deciding how much to study, the student would need to look at the improvement in his final grade that would result from each additional hour of study.

Using Graphs

In the model illustrated above, it was assumed that the person under study was male, a junior, 20 years of age, and taking Basic Economics in the fall semester. What would happen if we were to change one of these assumptions? Would the hypothesized relationship be any different if the course were Introduction to Health?

Assume that the same person is taking Introduction to Health. What does the relationship between study time and final grade look like now? College students generally agree that some courses are much easier than others and require much less work. We will assume that Introduction to Health is such a course. We still assume that the more the student studies, the better his final grade. But we will assume that he does not need to study as much to get the same grade in Health as in Economics. See Table 1.3.

In the table, the original hours-studied/final-grade schedule for Economics is presented in the first two columns. In the third column, the grade for this person taking Health is given. When the student does not study, he gets a grade of 50 percent, whereas in the economics course, he got a grade of only 30 percent. With only 2 hours of study, he will pass Health (with a grade of 70 percent) instead of possibly failing Economics (with a grade of 50 percent).

In Figure 1.4, the new hours-studied/final-grade curve is drawn. The original curve is labeled "Economics," and the new line, "Health." The new hours-studied/final-grade line has shifted up, indicating that for each hour studied the final grade received in Health will be higher. This particular person will require less study in Health to receive the same grade as that in Economics. For example, a grade of 70 percent can be achieved in Health for 2 hours of study per week. The same 2 hours of study per week would earn the student a final grade of 50 percent in Economics.

In this example we have distinguished between a *movement along* the hours-studied/final-grade curve and a *shift* of the curve. A movement along the curve in this example occurs whenever there is a change in the number of hours studied. On the other hand, whenever any of the assumptions made about the student are changed, the entire curve will shift.

Table 1.3
Relationship Between Study Time
and Final Grade for Two Different Courses

Study Time per Week (hours)	Final Grade in Economics (%)	Final Grade in Health (%)
0	30	50
2	50	70
4	65	85
6	80	90
8	90	95
10	92	98

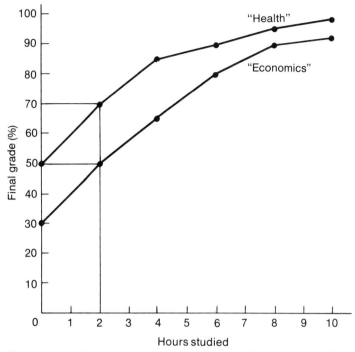

Figure 1.4. Graphing the Relationship Between Hours Studied and Final Grade Received for Basic Economics and Introduction to Health. A positive relationship exists between hours studied and final grade received. Every hour studied in the health course leads to a higher grade than in the economics course.

It is also possible for the curve for Economics to shift downward. What changes in the assumptions would cause such a shift? A downward shift means that for any number of hours studied, the expected grade for Economics will be lower. This might happen if the person taking the economics course were a freshman instead of a junior. As a freshman, a student might not study as well as someone who has been in college for more than two years. Therefore, with the same amount of time spent studying, the grade expected would be less.

Summary

The basic problem of economics is that of scarcity. Because we have limited resources, choices must be made. Economics is divided into microeconomics and macroeconomics. Microeconomics is the study of the behavior of households and firms. Microeconomics explores how decisions are made and how households and firms interact in the market. Macroeconomics is concerned with the "big picture." Macroeconomics examines the behavior of the entire economy and deals with the problems of unemployment, inflation, and growth.

Positive economics deals with "what is," while normative economics examines "what ought to be." Efficiency and equity are two goals that we may not be able to achieve simultaneously. Efficiency refers to the most productive use of resources. Equity refers to the issue of fairness and is difficult to determine since each person has his or her own conception of what is fair.

In order to understand the behavior of households and firms, economists use models. Following the scientific approach, economists first propose hypotheses about the relationships between economic variables. The next step is to test their validity. In the model-building process, economists rely heavily on the use of mathematics. Because of their ability to simplify the presentation of a relationship between variables, economists frequently use graphs to illustrate these models.

Key Concepts

economics
scarcity
microeconomics and macroeconomics
positive and normative economics
efficiency
equity
models
scientific method
theory
fallacy of composition
post hoc fallacy
intercepts
direct, inverse, and complex relationships
slope

Self-Test Questions: True or False

T   F   1. The central problem of economics is scarcity.

T   F   2. The following statement is an example of positive economics: "An unemployment rate of 6 percent is too high."

T   F   3. Microeconomics is the study of individual households and firms, whereas macroeconomics examines the performance of the entire economy.

T   F   4. The following statement is an example of normative economics: "Health care should be made available to all people."

T F   5. As long as the allocation of resources is efficient, equity will be achieved.

T F   6. According to the fallacy of composition, whatever is true for the individual is true for society.

T F   7. It is important to know the assumptions made about a model in order to understand fully what it is attempting to explain.

T F   8. An example of faulty reasoning due to the post hoc fallacy is, "since the stock market has risen almost every time the NFC has won the Super Bowl, the NFC victory is generally the cause of the increase in stock values."

Answer questions 9 and 10 on the basis of the following table and graph:

Combination	X	Y
B	0	5
C	1	4
D	2	3
E	3	2
F	4	1
G	5	0

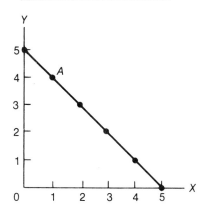

T F   9. Point A on the graph corresponds to combination F in the table.

T F   10. An inverse relationship between variables X and Y is illustrated in the table and graph.

Answers to Self-Test Questions

1. ***True.*** The basic problem of economics is that of scarcity. Since resources are scarce we must make choices as to how they should be used.

2. *False.* A positive statement is an objective proposition, capable of being tested. The statement that the unemployment rate is too high is a subjective comment. We may agree, but we cannot prove that it is right.

3. *True.* Microeconomics examines the behavior of individuals, whereas macroeconomics studies the entire economy or "the big picture."

4. *True.* A normative statement is a subjective proposition that cannot be tested. The statement that health care *should* be provided to all people involves a value judgment.

5. *False.* It is possible that the allocation of goods that results from the most efficient use of resources is not judged fair by society. As a result, government intervention may be considered necessary to improve the allocation decided by the market.

6. *True.* The fallacy of composition states that what is true for one person is necessarily true for society. For example, Phyllis may decide that the fastest way out of a burning theater is to run. If everyone in the theater thinks the same way, there will be such confusion that everyone will be delayed.

7. *True.* It is essential to know the assumptions made in constructing a model. For example, in the hours-studied/final-grade case, we needed to know what assumptions were made about the person and course studied, in order to understand fully their relationship.

8. *True.* The post hoc fallacy states that if one event occurs before another, the former event must have caused the latter. It is obvious that even though the performance of the stock market and the Super Bowl winner are related, there is no apparent causation from one to the other.

9. *False.* Combination F in the table has a value of 4 for X and a value of 1 for Y. However, point A on the graph corresponds to combination C in the table, where X equals 1 and Y equals 4.

10. *True.* An inverse relationship between X and Y means that increases in one variable are associated with decreases in the other. In this example, as X rises from 0 to 5, Y falls from 5 to 0.

Discussion Questions

1. Distinguish between the following economic concepts:
   a. macroeconomics and microeconomics
   b. positive and normative economics
   c. efficiency and equity

2. What is an economic model? Why do economists use models?

3. It is generally accepted that as altitude increases, temperature decreases. Construct a table illustrating a hypothetical relationship between altitude and temperature. Draw

the graph associated with the table. What type of relationship exists between these two variables? What assumptions did you make?

4. Given the accompanying table, describe the relationship between variables P and F. Draw the graph. What would happen to the curve drawn if all the values of F were to increase by 1 unit, as shown in the third column?

P	F	F'
0	0	1
1	3	4
2	6	7
3	9	10
4	12	13
5	15	16

Problems

Wylma's family goes to the supermarket each Saturday afternoon to buy food. When the price of chicken is $1.50 a pound, Wylma's family is willing to purchase 3 pounds of chicken a week. If the price of chicken rises to $1.70, they will buy only 2 pounds. If the price falls to $1.30, they will buy 4 pounds.

1. Derive the schedule illustrating the relationship between the price of chicken and the amount of chicken Wylma's family is willing to purchase.

Price	Amount Purchased

2. Draw the graph corresponding to this schedule, placing price on the vertical axis and the amount they are willing to purchase on the horizontal axis.

3. Now assume that Wylma's family decides to buy one additional pound of chicken at each of the three prices because their preference for chicken has increased. Derive the new schedule and curve for the price and quantity purchased, using the table and graph developed in problems 1 and 2.

Basic Economic Concepts

Objectives

Upon completion of this chapter, you should understand:

1. The different economic resources available to produce goods and services.

2. How to use the production possibilities model to demonstrate basic economic principles and to analyze economic problems.

3. The institutions of the private market system.

4. How three basic economic problems are solved by the private market.

5. Why all nations can benefit from international trade.

The ultimate goal of any economy is to allocate its scarce resources to produce those goods that are most valued by society. As we noted in the beginning of the previous chapter, *scarcity* will always exist because we have unlimited wants and limited resources with which to satisfy these wants. There are a number of important questions yet to be answered regarding the problem of scarcity. For example, what kinds of resources does an economy have to devote to production? How does the private market allocate these scarce resources to produce those goods most valued by society? What are the sources of economic growth? The answer to this question is vital because economic growth enables us to satisfy more of our wants. Finally, how is the problem of scarcity reduced through international trade?

The purpose of this chapter is to answer the above questions in order to provide you with a foundation for better understanding how our economy operates. First, we describe the different types of resources that our economy uses to produce goods and services. An economic model will then be developed (called production possibilities) to introduce the method of thinking used by economists as well as to demonstrate important principles. Next, we examine the overall operation of the private market economy, exploring how it solves three basic economic problems. The chapter concludes by describing the benefits that nations gain through trade when each nation specializes in producing those goods in which it has a comparative advantage.

2.1 Our Economic Resources

There are three overall types of *economic resources:* (1) labor, (2) capital, and (3) natural resources. Note that our economic resources are also called *inputs* or *factors of production.* They are factors that are combined in the production process to produce goods and services, called *outputs.*

Labor

The basic ingredient in the production process is *labor,* more accurately called *human resources.* Human resources consist partly of the ability of workers to perform physical tasks on the job, such as turning a screw or hauling materials to a particular site. In addition, our human resource base contains *human capital,* which refers to the skills and knowledge that people acquire during their lifetimes. The concept of human capital includes *entrepreneurship,* which refers to the ability of people who successfully run firms to develop new products and better methods of production as well as their willingness to take risks in launching new business ventures.

Capital

Capital is any *human-made input* used to produce goods. There are three types of capital: (1) *construction,* which includes large human-made structures such as factories, roads, bridges, and airports; (2) *machinery and equipment,* like computers and hammers; and (3) *inventories,* which are unsold goods, including goods in the process of being produced, such as an unfinished car on an assembly line. Inventories also include goods that have been fully produced but not yet sold. For example, car dealers need an inventory of cars on their lots for normal business purposes, whereas supermarkets must have a large assortment of vegetables, poultry, meat, ice cream, and other goods on their shelves. Note that when economists use the term *capital* they are referring to real (or physical) capital (i.e., any human-made input) not *financial capital* which includes instruments such as stocks, bonds, and commercial loans used to finance the resources made by people such as the construction of factories, machines and equipment, and to build up inventories.

Natural Resources

The third input used in the production process is **natural resources,** which are resources that exist in nature. They are not made by human beings. Natural resources include such ingredients as land, water, air, and the deposits of minerals (e.g., oil, natural gas, and bauxite). The whole ecology is a part of our natural resource base.

To be able to better distinguish the differences between our various economic resources, let's examine the sufferings of a drought-stricken wheat farmer in Kansas. Farmer Gray (a *human resource*) gets hopping mad one day, frustrated by the lack of rain. He hops up and down, kicks the dry dirt, and then finally sits on a log to think. Using his wits *(human capital),* the farmer finally decides to build an irrigation ditch. The next day, he rents a bulldozer *(real capital)* using money *(financial capital)* he borrowed from his bank. To dig the ditch, farmer Gray starts the engine of the bulldozer, pushing its gas pedal down with his foot *(physical labor)*. A week after the ditch is completed, a flash of lightning lights up the night sky, and a bolt of thunder jolts farmer Gray and his family out of a deep sleep. He joyfully runs outside with his family to watch the rain fill up the new irrigation ditch. The rain and the puddle the family is standing in are, of course, a *natural resource* (a gift of nature). But what is the ditch? Is the ditch also a natural resource? No, because the ditch was created by the farmer, it is real capital. The irrigation system represents a capital improvement on the land. In addition, note that farmer Gray is an *entrepreneur* — he took the risk of borrowing money to build the ditch.

Having examined our resource base, we now turn to the production possibilities model. Examination of this model will provide you with tools for analyzing important economic concepts.

2.2 Production Possibilities

The **production possibilities (PP) model** represents all possible combinations of two goods that an economy can produce. We will study production possibilities to demonstrate how economists build models of the economy. All **economic models** are based on assumptions drawn up in order to simplify the real world into a pattern that is easier for us to understand.

Therefore, the PP model will provide a tool for analyzing important economic concepts and will help you to become more familiar with the use of graphs and tables. The overall purpose of examining the PP model is to introduce you to a new way of thinking. It is something you will carry with you for the rest of your life, even if later you are unable to recall the details of this particular model.

Assumptions of the Model

First, we assume that only *two types of goods and services* are produced (e.g., civilian goods and military goods, or luxury goods and necessities). This assumption is made to simplify our view of reality so that we can better understand events in the "real world." By limiting the choice of goods to two, we are able to illustrate the PP model on a two-dimensional graph. The PP model could be expanded to include millions of goods, but that would bog us down, making it impossible to use graphical analysis.

Second, it is assumed that all inputs are *limited in amount.* The number of workers in the economy, the number of factories, the amount of machinery and equipment, and the supply of natural resources are assumed to be fixed in supply. In addition, these inputs are assumed to be *fully employed* in production.

Third, we assume that the state of technology is *not changing.* We also assume that the economy uses the *most efficient* technologies available. The term **technology** refers to a method of production. The production of different outputs requires different combinations of inputs. For example, the baking of biscuits requires such ingredients as flour, eggs, baking soda, and an oven, while the production of bricks uses clay and a kiln.

Examining the PP Curve

The PP curve illustrated in Figure 2.1 shows possible combinations of food and clothing that an economy can produce given the assumptions of the model. The PP curve is drawn from the hypothetical data presented in Table 2.1.

How do we interpret the various points on the curve? Note that at point *A* in Figure 2.1, all economic resources are being used to make 105 units of clothing and no food is grown. If, on the other hand, all resources were used in farming, 120 units of food could be made with no clothing produced (see point *G*). The points between these extremes represent the other *possible* combinations of these two goods that could be made with full employment of all resources and the use of the most efficient technologies. The *actual* combination produced depends on what society prefers to buy. If society wants to consume 20 units of food and 100 units of clothing, the actual location on the curve will be point *B*. If you have difficulty plotting these points, refer to Chapter 1 to review the graphing technique.

Using the PP Model to Demonstrate Basic Economic Concepts

Economists use the PP model to demonstrate many fundamental economic concepts. We begin by examining the problem of scarcity.

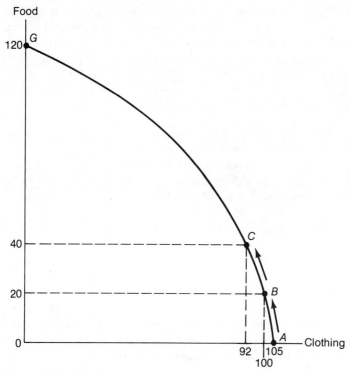

Figure 2.1. Production Possibilities Curve. The curve represents all possible combinations of food and clothing that can be produced. In order to produce more of one good, society must give up increasing amounts of the other good.

Scarcity and Increasing Opportunity Cost Movement along the PP curve illustrates the concept of *scarcity*. We noted earlier that because we have limited economic resources, we can never fully satisfy our unlimited wants. All economies, no matter how prosperous, must *choose* between alternative goods to produce. Each choice involves an ***opportunity cost***. In the context of the PP model, opportunity cost refers to the fact that to produce more of one good, we must give up the production of the other good.

As Table 2.1 and Figure 2.1 illustrate, the opportunity cost of producing the first 20 units of food is 5 units of clothing since society must decrease clothing production from 105 units to 100 units (represented by the move from point *A* to point *B*). What is the opportunity cost of the next 20 units of food? The move from point *B* to point *C* involves cutting clothing production back from 100 units to 92 units in order to release the resources needed to increase food production from 20 units to 40 units. Therefore, the opportunity cost of this 20-unit increase in food production is the 8 units of clothing that society must give up. Production of the third 20-unit increase in food involves a sacrifice of 12 units of clothing.

Table 2.1
Production Possibilities:
All Possible Combinations
of Food and Clothing
That May Be Produced

Food			Clothing	
	120	G	0	
+20				−40
	100	F	40	
+20				−25
	80	E	65	
+20				−15
	60	D	80	
+20				−12
	40	C	92	
+20				−8
	20	B	100	
+20				−5
	0	A	105	

In our example the sacrifice becomes greater as more and more of one good is produced. This illustrates the **_law of increasing costs,_** which states that to produce more and more of one good, society must give up an increasing amount of the other good.

This situation of increasing opportunity cost is partly a consequence of the nature of the different technologies used. It is assumed that food production is *land intensive,* which means that the amount of land used per unit of food produced is relatively higher than the amount of labor used per unit of food. Clothing production, on the other hand, is assumed to be *labor intensive,* which means that it requires relatively more labor and less land per unit of output than food production. Because the production of different goods requires different combinations of inputs, the substitution of one input (such as labor) for the other input (such as land) is said to be "imperfect." What is the effect of *imperfect substitution?* As food production is increased, clothing production must be reduced to provide the inputs required for farming. The decrease in clothing production releases relatively more labor than land since clothing production is labor intensive. Consequently, more and more units of clothes must be forgone to produce the same additional amount of food each time. This causes the PP curve to bow out, making it concave.

Unemployment   What would happen if people in the economy did not plan to buy the maximum amount of goods that could be produced? The result would be **_unemployment,_** which means that some people who are willing and able to work cannot find employment.

Unemployment causes the economy to produce below the PP curve. For example, at point U society is consuming 60 units of food and 65 units of clothing, as illustrated in Figure 2.2. If total spending were to change, moving the combination of goods purchased from point U to point C, previously idle resources would be employed to increase the production of clothing from 65 units to 80 units, with no change in the quantity of food produced. Note that any point on the PP curve represents full-employment production.

Three conclusions can be drawn from using this model. First, unemployment may be created by insufficient spending. If people in the economy do not attempt to buy the amount of goods that could be produced at full employment, firms will lay off workers and factories will operate at reduced capacity. This has occurred on numerous occasions in our economy. During the last decade we experienced several recessions, with the unemployment rate rising to double digits, led by massive layoffs in the automobile, steel, and housing industries.

Second, unemployment imposes on society a cost of lost output. This cost can be very high. For example, the possible production that our economy lost during the Great Depression of

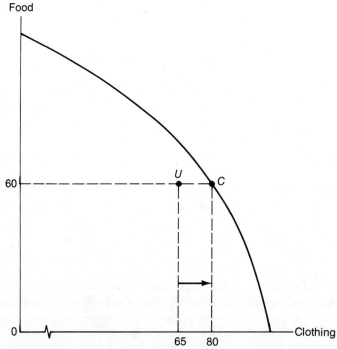

Figure 2.2.   Elimination of Unemployment by Producing More Clothing. Unemployment causes the economy to produce less than full employment output, represented by point U. The move from point U to point C represents the elimination of unemployment by producing 15 more units of clothing, with no change in the amount of food produced.

the 1930s has been estimated to be equivalent to our defense expenditures during World War II. All the goods that we could have produced during depressions and recessions can never be regained. They are lost forever.

Third, efforts to increase total spending in the economy can eliminate the problem of unemployment by moving us to a point located on the PP curve. Policy options designed to stimulate overall spending in our economy can be initiated by the federal government and our central banking system. Such options will be discussed in Chapters 10 and 11.

Inefficiency The PP curve is drawn assuming the most economically *efficient* use of inputs. This means that the most output is produced using the least costly combination of inputs. What would happen if the economy failed to employ its economic resources efficiently? Inefficient production creates ***underemployment,*** in which inputs are not used to their full potential (even though they may be employed full-time). For example, during an economic downturn some college graduates may be able to find work only in jobs that do not require higher education. This represents underemployment of human resources. Underemployment created by inefficiency results in economic waste. People in the economy lose the ability to consume goods when there is inefficiency, just as they do when there is unemployment. For example, in Figure 2.2, point U could also represent a loss of production due to inefficiency. The elimination of inefficiency would result in higher output given a sufficient increase in total spending, which is illustrated by a move from point U to any point on the PP curve.

Innovation: An Important Source of Economic Growth We initially drew the PP curve assuming that the available technologies did not change. In reality, the state of technology is constantly changing. The development of a better method of production is called ***innovation.*** Our economy has experienced many innovations, sometimes with a dramatic impact. For example, the agricultural sector of our nation experienced a revolution in the way in which food is produced. The small farm gave way to the large farm as more capital-intensive methods of production were introduced. As a result, agricultural productivity shot up dramatically. This situation is presented in Figure 2.3, which presents the PP curve for farm versus nonfarm goods. The inner curve represents the "before" situation. Innovation in farming permits more food to be produced with the same amount of input. This results in an outward shift in the PP curve at all points except at A. At point A all resources are employed in producing nonfarm goods, and since there has not been any assumed change in nonfarm technology, there is no change in the amount of nonfarm goods that can be produced.

This outward shift in the PP curve represents an increase in potential ***economic growth.*** To realize this growth potential there has to be a corresponding increase in total spending. What problem would be created if we were initially at point X and we remained there after the innovation in farming? Unemployment would result. Workers previously employed in farming are now laid off, replaced by machinery such as combines and tractors. Fewer workers are needed to produce the same amount of farm output. This change in technology, however, does not have to result in permanent unemployment. The idle resources could be employed if the spending for goods were to increase in step with the increase in potential output. One possible

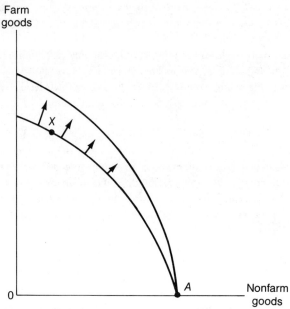

Figure 2.3.   Innovation in Agriculture. Improved methods of production in farming permit more food to be produced with the same amount of inputs.

path is illustrated in Figure 2.4 by the movement from point X to point Y. In this case, there is a shift in resources from the farm to the nonfarm sector made possible by innovation in agriculture.

This discussion demonstrates the profound change that actually occurred in the structure of employment in the United States. In 1910, about one-half of all workers were employed in farming. By 1987, the figure had dropped to 3 percent. Where did the displaced workers find jobs? They were employed primarily in the service sector, such as wholesale and retail trade, education, real estate, banking, and government.

We should be aware that the adoption of new methods of production is often viewed with suspicion by workers in industries where the technological change takes place. This is understandable, since those workers may become unemployed in that industry as a result of innovation. However, as we demonstrated using the PP model, those workers who become unemployed in one industry need not be unemployed forever. They can eventually find jobs in other industries, as long as total spending increases to purchase additional goods. These workers, of course, often have to retrain for the new positions that open up.

An Increase in Labor/Education and Training as a Source of Economic Growth   Until now we assumed that the amounts of labor, capital, and natural resources were fixed. What would happen if there were a sudden increase in the amount of labor or if the

30

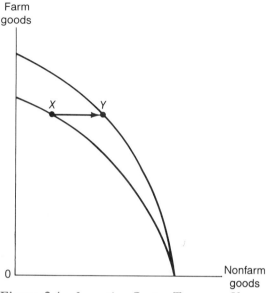

Figure 2.4. Innovation Creates Temporary Unemployment. Laid-off farm workers can find employment if spending increases in step with the growth in potential output.

same number of workers were to receive additional education and training? The overall effect would be to shift the entire PP curve outward, since the economy could produce more of both goods. Increases in the quantity and quality of the other inputs involved would have a similar impact.

Figure 2.5 illustrates the effect of an assumed increase in the amount of labor on the possibilities of producing food and clothing. Population growth due to increases in the net birth rate and migration has been an important source of economic growth in many countries, including the United States, Canada, and many European countries. However, certain economies in Asia, Africa, and Latin America appear to be suffering from overpopulation. Large extended families working small plots of land have caused negative returns to appear in certain farm sectors. To the extent that this has occurred, further population growth would cause the PP curve to shrink.

Investment and Economic Growth: Present Versus Future Satisfaction Resources can be allocated to satisfy the wants of the current generation rather than persons who will live in the future, and vice versa. Therefore, we must choose among the various types of goods that may be produced *over time*. The choice boils down to the production of more consumer goods or more capital goods. **Consumer goods** are called *final* goods because they satisfy the final wants of households. **Capital goods,** on the other hand, are called *interme-*

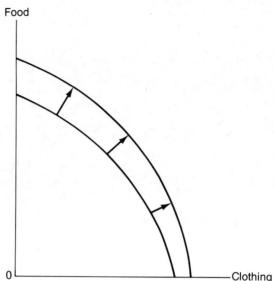

Figure 2.5. Impact of an Increase in the Supply of Labor. The economy can produce more of both goods with additional economic resources.

diate goods since they are human-made inputs. In other words, capital goods do not satisfy wants directly. Instead, they are created to produce more of other goods in the future (both consumer and capital goods).

Point *C* of Figure 2.6 illustrates the situation in which society has placed all of its resources into the production of consumer goods. No capital goods are being produced at point *C*. This maximizes the **present satisfaction** of society since *all* economic resources are being used to produce goods that satisfy the wants of households. The movement from point *C* to point *B* represents an increase in the production of capital goods and a decrease in the production of consumer goods. Therefore, the opportunity cost of producing more capital goods is the amount of consumer goods that society must give up.

In the example illustrated in Figure 2.6, society sacrifices *CC'* units of consumer goods in order to produce 0*K* units of capital goods. The increase in the stock of capital goods by 0*K* is called **investment.** The decrease in the amount of consumer goods *CC'* represents **saving** by households where saving *(CC')* is defined as total income (0*C*) minus expenditures on consumer goods (0*C'*). Households must save (postpone consumption) in order to release the scarce resources needed for investment (i.e., to produce capital goods).

What is the effect of this increase in capital goods? The move from 0 to *K* in Figure 2.6 increases the capital base of the economy, which means that we have more factories, machinery, and other human-made inputs with which to produce other goods in the *future*. Therefore, the effect of investment is to shift the entire PP curve outward. This is illustrated in Figure 2.7. The inner curve represents the production possibilities in 1989, which is the

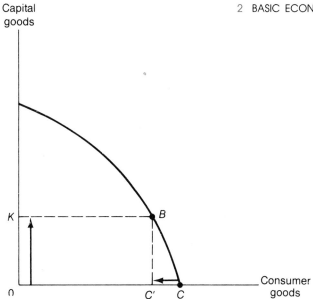

Figure 2.6. Investment and Saving. Households must postpone consumption in order to release the resources needed to produce additional capital goods.

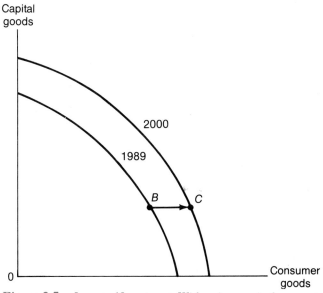

Figure 2.7. Impact of Investment. With an increase in the current production of capital goods, the economy is able to produce more of both goods in the future. In this example, the new capital goods are fully used to produce more consumer goods.

year in which the decision to increase the stock of capital goods was made (from 0 to K, which is the same as the situation illustrated in Figure 2.6). The outer curve demonstrates the increased growth potential by the year 2000. Investment has increased the economy's ability to produce both more consumer and more capital goods.

What combination of goods will the economy produce by 2000? The actual growth path taken depends on changes in spending. Suppose that society uses all of the new capital goods produced in 1989 to produce more consumer goods. The move from point B in 1989 to point C in 2000 demonstrates that the sacrifice of *present* consumption gives society more satisfaction in the *future*.

High rates of investment have been a major source of economic growth in the United States and all other industrialized nations. Unfortunately, many of the world's least developed countries have found it very difficult to follow such a path since a sharp cut in present consumption could push millions of families past the brink of starvation. We will now examine the overall behavior of the private market system.

2.3 An Overview of the Private Market System

The ***private market system*** is rooted in a number of important institutions. *Private property* is, of course, an essential ingredient. What is private property? It is simply the ownership of assets such as land and buildings by individuals, which is the opposite of public property owned by society through government, such as roads and military bases. The right to the ownership of property by individuals is granted by government through the *enforcement of contracts.* A contract is an agreement between two or more parties which is enforceable in a court of law. For example, if you sign a rental agreement for an apartment, you will probably be held liable for damage to the owner's property. In addition, the private enterprise system operates principally on the concept of *self-interest.* This means that persons are motivated to help themselves. We should be aware that while self-interest involves "greed," it is also consistent with "altruism" since many people gain satisfaction by helping others.

We do not live in a purely private market economy. Instead, we live in a ***mixed economy*** in which there is a private enterprise system *plus* a role for government. Whereas individuals act out of self-interest, government attempts to act in the *collective interest* of all members of society. In general, we believe that people acting out of self-interest will behave in a manner that benefits society in general. For example, people go to work to earn income for their families. The goods they help to produce benefit others in the economy. But decisions made on the basis of self-interest are not always in the interest of the group. Government is needed to provide certain goods and services that either will not be provided by the private market (e.g., national defense) or, if provided by the private market, will not be provided in sufficient quantity (e.g., education and health care). In addition, government has a number of other roles that cannot be performed adequately by the private market (e.g., enforcing contracts, decreasing pollution, and reducing poverty). The functions of government in a mixed economy are discussed in Chapter 7.

The Circular Flow

What is meant by the term *market*? A **market** is a place where buyers and sellers interact, establishing the price of goods and the quantity sold during a given period of time. There are two overall types of markets in the private enterprise system: the product market and the factor market. The **product market** refers to the market for goods and services produced such as houses, pizzas, and medical care. Note that we use the term *goods* as an abbreviation for the term *goods and services.* The **factor market,** on the other hand, refers to the market for the economic resources (also called inputs) used in production: the market for human resources, capital, and natural resources. It is called the factor market because the ingredients used in the production process are also called "factors of production."

There are two decision makers in a purely private market: the household and the firm. (Government is not included because we are not assuming a mixed economy.) The term **household** refers to the family unit, which makes such decisions as where to work and what goods and services to buy with the income earned. A *firm* is the production unit, which makes such decisions as what goods to produce and how many workers to employ.

As the **circular flow** diagram (Figure 2.8) indicates, households act as buyers in the product market (the upper loop) and as sellers in the factor market (the lower loop). Firms, on the other hand, act as sellers in the product market (the upper loop) and as buyers in the factor market (the lower loop). The arrows indicate the flow of income and physical outputs and inputs. The outer loop shows how money changes hands, with households receiving income payments from firms through the sale of inputs. Firms, in turn, receive income from households through the sale of goods. The inner loop shows the exchange of physical outputs and inputs, with households receiving goods and services and firms receiving labor services, capital, and natural resources.

The Interaction of Buyers and Sellers

Acting out of self-interest, households are assumed to want to *maximize total satisfaction.* This means that households want to buy that combination of goods in the product market and to sell that combination of inputs in the factor market which makes them as happy as possible. On the other hand, firms are assumed to want to *maximize total profit.* Total profit is the amount by which the total sales revenue (income) received by firms exceeds the total costs of production.

Every transaction involves a price and quantity. In the product market, firms sell a certain quantity of a good or service at a particular price. For example, if you were to buy three pizzas from Joe's Pizzeria for $7 each, the total revenue (income) earned by Joe would be $21. From your viewpoint, this $21 is a cost of purchasing the product. You want to pay the lowest

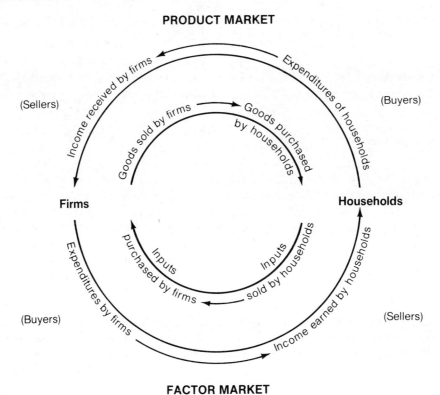

PRODUCT MARKET

(Sellers)   (Buyers)

Income received by firms

Expenditures of households

Goods sold by firms

Goods purchased by households

Firms   **Households**

Inputs purchased by firms

Inputs sold by households

Expenditures by firms

Income earned by households

(Buyers)   (Sellers)

FACTOR MARKET

Figure 2.8.   The Circular Flow Diagram Represents the Flow of Money (Outer Loop) and the Flow of Goods/Inputs (Inner Loop). Households buy goods from firms in the product market, earning the necessary income by selling inputs in the factor market. Firms buy inputs in the factor market, which are combined to produce goods for sale in the product market.

possible amount while Joe wants to receive the highest possible revenue (given the costs of production).

This interaction extends to the factor market, where the roles of the two decision makers are reversed. Most households sell labor services to firms, which combine these labor inputs with other resources to produce outputs for sale in the product market. For example, if you sell forty hours of labor services at a price of $5 per hour, the value of this transaction is $200. This $200 is income to you (the household) and a cost to the firm. Acting out of self-interest, you want to maximize the income earned through the sale of inputs (given everything else, such as the desired amount of leisure time), while the competitive firm wants to minimize the total cost paid (given the desired level of output sold in the product market). In the following section, we examine how this interaction of households and firms in the product and factor markets solves three basic economic problems.

36

2.4 The Private Market Solution to the Three Basic Economic Problems

All economies are concerned with allocating resources to produce and distribute goods. The way in which a particular economy produces and distributes goods depends on its **solutions to the three basic economic problems:** (1) what to produce and in what quantity, (2) how to produce, and (3) for whom to produce. In this section we examine the private market solution to these problems.

What to Produce and in What Quantity?

The first problem every economy must solve is that of choosing *what to produce and in what quantity*. When we examined the PP curve in Section 2.2, we concluded that an economy is capable of producing a wide variety of goods — such as capital goods or consumer goods, luxury goods or necessities, civilian goods or military goods, public goods or private goods. Since we have limited economic resources, an increase in the production of one good has an opportunity cost in that the production of other goods must be reduced. The actual combination of goods produced depends on the pattern of spending in the economy.

In a purely private market economy, the pattern of spending is determined largely by the **dollar votes** of consumers. When you go into a store to buy a particular good, the salesperson rings up the sale at the cash register which, in a sense, registers a vote for that product. For example, if more and more people play video arcade games, more game parlors will pop up across the country and fewer of the old-fashioned mechanical pinball machines will be produced. Therefore, the pattern of spending by consumers plays an important role in directing economic resources in our economy. This is because purchases by consumers generate revenue (income) for firms.

But decisions concerning what to produce and in what quantity also hinge on the costs of production. The decisive factor that motivates firms in the private market is the *expectation of profit*. For example, suppose that there are two goods, digital watches and tickets for off-Broadway shows, each selling for $30. Also suppose that the cost of producing a digital watch is $5 per watch while the cost of producing an off-Broadway show is $20 per seat. Since the owners of firms expect to make a higher return in producing watches than off-Broadway shows, the economic resources of the economy will be channeled more toward the production of watches.

How to Produce?

Production costs are important not only in deciding what goods to produce. They are also a crucial determinant in the decisions made by firms in deciding *how to produce* these goods. Production costs, in turn, depend on the alternative methods of production that are available and the relative costs of the various inputs that may be used in the production process. In a competitive market economy, firms will choose that method of production which *minimizes total costs*. By minimizing the cost of production, firms are maximizing total profit. Why?

Since profit is the difference between the revenue that firms receive from sales and the costs that they must pay out, total profit will increase (given total revenue) if the firm is able to reduce total costs.

To understand this better, see Table 2.2. The table assumes that there are two methods available for producing a one-mile stretch of roadway. *Method 1 involves a labor-intensive production process.* The roadway is built with *two hundred* workers who share various small tools, such as shovels, picks, wheelbarrows, and rakes. The total cost of labor per hour is $400 at a wage rate of *$2 per hour* or $2,000 at a wage rate of *$10 per hour*. The overall cost of the equipment is assumed to be unchanged at $100 per hour. *Method 2 is capital intensive,* involving a bulldozer, a steam roller, and a machine for laying hot asphalt, as well as numerous trucks for hauling steel reinforcement rods and cement. The cost of this heavy equipment is assumed to be a constant $900 per hour. Labor costs are a small portion of the overall cost of production. Only *fifty* workers are employed in this method of production. At a wage rate of *$2 per hour,* overall labor costs are $100 per hour. If the wage rate were to increase to *$10 per hour,* total labor costs would be $500 per hour.

How would the roadway be produced? The answer lies both in the *alternative technologies available* and the *relative cost of the inputs.* If the wage rate were *$2 per hour,* firms would choose to use the labor-intensive method of production (method 1) since the total cost of producing the roadway is $500 compared to $1,000 for method 2. On the other hand, if the wage happened to be *$10 per hour,* firms would choose the capital-intensive method of production since the total cost of method 1 is $2,100 and the total cost of method 2 is only $1,400.

Table 2.2
In Producing a Roadway, Firms Choose That Method
of Production Which Minimizes Total Costs

Method 1: LABOR-INTENSIVE TECHNOLOGY		Method 2: CAPITAL-INTENSIVE TECHNOLOGY	
Given a wage of $2		*Given a wage of $2*	
Labor costs	$ 400	Labor costs	$ 100
Capital costs	100	Capital costs	900
TOTAL	$ 500	TOTAL	$1,000
Given a wage of $10		*Given a wage of $10*	
Labor costs	$2,000	Labor costs	$ 500
Capital costs	100	Capital costs	900
TOTAL	$2,100	TOTAL	$1,400

The following are summaries of two articles which describe the socialist economy of the People's Republic of China and its experiment with the private enterprise system. For a detailed discussion of how China and other economies solve the three basic economic problems, see *Special Topic A: Comparative Economic Systems.*

An Experiment with Private Enterprise

For almost twenty years, the People's Republic of China had closed its door to foreign influence in an attempt to develop its economy solely through socialism. This policy changed in the late 1970s. China is now attempting to attract foreign investment, technology, and management by creating four Special Economic Zones.

These zones are being developed as new urban areas containing capitalist export centers for manufactured goods. The largest of these zones is Shenzhen. According to the Deputy Mayor of Shenzhen, Zhou Xi-wu, "We know the socialist economic system is not perfect, yet we cannot introduce an all-capitalist system. We shall persist in the socialist way. But we can introduce some advanced foreign economic experience, either capitalist or socialist, into our system — to reform it, change it, perfect it. If the experiment of the Special Economic Zones succeeds here, other parts of China can use the lessons. If they fail, other parts of China can avoid these experiments."

Source: John J. Putnam, "Special Economic Zones: China's Opening Door," *National Geographic,* July 1983, pp. 64–83.

An Update: Five Years Later

Only recently have growing numbers of foreign companies begun to make inroads into the huge Chinese market for consumer goods and services. In November, 1987, Kentucky Fried Chicken opened the first Western fast-food restaurant in China. The restaurant contains 500 seats and can fry 2,300 pieces of chicken an hour. Other foreign products being introduced are soft drink colas (Coca-Cola and Pepsi), cosmetics (Revlon, Max Factor, Mary Quant, and Christian Dior), color film (Kodak and Fuji), and coffee (Nescafé and Maxwell House).

Most of the one billion people cannot be reached by foreign firms because of distribution problems and wide regional variations in climate, language, and taste. Marketing drives are generally limited to the 20 percent of the people who live in the nation's more affluent cities. Other problems which hamper foreign sales are low per capita income and tight government controls over the extremely scarce foreign exchange currency needed to pay for imports.

Source: Maria Shao, "Laying the Foundation for the Great Mall of China," *Business Week,* January 25, 1988, pp. 68–69.

The adoption of the technology that minimizes the total cost of production is called *economic efficiency.* We should note that technology which is economically efficient may not necessarily be the most technically efficient method of production. ***Technical efficiency*** is an engineering concept that entails producing an output with the least amount of input. The capital-intensive technology for producing roads (method 2) may be more technically efficient than the labor-intensive technology (method 1), but when the wage rate is only $2 per hour it is not the most economically efficient method. The concept of economic efficiency helps to explain why developing economies (with relatively lower labor costs) build roads using labor-intensive techniques, whereas industrialized countries (with relatively cheaper capital costs) build roads using capital-intensive methods.

The solution to the "what" and "how" questions involves the *problem of production.* The solution to the "for whom" question is more controversial than the other two because it involves the *problem of distribution.* Who should benefit from the goods produced by the economy? In addition to economic efficiency, the economy wants to achieve ***allocative efficiency,*** which means that goods are produced in that combination which maximizes the total satisfaction of consumers. In a purely private market, the solution is largely the result of *dollar votes* in the product market. People who spend money in the product market get the satisfaction of consuming the goods and services which they buy.

But what determines the amount of dollar votes that different people make in the product market? In a purely private market, the answer lies primarily in the distribution of income and wealth. Those with the most income and wealth have the most votes as to what is produced. The distribution of income is determined in the factor market, where households earn income by selling their factors of production (labor, capital, and natural resources). Wealth is a stock of income accumulated over time, often being passed from one generation to the next through inheritance. This explanation is, of course, a cursory treatment of a complex question.

Why do countries trade with each other? We will note that nations engage in international trade because of the benefits that result from specialization. All nations can benefit from trade if each specializes in producing those goods in which it has a comparative advantage.

The forces shaping the distribution of income and wealth will be discussed at length in *Special Topic G: Income Distribution and Poverty.* See *Special Topic A: Comparative Economic Systems* for a description of how the economy of the Soviet Union and other economic systems solve the three basic economic problems.

2.5 Specialization and the Principle of Comparative Advantage: Why Nations Trade

To understand the basic cause of international trade, let us assume that there are only two countries, Javit and Xanda, and that each country produces only two goods, food and clothing. The *maximum* amount of either good that Javit and Xanda could produce is presented in Table 2.3. Javit can produce a maximum of 200 units of food or 600 units of clothing. On the other hand, Xanda can produce a maximum of 100 units of food or 200 units of clothing. This table (which is based on the production possibilities model presented in Section 2.2) assumes constant opportunity costs.

Since Javit has the ability to produce more of either good, why should it trade with Xanda? The answer lies in the difference in opportunity costs, which are calculated from Table 2.3. For example, Javit must give up 600 units of clothing to produce 200 units of food. Therefore, the opportunity cost of producing 1 unit of food in Javit is 3 units of clothing ($1F = 3C$), indicated at the top of Table 2.4. On the other hand, Xanda must give up the production of 200 units of clothing in order to produce 100 units of food. This means that the opportunity cost of producing 1 unit of food in Xanda is 2 units of clothing ($1F = 2C$).

While Javit has an **absolute advantage** in production since it can produce more of either good, Xanda has a *comparative advantage* in the production of food. Javit must give up 3 units of clothing to produce 1 unit of food, whereas Xanda must give up only 2 units of clothing to produce the same unit of food (shown at the top of Table 2.4). Javit, on the other hand, has a comparative advantage in the production of clothing. According to the **principle of comparative advantage,** each nation can gain through trade by specializing in the production of those goods that it can make *relatively* more efficiently. Javit should export clothing and import food, while Xanda should export food and import clothing.

The Benefits of International Trade

What are the **benefits of international trade?** To illustrate the potential gains from trade, let us assume that the two countries exchange food and clothing at the price of 1 unit of food for 2.5 units of clothing ($1F = 2.5C$). Both countries benefit since Javit can get 1 unit of food

Table 2.3
Maximum Amount of Either
Food or Clothing That Both
Countries Could Produce

	Food	Clothing
Javit	200	600
Xanda	100	200

Table 2.4
Differences in Opportunity Costs
Between the Two Countries

Opportunity cost of producing 1 unit of food
    (Xanda has a comparative advantage in food)
    Javit   1 unit of food = 3 units of clothing $(1F = 3C)$
    Xanda   1 unit of food = 2 units of clothing $(1F = 2C)$
Opportunity cost of producing 1 unit of clothing
    (Javit has a comparative advantage in clothing)
    Javit   1 unit of clothing = $\frac{1}{3}$ unit of food $(1C = \frac{1}{3}F)$
    Xanda   1 unit of clothing = $\frac{1}{2}$ unit of food $(1C = \frac{1}{2}F)$

for 2.5 units of clothing (domestically, the cost is 3 units of clothing) and Xanda can get 2.5 units of clothing for 1 unit of food (domestically, it could only get 2 units of clothing). Therefore, we can see that each country stands to benefit through trade by specializing in the production of the good in which it has a comparative advantage. Javit can consume more food by selling clothing to Xanda, and Xanda can consume more clothing by exporting food to Javit.

Summary

Economics studies how we can allocate our scarce resources in production to maximize the satisfaction of our unlimited wants. There are three types of inputs: human resources (which includes entrepreneurship), capital, and natural resources.

The production possibilities model represents all possible combinations of two goods that can be produced when resources are fully employed and the most efficient technologies are used. The PP model demonstrated the problem of scarcity — that we have to give up increasing amounts of one good in order to produce more of another good. We concluded that unemployment and inefficiency cause us to produce below the PP curve. We also discovered that innovation and increases in the stock of labor and capital raise the growth potential of our economy.

In the private enterprise system, firms and households interact in the product and factor markets to solve the three basic economic problems. Firms will produce those goods (in that amount) which the firms expect will make them the most profit. Likewise, firms will use those methods of production that minimize their total costs. The distribution of income and wealth largely determines to whom the goods are distributed.

Finally, we noted that nations trade with each other because of the benefits that result from specialization. All nations can benefit from trade if each nation specializes in producing those goods in which it has a comparative advantage.

Key Concepts

economic resources
inputs
factors of production
outputs
human resources (labor)
entrepreneurship
capital
financial capital
natural resources
production possibilities model
economic models
technology
opportunity cost
law of increasing costs
unemployment
underemployment
innovation
economic growth
consumer goods and capital goods
present versus future satisfaction
savings and investment
private market system
mixed economy
circular flow
market
product market
factor market
household
firm
solutions to the three basic economic problems
dollar votes
economic efficiency
technical efficiency
allocative efficiency
absolute advantage
principle of comparative advantage
benefits of international trade

Self-Test Questions: True or False

T **F** 1. All of the following are types of capital: construction, land, machinery and equipment, stocks and bonds.

T **F** 2. Innovation is defined as the creation of capital.

Answer questions 3 and 4 using the following PP curve:

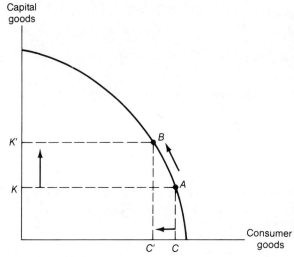

T **F** 3. The movement from point *A* to point *B* represents an increase in the production of capital goods. The opportunity cost involved in producing more capital goods is the amount of consumer goods forgone.

T **F** 4. The movement from point *A* to point *B* in the graph will cause the PP curve to shift outward in the future. If the economy were to remain at point *B*, unemployment would result.

T **F** 5. According to the circular flow diagram, households act as buyers in both the product market and the factor market.

T **F** 6. According to the purely private market solution, firms will decide "what to produce" based on dollar votes, given the costs of production.

Answer questions 7, 8, and 9 based on the following table, which represents the maximum amount of either food or clothing that both countries could produce.

	Food	Clothing
Bentol	100	300
Findal	400	800

T F   7. The opportunity cost of producing 1 unit of food in Findal is 2 units of clothing.

T F   8. Findal has an absolute advantage in the production of food and clothing.

T F   9. Findal has a comparative advantage in food production.

Answer questions 10 and 11 using the following table, which illustrates the production possibilities model.

Public Goods	Private Goods
90	0
75	30
60	55
45	75
30	90
15	100
0	105

T F   10. The opportunity cost of increasing the production of public goods from 45 to 60 units is 20 units of private goods.

T F   11. If this economy were producing 30 units of public goods and 80 units of private goods, then the economy is not using its resources to their fullest extent.

Answers to Self-Test Questions

1. *False.* Land as well as stocks and bonds are not types of capital. Capital is defined by economists as a human-made input. Land is an input, but it is not made by human beings — it is a natural resource. Stocks and bonds are not inputs since they are not used directly in the production process; instead, they are used to channel the savings of households to firms in order to finance the purchase of the three types of capital (construction, machinery and equipment, and inventories).

2. *False.* Innovation is defined as the development of a new technology (i.e., creating a new method of production or a new product). The creation of capital (human-made inputs) is called investment.

3. *True.* Households must save (postpone consumption by the amount CC') in order to release the economic resources required for investment by firms (the increase in capital goods by KK').

4. ***True.*** Investment increases our capital stock, which gives us more factories and machinery to use to possibly produce more consumer and capital goods in the future. This increase in potential economic growth is represented by the outward shift in the PP curve. However, if total spending in the economy were to remain unchanged, the economy would stagnate at point *B,* creating unemployment. To realize this growth potential, total spending would have to increase until the economy was located somewhere on the new PP curve.

5. ***False.*** Households do not act as buyers in the factor market — rather, they sell inputs to firms in the factor market. Households do this in order to earn the income to purchase goods from firms in the product market.

6. ***True.*** Firms will produce those goods which they expect will give them maximum total profit (i.e., the difference between total revenue and total costs). Given the total costs of production, total profit depends on total revenue which is generated by dollar votes in the product market.

7. ***True.*** The opportunity cost of producing 1 unit of food in Findal is 2 units of clothing. Given constant opportunity costs, to produce 400 units of food, Findal would have to give up the production of 800 units of clothing. Measured in terms of individual units, this is a loss of 2 units of clothing for every additional unit of food produced.

8. ***True.*** Findal has an absolute advantage since it can produce more food or clothing than Bentol.

9. ***True.*** Findal has a comparative advantage in food production since the opportunity cost of 1 unit of food in Findal is only 2 units of clothing — the cost in Bentol is 3 units of clothing.

10. ***True.*** In order to increase the production of public goods from 45 to 60 units, the production of private goods must be reduced from 75 to 55 units.

11. ***True.*** The economy is not using its resources to their fullest extent since the economy is capable of producing 10 more units of private goods given the production of 30 units of public goods. The economy may be operating below its production possibilities frontier either because it is experiencing unemployment or underemployment.

Discussion Questions

1. a. Define what economists mean by the term *capital* and list the three types of capital.

    b. Describe the relationship between savings and investment. How do changes in savings and investment affect present satisfaction versus future satisfaction? Why?

2. a. Describe the impact of innovation on the production of consumer goods (assuming no change in the method of producing capital goods), using the accompanying PP curve to illustrate your answer.

    b. If the economy were to remain at point *A*, what problem would be created? Why?

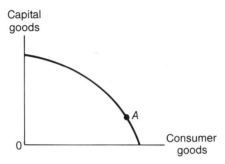

3. Draw the circular flow diagram. Describe how firms and households interact in both markets, indicating the financial flow of payments and income and the physical flow of outputs and inputs.

4. Describe the purely private market solution to the three basic economic problems.

Answer question 5 based on the following table which shows the maximum amount of either food or clothing that both countries could produce.

	Food	Clothing
Bentol	100	300
Findal	400	800

5. Since Findal can produce more of both food and clothing than Bentol, it will not benefit by trading with Bentol. Is this statement correct? Discuss.

Problems

Answer questions 1 through 3 using the following production possibilities schedule for Bantok in 1990:

Capital Goods	Consumer Goods
200	0
150	40
100	60
50	75
0	80

1. Graph the production possibilities curve. Suppose that Bantok is currently producing 100 units of capital goods and 60 units of consumer goods. Illustrate this combination on your graph.

2. What is the opportunity cost of increasing the production of capital goods from 100 units to 150 units in 1990? Illustrate this change on your graph.

3. Illustrate the impact of this investment on the production possibilities curve by the year 2000 on your graph. Explain the reason for this effect.

4. The following PP curves illustrate the impact of a drought on the economy's agricultural sector. Suppose that point *A* represents the initial combination of farm and nonfarm goods. How might the economy maintain the same level of farm goods production? Use the figure to illustrate your answer.

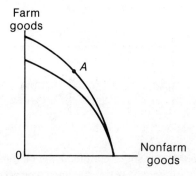

PART
TWO

Microeconomics

Supply and Demand in the Product Market

Objectives

Upon completion of this chapter, you should understand:

1. How to use supply and demand to analyze the process through which a market determines the price and quantity of goods sold.

2. How to analyze the impact of changes in market conditions on equilibrium price and quantity.

3. The effect of price floors and price ceilings on competitive markets.

Across the nation people wake up in the morning, have breakfast, and go off to work in order to earn the income to buy the goods that satisfy their wants. Firms employ these workers and other inputs to produce goods for sale in the product market in the expectation of making profit. This seemingly simple life pattern is repeated on a daily basis in the U.S. economy, involving about 122 million workers and over 17 million firms.

As a result of this interaction between firms and households, millions of goods are produced in the U.S. economy. The sales catalogs of major retailers such as Sears, L. L. Bean, and J. C. Penney represent only a small sample of the types of goods produced. In each individual market, firms must decide how much of the good to produce and what price to charge. Households, on the other hand, must decide how much of this product to buy and what price to pay. How does the private market coordinate this vast matrix of decisions that are made every day to determine the prices and quantities of goods sold in the economy?

The overall purpose of this chapter is to develop an economic model that helps to explain how such decisions are made in the product market. In Section 3.1 we introduce the purely competitive market structure, which describes how buyers and sellers would behave under perfect conditions. Next, in Sections 3.2 and 3.3 we introduce the model of "supply and demand," which economists have developed to analyze the behavior of buyers and sellers in the market. Supply represents the decisions made by firms acting as sellers, and demand represents the decisions made by households acting as buyers. In Sections 3.4 and 3.5 we bring the concepts of supply and demand together to discuss how competitive market forces determine the price and quantity of goods sold. Not all prices are the result of decisions made by buyers and sellers. In Section 3.6 we examine prices set by government and how they affect the market.

Note that many topics to be discussed throughout the remainder of this book hinge on the fundamental principles presented in this chapter. These principles introduce essential "building blocks" which are necessary to understand the inner workings of the private market economy.

3.1 Pure Competition

Economists have developed a model called **pure competition** to describe how buyers and sellers would interact in the market under perfect conditions. Pure competition is a standard that will be used in Chapter 5 to evaluate the behavior of the other less competitive market structures that characterize the private market economy.

The purely competitive market model is based on three major assumptions. First, we assume that there are *many households* and *many small firms* in the market acting *independently* of each other in their decisions to buy or sell. Second, each firm in a given industry is assumed to produce an *identical product*. For example, all the wheat produced by farmers is assumed to be of exactly the same quality. Third, we assume there are no barriers to hinder a firm from getting into business or out of business, given sufficient time. The result of these three assumptions is that the individual firm or household has *no control over price*. The price of the product is determined by the interaction of many buyers and sellers in the market, not by the decision of any single firm or household.

Why is the purely competitive firm not able to increase or decrease the price it charges for its product relative to the market price? Suppose that Joe decided to raise the price of pizza above the prevailing price charged by other pizzerias. Consumers would react by not buying pizza from Joe because they could get the same product elsewhere at a lower price. On the other hand, it would not be rational for Joe to lower his price below the price charged by the other pizzerias. He can sell all the pizza he wants to sell at the going market price because his pizzeria is small relative to the overall industry. Therefore, the purely competitive firm is a *price taker*, not a *price maker*.

The best examples of purely competitive industries are farming and some financial markets such as money market funds and checking accounts. Although many of the examples to be used do not strictly adhere to the purely competitive model because the products produced are not identical, they are all examples of highly competitive industries. The implications of imperfect competition are discussed in Chapter 5.

3.2 Demand

Whenever we walk through a large shopping mall on a Saturday afternoon, we will see a large crowd of people milling around tables and shelves filled with merchandise. To analyze the behavior of buyers in the market, economists have developed a model called *demand*.

The Law of Demand

What factors affect what we plan to buy? The price of the product, the amount of income we have, and the price of other goods certainly have an impact on our decision. In developing the demand curve, economists focus on the impact of the current *price of the product* because price is the only variable that both buyers and sellers share in the marketplace. According to the **law of demand**, households are willing and able to buy less of a good as the price of that good increases, assuming that all other influences do not change. For example, an increase in the price of a ticket to the movies will usually reduce attendance. An increase in price will ration some people out of the market since they may not be willing or able to pay the higher price. Conversely, a decrease in price will increase the amount that households plan to buy. People who are not willing to pay the full price to see a movie on a Saturday night may be induced to see the film at a bargain matinee.

The *demand schedule* for oranges presented in Table 3.1 is created by varying price and observing changes in the amount demanded by households (in a specific time period), keeping all other factors constant. Figure 3.1 shows the *demand curve* for oranges. The points on the demand curve correspond to the values in the demand schedule presented in Table 3.1. When the price is $4, households are willing and able to buy 175 thousand bushels (point *B*). If the price were to increase to $7, households would buy only 100 thousand bushels (point *E*). Price is always measured by the vertical axis, and quantity is always measured by the horizontal axis. Note that a "curve" may be a straight line, as is the straight-line curve illustrated by Figure 3.1.

Table 3.1
Demand for
Oranges
(thousands of
bushels)

	P	Q_d
A	$3	200
B	4	175
C	5	150
D	6	125
E	7	100
F	8	75

It is very important to note that an increase in price does not decrease "demand"; it decreases the "quantity demanded," represented by a movement down along the demand curve. "Demand," illustrated by the curve, has not changed. What factors will cause the demand curve to shift?

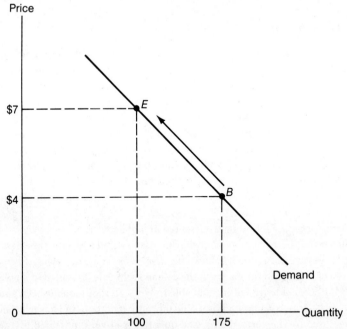

Figure 3.1.   Demand for Oranges (thousands of bushels). An increase in the current price of oranges will decrease the quantity demanded.

Nonprice Determinants of Demand

We noted that there are numerous factors other than the current price of the product that affect how much we plan to buy. They are called *nonprice determinants of demand* or *demand shift factors* because a change in any of them will shift the demand curve.

Tastes Some people crave chocolate candy, while others prefer to nibble on potato chips. Preferences or tastes are important in determining our willingness to purchase different types of goods. The demand for many goods, such as clothing and hair styles, changes frequently as fashions come and go. For example, what would happen if people suddenly desired to eat more oranges as an ingredient in a new fad dessert? Households would plan to buy more oranges at each price. There would be an increase in demand, which is illustrated in Figure 3.2 and Table 3.2. Note the outward shift to the right in the demand curve. Earlier, households had planned to buy 175 thousand bushels of oranges at a price of $4. When the orange dessert became a fad, they suddenly planned to buy 195 thousand bushels at the price of $4. At each price found in Figure 3.2 and Table 3.2, households plan to buy more oranges.

Income An increase in income will also cause an increase in our demand for most goods. For example, an increase in income would probably cause many people to buy more sirloin steak. If higher income causes an increase in the demand for a good, the product is a *normal good.*

But in some cases, the opposite will happen. If an increase in income causes a decrease in the demand for a particular good, it is called an *inferior good.* For example, when family income increases, the demand for certain types of food, such as pasta, potatoes, rice, and cheaper cuts of beef, decreases because the household can afford to buy more expensive food.

Population Since people are potential buyers, as population rises, the demand for most goods will also rise. For example, the migration of population to such urban centers as Los

Table 3.2
Increase in the
Demand for
Oranges
(thousands of
bushels)

P	Q_d	Q_d'
$3	200	**220**
4	175	**195**
5	150	**170**
6	125	**145**
7	100	**120**
8	75	**95**

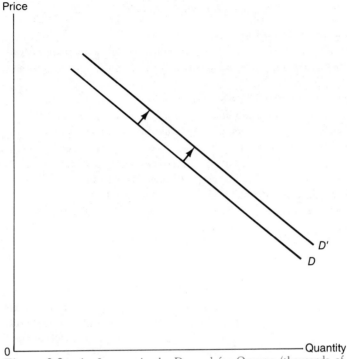

Figure 3.2.   An Increase in the Demand for Oranges (thousands of bushels). Households are planning to buy more oranges at each price.

Angeles and Atlanta has increased the demand for housing, restaurants, and automobiles in these cities.

The Prices of Other Goods   In purchasing consumer products, we must choose from a wide variety of goods. The demand curve for any particular good is drawn, given the prices of all other products, relative to the price of this good. Economists have classified these products into three major categories.

First, a ***substitute good*** is a good that we may use easily instead of another product (e.g., a submarine sandwich may be purchased instead of a pizza, and margarine may be bought instead of butter). An increase in the price of one of these goods will increase the demand for the other good. For example, the price of sirloin steak is a "nonprice" determinant of the demand for chicken. A sharp increase in the price of sirloin steak would tend to increase the demand for chicken (the substitute good).

Second, a ***complementary good*** is a product that we tend to buy along with the purchase of another good (e.g., hot dog buns are usually bought with hot dogs, tennis balls are purchased with tennis rackets). If the price of one of these products increases, the demand for the complementary good decreases. For example, if the price of hot dogs were to increase sharply, the quantity of hot dogs demanded would decrease (a movement along the demand curve for hot dogs). Since households would eat fewer hot dogs, the demand for hot dog buns would decrease (an inward shift to the left in the demand curve for hot dog buns). Therefore, the price of hot dogs is a nonprice determinant of the demand for hot dog buns (the complementary good).

Third, there are many goods in the economy that are neither substitute nor complementary goods. These goods are termed *independent goods.* If the price of one of these goods changes, it will not have a perceivable effect on the demand for the other (independent) good. For example, an increase in the price of pencils does not affect our demand for housing.

Expectations   What we think may happen in the future has a major impact on our current demand for goods. Expectations concerning future income and future prices are especially important. For example, when the economy slides into a recession, households threatened by layoffs attempt to save a larger portion of their current income. They would want to save more now in order to have a larger reserve of savings to live on later, during the expected period of reduced earnings. Their demand for many goods would decrease to permit them to increase their current savings.

Similarly, if the price of a particular good is expected to increase in the future, consumers may rush out to the stores to buy it. This occurred in the mid-1970s when people expected the price of beef to increase sharply. Many households bought freezers and stockpiled beef to beat the expected increase in the price of beef. Note that the expected future price of beef is a nonprice determinant of the current demand for beef.

Demand Versus Quantity Demanded

Failure to make the distinction between a change in the "quantity demanded" and a change in "demand" will make it difficult for you to understand the rest of this chapter. The demand curve is made up of numerous "quantity-demanded" points — which point is chosen depends on the current price of the product. Since price determines the quantity demanded, price cannot determine demand. Therefore, a *change in the quantity demanded* refers to a *movement* along a given demand curve. A *change in demand* refers to a *shift* in the demand curve itself. For example, in Figure 3.1, we noted that an increase in price from $4 to $7 would cause households to buy fewer oranges. The quantity demanded would drop from 175 thousand to 100 thousand bushels of oranges (a movement along the demand curve from point *B* to point *E*). Demand, which refers to the overall curve, has not changed. However, if people suddenly desired to eat more oranges, they would plan to buy more oranges *at each price*. There would be an increase in demand, represented by an outward shift to the right in the demand curve illustrated in Figure 3.2.

3.3 Supply

The huge variety of goods that appears on the shelves and tables of stores throughout the country depends on the decisions made by many producers. Economists analyze the behavior of competitive firms in selling their goods using the model of supply.

The Law of Supply

According to the **law of supply,** competitive firms will increase the amount they offer for sale as the price of their product increases, given all other influences. This increase in price gives firms the incentive to produce more. It enables them to earn the additional revenue required to buy more inputs in order to produce more goods for sale.

A *supply schedule* for oranges is illustrated in Table 3.3. It was created by varying price and observing the *change in the quantity supplied* by firms (in a specific time period), keeping all other factors constant. The data from this schedule were used to draw the *supply curve* in Figure 3.3. We can see that an increase in the price of oranges from $4 to $7 causes firms in the market to increase the quantity supplied from 75 thousand to 150 thousand bushels (a move from point *B* to point *E*). The slope of the supply curve is positive (upward sloping), not negative (downward sloping) as is the case with the demand curve. Note that Figure 3.3 represents *market supply,* which is the summation of the amounts that individual firms would plan to sell at each price.

Nonprice Determinants of Supply

Numerous factors other than the price of the product affect the production decisions of firms. These factors are called **nonprice determinants of supply** or **supply shift factors** since a change in any one of them will shift the supply curve.

Table 3.3
Supply of
Oranges
(thousands of
bushels)

	P	Q_s
A	$3	50
B	4	75
C	5	100
D	6	125
E	7	150
F	8	175

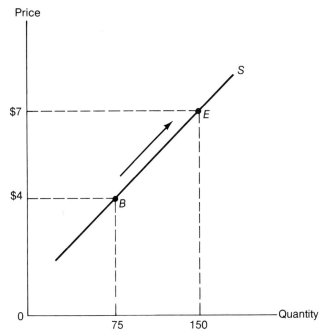

Figure 3.3. Supply of Oranges (thousands of bushels). An increase in the current price of oranges will increase the quantity supplied.

The Cost of Production The firm's decision as to how much to produce at a particular price is heavily dependent on the cost of running its business. A decrease in the cost of production increases the level of total profit. This increase in total profit gives the firm the incentive to purchase more inputs in order to expand production at each price. The resulting increase in the supply of oranges is represented by an outward shift to the right in the supply curve. Table 3.4 and Figure 3.4 illustrate this increase in supply since, at each price, firms plan to offer a larger quantity of the product for sale.

Why might the costs of producing different types of goods decrease? First, a drop in the price of inputs (labor, capital, and natural resources) will lower the cost of production. For example, the price of computers has dropped sharply over the last ten years, making it cheaper for firms to store and process information. Second, innovation will also cause production costs to decrease. With a better method of production, firms are able to combine inputs at less expense. For example, the automobile was first made affordable to a large number of persons when Henry Ford introduced mass assembly technology to the automobile industry in the early 1900s. This innovation caused the cost of producing cars to drop sharply. More recently, the development of prefabricated homes has made the price of housing lower for many families.

Table 3.4
Increase in the Supply of Oranges (thousands of bushels)

P	Q_s	Q'_s
$3	50	60
4	75	85
5	100	110
6	125	135
7	150	160
8	175	185

Expectations   The expectations of firms concerning the future price of their product may affect current production. If firms expect the price of their good to increase in the future, they might react in either one of two ways.

If they could stockpile the good, firms would increase production while withholding their product from the market. Firms would do this in order to have a large reserve of the product to

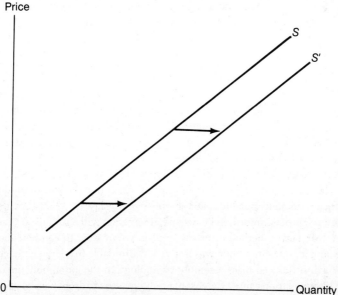

Figure 3.4.   An Increase in the Supply of Oranges (thousands of bushels). Firms are planning to sell more oranges at each price.

sell if the price actually should increase in the future. The withholding of goods from the market would decrease current supply (i.e., the supply curve would shift inward to the left). For example, oil companies hoarded oil during the oil embargo of 1975 in anticipation of a sharp increase in the price of oil.

If, however, firms could not stockpile the good (perhaps because it was perishable or too expensive to store), firms would tend to step up current production. They would attempt to reach full operation in order to be able to sell more goods in the event that the expected price increase did in fact occur. For example, egg farmers anticipating an increase in the price of eggs need time to build more hen houses and to raise more chickens. The result would be an increase in current supply (i.e., the supply curve would shift outward to the right).

Prices of Alternative Products   The prices of alternative products that the firms might have produced are also important. For example, suppose that farmers are contemplating what crop to plant. If the price of soybeans rises relative to the price of corn, the farmers will tend to switch from corn production to soybean production since it will be more profitable. The supply of corn will decrease, with the curve shifting inward to the left.

The Number of Firms in the Market   If more firms enter the market, the supply curve will increase. The quantity supplied at each price will be greater because there are more firms planning to sell their product in this industry.

Supply Versus Quantity Supplied

In Figure 3.3, we saw that an increase in price from $4 to $7 would induce firms to increase the ***quantity of oranges supplied*** from 75 thousand to 150 thousand bushels (a *movement* from point *B* to point *E* up the supply curve). *Supply* (the whole curve) would not change. A ***change in supply*** refers to a *shift* in the supply curve itself. An increase in the supply of oranges is represented by an outward shift to the right in the supply curve. Table 3.4 and Figure 3.4 illustrate an increase in supply since, *at each price,* firms plan to offer a larger quantity of the product for sale.

3.4 Market Equilibrium

How do buyers and sellers interact in markets to establish the price and quantity of goods sold? In order to understand such behavior, we must examine the concept of market equilibrium.

Equilibrium Conditions

A market is in equilibrium when buyers and sellers agree on the price and quantity sold, since there is no tendency for the actual price to change. ***Equilibrium price*** is defined as a position of stability toward which the ***actual price*** (the current price) moves. Once the actual price reaches equilibrium, it will tend not to change any further since it has achieved the *equilib-rium condition,* defined as the situation where the quantity demanded equals the quantity supplied.

Table 3.5 and Figure 3.5 illustrate the equilibrium price and equilibrium quantity sold in the market for oranges. The supply and demand schedules presented in Table 3.5 are the same as those we examined in Sections 3.2 and 3.3. We can see that the equilibrium condition is met at a price of $6 since firms are planning to sell 125 thousands of bushels of oranges, which is the amount that households plan to buy at this price. In other words, at the price of $6, the quantity sold of 125 thousands of bushels *clears* the market since neither too little nor too much is produced. This combination of $6 and 125 thousands of bushels is the only stable combination of price and output. At any other price the quantity demanded will either be greater or less than the quantity supplied. The resulting shortage or surplus, in turn, will cause the price to change. How do changes in price eliminate shortages and surpluses?

Case of a Shortage

Suppose one Saturday morning you are driving along a rural road and you spot a long line of cars parked outside an old building where an auction is taking place. After parking your car, you enter the front of the building. There is a large crowd of people, some standing and many seated, all watching the auctioneer chanting into a microphone at the end of the large hall. You discover that about ten people are bidding against each other in their attempt to buy an old rocking chair sitting on top of the auctioneer's table. "It's a real beauty . . . only one of its kind," the auctioneer says in a low voice. He then begins to eye the audience, "Do I hear $60, $60 . . . $65, $65 . . . $70, $70 . . . " The people bidding keep raising their arms in response, causing a flurry of price increases until eventually there is only one arm up in the air. "Going once, going twice, . . . sold for $95 to the gentleman in the red hat!," the auctioneer shouts.

This bidding process occurs in all markets whenever there is a *shortage* of goods available for sale. While we don't see consumers waving their arms in an attempt to buy the last head of lettuce in a grocer's bin, the dissatisfaction of customers facing a shortage of lettuce will cause the grocer to order more lettuce from the produce broker. As other grocers in the market phone in their orders for lettuce, a bidding process is initiated, causing the price of lettuce to increase.

To understand in more detail how price increases eliminate shortages, let us return to our market for oranges illustrated by Table 3.5 and Figure 3.5. Suppose that the actual price of oranges is $3. At this price, firms are willing to sell only 50 thousand bushels of oranges per day (point *A* on the supply curve), but households want to buy 200 thousand bushels of oranges per day (point *B* on the demand curve). Since the quantity demanded exceeds the quantity supplied, a shortage of 150 thousand bushels exists.

At the price of $3, firms are content because they are selling the amount they want to sell (50 thousand bushels). However, households are not content because, at the price of $3, they had wanted to purchase 200 thousand bushels. The plans of households have not been satisfied.

Table 3.5
Market Equilibrium: Supply and
Demand for Oranges (thousands
of bushels)

	P	Q_s	Q_d
Actual price	$3	50	200
	4	75	175
	5	100	150
Equilibrium	6	125	125
	7	150	100
	8	175	75

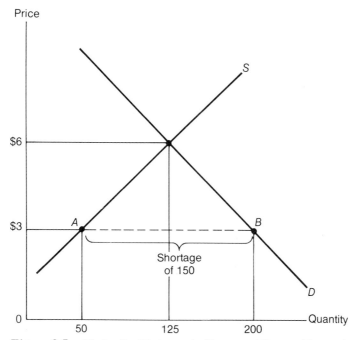

Figure 3.5. Market Equilibrium and a Shortage of Oranges (thousands of bushels). When the actual price is below the equilibrium position, households want to buy more than firms want to sell. The resulting shortage causes households to bid the price up. The resulting increase in price increases the quantity supplied while decreasing the quantity demanded.

What happens as a result of this shortage? Households bid the price of the good up, which brings into play the **role of prices.** As price increases to $6, it *signals* the need for the increased production of oranges (giving citrus growers the incentive to harvest and store their crops more carefully) while some households are *rationed* out of the market. Firms increase the quantity of oranges supplied by 75 thousand bushels (from 50 thousand to 125 thousand bushels) while some households are rationed out of the market, which decreases the quantity of oranges demanded by 75 thousand bushels (from 200 thousand to 125 thousand bushels). At the price of $6, both decision makers are in agreement (i.e., the quantity supplied equals the quantity demanded at 125 thousand bushels). Consequently, the actual price will stabilize at $6, making it the equilibrium price.

We can summarize how changes in price eliminate a shortage using the following notation:

$$\text{shortage} \rightarrow \text{households} \uparrow P \rightarrow \downarrow Q_d \text{ and } \uparrow Q_s \text{ until } Q_d = Q_s$$

Note that "↑" represents an increase, "↓" represents a decrease, and "→" represents the direction of causation. The notation above translates as follows. A shortage causes households to bid the price up, which in turn causes the quantity demanded to decrease and the quantity supplied to increase until the quantity demanded equals the quantity supplied.

Case of a Surplus

At the end of a long day, families holding garage sales typically begin marking down their prices because there are too many used toasters, stuffed animals, old clothes, and other stuff still piled on their tables. Many families decide it is better to sell at a lower price than not to sell at all. The same principle operates in all markets.

If the actual price of oranges lies above the equilibrium position, a **surplus** will occur. See Table 3.6 and Figure 3.6, where the actual price is assumed to be $8. This time firms are not

**Table 3.6
Market Equilibrium: Supply and
Demand for Oranges (thousands
of bushels)**

	P	Q_s	Q_d
	$3	50	200
	4	75	175
	5	100	150
Equilibrium	6	125	125
	7	150	100
Actual price	8	175	75

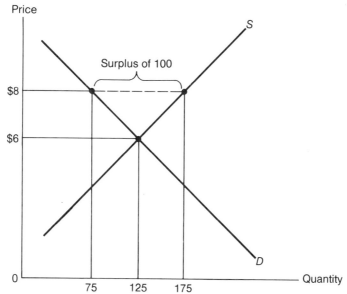

Figure 3.6. Market Equilibrium and a Surplus of Oranges (thousands of bushels). When the actual price is above the equilibrium position, households want to buy less than firms want to sell. The resulting surplus causes firms to lower prices. The resulting decrease in price decreases the quantity supplied while increasing the quantity demanded.

content with the price of $8 because they had planned to sell 175 thousand bushels, but they are only able to sell 75 thousand bushels (since households will buy only 75 thousand bushels of oranges at this price). There exists a surplus of 100 thousand bushels at the price of $8; therefore, it is not a stable price for oranges.

Once again, the role of prices is brought into play. Those firms with surplus oranges will attempt to attract new buyers by lowering their price. This causes the actual price to fall from $8 to $6 for all firms in the market. The decrease in price induces households to buy more (an increase in the quantity demanded by 50 thousand bushels, from 75 thousand to 125 thousand bushels). At the same time, this decrease in price causes firms to plan to sell less (a decrease in the quantity supplied by 50 thousand bushels, from 175 thousand to 125 thousand bushels). We can see that the downward movement along both curves in Figure 3.6 causes equilibrium to be reached at a price of $6, where households and firms agree to trade 125 thousand bushels of oranges. There is no reason for the price to fall further since both decision makers are in agreement. We may summarize this process as follows:

$$\text{surplus} \rightarrow \text{firms} \downarrow P \rightarrow \uparrow Q_d \text{ and } \downarrow Q_s \text{ until } Q_d = Q_s$$

The notation above translates as follows. A surplus causes firms to reduce price, which in turn causes an increase in the quantity demanded and a decrease in the quantity supplied until they are equal.

3.5 Changes in Market Conditions

In the preceding section, we assumed that supply and demand conditions were unchanged. However, in reality, market conditions do change. A sudden freeze in Florida will hurt the harvest of citrus fruit, decreasing the supply of oranges, lemons, limes, and grapefruit. Also, fads come and go. The demand for last season's fashions in clothes falls at the same time that the demand for new fashions rises. Any such change in one of the nonprice determinants of supply or demand will cause a shift in a curve and a change in equilibrium price and quantity.

Case of an Increase in Demand

Suppose that the price of beef were to rise suddenly. What impact would this increase in the price of beef have on the demand for chicken (assumed to be a substitute good)? As noted in Section 3.2, when two goods are substitutes, a rise in the price of one (beef) will increase the demand for the other (chicken).

Figure 3.7 illustrates the resulting increase in the demand for chicken (shown as an outward shift to the right in the demand curve from D_1 to D_2). We can see that the rise in demand creates a shortage at the original equilibrium price of $1. Households are not satisfied at the price of $1 because they are not able to buy the quantity of chicken they had planned to purchase. Firms are planning to sell only 30 units (point A) rather than the 70 units (point B) demanded by households. Therefore, there is a shortage of 40 units of chicken.

As a result of this shortage, households bid up the price of chicken. As the actual price rises it signals the need for increased production, causing the quantity of chicken supplied by firms to go up by 20 units. At the same time, the increase in the actual price of chicken rations some households out of the market, causing a decrease in the quantity of chicken demanded by 20 units. Once the actual price reaches the new equilibrium price of $2, both firms and households agree to buy and sell 50 units of chicken. The shortage has been eliminated, and a new equilibrium has been achieved.

This process can be summarized as follows:

$$\uparrow D \rightarrow \text{shortage} \rightarrow \text{households} \uparrow P \rightarrow \downarrow Q_d \text{ and } \uparrow Q_s \text{, until } Q_d = Q_s$$

These symbols may be translated as follows. An increase in demand causes a shortage, which in turn causes households to bid the price up. The increase in price causes a decrease in the quantity demanded and an increase in the quantity supplied until the market is cleared.

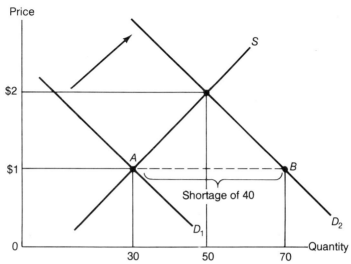

Figure 3.7. Case of a Shortage. An increase in the demand for chicken creates a shortage at the initial equilibrium price. Households bid up the price, which in turn eliminates the shortage by decreasing the quantity demanded and increasing the quantity supplied.

Case of an Increase in Supply

The effect of a change in supply is opposite to the effect caused by a change in demand. For example, an increase in supply creates a surplus, whereas an increase in demand creates a shortage. No matter what the cause of the shortage or surplus, actual price will move to eliminate the problem by bringing both decision makers into agreement. The equilibrium position will be reached when the market is cleared. To simplify the explanation, the figures used in the remainder of this chapter will no longer refer to specific numbers. Instead, equilibrium price and quantity will be indicated by the symbols P for price and Q for quantity.

To illustrate the impact of a change in supply, let us suppose that potato farmers have enough rain to grow an unusually large crop (called a bumper crop). Also, weather conditions during the harvest are dry, making it easy for the farmers to drive heavy machinery into the fields to dig the potatoes out of the earth. Given this situation, answer the following questions as a review of the inner workings of the competitive market:

1. How is supply affected?
2. What problem is created at the initial equilibrium price?
3. Which decision maker is not content with this situation?
4. How does a change in the actual price of potatoes eliminate the problem?

The answers to these questions are as follows:

1. Supply would increase, represented by a rightward shift in the supply curve (see Figure 3.8).

2. The increase in supply would create a surplus at the initial equilibrium price (*P*), represented by the distance between point *A* and point *B*.

3. The decision makers not content with this surplus would be the firms because they would not be able to sell the number of potatoes they had intended to sell at this price.

4. Firms with excess inventories would lower the actual price of potatoes. This decrease in the actual price of potatoes would increase the quantity demanded by households while decreasing the quantity supplied by farmers. Actual price would continue to fall until the quantity demanded equaled the quantity supplied at *P'*. This would establish a new equilibrium position. When the market is cleared, both decision makers are content; therefore, there is no tendency for actual price to change any further. Note that the equilibrium quantity sold would increase from *Q* to *Q'*.

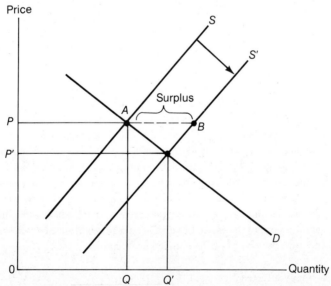

Figure 3.8. Case of a Surplus. An increase in the supply of potatoes creates a surplus at the initial equilibrium price. Firms decrease price, which in turn eliminates the surplus by increasing the quantity demanded and decreasing the quantity supplied.

Case of an Increase in Both Demand and Supply

Suppose that the conditions for growing and harvesting potatoes improve at the same time that people begin buying more baked potatoes (to eat with such toppings as sour cream, bacon, and cheese). What would happen to the equilibrium price and quantity of potatoes sold if there were a simultaneous increase in *both* the supply and demand for potatoes? Figure 3.9 illustrates the case in which demand increases by *more* than the increase in supply, resulting in a rise in the price of potatoes. On the other hand, Figure 3.10 illustrates the case in which demand increases by *less* than the increase in supply, driving the price of potatoes down. Note that the changes in equilibrium price illustrated in Figures 3.9 and 3.10 are in opposing directions. As a result, the change in equilibrium price is *uncertain* unless the relative sizes of the shifts in supply and demand are known. We can also see that the changes in equilibrium quantity are in the same rightward direction in both figures. Consequently, the equilibrium quantity sold will definitely increase.

The amount by which the equilibrium quantity of the goods sold changes *relative* to a change in equilibrium price depends on the elasticity of supply or demand. See *Appendix A: Price Elasticity* at the end of this chapter for a discussion of this concept.

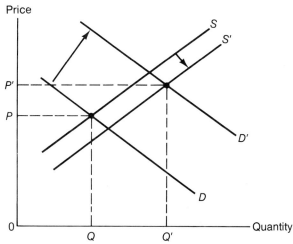

Figure 3.9. The Demand for Potatoes Increases by More Than the Increase in Supply. This causes the equilibrium price to increase and the quantity sold to increase.

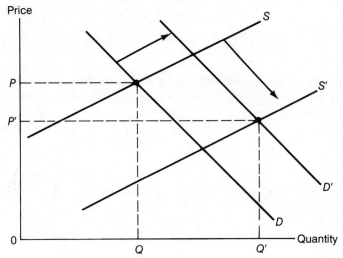

Figure 3.10. The Demand for Potatoes Increases by Less Than the Increase in Supply. This causes the equilibrium price to decrease and the quantity sold to increase.

Supply, Demand, and the Price of Stock

As the supply of stock shrinks, do stock prices necessarily rise? Most on Wall Street would answer "yes." They further maintain that the record decrease in the supply of stock in the past year (caused by the removal of blocks of stock through current buy-out and buy-back activity) is responsible for the recent increase in stock prices. Eugene Peroni, a technical analyst at Janney Montgomery Scott, believes that without the shrinkage of stock supplies, the Dow Jones Industrial Average might still be trading at the low levels at which it traded immediately following the October 1987 crash.

A minority of analysts disagree. According to economist A. Gary Shilling, "There is no statistical evidence that [establishes that] as you reduce the supply of stocks you're guaranteeing that prices will rise . . . if you reduce the supply, anyone would agree that the price would increase. But the effect of supply in this case is completely swamped by the changes that take place in demand." He warns people not to buy stock based on the advice of analysts whose predictions are based solely on decreases in stock supplies. Here's the rub: analysts concentrate on the supply side because the supply of stock is easy to quantify. Mr. Shilling argues that it is impossible to accurately forecast changes in stock prices because the most important factor, changes in demand, is very difficult to measure.

The above is a summary of an article, "As Supply of Stocks Shrinks, Do Prices Necessarily Rise?" by Douglas R. Sease, that appeared in *The Wall Street Journal,* April 10, 1989, pp. C1–C2.

So far we have examined how prices and the amount of goods sold are established in competitive markets through decisions made by buyers and sellers. But not all prices in our economy are "market" prices.

3.6 Price Floors and Price Ceilings

Our economy has numerous *institutional prices,* which are prices established by government. The focus of this section is on the impact of prices set by government on a competitive market.

Ceiling and Floor Prices

Figure 3.11 represents a purely competitive market for wheat. We can see that the market-clearing equilibrium price (P_E) is $4. Suppose that the government were to pass a law that made the price of wheat $5. An institutional price that is set above the market equilibrium price is called a ***price support*** or a ***floor price,*** since it prevents the actual market price from falling to the equilibrium position (i.e., the actual price hits the "floor" and stops). Note that a

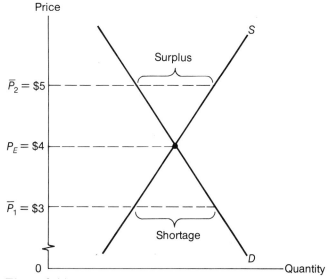

Figure 3.11. Ceiling and Floor Prices in a Competitive Market for Wheat. A floor price results in a surplus, and a ceiling price results in a shortage.

surplus is created at the floor price $(\overline{P}_2)$ of \$5, since at this price farmers plan to sell more wheat than households plan to buy.

On the other hand, if the institutional price $(\overline{P}_1)$ were set at \$3, a shortage would occur since households plan to buy more wheat than farmers offer for sale. An institutional price that is set below the equilibrium position is called a ***ceiling price*** because the actual market price hits against this limit as it attempts to move up to the equilibrium position (i.e., actual price hits the ceiling and cannot rise any further).

Why should the government impose price ceilings or price floors? In general, the government should establish institutional prices only when the private market fails to establish a price that is in the best interest of society. However, it is difficult for the government to determine exactly what is the best interest of society. In addition, special interest groups have been known to prevail upon Congress to pass laws that benefit them at the expense of the rest of society. The following discussion will illustrate the rationale and impact of ceiling prices imposed by government during World War II.

The impact of floor prices in agriculture is discussed at length in *Special Topic E: The Farm Problem and Public Policy.* Also, *Appendix B: The Issue of Protectionism Versus Free Trade* at the end of this chapter demonstrates how the imposition of a tariff on imported goods creates a floor price on the domestic goods being protected.

Price Controls During World War II

Government-imposed price controls were used extensively during World War II (1941 to 1945). Let us explore the rationale and impact of a price ceiling imposed on the civilian market for gasoline (i.e., gasoline for nonmilitary use).

The demand curve D_1 illustrated in Figure 3.12 represents the demand for gasoline by civilians during the Great Depression (1929–1941), which occurred just prior to World War II. Since unemployment was very high during the Great Depression, reduced income caused the demand to be low for most consumer goods, including cars and the gasoline used to drive them. When the United States entered World War II, unemployment dropped due to the huge increase in military expenditures. As a result, civilian demand increased for gasoline and other consumer goods. As Figure 3.12 indicates, civilian demand for gasoline rose from D_1 to D_2, where D_2 represents the higher demand for gasoline by civilians during World War II. Without government price controls, the price of civilian gasoline would have increased from P_1 to P_2 and the quantity of gas sold to civilians would have increased from Q_1 to Q_2. But these changes in price and the quantity of gasoline sold did *not* occur because the federal government imposed a ceiling price on civilian gasoline during World War II.

Rationale for Price Ceilings

Why did the federal government institute a ceiling price on civilian gasoline? It did so because Congress and President Roosevelt felt that during this national emergency, market pricing

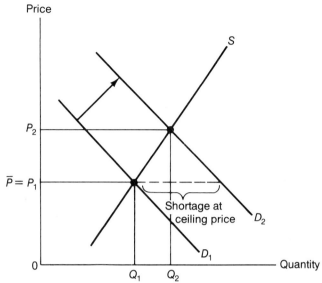

Figure 3.12. Civilian Market for Gasoline. The increase in demand creates a shortage at the price ceiling. Scarce gasoline was rationed to households through the use of coupons.

would not perform in the best interest of society. Without a ceiling, the price of civilian gasoline would have increased from P_1 to P_2, causing households to be *rationed* out of the market while *signaling* the need for increased gasoline production for civilian use. Because of the crisis caused by the war, the government felt that a sharp increase in the price of gasoline would have weakened the morale of many families and, therefore, would have hurt the war effort. The morale of lower- and middle-income families would have suffered most, because the increase in price would have rationed scarce civilian gasoline away from them to higher income families. In addition, the government did not want price to signal the need for increased gasoline production for civilian use since there was a more urgent need for gasoline for military use.

Alternative Methods of Rationing

To analyze the situation further, see Figure 3.12. We are assuming that the federal government placed the ceiling price (represented by $\overline{P}$) at the initial equilibrium level (P_1). After the increase in demand from D_1 to D_2, a shortage developed at the controlled price ($\overline{P}$). Since the government decided not to permit the private market mechanism to solve the problem of a shortage by raising price, Congress had to come up with an alternative method for rationing.

Since not enough gasoline was available to civilians at the ceiling price, the limited amount of gasoline could have been rationed out on a *first-come, first-served basis*. A major problem with that solution would have been inefficiency. People would have had to waste time waiting

73

in line for gasoline (which might not even have been available for them to purchase when they finally got to the front of the line).

The federal government came up with another solution. The government printed *coupon books* to ration gasoline to civilians. Under the price ceiling and ration book program, civilians needed two things to buy gasoline — money and coupons. The customer would tear out a coupon from the ration book, giving it to the gasoline attendant together with the necessary money. During this crisis, many other basic commodities were also sold through the rationing program. They included sugar, meat, butter, and milk.

Problems Created by Rationing with Coupons

Rationing through the use of coupons has a number of serious drawbacks. First, price controls are used in a private market only under special circumstances because they interfere with the normal workings of the market mechanism. Second, the coupon program is expensive both in terms of printing costs and the administrative expenses involved in running the program. Third, it is difficult for the government to determine just how many coupons to issue. During World War II, the government wanted to restrict the sale of civilian gasoline to Q_1, a level less than the equilibrium quantity (Q_2), illustrated in Figure 3.12. The target of Q_1 will be missed if the appropriate quantity of coupons is not issued. If too few coupons are distributed, there will be a surplus of civilian gasoline. On the other hand, if too many coupons are issued, some people with coupons will not be able to buy gasoline because of the shortage created. Fourth, rationing by coupon creates an equity problem. It is very difficult for the government to distribute coupons in a manner that most people would consider fair. The need for gasoline for civilian use varies extensively according to such factors as family size, occupation, location, and access to mass transit. Finally, price controls and rationing by coupon generally result in the development of an illegal market that would require the expense of additional law enforcement.

Summary

Pure competition is a standard used for describing and evaluating the behavior of the less competitive markets that make up the private market economy. Under pure competition it is assumed that there are many small firms and many households acting independently in the market, with each firm producing an identical product. As a result, the individual purely competitive firm has no control over price.

Buyers and sellers interact to determine the price and the amount of goods sold. According to the law of demand, an increase in price will result in a decrease in the quantity demanded, and according to the law of supply, an increase in price will increase the quantity supplied (given all other factors). A change in a nonprice determinant would cause the demand or supply curve to shift.

If the actual price is above the equilibrium level, a surplus will occur since firms plan to sell more than households want to buy. On the other hand, if the actual price is too low, a shortage

74

will occur, upsetting the plans of households since they would want to buy more than firms plan to sell at the current price.

Price plays an important role in eliminating shortages and surpluses. For example, if a shortage occurs, households will initiate an increase in actual price, which in turn causes the quantity demanded to decrease as households are rationed out of the market. This increase in the current price will also signal to firms the need for increased production, increasing the quantity supplied. Actual price will settle at the equilibrium position since this is the particular price at which buyers and sellers agree on the quantity to be sold. The equilibrium condition is met since the quantity demanded equals the quantity supplied.

An increase in demand (with supply unchanged) creates a shortage at the initial equilibrium price, causing equilibrium price and quantity to increase. An increase in supply (with demand unchanged) creates a surplus, causing a decrease in equilibrium price and an increase in the quantity sold. The effect of simultaneous changes in both supply and demand is more complex. If the relative sizes of the shifts in both curves are known, the changes in equilibrium price and equilibrium quantity can be determined. However, if the relative sizes of the shifts in both curves are not known, the direction of change in either equilibrium price or equilibrium quantity will be uncertain.

Not all prices are determined in the marketplace. Some prices are set by government. A floor price is an above-equilibrium institutional price, which creates a surplus. A ceiling price is set below the equilibrium price, which creates a shortage. Price controls were used extensively during World War II, and the government used rationing by coupon to distribute many consumer goods.

Key Concepts

pure competition
law of demand
nonprice determinants of demand
demand shift factors
normal and inferior goods
substitute, complementary, and independent goods
changes in quantity demanded
changes in demand
law of supply
changes in supply
nonprice determinants of supply
supply shift factors
equilibrium price
actual price
equilibrium condition

shortage
role of prices
surplus
impact of changes in market conditions
floor or support prices
ceiling prices
rationing by coupon

Self-Test Questions: True or False

T   F   1. Under conditions of pure competition, there are many firms acting independently in a given market, each producing an identical product. As a result, each firm in the market has no control over price since it can sell its product only at the equilibrium market price.

T   F   2. An increase in the price of hamburger will tend to decrease the demand for hamburger.

T   F   3. Suppose that goods *A* and *B* are substitute goods. An increase in the price of good *A* will tend to increase the demand for good *B*, while the quantity of good *A* demanded will decrease.

T   F   4. An increase in the cost of production will tend to shift the supply curve inward to the left.

T   F   5. The equilibrium condition is met when the quantity supplied equals the quantity demanded.

T   F   6. See the accompanying graph illustrating a competitive market for eggs. The shift in supply creates a surplus at the initial equilibrium price. The decision maker that would not be content with this situation is the firm.

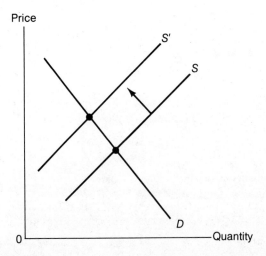

Answer Questions 7 and 8 by referring to the table below.

Price	Quantity Supplied	Quantity Demanded
$0.40	10	80
0.60	20	60
0.70	30	50
0.80	40	40
0.90	60	30
1.00	80	20

T F 7. If the actual price were $0.70, there would be a shortage of 20 units of eggs.

T F 8. If the actual price of $0.70 were to move to the equilibrium position, the quantity demanded would decrease by 10 units while the quantity supplied would increase by 10 units.

T F 9. If demand decreased at the same time that supply increased, equilibrium quantity would definitely increase and equilibrium price would decrease.

T F 10. If demand decreased by more than supply decreased, both equilibrium price and quantity would fall.

T F 11. A ceiling price results in a surplus in a competitive market.

T F 12. Each of the following would increase the demand for new housing: 1) an increase in population, and 2) an increase in the cost of lumber.

Answers to Self-Test Questions

1. *True.* Under conditions of pure competition, there are many firms acting independently in setting price, each producing a standardized product. The individual firm cannot charge an above-market price since households can buy an identical product from other firms at a lower price. Also, it would not be rational for the individual firm to offer the product for sale at a below-market price since the firm can sell all the goods that it wants to sell at the higher market price. Therefore, the single firm is a price taker.

2. *False.* Demand will not change since there has not been a change in a nonprice determinant (i.e., the demand curve will not shift). An increase in price will decrease the quantity demanded, an upward movement to the left along a given demand curve.

3. **True.** For example, an increase in the price of orange juice (good *A*) will tend to increase the demand curve for grapefruit juice (good *B*), shifting the demand curve for grapefruit juice outward to the right. An increase in the price of orange juice will tend to decrease the quantity of orange juice demanded (a movement up the demand curve for orange juice).

4. **True.** The cost of production is a nonprice determinant of supply. With an increase in production costs, supply will decrease. Firms are less willing to purchase inputs, causing them to produce less output at each price.

5. **True.** Actual price reaches the equilibrium position when the market is cleared (i.e., when the quantity supplied equals the quantity demanded). When households plan to buy the amount that firms plan to sell at the current price, both decision makers are in agreement. Consequently, there is no reason for the actual market price to change any further.

6. **False.** The shift in supply illustrated in the graph represents a decrease in supply. This decrease in supply creates a shortage at the initial equilibrium price. Households would not be content with this situation since they would plan to buy more at this price than firms are willing to sell. As a result of the shortage, households would bid price up.

7. **True.** At the actual price of $0.70, the quantity supplied is 30 units and the quantity demanded is 50 units. There is a shortage of 20 units.

8. **True.** If the actual price of $0.70 moved to the equilibrium position of $0.80, some households would be rationed out of the market, causing the quantity demanded to drop from 50 units to 40 units. The increase in price from $0.70 to $0.80 would also signal to firms the desire for increased production, causing the quantity supplied to rise from 30 units to 40 units. At the equilibrium price of $0.80, the market is cleared since both households and firms plan to buy and sell 40 units of eggs.

9. **False.** Equilibrium price would definitely decrease; however, the change in the equilibrium quantity sold is uncertain. Equilibrium quantity would increase only if the increase in supply was greater than the decrease in demand.

10. **True.** Equilibrium price would definitely decrease because it was known that demand decreased by *more* than the decrease in supply. The fall in price caused by the drop in demand would more than offset the increase in price caused by the drop in supply. Since households want to buy less and firms want to sell less, the quantity sold would also decrease.

11. **False.** A ceiling price is below the equilibrium price. Since the actual price is not permitted to rise to the equilibrium position, a shortage exists.

12. **False.** The demand for new housing would rise with an increase in population. However, because the cost of lumber is a *nonprice determinant of supply,* an increase in the cost of producing new housing would not directly affect the demand for new housing—it would decrease the supply of new housing.

Discussion Questions

1. Describe the difference between a change in the quantity demanded and a change in demand. List the factors that will cause such changes.

2. Define the following terms:
   a. equilibrium price
   b. equilibrium condition
   c. the role of price in eliminating a shortage

3. How will an increase in the price of gasoline affect the demand for gasoline? How will the demand for large and small cars be affected by this increase in the price of gasoline? Use a graph to illustrate your answers.

4. Suppose that there is an increase in the income of households in a given area and an increase in the cost of oil used in making plastic siding for houses. Describe how the equilibrium price and the quantity of plastic siding will be affected by these changes. Use a graph to illustrate your answer.

5. What is the effect of a floor price on a competitive market? Why?

Problems

Answer questions 1 through 6 using the following competitive market schedule for new housing units:

Price	Quantity Supplied	Quantity Demanded
$60,000	100	500
70,000	200	400
80,000	300	300
90,000	400	200

1. Graph these market data.

2. What is the equilibrium price and quantity of new housing? Draw a graph to illustrate your answer.

3. Suppose that a sharp increase in the mortgage interest rate causes the quantity of new housing demanded to decrease by 200 units at each price. Plot the new demand curve on your graph. Assume that the supply curve for new housing remains unchanged.

4. Given the initial equilibrium price, what problem does this decrease in demand create?

5. What is the new equilibrium price and quantity of new housing? Indicate your answers on the graph.

6. Describe the signaling and rationing function of prices, explaining how this new equilibrium position was achieved.

Appendices

A: Price Elasticity

The purpose of this appendix is to extend the discussion of supply and demand in Section 3.5. How do we measure the responsiveness of the change in the quantity demanded or supplied relative to the change in price?

Measurement of Price Elasticity

The degree of elasticity is measured using the ***elasticity coefficient*** (*E*), which is calculated by dividing the percentage change in the quantity supplied or demanded (%Δ*Q*) by the percentage change in price (%Δ*P*) or

$$E = \frac{\%\Delta Q}{\%\Delta P}$$

(Note that the plus and minus signs are ignored.) Table 3.7 gives us an overview of the three primary categories of elasticity, and an example showing how we calculate the elasticity coefficient for supply.

Table 3.7
Overview of the Elasticity of Supply and Demand

Category	Definition	Coefficient	Example
Inelastic	%Δ*Q* less than %Δ*P*	*E* less than 1	$25\%/100\% = \frac{1}{4}$
Elastic	%Δ*Q* greater than %Δ*P*	*E* greater than 1	$100\%/25\% = 4$
Unitary	%Δ*Q* equal to %Δ*P*	*E* equal to 1	$20\%/20\% = 1$

Inelastic Supply and Demand

Supply or demand is **_inelastic_** when the percent change in the quantity demanded or the quantity supplied is less than the percent change in price. As a result, the elasticity coefficient is less than 1. As we can see in Figures 3.13a and 3.13b, when demand or supply is inelastic, the change in quantity is not very responsive to a change in price. Suppose that a 100 percent increase in price causes a 25 percent decrease in the quantity demanded, while the quantity supplied increases by 25 percent. The elasticity coefficient is $\frac{1}{4}$ (or 25 percent/100 percent) in each case. Since the coefficients are less than 1, both supply and demand are inelastic.

Elastic Supply and Demand

When demand or supply is **_elastic_,** the coefficient is greater than 1, indicating that the percentage change in the quantity demanded or the quantity supplied is greater than the percentage change in price. As Figures 3.14a and 3.14b indicate, a 25 percent increase in price causes a larger percent change in both the quantity supplied and the quantity demanded. For

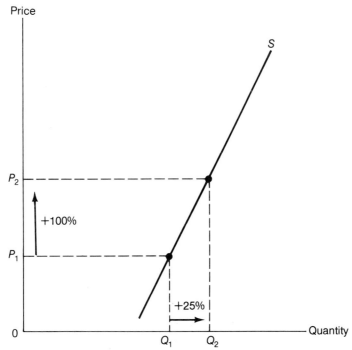

Figure 3.13a. Inelastic Supply. Supply is inelastic when the percentage change in the quantity supplied is less than the percentage change in price.

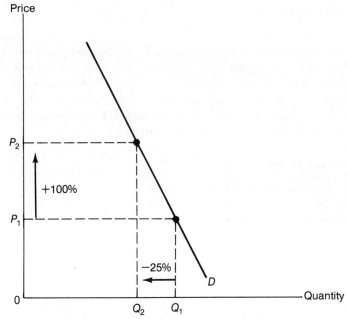

Figure 3.13b.   Inelastic Demand. Demand is inelastic when the percentage change in the quantity demanded is less than the percentage change in price.

example, the elasticity coefficient for supply is 4 (or 100 percent/25 percent). Since the coefficient is greater than 1, supply is elastic.

Unitary Elasticity

The third category of elasticity is called unitary elasticity. When demand or supply is of *unitary elasticity,* the coefficient is equal to 1. This indicates that the percentage change in the quantity demanded or the quantity supplied is equal to the percentage change in price (not illustrated). For example, if price increased by 20 percent, causing a 20 percent change in the quantity supplied or demanded, the elasticity coefficient would be 1 (or 20 percent/20 percent).

Determinants of Elasticity

What determines the amount of a good that households and firms would buy and sell as a result of a change in price? The following discussion examines the determinants of the elasticity of demand and supply.

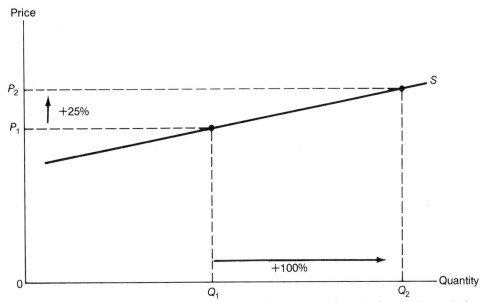

Figure 3.14a. Elastic Supply. Supply is elastic when the percentage change in the quantity supplied is greater than the percentage change in price.

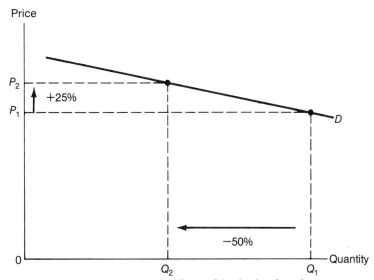

Figure 3.14b. Elastic Demand. Demand is elastic when the percentage change in the quantity demanded is greater than the percentage change in price.

83

Demand

The overall relative cost of the product, measured as a proportion of family income, is an important determinant of the elasticity of demand. Demand tends to be less elastic the smaller the *cost of the good as a proportion of family income,* simply because a change in the prices of lower cost items has a smaller impact on family finances. For example, a 20 percent increase in the price of pencils may not affect the purchase of pencils very much since the total expenditure for pencils is a very small part of the family budget. On the other hand, a 20 percent increase in the price of new housing may ration a large number of families out of the new housing market, causing them either to buy older houses or to rent housing because they cannot afford or are not willing to pay the higher price of new houses.

In addition, demand tends to be less elastic the fewer the *number of close substitutes* for the product in a given time period. This is because households are less able to switch to lower priced substitutes as the price of the product increases. The lack of available substitutes makes the quantity demanded for the good less sensitive to changes in price. For example, the demand for natural gas to heat homes tends to be more inelastic than the demand for steak in a given year. A 20 percent increase in the price of both goods would generally result in consumers cutting back on their purchase of steak by relatively more than their reduction in the consumption of natural gas, simply because other goods can be more easily substituted for steak (e.g., chicken or hamburger) than for natural gas (e.g., wood or solar energy).

Finally, demand tends to become less elastic the *shorter the time period,* since households have less opportunity to adjust to market changes. Therefore, demand tends to be more elastic the longer the time period. Given sufficient time, households tend to switch away from purchasing higher priced goods to purchase lower priced substitutes. For example, suppose that the price of natural gas were to increase 800 percent. Given enough time to convert their home heating systems, households might use wood, solar energy, or synthetic gas made from coal instead of heating their homes with the relatively higher priced natural gas.

Supply

Time is the primary determinant of the elasticity of supply. Supply is more elastic (or less inelastic) the longer the period of time because the industry has greater ability to adjust output to changes in price. We will note in Section 4.1 of Chapter 4 that economists define time in terms of three periods: the market period, the short run, and the long run (where the market period is the shortest time period).

B: The Issue of *Protectionism* Versus Free Trade

Despite its substantial benefits described in Section 2.5 of Chapter 2, world trade is hindered by a maze of trade barriers in the form of tariffs and quotas. A tariff is simply a tax that a nation places on imports. By raising the price of imports to consumers, the tariff discourages people living in that country from buying goods from other nations. Quotas set by government, on the other hand, directly restrict trade by limiting the volume of certain goods that can be legally imported. Given the benefits that result from specialization and trade, why would nations erect barriers designed to inhibit trade?

Arguments For and Against Protection

There are three major arguments for imposing tariffs and quotas in international trade. First, the owners of firms and the workers in an industry that is threatened by lower priced imported substitute goods tend to petition Congress for relief from "ruinous competition." The steel and automobile industries have used this argument vigorously during the last decade. They claim that we should impose trade barriers against foreign steel and automobile producers in order *to protect jobs and domestic living standards.* Although such protection is in their own self-interest, it is not likely to be in the collective interest of society. The tariff will drive the cost of the product up and reduce the benefits of specialization through trade. The economic impact of tariffs will be examined in more detail after we finish this discussion.

Second, protection is occasionally needed to support industries that are necessary for *military self-sufficiency.* Nations reliant on essential goods supplied by friendly nations may find their normal trade patterns disturbed by war. These potential disruptions in trade relations reduce the benefits of international specialization in goods vital to national defense. Some argue that tariffs should be erected to promote production of these goods domestically. This argument has been used in the United States by the steel, electronics, and shipping industries.

Finally, according to the *infant-industries argument,* new industries must initially be protected against foreign competition if they are likely to grow into healthy competitors in the future. This argument is valid for industries having economies of scale in which the average cost of production decreases as the size of the plant increases (discussed in Chapter 5). There is one serious problem with this reasoning — once protection is granted to an industry, it is very difficult to remove. Infant industries that mature fully often have the political clout to preserve the protective measures beyond the years needed for survival. The infant-industries argument is used primarily in developing economies that are attempting to build basic industries such as steel, heavy manufacturing, and chemicals.

The Economic Impact of a Prohibitive Tariff

What is the *economic impact of a tariff* on the domestic economy? Figure 3.15 illustrates the domestic supply (*S*) and demand (*D*) conditions in Javit for food, where the equilibrium price without international trade is P_2. Suppose that the international price of food is P_1 before any trade barriers are imposed. How much food will Javit import? Given the international price of P_1, consumers will want to buy Q_d units of food overall (see point *A*). Domestic producers in Javit will want to produce only Q_s units of food at the P_1 price (see point *B*). Therefore, the excess demand (measured by the distance $A - B$) is satisfied through imports.

Now suppose that food producers in Javit succeed in getting their government to erect a tariff that raises the price of imported food from P_1 to P_2. This tariff is said to be a *prohibitive*

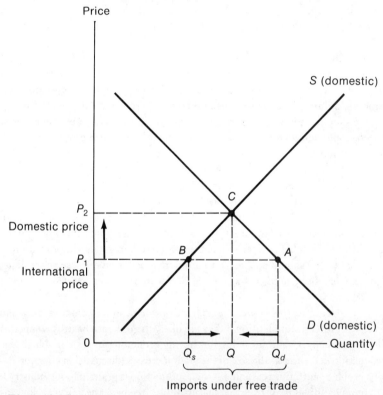

Figure 3.15.   The Economic Impact of a Prohibitive Tariff. The tariff raises the price of imports to consumers, which decreases the quantity they plan to buy. This higher price also subsidizes domestic producers, causing them to increase the quantity supplied. A tariff is prohibitive when it raises the international price of a good to the domestic level, eliminating all imports.

tariff since Javit will no longer import food from other nations. Why? The tariff raises the international price of food to the level that would have prevailed in Javit without trade. Imports fall to zero (indicated by point C).

What is the economic impact of this tariff? It benefits food producers and the workers employed in this industry because the resulting price increase (from P_1 to P_2) raises domestic food production in Javit (from Q_s to Q). On the other hand, consumers in Javit are hurt since they must now pay a higher price for less food. Because of the artificial price increase, buyers reduce the quantity of food demanded (from Q_d to Q). Therefore, the tariff has the effect of aiding food producers and agricultural workers at the expense of consumers. In addition, the overall economy suffers from a reduction in economic growth since we are not able to benefit from the gains of specialization explained by the principle of comparative advantage (described in Section 2.5 of the previous chapter).

There is also the prospect that the imposition of the tariff might initiate a trade war. If Javit imposes a tariff on food, Xanda may retaliate by placing a tariff or quota on clothes imported from Javit. This might induce Javit to erect even further restrictions on trade. If the situation became explosive, the rising barriers could drastically reduce the volume of international trade. Consequently, all countries might eventually suffer from the resulting loss in economic growth.

The last major trade war occurred in the 1930s during the Great Depression. Trading nations raised tariff barriers in a futile effort to "protect jobs and domestic living standards." At one point, tariff duties in the United States stood at over 60 percent of the value of dutiable imports. The tariff duties were only about 10 percent during the 1980–1987 period.

Pure Competition: The Firm's Short-Run Production Decision/ Long-Run Market Behavior

Objectives

Upon completion of this chapter, you should understand:

1. The three economic time periods.

2. A fundamental production problem called the law of diminishing returns.

3. How to measure the profit and loss of a firm.

4. How the individual competitive firm decides how much to produce in the short run.

5. The long-run pricing and output behavior of competitive industries and how market forces allocate scarce resources.

The discovery of the microcomputer chip has spawned a whole new industry. Steve Jobs developed the first Apple personal computer in a garage with a friend, Stephen Wozniak, in 1977. Since then the personal computer industry has exploded with activity. The huge profits, which had mushroomed in the personal computer market, enticed new rivals into this market. There are now numerous firms producing personal computers in addition to Apple, such as IBM, Tandy, Zenith, Compaq, Atari, and Commodore.

While many of the firms in the personal computer industry enjoy high profits, producers in other industries may experience economic loss, forcing them to cut back production. If the losses persist, the firms are eventually forced out of business, leaving a trail of vacant buildings and jobless workers. Such has been the fate of a multitude of small farmers, gasoline stations, family-run restaurants, and neighborhood grocery stores. Basic maufacturers in the United States, such as the steel companies, have also felt the pinch. With the passage of time, these idle resources become employed in industries producing goods that are in relatively greater demand.

This chapter begins by exploring the impact of time on production. We then describe how to measure the profit or loss of a firm. Marginal analysis is used to exlore the production decision of the purely competitive firm. Next, the significance of the role of profit and loss is examined. A primary objective of this chapter is to examine the behavior of the purely competitive firm and the industry it occupies when each has sufficient time to adjust completely to changes in market conditions. This foundation will provide a basis for understanding how market prices serve to allocate scarce economic resources among the millions of alternative uses that exist in our economy.

4.1 The Three Time Periods and the Law of Diminishing Returns

Time is important to all of us since we all have deadlines to meet and schedules to plan. Businesses are time conscious, too, especially when the decisions they are making involve a possible long-term commitment of resources, such as whether to build a new factory or to purchase an expensive piece of equipment. The purpose of this section is to examine how economists measure time. We will also analyze a fundamental production problem that occurs when firms do not have sufficient time to acquire all the resources they desire (called the law of diminishing returns).

The Three Time Periods

In economics, there are three time periods, called the market period, the short run, and the long run. These periods are not measured in terms of hours, weeks, months, or years. Instead, each is a measure of the relative ability of an industry to adjust production to changes in market conditions. The longer the time period, the greater the ability of an industry to expand output in response to an increase in demand. This is partially because a longer time period gives existing firms more opportunity to employ increasing amounts of inputs with which to increase production. They may have to decide whether to hire another accountant, secretary, or lathe operator. In addition, new firms will eventually be able to enter the market, given sufficient time to construct new plant facilities. In the following discussion, we examine the characteristics of each of these three time periods.

Market Period   The *market period* is defined as that period in which a given amount of output has been produced and is ready to be sold on the market. For example, the market period begins at the moment farmers place their ripe tomatoes on the market for sale. The quantity of fresh tomatoes supplied is fixed. As we can see in Figure 4.1, the supply curve is represented by a vertical line in the market period. What would happen if suddenly we were to attempt to buy more tomatoes? As Figure 4.1 demonstrates, a rise in demand (D_1 to D_2) causes

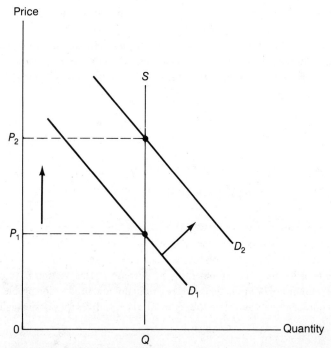

Figure 4.1.   The Market Period Supply Curve. The quantity supplied is fixed since the amount of tomatoes offered for sale has just been placed on the market. There is not sufficient time to produce more tomatoes in this time period.

the price to increase (P_1 to P_2). Note that the quantity farmers are able to offer for sale *(Q)* does not increase since there is insufficient time for more tomatoes to ripen and for farmers to pick more tomatoes. Similarly, a decrease in demand (D_2 to D_1) will cause the price to fall (P_2 to P_1). The quantity of fresh tomatoes offered for sale will remain at the same level *(Q)*. In this brief period of time, the only alternative the farmers have is to let their crops rot.

Short Run   The ***short run*** is defined as a time period in which there are (1) both variable and fixed inputs, and (2) no entry or exiting of firms. This time period is longer than the market period since firms have some ability to adjust production to changes in market conditions.

The first major characteristic of the short run is the existence of both fixed inputs and variable inputs. ***Fixed inputs*** are factors of production that cannot be increased or decreased in order to adjust output. Inputs that are fixed in the short run include buildings, machinery and equipment, and land, since it takes firms more time to acquire or to sell these assets than is available in this time period. The short run, however, is sufficiently long for firms to employ either larger or smaller quantities of other types of inputs, such as labor, materials, supplies, and services. These factors are called ***variable inputs*** since they can be increased or decreased by firms in order to adjust production in response to a change in market conditions. For example, an increase in the demand for tomatoes might cause existing farmers to hire additional workers and to employ a larger quantity of other variable inputs in order to increase production. However, the extent to which they can expand output is constrained in the short run by the size of their farms as well as by the amount of machinery and equipment on hand.

The second major characteristic of the short run is that there is *no **entering** or **exiting of firms*** to or from the market. Since there is not enough time to buy more land or to construct buildings, new firms are not able to enter the market. Existing firms cannot leave the market because they do not have sufficient time to sell their land or buildings. The owners of these firms can *shut down* their operations by laying off their entire work force, but they cannot go *out of business* in the short run because they do not have sufficient time to sell their plant facilities. Therefore, the entry or exit of firms is impossible in the short run.

Long Run   The ***long run*** is defined as the time period in which (1) all inputs are variable, and (2) there is entry and exiting of firms. All adustments in production are possible in the long run because firms are assumed to have sufficient time to employ more or less of any input (including capital and land). Therefore, in the long run all inputs are variable. In addition, firms are able to get into or out of business because there is enough time to construct new buildings, buy more land, or sell buildings and land. For example, in response to an increase in demand, existing tomato farmers are able to expand production in the long run by purchasing more land, buildings, machinery, and equipment in addition to hiring more labor. Also, new firms are able to enter the tomato industry. Note that references to short-run and long-run time periods will be made throughout this chapter as we explore the pricing and output behavior of the firm and the industry under conditions of pure competition. We now turn to a fundamental production problem which occurs in the short run, called the law of diminishing returns.

The Law of Diminishing Returns

Have you ever heard the phrase "too many cooks spoil the broth"? This simple adage illustrates a fundamental law of production which occurs in the short-run time period. Suppose that Charlie opens a restaurant, called the Soup Kitchen, which is an immediate success. Customers flock to his restaurant in droves, especially to taste his famous Scottish broth. Since Charlie is initially understaffed for such a large crowd of customers, he immediately begins to hire more cooks. At first the additional staff improves the efficiency of the overall operation since previously unused kitchen facilities become involved in making soup. At some point, however, the additional number of cooks hired begins to exceed the optimal capacity of the fixed kitchen space. The cooks begin to get in each other's way. Some become annoyed at having to wait in line to use the stoves. Others begin to complain of the lack of space in the refrigerators. Then, one sad day, Charlie finds his customers in an uproar — the soup tastes awful. Some customers complain there is too much salt in the soup, while others say it tastes like dishwater (which it actually had been before it was accidentally served to an impatient crowd in the back of the restaurant). Charlie becomes very upset and runs into his crowded kitchen shouting at the top of his lungs, "Who spoiled my broth!" Of course, the answer is "too many cooks."

The problem that occurred in Charlie's kitchen that fateful day illustrates what eventually happens in *any* production process when too many variable inputs (the cooks in this example) are combined with a fixed input (the kitchen facilities) to produce an output (the bowls of soup being rushed to the tables). This production problem was first noted in agriculture in the nineteenth century by David Ricardo. The problem is caused by the ***law of diminishing returns,*** which states that, as more units of a variable input (such as labor) are combined with a fixed input (such as land or capital), eventually the *extra* output per additional variable input will fall.

Table 4.1 illustrates the basic elements of this law. We are assuming that a farmer growing corn has a fixed amount of land and can increase the total production of corn (shown in column 2) by hiring more workers (shown in column 1). We can see that the first worker produces 10 units of corn. If the farmer hires a second worker, both workers together produce 30 units of corn. If a third worker is hired, the total production of corn of all three workers is 60 units. Column 3 shows the contribution that each additional worker makes to corn production, called the ***marginal physical product of labor (MPP$_L$),*** which is measured as the change in total output divided by the change in labor. As column 3 shows, the marginal physical product of the first worker is 10 units (where $MPP_L = +10/+1 = 10$). The second worker causes total output to increase by 20 units, which means that the marginal physical product of this worker is 20 units.

Initially, each additional worker contributes more to total production than did the previous workers. This occurs until the addition of the fourth worker. Diminishing returns first sets in with the hiring of the fourth worker since this worker only contributes 15 units of output, which is below the 30 additional units of corn produced by the third worker. We can

Table 4.1
Calculation of the
Marginal Physical
Product of Labor
in Corn Production

(1) Labor	(2) Total Output	(3) MPP$_L$
0	0	
1	10	10
2	30	20
3	60	30
4	75	15
5	85	10
6	90	5
7	90	0
8	85	-5

see that each extra worker hired after the third worker causes additional production to fall. Note that total production is still increasing (at a decreasing rate) until the seventh worker is hired, at which point the marginal physical product is zero. *Negative returns* begin with the addition of the eighth worker, since the contribution of this worker is − 5 units total output has actually decreased from 90 to 85. Therefore, diminishing returns start with the addition of the fourth worker, and negative returns set in with the hiring of the eighth worker.

What accounts for the law of diminishing returns? After a certain point, the variable inputs have less of the fixed inputs with which to work. In the example of Charlie's restaurant, "too many cooks spoiled the broth" because of the lack of adequate kitchen facilities. In the case of farming, the addition of more workers eventually caused the extra units of corn produced to fall because of the lack of sufficient land. In the next section we explore how economists measure the profit and loss of a firm.

4.2 Measuring the Profit and Loss of a Firm

Do you ever dream of starting your own business? It's fascinating to imagine all of the wonderful things you could do with your first million dollars. Unfortunately, most small businesses go bankrupt after two years of trying to make a go of it. Why? Very often the owners begin their business thinking only in terms of the money they need to pay their bills. They often neglect to consider the value of their own personal resources until it is too late.

The Explicit and Implicit Costs of a Firm

Suppose that Opal opens a semi-fast food restaurant called Opal's Hamburger Palace. In trying to make the best hamburgers available on Route 66, Opal is constantly barraged with bills. She has to pay the head chef, cooks, and waitresses, in addition to paying her suppliers for such items as ground meat, buns, onions, pickles, and ketchup. In addition, Opal has to consider the value of all her own resources used in the business, including time she spends at the restaurant. The annual costs of this representative firm in producing a given number of hamburgers are illustrated in Table 4.2. Note that the *total costs* of production are broken down into two overall categories: explicit costs and implicit costs.

Explicit costs are the expenditures for resources used in the restaurant that are *not owned by the owner of the business* (i.e., they are the bills that Opal must pay including payroll). As Table 4.2 indicates, Opal must pay $200,000 in labor costs to people she has hired, $280,000 for supplies purchased from other firms (e.g., hamburger meat, buns, and ketchup), and $20,000 for contracted services (e.g., advertising, telephone, and the services of a tax account-ant). Total explicit costs in this example are $500,000.

Implicit costs are the opportunity costs of the personal resources of the firm's owner. The opportunity cost of an economic resource is the value of that resource in its next best alternative use. For example, in Table 4.2 the opportunity cost of the time Opal spent in her business last year is estimated to be $60,000 based on the highest annual salary she could earn if she worked for another firm. In addition, she owns land and a building that could be rented together for $140,000 per year. Therefore, by staying in business, Opal gives up a total of

Table 4.2
Explicit and Implicit Costs of
Opal's Hamburger Palace

Explicit costs	
Value of resources purchased by	
the owner from other persons	
Labor	$200,000
Supplies	280,000
Contracted services	20,000
Subtotal	$500,000
Implicit costs	
Value of resources owned by owner	
Work time of owner	$ 60,000
Land	40,000
Building	100,000
Subtotal	$200,000
Total costs	$700,000

$200,000 — the value of all her resources in their next best use. Her implicit costs of $200,000 do not show up in Opal's financial statements, whereas explicit costs do appear as money paid "out of pocket." Nevertheless, implicit costs are just as important as explicit costs to the owner of a firm in gauging the success or failure of his or her business. The *total cost* that Opal faces in producing hamburgers is $700,000.

Economic Profit, the Breakeven Point and Normal Profit, or Loss?

How successful is Opal's Hamburger Palace? Given the costs of production represented in Table 4.2, the fate of her business depends on the amount of total revenue (income or sales receipts) she is able to earn over the year. In the discussion that follows we will assume three different levels of total revenue in order to illustrate how we measure economic profit, the breakeven point and normal profit, and loss.

Economic Profit *Total economic profit* is equal to the amount by which total revenue *(TR)* exceeds total cost *(TC)*. If total revenue were $800,000, Opal would receive $100,000 in total economic profit. We calculate total economic profit as follows:

$$\text{Total Economic Profit} = TR - TC = \$800,000 - \$700,000 = \$100,000$$

The Breakeven Point and Normal Profit On the other hand, if total revenue were $700,000, Opal's firm would be at the ***breakeven point*** because total revenue and total cost are both equal. Total economic profit is zero, since

$$\text{Total Economic Profit} = TR - TC = \$700,000 - \$700,000 = \$0$$

It is *very important* to note that when total economic profit is zero, the firm is making normal profit. *Normal profit* is the return necessary to cover the opportunity costs of the resources owned by Opal (the firm's owner) after all the bills are paid. As Table 4.2 indicates, when total revenue is $700,000, Opal is making $200,000 in normal profit since she is receiving a return just sufficient to cover the opportunity cost of her own resources (her implicit costs) after she pays all her out-of-pocket expenses which amounted to $500,000 (her explicit costs). This can be represented as follows:

$$\begin{aligned} \text{Total Economic Profit} = TR - TC &= TR - (\text{Explicit Costs} + \text{Implicit Costs}) \\ &= \$700,000 - (\$500,000 + \$200,000) = 0 \end{aligned}$$

Note that Opal would stay in business in the long run if economic profit were zero since she could not make a higher return on her own resources in the next best use. Also note that if total revenue were $800,000 she would make economic profit of $100,000 — which is a return of $100,000 above the value of her own resources. Therefore, economic profit is also called *above-normal profit.*

95

Loss   If Opal received only $550,000 in revenue, she would be taking a total *loss* of $150,000 calculated as the amount by which total revenue is less than total cost:

$$\text{Total Loss} = TR - TC = \$550,000 - \$700,000 = -\$150,000$$

Note that Opal would make $150,000 more by going out of business. Why? Although this $550,000 in total revenue is enough to pay all her bills (explicit costs) of $500,000, it is not sufficient to cover all the opportunity costs of her own resources (implicit costs). If Opal puts her own resources into the next best alternative use (i.e., if she worked for another firm and leased her land and building), she could earn $200,000 which is $150,000 more than the $50,000 she would receive if she stayed in business. We will now turn our attention to the method used by a firm in deciding how much output to produce.

4.3 The Short-Run Production Decision of the Purely Competitive Firm

Opal was delighted when her youngest brother, Bert, agreed to help her build the Hamburger Palace. He also helped in the kitchen — which led to his weight problem. To lose the extra pounds, Bert decided to diet and to exercise more. He took up hiking. Within a week of hiking along the roads and trails of his hometown, Bert became very enthusiastic about the sport — so enthusiastic in fact that he quit Opal's restaurant to open his own business making boots, which he proudly named The Hiking Experience. The purpose of this section is to analyze how many hiking boots Bert should make per day. However, before turning to the production decision of the firm, let's review two critical assumptions.

A Review: Pure Competition and the Short-Run Time Period

Note that we are assuming Bert operates his company, The Hiking Experience, in a purely competitive market. Bert has no control over the price he can charge for the boots he sells because his firm faces intense competition and all hiking boots produced in the industry are assumed to be identical — they look the same, they wear the same, then even smell the same (before being worn). As we described in Chapter 3 (Section 3.4), the competitive equilibrium price of a good is determined by the interaction of many households and firms, each acting independently in buying or selling a standardized product. In addition, we assume there are no barriers to hinder a firm from getting into business or out of business, given sufficient time. What would happen if Bert attempted to charge $61 for a pair of hiking boots that could be purchased from other firms for only $60? Bert would lose all of his potential customers — people would not be willing to pay his $61 for a pair of hiking boots when they could easily buy an identical pair from other firms at the lower market price of $60.

In addition, we are assuming the firm is operating in the short-run time period, which means that Bert can produce additional boots by hiring more workers and by buying more leather, cloth, and other supplies (i.e., employing more variable inputs), but the production of boots is limited by the size of his shop and the amount of equipment he has inside (his fixed inputs). Moreover, because there is not sufficient time for the purchase (or sale) of capital and land, firms do not have enough time to enter (or leave) the industry — the number of firms in the industry is fixed in the short run. The final section of this chapter will explore how the competitive firm interacts with the market over the long run, a period of time long enough for firms to make any adjustments to changes in market conditions. (See Section 4.1 of this chapter for a review of the different time periods.)

How many pairs of hiking boots should Bert make per day? In deciding how much to produce, Bert uses marginal analysis — balancing the cost of producing an additional pair of boots against the extra revenue to be gained. We call this method of reasoning *marginal analysis* because all firms increase production in small increments (i.e., marginal or "extra" amounts) as they search for the level of output that will maximize total economic profit.

Short-Run Production Costs

Bert's production costs change as he expands output. Table 4.3 shows the *total cost of production* (column 3), which includes all of Bert's explicit and implicit costs for the overall number of boots produced in a given day. For example, Bert can produce two pairs of boots at a total cost of $116. In column 2, we can see the *average cost of production,* the cost per unit of output. Average cost is calculated by dividing total cost by the number of units produced. For example, the average cost of producing two pairs of boots is $58 per pair (or $116/2). Bert's primary concern is how his total costs change as he changes production. Column 4 shows the *marginal cost of production,* which is defined as the cost of producing one *additional* unit of output. Marginal cost is calculated by dividing the change in total cost (column 3) by the

Table 4.3
The Firm's Short-Run Cost Schedule

(1) Quantity	(2) Average Cost	(3) Total Cost	(4) Marginal Cost
0	—	$ 70	—
1	$95	95	$25
2	58	116	21
3	48	144	28
4	45	180	36
5	45	225	45
6	46	276	51
7	48	336	60
8	51	408	72
9	55	495	87

change in output (column 1). For example, if Bert expands production from one pair to two pairs of boots, total cost increases from $95 to $116 (column 3). Therefore, the marginal cost of the second pair is $21. The marginal cost of the third pair is $28, since an increase in output from two pairs to three pairs causes total cost to increase from $116 to $144.

Figure 4.2 illustrates the average and marginal cost information presented in Table 4.3. Note that the marginal cost of production begins to increase in the short run with the third unit of output because of the law of diminishing returns. Why? In Section 4.1 we noted that as Charlie hired more cooks for his Soup Kitchen, the extra amount of soup produced by each additional cook eventually diminished because each new cook had less equipment and kitchen space with which to work. Bert faces the same production problem in the short-run time period. He has a fixed number of work benches, a given amount of boot-making equipment, as well as a restricted amount of work space in his shop. If he expands production by hiring more workers, eventually the marginal and average costs of production will rise. This is because

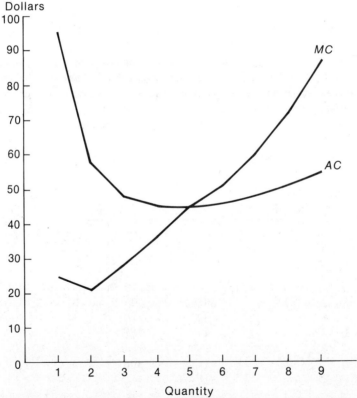

Figure 4.2.   The Firm's Short-Run Average Cost *(AC)* and Marginal Cost *(MC)* Curves. These cost curves are "U-shaped" because they follow the law of diminishing returns.

Bert has to pay each additional worker the same wage even after the output per additional worker falls (i.e., after the law of diminishing returns sets in). This makes the marginal cost and average cost curves "U-shaped" in the short run, as Figure 4.2 illustrates.

Revenue Received by a Firm

In deciding how many units of output to produce, Bert must also consider his revenue. From Bert's viewpoint, the price paid by a customer is the *average revenue* received by his firm, where average revenue is defined as the revenue received per unit of output. Given a market price of $60, we can see in column 2 of Table 4.4 that Bert receives $60 in revenue for each pair of hiking boots sold.

Total revenue is shown in column 3, calculated as the price of the product (column 2) multiplied by the quantity of boots sold (column 1). For example, if Bert sells two pairs of boots he will earn $120 in total revenue (or $60 × 2). Column 4 shows *marginal revenue,* the revenue received from selling one *additional* unit of output. Marginal revenue is calculated by dividing the change in total revenue (column 3) by the change in output (column 1). For example, if Bert expands production from one pair to two pairs of boots, total revenue increases from $60 to $120 — and the marginal revenue of the second pair is $60. The marginal revenue of the third pair is also $60 since an increase in output from two pairs to three pairs causes total revenue to increase from $120 to $180.

As we noted in the introduction to this section, Bert has no control over the price of boots because the market is assumed to be purely competitive. The Hiking Experience is a *price*

Table 4.4
The Competitive Firm's Revenue Schedule
(assuming a market price of $60)

(1) Quantity	(2) Price, Average Revenue	(3) Total Revenue	(4) Marginal Revenue
0	—	$ 0	—
1	$60	60	$60
2	60	120	60
3	60	180	60
4	60	240	60
5	60	300	60
6	60	360	60
7	60	420	60
8	60	480	60
9	60	540	60

taker. If Bert tries to charge more than the market price of $60 per pair, households will refuse to buy any of his boots; instead, they will buy identical boots from his competitors at the lower market price.

See Figure 4.3, which illustrates the average and marginal revenue data presented in Table 4.4. Since Bert can sell all of his boots at the market price of $60, this price *(P)* represents his firm's demand curve *(d)*. Note that Bert's demand curve also represents his average and marginal revenue curves *(d = AR = MR)*. Why? His average revenue *(AR)* curve is horizontal in Figure 4.3 because Bert receives the same $60 in revenue per unit regardless of the additional quantity sold. Marginal revenue *(MR)* is equal to average revenue because every time he sells one more unit of output, he receives $60 in *additional* revenue. We will now examine the cost and revenue data using marginal analysis to determine how many hiking boots Bert will produce in the short run.

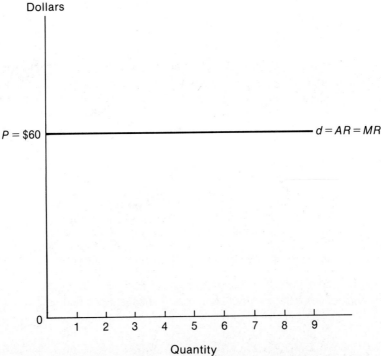

Figure 4.3.   The Firm's Demand *(d)*, Average Revenue *(AR)*, and Marginal Revenue *(MR)* Curves. The market price *(P)* is the firm's demand curve since the firm can sell all of its output at this price. The firm's demand curve also represents its average and marginal revenue curves since the firm receives the same $60 in revenue per unit regardless of the additional quantity of boots sold per day.

The Short-Run Production Decision: How Much Should a Firm Produce?

To analyze the production decision under different market conditions, we will assume that the costs of production remain the same; the only change to be made will be on the revenue side. We will first assume that the market price of hiking boots is $60 to illustrate the case of economic profit. We will then demonstrate the situations in which the firm would take a loss or break even (assuming prices of $28 and $45, respectively).

Bert's Success Story: Maximizing Total Profit When Price Is $60   All firms want to maximize total profit, the amount by which total revenue exceeds the total cost of production. (Note that the term *profit* in this section refers to economic profit, not normal profit.) In order to maximize total profit, the firm should continue to increase production until the revenue obtained from an additional unit of output equals the cost of producing it. Therefore, the firm will produce that level of output at which marginal revenue *(MR)* equals marginal cost *(MC)*. This is called the **MR = MC rule.**

To understand the reasoning behind the *MR = MC rule,* see Table 4.5, which reproduces the marginal cost and marginal revenue data presented in Tables 4.3 and 4.4. Because Bert does not have all the information in Table 4.5 as he begins to increase production, he must reach the optimum level of production through a trial-and-error process — balancing the

Table 4.5
The Production Decision (Bert maximizes *total* economic profit by producing that amount of output where *MR* equals *MC*.)

(1) Quantity	(2) Marginal Revenue	(3) Marginal Cost	(4) Marginal Profit
0	—	—	—
1	$60	$25	$35
2	60	21	39
3	60	28	32
4	60	36	24
5	60	45	15
6	60	51	9
7	60	60	0
8	60	72	−12
9	60	87	−27

extra revenue to be gained against the extra cost to be paid when he produces one additional pair of boots.

For example, when Bert produces the fourth pair (column 1), he adds $60 to his total revenue (column 2) and $36 to his total cost (column 3). Therefore, the fourth pair adds $24 to his total profit (column 4), which is the marginal profit of the fourth pair. *Marginal profit* is defined as the change in total profit per additional unit of output, which may be calculated by subtracting the marginal cost of production (column 3) from marginal revenue (column 2). Bert will also produce the fifth and sixth pairs of boots since they add $15 and $9, respectively, to his total profit (column 4). As long as marginal revenue exceeds marginal cost, Bert will have the incentive to expand production since total profit will increase as additional units of output are produced. When Bert produces the seventh pair, he finds that there is no change in total profit. He discovers that total profit cannot be increased any further when he produces the eighth pair of boots. He sees that the production of the eighth pair adds $60 to his firm's total revenue (column 2) and $72 to total cost (column 3) — causing total profit to fall by $12 (column 4). Therefore, Bert will cut back production, maximizing total profit by producing seven pairs of boots per day, where marginal revenue equals marginal cost. Note that all firms want to maximize *total* profit, not *marginal* profit. Marginal profit is only useful as a guide to indicate the direction of change in total profit — when marginal profit is positive, total profit is increasing; when marginal profit is negative, total profit is decreasing; and when marginal profit is zero, total profit is at a maximum.

We can verify the logic behind the $MR = MC$ *rule* by examining total profit in Table 4.6. Total profit (column 6) is calculated by subtracting total cost (column 5) from total revenue (column 4). When Bert increases production from four pairs to five pairs, total profit increases from $60 to $75. As long as total profit is not decreasing, Bert will continue to expand production. When he produces the seventh pair, total profit remains unchanged at the maximum of $84. Since production of the eighth pair would cause total profit to fall to $72, he will decide to produce only seven pairs of boots per day. (As Table 4.6 shows, production of the sixth pair also results in $84 in total profit, the same as the seventh pair. We assume that the firm will continue to increase production until total profit *begins* to fall. Since this occurs with the eighth pair, Bert will stop his search for even more profit. He will cut back production and will make only seven pairs of boots per day.)

The production decision can be analyzed graphically. Figure 4.4a and Figure 4.4b illustrate the average and marginal data presented in Table 4.6 (see columns 2, 3, 7, and 8). As Figure 4.4a indicates, the firm will produce seven pairs of boots per day because at this level of output marginal revenue equals marginal cost (both are $60). The resulting maximum total profit is illustrated in Figure 4.4b, where the average revenue of $60 exceeds the average cost of $48 given the production of seven pairs of boots. Total profit is $84 per day, calculated as the amount by which average revenue ($60) exceeds average cost ($48) multiplied by the seven pairs of boots produced (or $12 × 7).

We noted that all firms want to maximize total profit. However, if the owners of a firm sadly discover that the market price for their product is too low for their company to make economic profit or to break even, then they will try to minimize their loss in the short run. In

Table 4.6
The Case of Economic Profit (Given a market price of $60, Bert will
maximize total economic profit by producing that amount of output
where MR equals MC.)

(1)	(2)	(3)	(4)	(5)	(6)	(7)	(8)
	Price,						
	Average	Average	Total	Total	Total	Marginal	Marginal
Quantity	Revenue	Cost	Revenue	Cost	Profit	Revenue	Cost
0	—	—	$ 0	$ 70	$−70	—	—
1	$60	$95	60	95	−35	$60	$25
2	60	58	120	116	4	60	21
3	60	48	180	144	36	60	28
4	60	45	240	180	60	60	36
5	60	45	300	225	75	60	45
6	60	46	360	276	84	60	51
7	60	48	420	336	84	60	60
8	60	51	480	408	72	60	72
9	60	55	540	495	45	60	87

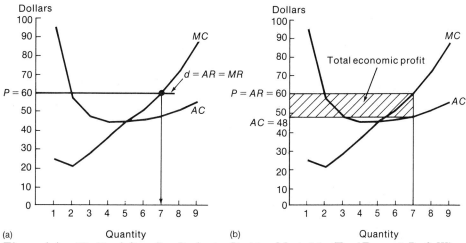

Figure 4.4. The Firm's Short-Run Production Decision: Maximizing Total Economic Profit When Price is $60. (a) The firm will produce 7 pairs of boots per day since, at this level of production, marginal revenue *(MR)* of $60 equals marginal cost *(MC)*. (b) Given this level of production, the firm has maximized total economic profit ($84 per day), calculated as the amount by which average revenue ($60) exceeds average cost ($48), multiplied by the pairs of boots produced per day (7).

other words, the company will strive to reduce the amount by which total cost exceeds total revenue as much as possible.

Minimizing Total Loss After Price Has Dropped to $28

To illustrate how a firm minimizes its total loss in the short run, let's assume that the market demand for hiking boots decreases, causing the price of hiking boots to fall from $60 to $28. Bert is disgusted. He set out to get rich, but the drop in the price of hiking boots to $28 has forced him into a position of trying to cut his losses. He doesn't have time to get out of the business in the short run because there is not sufficient time to sell his shop, equipment, and land. What can he do? Take a vacation? No, that won't help. He must decide how many boots to produce per day until he has time to sell The Hiking Experience.

In order to minimize his loss, Bert will continue to adjust production until the revenue obtained from an additional unit of output equals the cost of producing it. He will produce that level of output at which marginal revenue *(MR)* equals marginal cost *(MC)*. Therefore, the *MR = MC rule* applies to the minimization of loss as well as to the maximization of profit.

We can verify the logic behind the *MR = MC rule* by examining Table 4.7, which represents the firm's total loss (column 6), calculated by subtracting total cost (column 5) from total revenue (column 4). We are assuming that the cost of producing hiking boots remains unchanged. The total revenue presented in Table 4.7 is less than the original total revenue (Table 4.4) because we are assuming that the price of hiking boots has fallen from $60 to $28 (column 2).

Table 4.7
The Case of Loss (Given a market price of $28, Bert minimizes his total loss in the short run by producing that amount of output where *MR* equals *MC*.)

(1) Quantity	(2) Price, Average Revenue	(3) Average Cost	(4) Total Revenue	(5) Total Cost	(6) Total Loss	(7) Marginal Revenue	(8) Marginal Cost
0	—	—	$ 0	$ 70	$−70	—	—
1	$28	$95	28	95	−67	$28	$25
2	28	58	56	116	−60	28	21
3	28	48	84	144	−60	28	28
4	28	45	112	180	−68	28	36
5	28	45	140	225	−85	28	45
6	28	46	168	276	−108	28	51
7	28	48	196	336	−140	28	60
8	28	51	224	408	−184	28	72
9	28	55	252	495	−243	28	87

If Bert were to shut down his business (laying off his workers and canceling his orders for leather and other supplies), he would lose $70 per day (column 6). Why? As we can see in Table 4.7, if Bert produced zero pairs of hiking boots, he would receive no revenue (column 4) and the total cost of his fixed inputs would be $70 (column 5). Note that, even if he has shut down his operation, Bert is still considered to be in business because he is still the owner of The Hiking Experience. Remember, he doesn't have time to sell his property in the short run. While waiting for someone to buy his building, equipment, and land, Bert will experiment to see if he can cut his loss. He discovers that the production of the first pair of hiking boots causes his loss to fall to $67 per day (column 6). When he increases production from one to two pairs of boots, his loss falls even further (from $67 to $60). Bert will continue to produce additional pairs of boots until his total loss begins to increase. Bert does not realize that he has minimized his loss until he produces the fourth pair of boots, which causes his total loss to increase from $60 to $68. He will therefore cut back production to three pairs where his total loss is at a minimum of $60 per day. Bert will continue to operate in the short run as long as his total revenue is able to cover all of his total variable costs and at least some of his total fixed costs. As we noted above, if Bert were to shut down, his loss would be $70 per day (the amount of his daily total fixed costs). By keeping his business in production, Bert is only losing $60 per day.

Figure 4.5a and Figure 4.5b (which are based on Table 4.7) illustrate graphically how a firm minimizes its total loss in the short run. Assuming that the market price of hiking boots (P_2) is now only $28, Figure 4.5a indicates that Bert will produce three pairs of boots because

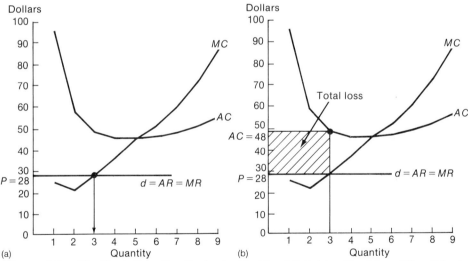

Figure 4.5. The Firm's Short-Run Production Decision: Minimizing Total Loss When Price is $28. (a) The firm will produce 3 pairs of boots per day since at this level of production, marginal revenue *(MR)* of $28 equals marginal cost *(MC)*. (b) Given this level of production, the firm has minimized total loss ($−60 per day), calculated as the amount by which average cost ($48) exceeds average revenue ($28), multiplied by the pairs of boots produced per day (3).

105

at this level of output marginal revenue equals marginal cost (both are $28). The resulting minimum total loss is illustrated in Figure 4.5b, where the average cost of $48 exceeds the average revenue of $28 given the production of three pairs of boots. Bert's total loss is $60 per day (calculated as the amount by which average cost [$48] exceeds average revenue [$28] multiplied by the three pairs of boots produced, or $20 × 3).

Breaking Even: Bert Would Make Normal Profit If the Price Were $45   Bert was able to make economic profit when the market price of hiking boots was $60 per pair. However, he discovered that when the market price of boots fell to $28, the best he could do was to minimize his loss in the short run. A third possibility is called the *breakeven case,* in which Bert is making neither *economic* profit nor loss; rather, he is making *normal* profit. As we described in the previous section, normal profit is the return that the owner must receive on his or her own resources (called implicit costs) after all the bills are paid (the explicit costs).

The breakeven case would occur if the market price of hiking boots were $45 per pair (assuming the same costs of production). As we can see in Table 4.8, when the market price is $45 (column 2), Bert will take a loss of $70 per day if he produces no boots at all (column 6). We can see that when he produces the first pair of boots, his total loss decreases to $50.

Bert will continue to produce additional pairs of boots as long as his total loss is decreasing. Production of the fourth pair causes his loss to fall to zero. We assume that Bert will

Table 4.8
The Breakeven Case (Given a market price of $45, the best Bert can do in the short run is to break even making normal profit — by producing that amount of output where *MR* equals *MC*.)

(1) Quantity	(2) Price, Average Revenue	(3) Average Cost	(4) Total Revenue	(5) Total Cost	(6) Total Loss	(7) Marginal Revenue	(8) Marginal Cost
0	—	—	$ 0	$ 70	$−70	—	—
1	$45	$95	45	95	−50	$45	$25
2	45	58	90	116	−26	45	21
3	45	48	135	144	−9	45	28
4	45	45	180	180	0	45	36
5	45	45	225	225	0	45	45
6	45	46	270	276	−6	45	51
7	45	48	315	336	−21	45	60
8	45	51	360	408	−48	45	72
9	45	55	405	495	−90	45	87

experiment to see if he can do better than simply break even (making zero loss) by increasing production further. Bert discovers that the production of the sixth pair of boots causes his loss to increase to $6. Since this is the first time that he has observed an increase in his total loss, Bert will cut back production to five pairs where he is now satisfied to be able to break even. Note that the *MR = MC rule* applies to the breakeven case as well as to the minimization of loss and the maximization of profit. We can see in column 6 of Table 4.8 that the firm's total loss is zero with the production of the fifth pair of boots where marginal revenue equals marginal cost (both are equal to $45).

Figure 4.6 (which is based on Table 4.8) illustrates graphically that the best the firm can do is to break even when the market price of boots is $45. As Figure 4.6 indicates, when Bert

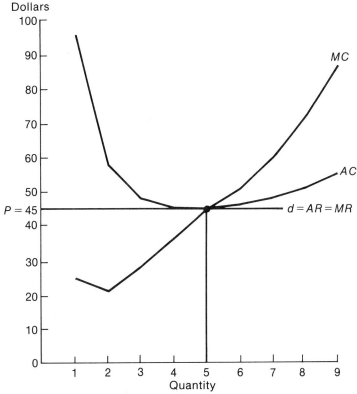

Figure 4.6. The Firm's Short-Run Production Decision: Breaking Even (making normal profit) When Price is $45. The firm will produce 5 pairs of boots per day because at this level of production, marginal revenue *(MR)* of $45 equals marginal cost *(MC)*. The production of 5 pairs of boots per day causes the firm's total economic profit per day to be zero since average revenue ($45) equals average cost.

produces five pairs of boots, marginal revenue equals marginal cost. He is breaking even at this level of production because the average cost of production equals the average revenue received (both are $45).

Having examined the production decision of an individual firm in the short run, we will now explore how the firm interacts with the market over the long-run time period.

4.4 The Long-Run Pricing and Output Behavior of Competitive Markets

Perhaps you have heard of the "horse and buggy" days. In the early twentieth century, most people either walked or drove a horse and carriage to their destinations. Milk wagons were pulled by horses around neighborhoods until the 1950s, when they were finally replaced by gas-powered trucks. More recently, personal computers, pocket calculators, digital watches, video recorders, compact discs, and handheld televisions have become new growth industries as other industries have declined. Industries rise and fall in response to the appearance of economic profit and loss in the marketplace. We now turn our attention to the impact of economic profit and loss on the long-run behavior of competitive markets.

The Role of Economic Profit in the Long Run

Suppose the demand for hiking boots increases, causing firms in the market to make economic profit. How would the appearance of economic profit affect competitive market behavior? In the short run, firms can expand the production of hiking boots only by employing more variable inputs, such as labor. They do not have sufficient time to employ more fixed inputs by building new factories or buying more land. There is also not enough time for firms to enter the market.

In the long-run time period, however, firms have enough time to build new factories and to buy new land. Since all inputs are variable (including capital and land), there is sufficient time for firms to enter the industry in pursuit of economic (above-normal) profit. The entry of new firms will cause supply to increase, which in turn will drive the market price down. See Figure 4.7a which illustrates the increase in the market supply curve (from S_1 to S_2).

As we can see in Figure 4.7a, the price of hiking boots has fallen from $60 to $45 ($P_1$ to P_2), and the quantity sold has increased. Entry will stop when the firms in the market are just breaking even (making normal profit rather than economic profit). Economic profit is eliminated in the long run since the price of hiking boots is ultimately driven to the average cost of production. The *long-run equilibrium position of the purely competitive firm* is illustrated in Figure 4.7b, which represents the breakeven case we described in the previous section (illustrated by Figure 4.6). We noted that Bert was able to break even (making normal profit) by producing the amount of output at which marginal revenue equaled marginal cost.

The impact of the appearance of economic profit on the *long-run pricing and output behavior of a purely competitive market* can be summarized as follows:

$$economic\ profit \rightarrow LR\ entry \rightarrow \uparrow S \rightarrow \downarrow P\ until\ P = AC$$

We can interpret this as follows: The appearance of economic profit induces firms to enter the market in the long run, which causes an increase in supply $(\uparrow S)$, which in turn forces price to decrease $(\downarrow P)$ until firms in the industry break even $(P = AC)$, making only normal profit.

The Role of Loss in the Long Run

Suppose the demand for hiking boots decreases, causing the firms in the industry to take a loss. How would the appearance of loss affect competitive market behavior? In the short run, firms would reduce production by employing fewer variable inputs, such as labor. Firms would not have sufficient time to sell their factories, land, and other inputs that are fixed in the short run. Consequently, they do not have enough time to get out of business.

In the long-run time period, however, firms have enough time to leave the market in response to loss. The departure of firms will cause the supply of hiking boots to decrease, which in turn will drive the market price up. The decrease in supply over the long run is illustrated in Figure 4.8a by the shift in the market supply curve from S_1 to S_2.

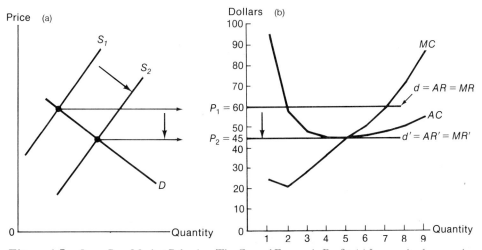

Figure 4.7. Long-Run Market Behavior: The Case of Economic Profit. (a) In pursuit of economic (above-normal) profit, firms will enter the market in the long run, which causes market supply to increase from S_1 to S_2. This increase in supply causes price to fall from P_1 to P_2. (b) When price equals average cost (AC), total economic profit is zero. Firms can only break even (make normal profit) in the long run under conditions of pure competition.

The Development of New Market Centers

Boom towns are developing outside the traditional suburbs of many cities in every region of the United States. These new market centers are suburbs of the old suburbs which turned into "cities" as branches of big accounting firms, law firms, and corporate headquarters arrived. Most of the growth of these boom towns is the result of smaller companies seeking lower rent for office space, less congestion, and cheaper housing. This new urban trend has also been helped by the proliferation of personal computers and facsimile machines which make remote locations convenient for entrepreneurs by lowering the cost of obtaining information.

The pasture lands of Marrieta/Roswell, located twenty miles north of Atlanta, Georgia, have been totally transformed by the construction of office buildings, warehouses, light manufacturing factories, and retail shops. In addition to the 20,000 jobs created over the last five years, it is predicted that 51,000 new jobs will be generated in this area during the 1988–1993 period.

Troy, a distant suburb of Detroit, is experiencing all-out growth due to the corporate "downsizing" of the Big Three auto companies. Hundreds of specialized small companies have clustered in Troy to perform former in-house tasks which are now being farmed out by the Big Three. Other boom towns include Scottsdale/Sun City, Arizona; Herndon/Manassas, Virginia; Virginia Beach/Chesapeake, Virginia; Orlando/Kissimmee, Florida; Newport Beach/Laguna, California; Dallas/Richardson, Texas; East Brunswick, New Jersey; and Santa Ana/Costa Mesa, California.

The above is a summary of an article, "The New Boom Towns" by Bernard Wysocki Jr., which appeared in *The Wall Street Journal,* March 27, 1989, pp. B1–B2. It illustrates the process by which new market centers are created via the long-run adjustment process of firms seeking to locate in areas that offer relatively lower costs and higher revenue.

Price will continue to rise until it equals average cost. The *long-run equilibrium position of the purely competitive firm* is illustrated in Figure 4.8b. Once the firms in the market are just breaking even (making normal profit rather than loss), exiting from the market will cease. We can see in Figure 4.8a that the price of hiking boots has risen from \$28 to \$45 (P_1 to P_2) and the quantity sold has decreased.

The *long-run pricing and output behavior of a purely competitive market* can be summarized as follows:

$$\text{loss} \rightarrow LR \text{ exiting} \rightarrow \downarrow S \rightarrow \uparrow P \text{ until } P = AC$$

The appearance of loss forces firms to leave the market in the long run, which causes a decrease in supply $(\downarrow S)$, which in turn causes price to increase $(\uparrow P)$ until firms in the industry are breaking even $(P = AC)$, making normal profit.

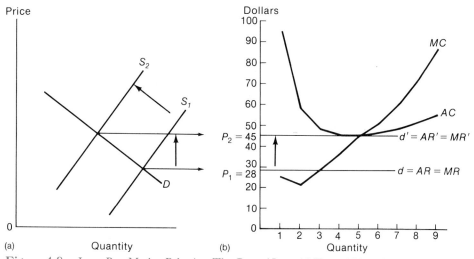

Figure 4.8. Long-Run Market Behavior: The Case of Loss. (a) To avoid loss, firms will leave the market in the long run, which causes market supply to decrease from S_1 to S_2. This decrease in supply from S_1 to S_2 causes price to increase from P_1 to P_2. (b) When price equals average cost *(AC)*, total loss has been eliminated. Firms can only break even (make normal profit) in the long run under conditions of pure competition.

Market Forces and the Efficient Allocation of Scarce Resources

We can draw several important conclusions from the long-run behavior of competitive markets.

Allocative Efficiency First, the competitive market mechanism serves to allocate economic resources efficiently among their alternative uses. We noted in the previous section that a firm will produce that level of output where marginal revenue (which is also the price of the product) equals the marginal cost of production. The *MR = MC rule* applies to both the short run and the long run. Therefore, price will always equal the marginal cost of production *(P = MC)* when the market is purely competitive. This equality is very significant to the well-being of society. It indicates that we have achieved **allocative efficiency,** which means that resources in the economy have been allocated to produce those goods that society wants the most (described earlier in Chapter 2, Section 2.4).

From society's viewpoint, price is a measure of the extra benefit society receives from the consumption of the last unit of the good produced. For example, if you (as a member of society) pay a price of $8 for a pizza, your purchase implies that the pizza gives you $8 worth of pleasure. It will be irrational for you to pay $9 for a pizza if it gives you only $8 worth of satisfaction. On the other hand, (from society's viewpoint) marginal cost measures the opportunity cost of producing the last unit of output. The extra cost to society is measured in terms of the other goods sacrificed when resources are used to produce an additional unit of pizza.

The competitive market will continue to allocate more resources to the production of a good as long as the extra benefit exceeds the extra cost, because each additional unit produced increases the well-being of society. Society maximizes its total satisfaction when it allocates resources to produce each good up to the point where the extra benefit received from a good *(P)* equals the extra cost of producing it *(MC)*.

Economic Efficiency   Second, under conditions of pure competition, the private market will achieve *economic efficiency* (described in Chapter 2, Section 2.4). Purely competitive firms are forced to produce output using the *least-cost combination of inputs*. Why? Inefficient firms have to charge a higher price than their more efficient rivals to cover their higher costs of production. Since households are not willing to buy goods from firms that charge higher prices, these inefficient, high-cost firms are eventually driven out of business.

The breakeven point illustrated in Figure 4.9 is the long-run equilibrium position of the purely competitive firm. As the figure indicates, price is driven to the *minimum* average cost

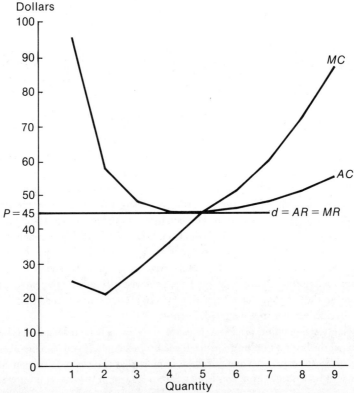

Figure 4.9.   Long-Run Equilibrium Position of the Purely Competitive Firm: The Breakeven Point. The long-run entry and exit of firms under pure competition result in allocative efficiency and economic efficiency.

of production in the long run, which means that the firm is producing at optimal capacity. Since the market price is driven to the firm's minimum average cost of production in the long run, we pay the lowest possible price for the goods bought in the market.

Summary

In the market period, the level of production is fixed since the product is on the market awaiting sale. Production can be increased or decreased in the short-run time period by altering the amount of variable inputs. Firms are not able to enter (or exit) an industry since they do not have sufficient time to buy (or sell) fixed inputs such as capital and land. In the long-run time period, all inputs are variable; therefore, the entry and exit of firms is possible.

We analyzed the short-run production decision of the purely competitive *firm.* In order to maximize total economic profit (or minimize total loss), a firm should increase production until the cost of the extra unit of output is equal to the extra revenue obtained. In other words, the firm should produce that level of output at which marginal revenue equals marginal cost (called the *MR = MC rule*).

Price equals the marginal cost of production *(P = MC)* when the purely competitive firm is in long-run equilibrium, which indicates that we have achieved allocative efficiency. Resources in the economy have been allocated to produce those goods that society wants the most. In addition, price is driven to the minimum average cost of production (the breakeven point), which means that the firm is producing at optimal capacity, making normal profit. The minimization of total costs is called economic efficiency. Households are able to buy the good at the lowest possible price.

We have also examined the behavior of the whole *industry.* An increase in demand will cause market price to increase, creating economic profit. This above-normal profit attracts firms into the market in the long run. As market supply increases in the long run, price falls until it equals the minimum average cost of production. Just the opposite occurs when demand decreases in a particular industry, creating economic loss. When firms are breaking even, they are making normal profit, which is the return necessary to cover the opportunity cost of the owner's own resources (called implicit costs). •

Key Concepts

market period
short run
fixed and variable inputs
entering and exiting of firms
long run
law of diminishing returns
marginal physical product of labor

explicit and implicit costs
total economic profit (above-normal profit)
breakeven point
normal profit
loss
marginal analysis
total, average, marginal costs of production
total, average, marginal revenue
price taker
MR = MC rule
marginal profit
role of profit and loss in the long run
long-run equilibrium position of the purely competitive firm
long-run pricing and output behavior of a purely competitive market
allocative efficiency
economic efficiency

Self-Test Questions: True or False

T   F   1. Land is a variable input in the long-run time period.

T   F   2. Suppose that the total cost of producing pizza at Joe's Pizza Place is as follows: total cost = explicit cost ($30,000) + implicit cost ($70,000). If Joe earns $100,000 in total revenue, he is making zero normal profit.

T   F   3. See Question 2. Suppose that business sales slack off, causing Joe's total revenue to fall to $90,000. After paying all his bills, Joe earns $60,000. This is $10,000 less than Joe would receive if he were to go out of business, putting all his resources into use in their next best opportunity.

T   F   4. Firms will go out of business in the short run if they are taking an economic loss.

T   F   5. Suppose that the industry manufacturing rubber ducks produces 20 million ducks at a cost of $4 each. If the price of each rubber duck is $6, the industry is making an economic profit of $40 million.

T   F   6. The long-run pricing and output behavior of a purely competitive market was emphasized in this chapter. The sequence of events initiated by the appearance of economic profit can be summarized as follows:

$$\text{economic profit} \rightarrow LR \text{ entry} \rightarrow \uparrow S \rightarrow \downarrow P$$

T   F   7. Price is driven to the minimum average cost of production of the firm in the long run under conditions of pure competition. In the long run, purely competitive firms can only break even, making zero economic profit.

T   F   8. Suppose that the marginal revenue of the fifth unit of output for the firm is $20 while the marginal cost is $15. The fifth unit will contribute $5 to the firm's total profit.

Note that questions 9 and 10 refer to the long-run equilibrium position of the purely competitive firm described in Section 4.4.

T   F   9. Society maximizes its total satisfaction when it allocates resources to produce each good up to the point where the price of the good equals the marginal cost of producing it $(P = MC)$.

T   F   10. Price is equal to the firm's minimum average cost, which means that the firm is operating at optimal capacity.

Answers to Self-Test Questions

1. **True.** In the long run, *all* inputs are variable since firms have sufficient time to buy or sell any input, including land and capital.

2. **False.** Since total revenue equals total cost (both being equal to $100,000), Joe's Pizza Place is breaking even, making zero *economic* profit. *Normal* profit is the return necessary to cover the opportunity cost of Joe's own resources, which in this case is $70,000 (his implicit costs).

3. **True.** If Joe earns $90,000 in total revenue and pays the $30,000 that he owes others for their goods and services (his explicit costs), he has $60,000 left over. Since the income he could earn by going out of business and employing his personal resources in their next best opportunities is $70,000 (his implicit costs), Joe would receive $10,000 less by staying in business. Joe will go out of business when he has sufficient time to sell his assets (the long run).

4. **False.** Firms cannot go out of business in the short run since they do not have time to sell their land and capital (their fixed inputs). Firms are able to shut down by reducing their variable inputs (such as labor) in the short run. But as long as they still own their plant facilities and other assets, these firms are still in business.

5. **True.** Economic profit is calculated as the amount by which total revenue exceeds total costs. Economic profit in this case equals $Q(AR - AC)$ or 20($6 - $4) or $40 million.

6. **True.** In the long run, this above-normal profit attracts new firms into the market. As firms enter, supply increases, which in turn drives the market price down.

7. **True.** Economic profit attracts new firms into the market, which in turn causes output to increase, driving prices down. The process stops when price equals minimum average cost since at this breakeven point, firms no longer have the incentive to enter the market. Firms are making normal profit when economic profit is zero. The same logic applies when firms are taking an economic loss.

8. **True.** The fifth unit adds $20 to total revenue and $15 to total cost, causing total profit to increase by $5.

9. **True.** From society's viewpoint, price measures the extra benefit of the last unit of output produced. Marginal cost measures the opportunity cost of this last unit of output in terms of the goods we have given up in producing it. As long as the extra benefit *(P)* exceeds the extra cost *(MC)*, total satisfaction increases as more of this good is produced. Total satisfaction is at the maximum when the extra benefit received equals the extra cost paid *(P = MC)*.

10. **True.** The entry of firms in the long run increases market supply, which in turn drives the price of the product down until the firms in the market are breaking even. As Figure 4.7 illustrates, the breakeven point for the firm occurs at that level of production where price equals minimum average cost. The firm is producing at optimal capacity.

Discussion Questions

1. Describe the characteristics of the three time periods.

2. Discuss the law of diminishing returns. How does the law of diminishing returns affect the firm's short-run average cost of production? Why?

3. Society has not maximized its total satisfaction if the price of a product exceeds the marginal cost of production. Is this statement true or false? Explain your reasoning.

Problems

1. Answer the next three questions using the following cost information for Joe's Pizzeria in 1989.

Explicit Costs		Implicit Costs	
Labor	$50,000	Work Time	$30,000
Supplies	$20,000	Land	$ 3,000
Subtotal	$70,000	Building	$15,000
		Equipment	$ 2,000
		Subtotal	$50,000

a. If Joe were to sell 20,000 pizzas at $6 each, what is the amount of normal profit? Is Joe making any economic profit? Describe the difference between the two concepts of profit.

b. If Joe had sold the 20,000 pizzas at a price of $5 each, would he be making an economic profit, breaking even, or taking an economic loss? Why?

c. If Joe were to sell his business, how much would he receive for his resources?

2. Answer the next two questions using the following table, which represents the short-run cost schedule of a firm making picture frames:

(1) Quantity	(2) Total Cost
0	$ 55
1	85
2	105
3	180
4	300

a. What is the average cost of producing three picture frames?

b. What is the marginal cost of producing the third picture frame?

3. Answer the next three questions using the following table, which represents Bert's cost and revenue schedule as he expands the production of hiking boots:

(1) Quantity	(2) Price, Average Revenue	(3) Average Cost	(4) Total Revenue	(5) Total Cost	(6) Total Profit or Loss	(7) Marginal Revenue	(8) Marginal Cost
0	—	—	$ 0	$ 70		—	—
1	$36	$95	36	95		$36	$25
2	36	58	72	116		36	21
3	36	48	108	144		36	28
4	36	45	144	180		36	36
5	36	45	180	225		36	45
6	36	46	216	276		36	51
7	36	48	252	336		36	60

a. How much total profit or loss would Bert receive if he produced five pairs of hiking boots?

b. What would happen to total profit or total loss if Bert were to expand the production of hiking boots from five to six pairs?

c. Using the $MR = MC$ *rule,* calculate how many pairs of boots Bert should produce in the short run. Explain your reasoning.

4. The following figure represents the purely competitive market for potato chips in the short run. Using this graph to illustrate your explanation, describe the long-run pricing and output behavior of this industry.

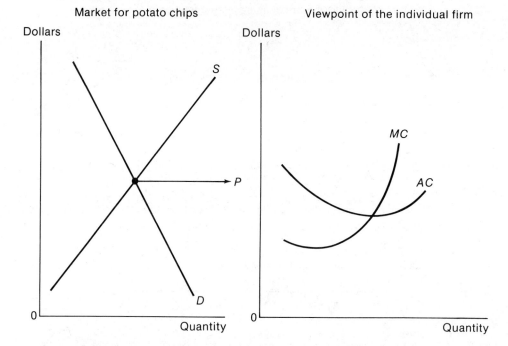

CHAPTER
5

Imperfect Competition

Objectives

Upon completion of this chapter, you should understand:

1. How a pure monopoly decides how much to produce and what price to charge.

2. The impact of monopoly on the allocation of resources and the distribution of income.

3. The behavior of firms under conditions of monopolistic competition and oligopoly.

4. The various barriers to entry and how they reduce competition.

5. The use of concentration ratios to measure the extent of competition.

The federal government ended a seven-year battle with the American Telephone & Telegraph Company with the settlement of an antitrust suit, resulting in the breakup of the world's largest private corporation. Under terms of the settlement, AT&T agreed to give up ownership of its twenty-two operating subsidiaries, which provide the bulk of the nation's local telephone service.

Shortly after settlement of the AT&T case, the federal government dropped its antitrust suit against International Business Machines, the world's leading producer of computers. The government withdrew the suit against IBM, claiming that since the filing of the case in 1969, the computer market had become more competitive. The government claimed that the entrance of new firms had reduced IBM's control of this industry.

The breakup of AT&T and the dropping of the suit against IBM both occurred in 1982. In the same year, the federal government permitted Dupont to buy a controlling share of Conoco stock, and U.S. Steel took over Marathon Oil. More recent megamergers among the largest oil companies include Chevron-Gulf (acquisition price, $13.4 billion), Texaco-Getty ($10.1 billion), Mobil-Superior ($5.7 billion), and Occidental-Cities Service ($4 billion).

Profound changes also occur daily among the many small businesses in our economy. Some are quietly entering the market at the same time that others are leaving. While the birth or death of any particular small business may go unnoticed by most, the cumulative effect of such market changes has an important role in allocating the resources of the economy.

Some markets are dominated by a few giants like AT&T and IBM, companies that may eventually lose some of their market power through government action or the entry of firms into the market. There are also markets in which numerous firms, such as small restaurants and gift shops, constantly struggle to stay afloat with their rivals in the industry. What are the economic implications of the different market structures that characterize the U.S. economy?

The purpose of this chapter is to describe the performance of markets under conditions of *imperfect competition.* Economists have constructed a number of market models to analyze the various ways in which buyers and sellers interact in determining price and output in product markets. Our primary focus is the comparative performance of pure monopoly and pure competition. Knowledge of the differences between pure competition and pure monopoly will make it easier for us to understand the behavior of the other imperfect market structures that lie between these polar opposites. We then examine methods of measuring the degree of competition in the U.S. economy.

5.1 Pure Monopoly

What are the characteristics of monopoly? How does a monopolist set price and the level of production?

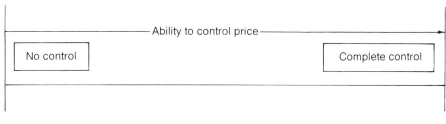

Pure competition:
1. Many sellers acting independently
2. Standardized product
3. Free entry

Monopoly:
1. Single firm
2. Unique product
3. No entry

Figure 5.1. Scale Measuring the Ability of a Firm to Control Price.

Characteristics

Pure competition and pure monopoly are at opposite ends of the scale by which we attempt to measure market performance (see Figure 5.1). *Pure competition* is a model describing the interaction of buyers and sellers under perfect conditions. Because purely competitive markets contain many small independent buyers and sellers of a standardized product and there are no barriers to entry, individual decision makers have no control over price.

At the opposite end of the scale is ***pure monopoly,*** in which there is only one firm selling a unique product, which means that there are no close substitutes for the good. The monopolist can charge a price above the level that would prevail under purely competitive conditions because customers have no alternative — either they buy at the monopoly price or they must do without. The monopolist can remain as the only seller due to barriers that prevent rival firms from entering the market (discussed in Section 5.3).

Monopolies are not very common. We will emphasize this market structure because the comparison of it to pure competition helps us to understand the behavior of other forms of imperfect competition which more typically characterize our economy. Electric power companies, mass transit in urban areas, and sewage treatment facilities are examples of monopolies that are regulated by government.

Price and Output Determination

How much will a monopoly produce, and what price will it charge for its product? The profit-maximizing combination of output and price depends on the firm's revenue and cost curves.

In Chapter 4 (Section 4.3), we noted that the purely competitive firm balances the extra revenue to be gained against the extra cost to be paid in deciding whether or not to produce an additional unit of output. The monopoly's *production* decision-making process is identical to that of a purely competitive firm. Each decision maker is using *marginal analysis,* seeking to produce that level of output where marginal revenue equals marginal cost in order to maximize total profit.

While both a purely competitive firm and a monopoly use the same production decision-making process, there is a major difference in how each decides what *price* to charge for its product. As we emphasized throughout Chapter 4, the purely competitive firm has no control over price — it is a price taker. A monopoly, on the other hand, has control over prices. After deciding how much to produce, the monopoly then searches to find the price which will enable it to sell this profit-maximizing level of output, given the demand for its product.

The Demand and Revenue Schedules of a Monopoly Suppose that the Gotham Cable Company is a monopoly, being the only firm providing cable television in Gotham City. Because there is only one firm in the area, Gotham Cable's demand is the overall demand for cable television in this area. Note that the monopoly is able to sell more of its output if it lowers its price. For example, Table 5.1 shows that if Gotham Cable were to reduce its price from $10 to $9 (column 2) the amount of cable television service demanded per month would increase from 2 units to 3 units (column 1).

Figure 5.2 illustrates Gotham Cable's demand curve *(d)*, which represents the quantity of cable service demanded at various prices. This figure is based on the data presented in Table 5.1 (columns 1 and 2). Because the price paid by a customer is also the average revenue received by the firm, the monopoly's demand curve is also its average revenue curve. The firm's average revenue *(AR)* curve is downward sloping, which indicates that Gotham Cable receives less revenue per unit as the quantity sold increases.

Table 5.1 presents the firm's marginal revenue *(MR)* in column 4, where marginal revenue is defined as the revenue received from the production of one *additional* unit, calculated as the change in total revenue divided by the change in output. As Table 5.1

Table 5.1
Revenue Schedule of a Pure Monopoly

(1) Quantity	(2) Price, Average Revenue	(3) Total Revenue	(4) Marginal Revenue
0	—	$ 0.00	—
1	$11.00	11.00	$11.00
2	10.00	20.00	9.00
3	9.00	27.00	7.00
4	8.00	32.00	5.00
5	7.00	35.00	3.00
6	6.00	36.00	1.00
7	5.00	35.00	−1.00
8	4.00	32.00	−3.00

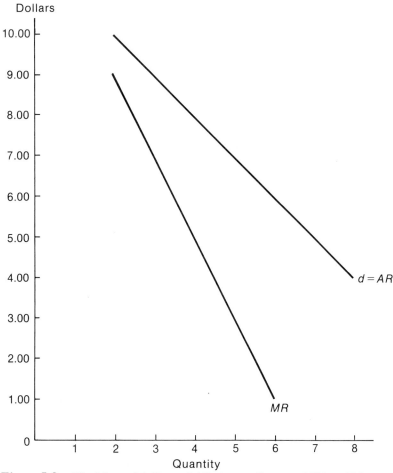

Figure 5.2. The Monopoly's Demand *(d)*, Average Revenue *(AR)*, and Marginal Revenue *(MR)* Curves. The monopoly's demand curve is also its average revenue curve. The monopoly's marginal revenue curve is below its average revenue as the firm expands production.

indicates, marginal revenue is less than average revenue as the firm expands production beyond the first unit because every time the firm chooses to sell one more unit, it must lower the price on the previous units that could have been sold at a higher price. For example, to increase cable television sales from 2 units to 3 units, Gotham Cable must lower its price from $10 to $9. Because the firm loses $2 on the first 2 units (each of which is now being sold for a dollar less) while gaining $9 from the extra third unit sold, the marginal revenue of the third unit is $7. Therefore, the marginal revenue of the third unit is below the $9 in average revenue received from this unit. Note that Figure 5.2, which is based on Table 5.1, shows that the marginal revenue curve of the monopoly is below its average revenue curve.

123

The Short-Run Production Costs of a Monopoly   In addition to examining its revenue, Gotham Cable must also consider its production costs in deciding how many units of service to produce each month. Note that the following discussion is a review of the cost concepts described in Section 4.3 of Chapter 4. Table 5.2 shows the average cost of production, defined as the cost per unit of output (column 2). Average cost is calculated by dividing total cost (column 3) by the number of units produced (column 1). For example, the average cost of producing 2 units of cable television service is $7.50 (or $15/2).

The monopoly's primary concern is how its total costs change as the company changes the number of units produced. Column 4 shows the marginal cost of production, which is defined as the cost of producing one *additional* unit of output. Marginal cost is calculated by dividing the change in total cost by the change in output. For example, if Gotham Cable expands its television service from 2 units to 3 units, total cost increases from $15 to $20. Therefore, the marginal cost of the third unit is $5. The marginal cost of the fourth unit is also $5, because an increase in service from 3 units to 4 units causes total cost to increase from $20 to $25.

Figure 5.3 is based on the average and marginal cost information presented in Table 5.2. As the figure indicates, in the short run the monopoly's marginal cost of production first decreases and then eventually begins to increase with additional units of output produced, which in turn causes the average cost of production to decrease and then to eventually increase. In Section 4.2 of Chapter 4, we saw that both the average and marginal short-run cost curves of the purely competitive firm eventually turn upward because of the law of diminishing returns. This same "U-shaped" pattern in the average and marginal cost curves exists in the short run for all firms, regardless of market structure.

Table 5.2
Cost Schedule of a Pure Monopoly

(1) Quantity	(2) Average Cost	(3) Total Cost	(4) Marginal Cost
0	—	$ 3.50	—
1	$9.50	9.50	$ 6.00
2	7.50	15.00	5.50
3	6.67	20.00	5.00
4	6.25	25.00	5.00
5	6.00	30.00	5.00
6	6.00	36.00	6.00
7	6.30	44.10	8.10
8	6.90	55.20	11.10

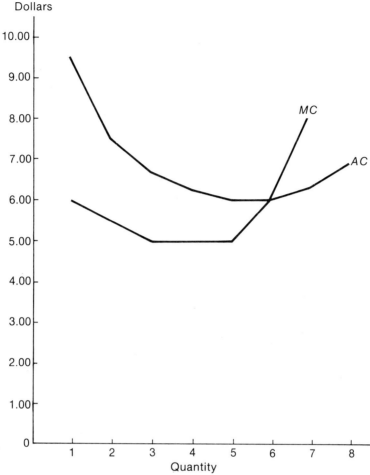

Figure 5.3. The Monopoly's Short-Run Average Cost *(AC)* and Marginal Cost *(MC)* Curves. These cost curves are "U-shaped" because they follow the law of diminishing returns.

The Production and Pricing Decision   How much should a monopoly produce? Gotham Cable wants to maximize total profit, which is the amount by which total revenue exceeds total costs. In order to maximize total profit, Gotham Cable should increase production as long as the revenue obtained from the additional unit sold exceeds the cost of producing it (in other words, as long as marginal revenue exceeds marginal cost). The firm will ultimately produce that level of output at which marginal revenue *(MR)* equals marginal cost *(MC)*. Therefore, in deciding how much to produce, a monopoly follows the *MR = MC rule* described in Chapter 4, Section 4.3.

125

Table 5.3
The Production and Pricing Decision of a Pure Monopoly

(1) Quantity	(2) Price, Average Revenue	(3) Average Cost	(4) Total Revenue	(5) Total Cost	(6) Total Profit	(7) Marginal Revenue	(8) Marginal Cost
0	—	—	$ 0.00	$ 3.50	$− 3.50	—	—
1	$11.00	$ 9.50	11.00	9.50	1.50	$11.00	$ 6.00
2	10.00	7.50	20.00	15.00	5.00	9.00	5.50
3	9.00	6.67	27.00	20.00	7.00	7.00	5.00
4	**8.00**	**6.25**	**32.00**	**25.00**	**7.00**	**5.00**	**5.00**
5	7.00	6.00	35.00	30.00	5.00	3.00	5.00
6	6.00	6.00	36.00	36.00	0.00	1.00	6.00
7	5.00	6.30	35.00	44.10	−9.10	−1.00	8.10
8	4.00	6.90	32.00	55.20	−23.20	−3.00	11.10

To better understand the decision-making process, see Table 5.3, which combines the monopoly's revenue and cost data presented in Table 5.1 and Table 5.2. When Gotham Cable increases production from 2 to 3 units, it adds $7 to its total revenue and $5 to its total cost (see columns 4 and 5 in Table 5.3). Therefore, the third unit adds $2 to Gotham Cable's total profit. We can see in column 6 that total profit has increased from $5 to $7 as production increases from 2 to 3 units. As long as marginal revenue exceeds marginal cost, total profit will increase as additional units of output are produced. The monopoly discovers that the production of the fifth unit causes total profit to fall by $2 (from $7 to $5). At this point, Gotham Cable will reduce production by 1 unit. The firm realizes that it had maximized total profit by producing 4 units, where marginal revenue equals marginal cost (both are $5).

The production decision can be analyzed graphically. As Figure 5.4 indicates, the firm will produce Q (4) units of cable television because at this level of output marginal revenue equals marginal cost. Given this level of production, Gotham Cable will price its product based on consumer demand. As Figure 5.5 indicates, the firm can sell Q (4) units of cable television at the price of P ($8)—measured by the vertical line from Q to the monopoly's demand curve. The resulting maximum total profit of $7 is illustrated in Figure 5.6. Total profit is calculated as the amount by which average revenue ($AR = $8) exceeds average cost ($AC = $6.25) multiplied by the units of cable television service sold ($Q = 4$).

Note that under pure monopoly, the appearance of economic profit illustrated in Figure 5.6 does not result in the expansion of output in the long-run time period because firms are assumed to be barred from entering the industry. Gotham Cable's economic profit is called *monopoly profit* because it is received as a result of the firm's market power. We will now describe how barriers to entry (discussed in Section 5.3) cause the monopoly market structure to misallocate resources.

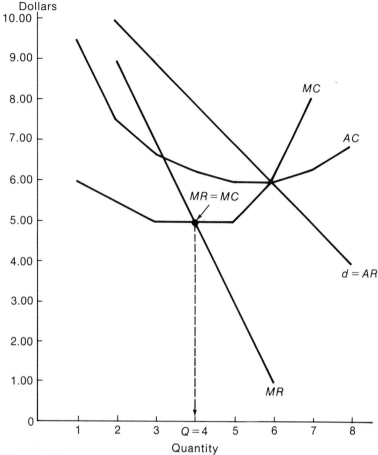

Figure 5.4. The Monopoly's Short-Run Production Decision. The firm will produce 4 units per day since at this level of production *(Q)*, marginal revenue *(MR)* equals marginal cost *(MC)*.

An Evaluation of Long-Run Pricing and Output Behavior: Pure Monopoly Versus Pure Competition

The lack of competition from other firms causes the monopoly market structure to fail to achieve both allocative and economic efficiency.

Allocative Efficiency To better understand how a monopoly misallocates resources, let's review the long-run breakeven position of a purely competitive firm (described in Chapter 4, Section 4.4). Figure 5.7 indicates that, in the long run, the purely competitive firm can only break even, making normal profit (see point *A*).

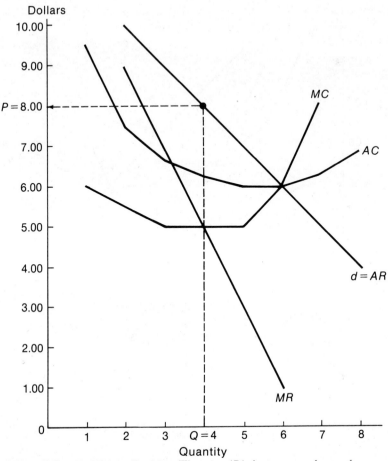

Figure 5.5.   The Pricing Decision. The price *(P)* that a monopoly can charge to sell *Q* units per day depends on its demand curve *(d)*. To sell 4 units Gotham Cable will charge a price of $8.

We noted in Chapter 4 that price will always equal the marginal cost of production *(P = MC)* when the market is purely competitive. This equality indicates that we have achieved *allocative efficiency,* which means that resources in the economy have been allocated to produce those goods that society wants the most. From society's viewpoint, price is a measure of the extra benefit society receives from the consumption of the last unit of the good produced. On the other hand, marginal cost measures the opportunity cost of producing the last unit of output. The competitive market will continue to allocate more resources to the production of a good as long as the extra benefit exceeds the extra cost — each additional unit produced increases the well-being of society. Society maximizes its total satisfaction when it allocates resources to produce each good up to the point where the extra benefit received from a good *(P)* equals the extra cost of producing it *(MC)*.

Under pure monopoly, the appearance of economic profit illustrated in Figure 5.6 does not result in the expansion of output in the long-run time period because firms are assumed to be barred from entering the industry. Barriers to entry cause the monopoly market structure to *under*allocate resources; society receives less output in comparison to the long-run output behavior of a purely competitive market. As we can see in Figure 5.6, the price charged by the monopoly *(P)* exceeds the marginal cost of production at the *Q* level of output. Society would

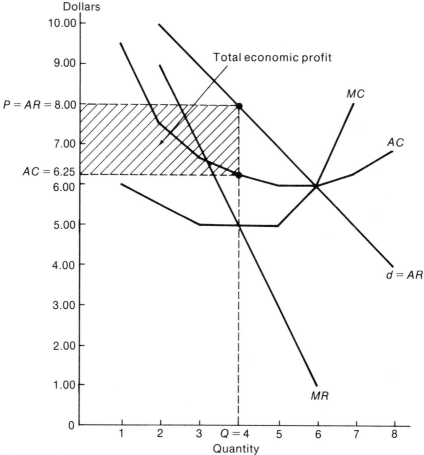

Figure 5.6. Measuring Total Economic Profit. Total economic profit is calculated as the amount by which average revenue *(AR)* exceeds average cost *(AC)*, multiplied by the amount of cable service provided per day *(Q)*. The resulting total economic profit made by Gotham Cable per day is $7 calculated as ($8 − $6.25) × 4 units.

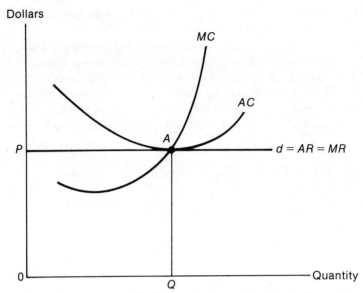

Figure 5.7.   Long-Run Equilibrium Position of the Purely Competitive Firm: The Breakeven Point (see point A). The long-run entry and exit of firms under pure competition results in allocative efficiency and economic efficiency.

be better off if the firm were to increase production because at the Q level of output, the extra benefit of another unit of output to society would exceed the extra cost of production. The monopoly is not willing to increase production because it would result in less total profit. Therefore, the lack of competitive entry hurts society.

Economic Efficiency   Under conditions of pure competition, the private market will also achieve *economic efficiency,* which means that firms are forced to produce output using the least-cost combination of inputs (described in Chapter 4, Section 4.4). As Figure 5.7 indicates, price is driven to the *minimum* average cost of production in the long run, which means that the firm is producing at optimal capacity. Because the market price is driven to the firm's minimum average cost of production in the long run, we pay the lowest possible price for the goods bought in the market.

As we noted above, the appearance of economic profit does not result in the expansion of output in the long run under pure monopoly because firms are assumed to be barred from entering the industry. As we can see in Figure 5.6, Gotham Cable Company's monopoly price *(P)* exceeds the firm's minimum average cost of production, which means that the firm is not operating at optimal capacity. Because of barriers to entry, society pays a higher price for less output than would occur under purely competitive market conditions.

As we noted earlier, monopolies are not very common. We have emphasized this market structure because the comparison of it to pure competition indicates the general behavior of other forms of imperfect competition that do characterize our economy.

5.2 Other Models of Imperfect Competition

There are two major market models between pure competition and pure monopoly called oligopoly and monopolistic competition.

Oligopoly

As Figure 5.8 indicates, oligopoly lies close to pure monopoly on the scale measuring the ability of the firm to control price under different market conditions. It is different from monopoly in that the industry is dominated by a few large firms instead of one. In addition, we assume in the oligopoly model that there are significant barriers to entry (rather than complete barriers which we assume in the monopoly model).

Characteristics   There are two types of oligopolies: differentiated and pure. In a ***differentiated oligopoly,*** firms produce products that are good substitutes for each other but are in some way different. An example is the automobile industry, where we find products that are highly substitutable (e.g., Ford, Chevrolet, Dodge) but that differ in perceived quality or design. In a ***pure oligopoly,*** firms produce identical products. Therefore, the only reason for customers to buy one firm's product over another's is *price difference.* Examples are the steel, aluminum, and cement industries.

The number of sellers in an oligopoly is small enough for the activities of a single seller to affect other firms. This is the chief characteristic of oligopoly — ***interdependence in pricing.*** For example, suppose that there are three dominant producers, firms X, Y, and Z. If firm X reduces its price in order to expand its share of the market, rivals Y and Z will be forced to follow suit. The result will probably be a price war in which all three producers will lose. Consequently, each of the dominant firms must consider the effects of its pricing decision on its rivals and the possible reactions of these rivals to its price change.

Price Leadership and Collusion   Since oligopolists are hurt by price wars, it is unlikely that they would practice such behavior frequently. It is more rational to expect that the oligopolists would adopt pricing policies mutually determined by the joint interest of the group. Again, suppose that firms X, Y, and Z are the dominant producers. Since each producer must consider the consequences of its pricing policy on the other major producers, the resulting oligopoly price will be the one most likely to maximize the joint profit of these firms. The process by which such an agreed-upon price is established occurs primarily through ***price-leadership behavior.*** This means that if firm X decides to increase its price, the other two firms simply agree to follow suit. Price leadership is not an illegal practice since it does not involve overt collusion to restrain trade. Overt ***collusion*** occurs if the dominant producers formally agree on what prices to charge for their products. Collusive contracts are not enforceable by the courts and are illegal. They may occur, however, when the rewards of excessively high profits offset the risk of penalties imposed by the government to inhibit such behavior.

131

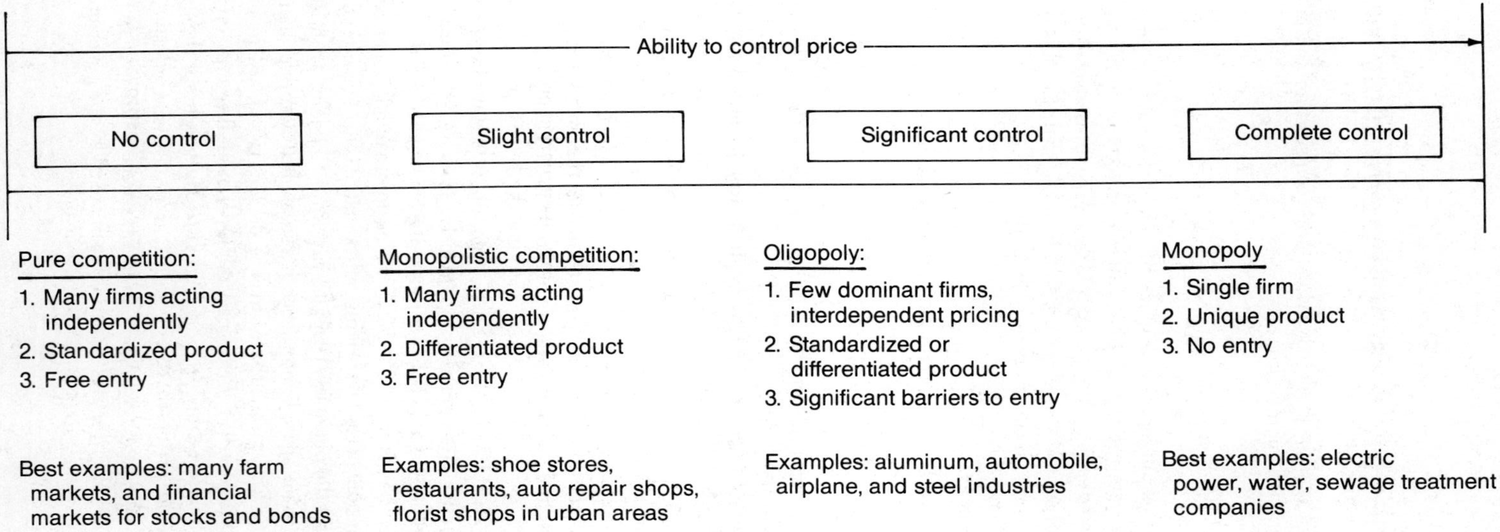

Ability to control price

No control	Slight control	Significant control	Complete control

Pure competition:
1. Many firms acting independently
2. Standardized product
3. Free entry

Best examples: many farm markets, and financial markets for stocks and bonds

Monopolistic competition:
1. Many firms acting independently
2. Differentiated product
3. Free entry

Examples: shoe stores, restaurants, auto repair shops, florist shops in urban areas

Oligopoly:
1. Few dominant firms, interdependent pricing
2. Standardized or differentiated product
3. Significant barriers to entry

Examples: aluminum, automobile, airplane, and steel industries

Monopoly
1. Single firm
2. Unique product
3. No entry

Best examples: electric power, water, sewage treatment companies

Figure 5.8. Scale Measuring the Ability of a Firm to Control Price.

Impact of Oligopoly The result of both price leadership and collusion is the establishment of a price close to the level that would have appeared if there had been only one producer in the industry. The impact on society is the same as that of monopoly pricing. Oligopoly tends to underallocate resources and redistribute income to owners of the companies that are the dominant producers.

Federal laws regulating the pricing practices monopoly are discussed in *Special Topic F: Government Regulation.*

Monopolistic Competition

Although monopolistic competition accounts for a smaller share of total production in the United States than oligopoly accounts for, this market model represents the behavior of the majority of firms in terms of number. Monopolistic competitors include the many small clothing stores, florists, barber shops, restaurants, bars, auto repair shops, and gasoline stations found in the downtown areas of most cities.

Characteristics Monopolistic competition lies close to pure competition on the scale represented by Figure 5.8. Like pure competition, *monopolistic competition* assumes that there are many small independent firms and that there is easy entry into the market in the long run. The only difference between the two models is that monopolistic competition allows for *product differentiation* (i.e., differences in the products produced in a particular industry). Product differentiation gives each firm a slight degree of control over price. Under conditions of pure competition, we assumed that all firms in a given market produce an identical product, which causes customers to buy from firms charging the lowest price.

Why does product differentiation give an individual firm some power to decide on price? Buyers develop preferences for certain products. The quality difference of a particular product might be "real" in the sense that it performs better, lasts longer, or tastes better. The quality difference might be "imagined" in the sense that we simply believe that it is a better product because of successful advertising campaigns. Whether the differences between products are real or imagined, the preferred products are more attractive to buyers. This gives firms some degree of control over price, since customers are willing to pay more to buy their favorite products.

For example, exclusive restaurants in New York City, such as The Four Seasons, Lutece, and the Rainbow Room, have reputations for superior food, service, and ambience which allow them to charge higher prices than eating places like Nathan's, which is famous for its hot dogs. Nathan's maintains a successful business by selling "fast food" at modest prices. The exclusive restaurants and Nathan's are monopolistic competitors, each offering a different product within the restaurant business for different prices.

Impact of Monopolistic Competition Since there are no barriers to entry, any above-normal profit that appears under monopolistic competition is eliminated by new firms that attempt to imitate the most successful producers. The entry of new firms (attracted by economic profit) increases market supply, which causes price to be driven down to the average cost of production.

A problem with monopolistic competition, however, is that the average cost of producing the profit-maximizing level of production is higher than that for a purely competitive firm. The higher production cost is due to product differentiation. It was noted that the loyalty of customers in buying a particular firm's product permits the firm to raise its price above the purely competitive level. From the firm's viewpoint, the price increase is sufficient to offset its corresponding loss in sales volume. However, the price increase does cause the firm to produce at a level that is below its plant's optimal capacity. For example, when you pass by barber shops you will frequently see vacant chairs. If the number of barbers were reduced (perhaps due to a strict licensing law), there would be fewer vacant chairs in the shops that remain — each shop would be operating closer to optimal capacity. Therefore, under monopolistic competition, there tends to be "overentry." Each firm operates below optimal capacity, which results in a higher average cost of production. Thus, under monopolistic competition, buyers pay a higher price than they would pay under purely competitive conditions.

On the other hand, monopolistic competition has a big advantage over pure competition in that buyers are faced with a wider choice in their decisions concerning what goods to purchase. Their selection of goods is not limited to a "standardized" product as is the case under conditions of pure competition. The higher prices that the customers have to pay for differences in product quality may be offset by this increased freedom of choice. In other words, consumers are generally willing to pay a higher price for diversity. We will now examine the barriers to entry that tend to sustain monopoly and oligopoly.

For a more detailed discussion of the behavior of the firm under conditions of monopolistic competition and oligopoly, see *Appendix A: Graphic Analysis of the Firm's Production Decision — Monopolistic Competition and Oligopoly.*

5.3 Barriers to Entry

If potential rivals are effectively kept out of the market, firms with market power are able to maintain above-normal profit. What are the ***barriers to entry*** that make it difficult for firms to enter a market?

Economies of Scale

In some industries, the average cost of production decreases as a firm increases the size (scale) of its plant. The decrease in average production costs that comes with plant expansion is termed *economies of scale.* This decrease in production costs will occur if a plant expands by employing highly skilled workers, or by using specialized machinery and equipment.

For example, when Henry Ford introduced mass assembly technology to the production of automobiles in the early twentieth century, the average cost of producing cars dropped sharply. There were about 88 auto companies in 1923. Most were driven out of business. Economies of scale made it possible for larger auto manufacturers to sell cars at a lower price than that charged by smaller, less efficient rivals.

In certain circumstances, economies of scale may be so important that only one producer in the market is desirable for efficiency. Such **natural monopolies** may include firms providing electric power, mass transit, sewage and water treatment, and telephone service in local areas. Provision of these goods or services by more than one firm may be inefficient because of the duplication of expensive overhead capital (e.g., the crossing of competing electric power lines).

A potential competitor needs to raise a huge sum of money to purchase the plant space and the machinery and equipment required to begin production since it must start up large in order to capture the economies of scale needed to enter the industry. In addition, it may incur massive advertising costs to reach the national and perhaps worldwide markets required to sell such a large volume of output. Therefore, rival firms face significant financial barriers in their attempt to begin competing with the older firms, which have already established a sound performance record. Their lack of being established and the high risk of failure make it difficult for these potential competitors to finance the required investment either through borrowing from lending institutions or through the sale of stocks and bonds.

Legal Barriers Created Through Government

Government is frequently a source of barriers to entry. Legal barriers created through government include the granting of patents and copyrights, licensing, establishment of regulatory agencies, and the imposition of tariffs and import quotas.

Patents and Copyrights   When government grants a *patent* to a firm that develops a new product or a better method of production, it gives the firm the exclusive right to use the innovation for a period of seventeen years. The seventeen-year ban against imitation of the patented technology rewards the innovator with a temporary monopoly. For example, Polaroid received a patent when it introduced instant film, which has helped to protect its position in the photography industry. Similarly, *copyrights* are granted for at least twenty-eight years in the United States, giving exclusive property rights to such creators as the writers of novels, plays, textbooks, poetry, and television series.

Licensing   Government may also encourage monopoly power through *licensing.* The licensing of such professionals as lawyers, doctors, accountants, and barbers limits the number of persons entering the profession, resulting in higher prices for services rendered. Government regulation may be necessary to protect the public from fraudulent or incompetent practitioners, but such regulation may lead to abuse. Tight restrictions on entry into licensed professions cause the earnings of those employed in the professions to be artificially high. As a result, these persons have the incentive to petition government for legislation more stringent than that required to protect the public interest.

Regulatory Agencies   Government has established certain *regulatory agencies* to protect the public from monopoly practices. Unfortunately, these regulatory agencies sometimes serve the interests of the firms they were intended to regulate. Instead of acting to keep prices down to protect consumers through regulation of rates, regulatory agencies may act as a monopoly by decreeing artificially high prices and by erecting artificial barriers to entry. For example, the Civil Aeronautics Board (CAB) granted franchises to individual airlines, which restricted flights in specific areas, resulting in excessively high fares. The Carter administration deregulated the air transport industry, permitting airlines to enter previously restricted market areas, with a resulting decrease in price on major routes. Air Florida operated only in Florida before deregulation. Afterward, this airline was one of the first to expand its services to other market areas, such as New York, Washington, D.C., and Pittsburgh, offering "no frills" service at a reduced fare.

Tariffs and Import Quotas   Government restricts foreign competition through the imposition of *tariffs and import quotas.* For example, the plight of the U.S. automobile industry caused the Reagan administration to negotiate restrictions on the number of cars imported for sale in the United States. While these quasi-quotas were intended to give the U.S. auto manufacturers more time to retool the design of their cars to meet the demand for smaller, more fuel-efficient cars, they permitted U.S. auto companies to sell cars at higher prices. In another example, the federal government set minimum prices on steel imported into the United States in response to the heavy losses of domestic steel companies.

Cartel Agreements

Government has also occasionally established or openly encouraged the formation of cartels for the purpose of maintaining above-market prices. A *cartel* is a group of firms which reaches a formal agreement that permits it to control prices. For example, the government presently encourages the formation of private marketing boards to raise the income of farmers. Citrus growers in California have created such a board, which is beneficial to the orange growers. Surplus oranges that cannot be sold at the artificially high price set by the board are withdrawn from the market and left to rot. Another example of a cartel is the Organization of Petroleum Exporting Countries (OPEC), which formed a cartel agreement in late 1973. Oil prices had been falling relative to other goods for several decades prior to the formation of this cartel. By 1974, OPEC quadrupled the international price of oil, causing an international energy crisis. The failure of OPEC to maintain this agreement caused world oil prices to tumble during the 1980s. At the time of writing, OPEC has succeeded in driving oil prices up due to a new cartel agreement.

Ownership of Essential Resources

Firms can also prevent new firms from entering the market through exclusive ownership of key ingredients used in the production process. For example, Alcoa Aluminum was once the sole U.S. owner of high-grade bauxite (the ore required to produce aluminum). New sources of bauxite were then discovered by Kaiser and Reynolds. These discoveries, coupled with antimonopoly action taken by the federal government, broke Alcoa's monopoly in the aluminum market. The current ownership of the available bauxite by only a few firms, however, prevents further entry into this industry. Another example is OPEC, just discussed. The initial success of this international monopoly in raising the price of oil hinged on its ownership of the majority of the world's crude oil.

For a discussion of the controversy over firms that have a high degree of market power, see *Appendix B: Pros and Cons of Big Business.*

5.4 Measuring the Extent of Competition

How competitive is the U.S. economy? The best criterion for measuring the degree of competition in a market is the amount of control firms have over the price they charge for their product. Unfortunately, it is very difficult to estimate the degree of price control exercised by firms. As an alternative, economists have developed the concentration ratio as a tool for measuring the degree of competition in a given industry.

The Concentration Ratio

The ***concentration ratio*** measures the percent of total sales in the market accounted for by the largest firms in an industry. In Table 5.4 we can see the concentration ratios of the four largest firms in selected manufacturing industries in the U.S. economy. For example, in the chewing gum industry, the four largest firms accounted for 95 percent of total industry sales. The book publishing industry has a lower ratio, with the top four firms accounting for 17 percent of total sales.

An industry is classified as having high concentration if the top four firms produce 50 percent or more of the total industry sales. If the ratio is less than 30 percent, there is low concentration, and if the ratio falls between 30 and 49 percent, the industry is classified as having medium concentration. In general, higher concentration ratios indicate lower degrees of competition.

Economists generally agree that industries are likely to be oligopolies when the top four firms account for at least 50 percent of total industry sales. High concentration makes it more

Table 5.4
Percentage of Total Industry Sales Accounted For by
the Four Largest Firms (Concentration Ratios) in 1982
for Selected Manufacturing Firms

Industry	Concentration Ratio
High concentration (50% or more)	
Chewing gum	95
Motor vehicles and car bodies	92
Electric lamps	91
Cereal breakfast foods	89
Vacuum cleaners	80
Malt beverage	77
Photographic equipment	74
Tires and inner tubes	66
Soap and other detergents	60
Farm machinery and equipment	53
Medium concentration (30 – 49%)	
Radio and television sets	49
Blast furnaces and steel mills	42
Construction machinery	42
Electronic computing equipment	40
Hardware	35
Bread, cake, and related products	34
Toilet preparations	34
Low concentration (less than 30%)	
Petroleum refining	28
Mattresses and box springs	23
Newspapers	22
Periodicals	20
Men's and boys' shirts and nightwear	19
Book publishing	17
Fluid milk	16
Bottled and canned soft drinks	14
Women's and misses' dresses	6

Source: U.S. Department of Labor, Bureau of the Census, 1982 Census of Manufacturers, April 1986, Concentration Ratios in Manufacturing (MC 82-S-7).

likely that the leading firms will be able to adopt price-leadership behavior or to collude. On
the other hand, industries having low concentration are generally classified under the monopolistically competitive market structure. When the top four firms account for less than 30
percent of sales, they are not in a position to manipulate the market price.

Candy Wars

The U.S. confectionary market (which includes candies and chocolates) is dominated by two producers, Hershey Foods (makers of Kit Kat, Reese's Peanut Butter Cups, and Hershey's Milk Chocolate Bars), with 20.8 percent of the market share, and Mars Inc. (makers of Snickers, M & M's, and Milky Way), with 18.5 percent of the market share. In the chocolate-bar market, Hershey and Mars together account for 81 percent of total sales.

Recently Mars' candy division has been introducing new confections at a frantic pace. Why? While Mars had been the market leader since the early 1970s, Hershey's purchase of the U.S. confectionary division of Cadbury Schweppes Foods (producers of York Peppermint Patties, Almond Joy, and Mounds) catapulted it to the number one position in the industry. In addition, competitors were able to successfully copy Mars' best products and marketing strategies.

Mars seems intent on being "No. 1" again. For years, Mars concentrated on producing a few large-selling products. But recently this strategy has changed. Mars is now making a strong attempt to vary its product line. In January 1989, Mars introduced Bounty, a substitute for Hershey's Mounds/Almond Joy. The bar had been successful in Europe for a long time but had previously failed in the United States in the 1970s. Another venture is their new premium chocolate, Suissande, aimed at Hershey's Golden Almond. While both of these products are targeted squarely at Hershey's strengths, their chances of success are rated slim by candy market experts. Mars has recently begun selling peanut butter M & M's. This product, an imitation of Reese's Pieces, is expected to succeed because it combines real milk chocolate and peanut butter. As a competitor notes, "their current marketing theory is to throw everything against the wall and see if something sticks."

The above is a summary of an article, "Mars Struggles to Reclaim Candy Crown" by Alix M. Freedman, which appeared in *The Wall Street Journal,* March 29, 1989, p. B1. The reader should note the confectionary industry is classified as highly concentrated since the four largest producers account for about 53 percent of total sales.

Problems in Measurement

The concentration ratio is only a proxy for measuring the degree of competition in a particular industry. The ratio may either underestimate or overestimate the true extent of control that leading firms have over price in a given industry.

Underestimation of Competitiveness The concentration ratios computed for U.S. industry exclude the sales of foreign producers. Consequently, an industry classified as having high concentration because it has relatively few firms producing domestically may be facing intense competition from foreign companies. Therefore, concentration ratios do not take into account competition that U.S. firms face from imported goods. In addition, the ratios do not illustrate the competition that may exist between industries. For example, the cereal breakfast foods industry is highly concentrated, with the top four firms producing 89 percent of total sales. Yet cereal producers are in direct competition with firms that sell doughnuts, bread, eggs, bacon, and pancakes. The competition of firms *between* industries is termed **contestable markets.**

Overestimation of Competitiveness Low concentration ratios may falsely indicate a high degree of competition when, in fact, the industry is not very competitive. This is because the ratios are calculated for industries on a nationwide basis, which obscures concentration ratios that may occur within local areas. Concentration ratios may be low because the top four firms account for only a small percentage of the industry's sales nationally, while the industry may actually be highly concentrated in smaller local markets. For example, in 1982, the four largest newspapers accounted for only 22 percent of total sales in the nation, indicating low concentration. However, most cities are served by only one or two newspapers. Similarly, the four-firm concentration ratio for fluid milk was only 16 percent nationwide in 1982, yet local areas are served by only a few milk producers.

Thus, large firms are not necessarily oligopolists, and small firms are not necessarily highly competitive. The true measure of competition is the degree of control the firm has over price. The degree of control cannot be precisely measured by either the size of the firm or the firm's share of the national market in a particular industry. Concentration ratios are useful only as a first approximation of the nature of market structures.

Summary

A pure monopoly is a single seller of a unique product, protected from other firms by barriers to entry. The list of barriers to entry includes economies of scale, legal barriers, cartel agreements, and ownership of essential resources. A monopoly restricts production and charges an above-competitive price, which results in economic profit. In comparison to a purely competitive market structure, a monopoly is inefficient. It causes an underallocation of resources. It also redistributes income from consumers to the owners of the monopoly.

The chief characteristic of oligopoly is mutual interdependency in pricing. Because there are a few dominant firms in the market, each of the major producers must consider the reaction of its rivals when it changes price. As a result, oligopoly pricing patterns tend to be established through price-leadership behavior and collusion.

Monopolistic competition is close to pure competition, and it describes many firms in our economy. The chief characteristic is product differentiation. Because each firm produces a slightly different product, it has a slight degree of control over price. Monopolistic competitors cannot make economic profit in the long run because there are no barriers to entry.

The role of "big" business in our economy is controversial. There is currently no procedure to measure precisely the degree of competition in our economy. The concentration ratio (which measures the percent of total sales in the market produced by the largest firms in an industry) is subject to numerous errors that can both underestimate and overestimate the true degree of competition in our economy.

Key Concepts

imperfect competition
pure monopoly
monopoly profit
differentiated versus pure oligopoly
interdependence in pricing
price-leadership behavior
collusion
monopolistic competition
product differentiation
barriers to entry
natural monopolies
concentration ratio
contestable markets
problems in measuring competition

Self-Test Questions: True or False

T F   1. The marginal revenue received by a monopoly is less than its average revenue as the firm expands production beyond the first unit because every time the firm chooses to sell one more unit, it must lower the price on the previous units that could have been sold at a higher price.

T F   2. A monopoly will ultimately produce that level of output at which marginal revenue *(MR)* equals marginal cost *(MC)*.

T F   3. Suppose that there are three dominant firms in a market. If the leaders of these three firms meet to agree formally on the price they will charge, this pricing practice is called "price leadership."

T F 4. Economies of scale occur when the average cost of production increases as the size of the plant increases.

T F 5. Assume that a pure monopoly sells 200 million units of output at a price of $10. If the average cost of production is $8, the monopoly is making an economic profit of $400 million.

T F 6. All of the following were mentioned as potential barriers to entry: patents, licensing by government, regulatory agencies, economies of scale, cartels, tariffs, import quotas, and the ownership of essential resources.

T F 7. Monopolistic competition is characterized by interdependency in pricing.

T F 8. Low concentration ratios indicate a high degree of competition when, in fact, an industry may not be very competitive.

T F 9. According to the efficiency criteria, a pure monopoly is inefficient because it produces a level of output that is less than the amount desired by society.

T F 10. A natural monopoly is created primarily by the ownership of essential natural resources.

Answers to Self-Test Questions

1. ***True.*** The marginal revenue received by a monopoly is less than its average revenue because the firm has to lower the price on previous units if it is to sell one additional unit. For an example, see Table 5.1 in Section 5.1 of this chapter. To increase cable television sales from 4 units to 5 units, Gotham Cable must lower its price from $8 to $7. Since the firm loses $4 on the first 4 units (each of which is now being sold for a dollar less) while gaining $7 from the extra unit sold, the marginal revenue of the fifth unit is $3. Therefore, the marginal revenue of the fifth unit is below the $7 in average revenue received from this unit.

2. ***True.*** In order to maximize total profit, a monopoly will increase production as long as the revenue obtained from the additional unit sold exceeds the cost of producing it. The firm will ultimately produce that level of output at which marginal revenue *(MR)* equals marginal cost *(MC)*.

3. ***False.*** They are engaging in overt collusion. Price leadership occurs when two of the three firms follow whatever price changes are made by the third firm without a formal agreement.

4. ***False.*** Economies of scale occur when the average cost of production decreases (rather than increases) as the size of the plant increases. Diseconomies of scale occur when average cost increases as plant size increases.

5.   ***True.*** Economic profit is calculated as the quantity sold *(Q)* multiplied by the positive difference between average revenue *(AR)* and average cost *(AC)* or $Q(AR - AC)$, which in this example is 200 million ($10 − $8). Note that product price always equals average revenue (e.g., the $10 price paid by the customer for a good equals the $10 in revenue received by the seller).

6.   ***True.*** They were all mentioned as being a potential barrier to the entry of new firms into the market.

7.   ***False.*** Under conditions of monopolistic competition, there are many small firms in the market, each acting independently in setting the price of its product. Because of product differentiation, firms have a slight degree of control over price. "Interdependency" in pricing occurs under oligopoly where a few firms dominate the market.

8.   ***True.*** The concentration ratios, which are reported for industries on a nationwide basis, do not indicate the high degree of concentration that may exist in local areas. As noted in the text, the four-firm concentration ratio for milk was low, yet local areas are served by only a few milk producers.

9.   ***True.*** Pure monopoly produces less than the amount of the good desired by society because it restricts production in order to charge a higher price in comparison to the purely competitive market model.

10.   ***False.*** A natural monopoly is created by the existence of economies of scale, which means that the average cost of production decreases as the plant grows in size.

Discussion Questions

1.   What are the characteristics of the four market structures? How do the differences in the models affect the ability of the firm to control price?

2.   List and briefly describe the various barriers to entry.

3.   How would the appearance of economic profit affect the pricing and output behavior of a pure monopoly in the long run? How would the effect on price and output be different in the long run if this industry had been purely competitive?

4.   Use the efficiency criteria to evaluate the long-run pricing and output behavior of pure monopoly.

5.   Define or discuss the following terms:
     a.   natural monopoly
     b.   cartel agreements
     c.   concentration ratio

Problems

1. List the assumptions of the different market structures in the following diagram:

|——————————————Ability to control price ——————————————→|

| No control | Slight control | Significant control | Complete control |

Pure competition:	Monopolistic competition:	Oligopoly:	Monopoly:
1.	1.	1.	1.
2.	2.	2.	2.
3.	3.	3.	3.

Answer questions 2 through 5 using the following revenue and cost schedule for a monopoly:

(1) Quantity	(2) Price, Average Revenue	(3) Average Cost	(4) Total Revenue	(5) Total Cost	(6) Total Profit	(7) Marginal Revenue	(8) Marginal Cost
0	—	—	$ 0.00	$ 1.00	___	_____	_____
1	$9.00	$8.00	9.00	8.00	___	_____	_____
2	8.50	6.50	17.00	13.00	___	_____	_____
3	8.00	6.33	24.00	19.00	___	_____	_____
4	7.50	6.25	30.00	25.00	___	_____	_____
5	7.00	6.20	35.00	31.00	___	_____	_____
6	6.50	7.00	39.00	42.00	___	_____	_____

2. Calculate the marginal revenue and the marginal cost of production.

3. Indicate the amount of output that the monopoly would produce.

4. What price would the monopoly charge?

5. Given this level of production and price, is the firm making economic profit, breaking even, or taking a loss? By how much?

6. Using the following figure to illustrate your answer, describe the pricing and output decision of a pure monopoly. Indicate the amount of monopoly profit on the graph.

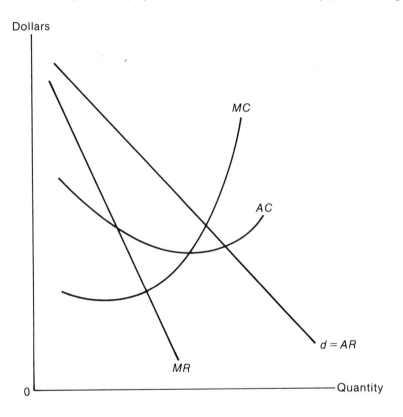

Dollars

MC

AC

d = AR

MR

0   Quantity

Appendices

A: Graphic Analysis of the Firm's Production Decision — Monopolistic Competition and Oligopoly

We use graphic analysis in this appendix to illustrate how marginal analysis can be used to explain the firm's short-run production decision under conditions of monopolistic competition and oligopoly. We also examine the long-run output and pricing behavior of these market structures.

An Overview: All Firms Use Marginal Analysis

We noted that both the purely competitive firm and the monopoly balance the extra revenue to be gained against the extra cost to be paid in trying to decide whether to produce an additional unit of output. (See Section 4.3 in Chapter 4 and Section 5.1 in this chapter.) The decision-making process is identical for all firms regardless of the market structure. First, each decision maker is using marginal analysis, seeking to produce the profit-maximizing level of output, which occurs where marginal revenue equals marginal cost. Second, after deciding how much to produce, each decision maker in an imperfectly competitive industry searches to find the price that enables it to sell this profit-maximizing level of output, given the demand for its product. Third, the profit (or loss) the firm makes then depends on the amount by which its average revenue exceeds (is less than) the average cost of production. It is then a simple matter to calculate total profit (loss) by multiplying the difference between the firm's average revenue and its average cost by the total number of units produced.

Monopolistic Competition

Under monopolistic competition, the individual firm has a slight degree of control over price because of product differentiation. As we noted in Section 5.2 of this chapter, one firm may be able to charge a higher price than its nearest competitor because it has chosen to advertise more extensively to establish brand loyalty or because it has decided to produce a better product. In addition, each firm (regardless of its relative standing in the industry) is able to sell more of its output if it lowers its price.

Demand and Revenue

Figure 5.9 illustrates the demand curve (d) for Lisa's Fudge Shop. The downward slope of this demand curve demonstrates that Lisa has some choice over what price to charge. This is not true under pure competition because all firms in the same industry were assumed to produce an identical product. The price that the purely competitive firm could charge was determined by supply and demand conditions in the market.

The monopolistic competitor's demand is more elastic than the monopoly's demand because customers can choose from whom to buy. Choice is lacking when there is a monopoly since there is only one firm in the market. (See Appendix A to Chapter 3 for a more detailed discussion of the price elasticity of demand.) As Figure 5.9 indicates, marginal revenue (MR) is less than average revenue (AR) as Lisa's Fudge Shop expands production because (as was

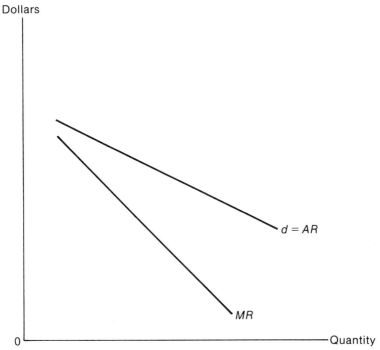

Figure 5.9. The Firm's Demand Curve *(d)* Under Monopolistic Competition. The demand curve slopes downward because every time the firm chooses to sell one more unit of output, it must lower the price on the previous units of output that could have been sold at a higher price. Marginal revenue *(MR)* is less than average revenue *(AR)* as the firm expands production.

the case with the Gotham Cable Company) every time the firm chooses to sell one more unit of output, it must lower the price on the previous units of output that could have been sold at a higher price.

The Short-Run Production Decision

How much should the monopolistic competitor produce? In order to maximize total profit, Lisa will increase fudge production as long as the revenue obtained from the additional unit of output exceeds the cost of producing the extra unit. As Figure 5.10 indicates, the firm will ultimately produce Q pounds of fudge because at this level of output marginal revenue *(MR)* equals marginal cost *(MC)*. To sell Q pounds of fudge, Lisa will charge price P, given the demand curve she faces. The resulting maximum total profit is illustrated in Figure 5.10, where total profit is calculated as the amount by which average revenue *(AR)* exceeds average cost *(AC)* multiplied by the number of pounds of fudge produced *(Q)*.

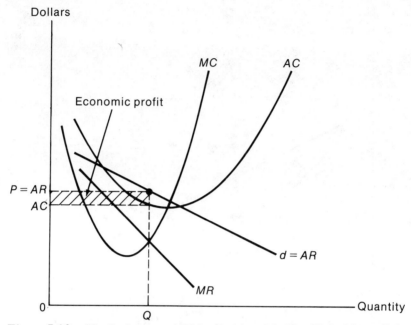

Figure 5.10.   The Production and Pricing Decision of the Firm Under Monopolistic Competition. The firm will produce the level of output *(Q)* where marginal revenue *(MR)* equals marginal cost *(MC)*. To sell this amount of output, the price *(P)* that the firm will charge depends on the demand curve. The resulting maximum total economic profit is calculated as the amount by which average revenue *(AR)* exceeds average cost *(AC)* multiplied by the number of units produced *(Q)*.

Long-Run Equilibrium

The main difference between the pricing and output behavior of Lisa's Fudge Shop and the Gotham Cable Company occurs in the long run. Assuming that Gotham Cable, a monopoly, has no potential rival firms, it will continue to make economic profit in the long run. Its output and price will remain at *Q* and *P* illustrated by Figure 5.6 in Section 5.1. But Lisa is in a highly competitive business. She learned her fudge recipes from her grandmother and her grandfather. Since the monopolistic competition model assumes free entry and exit of firms in the long run, other firms will try to imitate her recipes as long as there is above-normal profit in the industry. The entry of new firms into the market causes Lisa's Fudge Shop and other similar firms already in the market to lose customers.

As Figure 5.11 illustrates, Lisa faces a demand curve that decreases (shifts inward) as she loses customers to new firms as they enter the market. Note that in the long run, entry stops when all firms are breaking even, making only normal profit. Figure 5.11 illustrates Lisa's

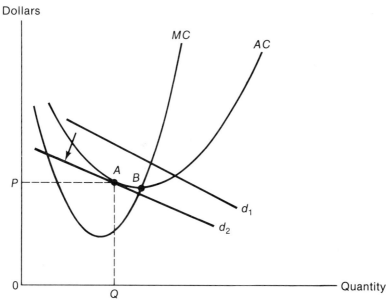

Figure 5.11. The Long-Run Adjustment Process. The firm's demand curve decreases from d_1 to d_2 as new firms enter the market. Entry stops when all firms are breaking even, making only normal profit. The firm's long-run breakeven position (point A) indicates that the firm produces below the level of output that would be produced if it were operating at optimal capacity (indicated by point B).

long-run breakeven position at point A, after demand decreased from d_1 to d_2. Note that her average revenue equals the average cost of production at point A. In the long run, she produces below the level of output that would be produced if she were operating her fudge shop at optimal capacity where average cost is minimized (indicated by point B). Overentry has caused each firm in the monopolistically competitive market to produce its product at higher average cost than would have prevailed under purely competitive market conditions.

Oligopoly

The primary difference in the results of the price and output decision made by an oligopoly compared to that of a firm operating under conditions of monopolistic competition is that the oligopoly is competing with only several other dominant firms in the market, not with many other firms as in the case of the monopolistic competitor. Therefore, any oligopolist is very aware of the potential reaction of the other dominant firms in the market when it attempts to change its price. Mutual interdependency in pricing is the chief characteristic of oligopoly.

Demand and Revenue

Suppose that there are only three companies making refrigerators; let's call them firms X, Y, and Z to simplify the discussion. Figure 5.12 illustrates the two potential demand curves that firm X (one of the oligopolists) faces, where the shape of each curve depends on the possible reactions of its rivals. Do the other firms, Y and Z, follow firm X when X tries to change its price?

Assume that firm X initially prices its refrigerators at P. We also assume that any price increase above the initial price (P) will not be followed by Y and Z since they want to raise their share of the market by taking customers away from X. Firm X's demand curve d_1 is more elastic than d_2 simply because households are able to buy refrigerators at a lower price from

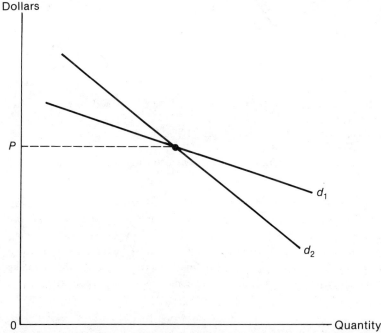

Figure 5.12. The Two Potential Demand Curves that Firm X (one of the oligopolists) Faces. The shape of each curve depends on the possible reactions of its rivals to a price change by firm X. Assume that firm X initially prices its product at P. Firm X's demand curve is d_1 if firms Y and Z do not follow X's price increase. Firm X's demand curve d_1 is more elastic than firm X's demand curve d_2 because households are able to buy the product at a lower price than X's rivals. Firm X's demand curve is d_2 if Y and Z will follow any price reduction by X. Because customers have less choice, X faces the more inelastic demand curve d_2 if it lowers its price.

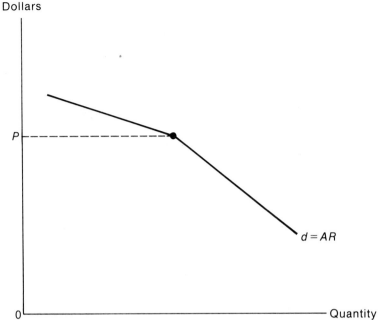

Figure 5.13.   Firm X's Actual Demand Curve *(d)*. Firm X's actual demand curve is based on its potential demand curves shown in Figure 5.12, redrawing d_1 above and d_2 below the initial price *(P)*. This kinked demand curve is also the firm's average revenue curve *(d = AR)*.

X's rivals if Y and Z do not follow X's price increase. (See Appendix A to Chapter 3 for an explanation of demand elasticity.)

In addition, let's assume that Y and Z will follow any price reduction by X below its initial price P since both of the rivals want to avoid losing customers to X. If firms Y and Z do follow any decrease in firm X's price, then households have *less choice* since relative prices remain the same. Therefore, the households are less responsive to X's price decrease. Since customers have less choice, X faces the more inelastic demand curve d_2 if it lowers its price.

What then does firm X's actual demand curve look like? It is peculiar looking, since it is kinked at the initial price P. Figure 5.13 represents firm X's actual demand curve *(d)* by reproducing the relevant segments of X's potential demand curves from Figure 5.12, redrawing d_1 above and d_2 below the initial price *(P)*.

Given the kinked demand curve (which is also the firm's average revenue curve, AR) in Figure 5.13, we end up with an even odder looking marginal revenue *(MR)* curve, which is illustrated in Figure 5.14. Note that marginal revenue drops abruptly at the kink in the demand curve since average revenue is discontinuous at this break in the curve (point A).

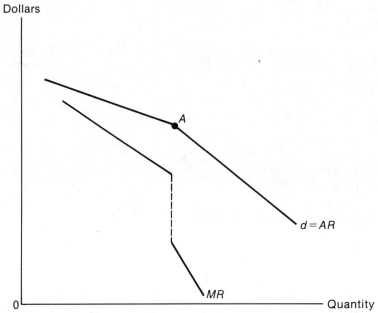

Figure 5.14.   Firm *X*'s Marginal Revenue *(MR)* Curve. Since average revenue *(AR)* is discontinuous at the kink in the demand curve (point *A*), marginal
revenue drops abruptly.

The Short-Run Production Decision

How much should an oligopolist produce to maximize total profit? The production decision is
analyzed graphically in Figure 5.15, where the firm's "U-shaped" average and marginal cost
curves are drawn relative to its revenue curves.

   As Figure 5.15 indicates, the firm will produce *Q* number of refrigerators since at this level
of output marginal revenue equals marginal cost. The resulting price *(P)* is located at the
kink in firm *X*'s demand curve. Note that the oligopolist is making economic profit since its
average revenue exceeds its average cost at this level of production (not shown).

Sticky Prices

The unique feature of the oligopoly model is that the price that initially emerges in the market
tends to stick at that price level over time. Why? Once the oligopolists reach an agreement
over what price to charge for their product, they want to avoid competitive price reductions
that tend to lead to a price war. Each firm is very conscious of the reaction of its rivals, which
inhibits the firm from changing its pricing policy. As Figure 5.16 illustrates, even a change in
firm *X*'s marginal cost curve from MC_1 to MC_2 in the long run does not affect its price *(P)*
since the firm still maximizes total profit by producing *Q* (since at this level of output marginal
revenue equals marginal cost).

152

Dollars

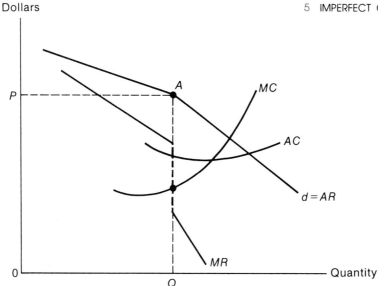

Figure 5.15. The Production and Pricing Decision of the Firm Under Oligopoly. Firm X will produce that amount of output (Q) where marginal revenue equals marginal cost. The resulting price (P) is located at the kink in firm X's demand curve (point A).

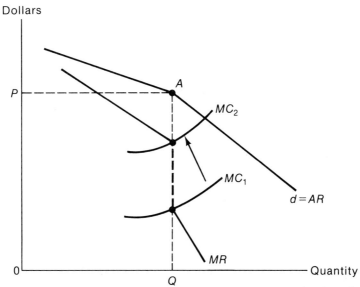

Figure 5.16. Sticky Prices. The price that initially emerges under oligopoly tends to stick at that price level over time. A change in firm X's marginal cost curve from MC_1 to MC_2 in the long run does not affect its price (P) since marginal revenue remains equal to marginal cost at the same level of output.

B: The Pros and Cons of Big Business

Are some businesses too big? There is currently a heated debate concerning the role of big business. Note that we are using the term *big* here in reference to market power rather than absolute size. Firms that are large in absolute terms may be small *relative* to their market, making them highly competitive. Also, the issues raised are broad-ranging because of the variety of viewpoints involved in the controversy. The parties affected include owners of big businesses, their employees, customers, and other members of society. Do not expect any conclusions to be drawn here.

Arguments Defending Big Business

A number of arguments have been made in defense of big business. They include the arguments concerning workable competition, economies of scale, and technological progress.

Workable Competition

According to this argument, there are forms of competition which are more subtle than simple "price" competition within a given industry.

First, there is *interproduct competition* between industries in cases where goods produced may easily be substituted for each other. For example, steel may be used instead of aluminum. If the price of aluminum rises due to a lack of price competition between aluminum manufacturers, customers may buy steel instead of aluminum. As a result, aluminum companies would be forced to lower their prices.

Second, there may be the *threat of potential competition* to firms that currently dominate a given industry. If these firms use their market power to push prices too high, they might induce producers in other industries to penetrate their market. According to this argument, if profits become excessive, firms outside the market will have sufficient incentive to surmount extremely high barriers to entry. IBM, which once held a monopoly in the international market for mainframe computers, now competes with other companies, such as Honeywell, Control Data, and Burroughs.

Third, the *countervailing power argument* claims that if the growth of firms creates abuses, antagonistic groups will form to counter the excessive power of these dominant firms. For example, if big business in a given industry antagonizes workers, labor unions will be formed. If consumers become upset, consumer protection groups will emerge. Political pressure groups may form to demand that government hold big business "socially accountable" for its actions in terms of protecting the environment, guaranteeing safer and healthier working conditions, and ensuring product safety.

Fourth, the *innovative competition* argument claims that, while big business may not face intense "price" competition, it does confront the persistent threat that rival firms may invent better products or discover better methods of production. This threat continually spurs big business to innovate or to face eventual extinction. Some feel that the plight of U.S. steel producers is due partially to their failure to adopt new technologies.

Economies of Scale

As noted in Section 5.3, the average cost of production may fall as a given firm expands the size (scale) of its operations. A larger plant might be able to adopt mass assembly techniques of production, hire more specialized workers, and use more sophisticated equipment. It might also be able to acquire supplies at discount prices, since it can buy in bulk. As a result, large firms may sell their products at prices that are lower than those charged by smaller, less efficient firms. Economies of scale are significant in many goods-production industries, such as automobiles, basic steel, electric power, and agriculture.

Technological Progress

According to John Kenneth Galbraith, the rapid development of technology over the last several decades has made the growth of large corporations inevitable, since technological change has made the production process more complex and more capital intensive. The result is the increased importance of large corporations because, through the sale of stocks and bonds, they can raise the money needed to finance the enormous amounts of capital required by modern production techniques. He argues further that large conglomerates (firms that own plants producing a variety of unrelated products) are in a better position to take the necessary risks for continued high levels of innovation. The profits gained in one market can offset the possible losses in another market in order to permit the company to survive.

Arguments Against Big Business

On the other side of the coin, there are those who argue that big business is hurting the economy. They claim that the following problems are caused by big business.

Inefficiency and Inequity

We noted earlier that monopolies and oligopolies use their market power to restrict production in order to charge higher prices for their products. Profits are not the reward for doing well, but rather are simply the consequence of market power. The result is inefficiency since there is an underallocation of resources to the production of the good provided by monopolies and oligopolies. Inequity may also result if there is an unfair distribution of income away from the customers who have to pay a higher price for less output to the owners of these companies.

Diseconomies of Scale

Big business may have surpassed the "economies of scale" discussed previously (i.e., average costs decrease as plant size increases). Some plants may have become too large. Further increases in plant size may result in higher average costs of production, called *diseconomies of scale.* According to this argument, the resulting large private bureaucracies have created a maze of "red tape," hindering the lines of communication needed for effective decision making. The rewards for doing well and the punishment for doing poorly may be lost in the large impersonal corporate structure, creating a sense of alienation among both workers and management. The resulting loss of incentive to perform well causes a reduction in productivity and therefore results in higher costs.

Lack of Incentive to Innovate

If firms are insulated from the discipline of competitive market forces, they will not have the incentive to develop new technology. Rather, they will suppress technological advances until their existing machinery and equipment have worn out. They will be receptive to innovation only when they have recouped the cost of previous investment.

The Benefit of Lower Production Costs May Not Go to Customers

Even if big business were to innovate and to achieve economies of scale, some economists believe that firms would continue to exert their market power to maintain excessively high prices. Therefore, the rewards of lower costs would go primarily to the owners of the companies in the form of higher profits, rather than to the buyers in the form of lower prices.

Economic Power Begets Political Power

Businesses with market power may exert influence over politicians, causing politicians to serve the interests of big business rather than those of the general public. Firms may gain political leverage by lobbying, financing the campaigns of politicians, offering them high-paying jobs upon retirement from public service, and through outright bribery. The normal interaction of executives in their roles in government and business creates an overlap in decision making which may result in benefits to big business. These benefits might appear in the form of large cost-plus government contracts, tax loopholes, protection from foreign competitors through tariff and quota barriers, a variety of subsidies, and reduced government regulations.

The Market for Labor and Other Factors of Production

Objectives

Upon completion of this chapter, you should understand:

1. How households and firms interact in the product and factor markets as buyers and sellers.

2. The decision-making process used by the individual firm in choosing how many workers to hire.

3. The behavior of the competitive labor market in determining employment and wages in an industry

4. The role of wages, interest, rent, and profit in allocating scarce resources.

The composition of our industrial work force has changed dramatically since the turn of the century. In 1900, over two-thirds of all workers were employed in goods production (agriculture, construction, manufacturing, and mining). Less than one-third of all workers were employed in industries providing services (e.g., trade, education, government, health care, and real estate). Today, these proportions have been reversed, with two-thirds of our current work force engaged in providing services and only one-third in producing goods. As a result, white-collar workers now outnumber blue-collar workers.

What are the causes of such profound shifts in employment? Significant changes in technology account for part of the change. While the service sector has tended to remain labor intensive, the goods-producing sector has increased the use of machinery and other forms of capital relative to labor. This has been especially true in agriculture. In addition, our economic resources have been redirected by major changes in the pattern of consumer spending. The growth in per capita income has caused people to buy more services, such as education and health care, and relatively fewer goods.

The purpose of this chapter is to explore the basic principles that govern the behavior of our markets for labor, capital, and natural resources. First, we review the relationship between the factor and product markets (initially described in Section 2.3 of Chapter 2). Second, we explain how individual firms decide what wage rate to pay and how many workers to hire. We then examine the overall operation of the market for labor. Finally, we extend this analysis to the markets for capital and natural resources.

6.1 An Overview: The Product and Factor Markets

All across America when the factory whistle blows Friday afternoon, the highways become crowded with workers looking forward to the weekend. Many families spend part of their weekend walking around the malls going from store to store, looking at the merchandise and spending their hard-earned money. Economists attempt to study such behavior using models that show how households and firms interact in product and factor markets.

The Circular Flow of Inputs and Outputs

The primary objective of this chapter is to extend supply and demand analysis to the factor market. Figure 6.1 modifies the original *circular flow diagram* described in Chapter 2 (see Figure 2.8) by incorporating the concepts of supply and demand discussed in Chapter 3. Households are on the supply side of the factor market (as sellers of inputs), and firms are on the demand side of this market (as buyers of these inputs).

Households have a demand for pizza, cars, and other goods produced by firms in the product market. To earn the income to buy these goods, households supply inputs in the factor market. They sell labor services to firms, going to work as auto mechanics, computer programmers, parking lot attendants, and so on. Households also receive income as the ultimate owners of the capital and natural resources used in production. For example, they

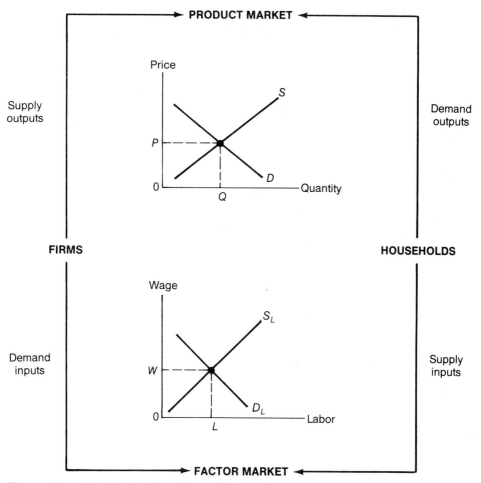

Figure 6.1. The Circular Flow Diagram. Households have a demand for outputs in the product market. To earn the income to purchase these outputs, households supply inputs in the factor market. Firms, in turn, demand inputs in the factor market, which they combine to supply outputs in the product market.

receive dividends on the stock they have in such corporations as GM and IBM. On the other hand, firms have a demand for inputs in the factor market which they combine to produce goods that they supply in the product market.

As we can see in the upper loop of Figure 6.1, the intersection of the supply and demand curves represents how households and firms interact to establish the price *(P)* and quantity of goods sold *(Q)* in the product market. Corresponding supply and demand curves in the factor market are represented in the lower loop of Figure 6.1. In the labor market, the intersection of these curves results in an equilibrium wage rate *(W)* and an equilibrium quantity of labor

159

employed *(L)*. Therefore, the markets for the factors of production (labor, capital, and natural resources) determine the prices (wages, interest, and rent) that the owners of these resources receive.

The study of the markets for labor, capital, and natural resources is important since the relative costs of these different inputs help determine the production processes used by firms. For example, firms tend to employ more machinery and fewer workers when the wage rate is higher relative to the cost of capital. As we noted in Chapter 2 (Section 2.4), developing economies (with relatively lower labor costs) tend to use labor-intensive methods to build roads, whereas industrialized countries (with relatively lower capital costs) build roads using capital-intensive methods.

In addition, the relative prices and ownership of these productive services determine the distribution of income in our economy. People with college degrees generally earn more than do persons without higher education. But this is not always the case. H. L. Hunt, for example, dropped out of high school and became a multibillionaire by purchasing land that later became extremely valuable because of the oil it contained.

The Functional Distribution of Income

The **functional distribution of income** breaks the income earned in the overall economy (called national income) into components according to the source of income. As we can see in Table 6.1, most income earned in the economy is through the sale of labor services. The compensation paid employees (wages, salaries, and fringe benefits) accounted for 73.3 percent of national income in 1988, which is up from the 65.2 percent that labor earned in 1950. Proprietors' income, which is the income earned by small businesses, fell from 16.3 percent of national income in 1950 to only 8.2 percent in 1988. The income earned by the owners of

Table 6.1
Functional Distribution of Income: Percent Distribution of National Income, by Type, 1950–1988

Type of Income	Percent Distribution				
	1950	1960	1970	1980	1988
Compensation of employees	65.2	71.0	75.5	75.5	73.3
Proprietors' income	16.3	11.4	8.2	5.5	8.2
Rental income	3.0	3.5	2.4	1.6	0.5
Corporate profits	14.3	11.5	8.8	8.6	8.2
Net interest	1.3	2.8	5.1	8.9	9.9
National income total	100	100	100	100	100

Source: 1950–1980, U.S. Department of Labor, Bureau of the Census, *Statistical Abstract of the United States, 1982* (Washington, D.C.: U.S. Government Printing Office), p. 425; 1988, U.S. Department of Commerce, Bureau of Economic Analysis, *Survey of Current Business*, February 1989 (Table 1.14).

corporations also declined during the last three decades. In 1950, corporate profits accounted for 14.3 percent of national income. By 1988, the share of corporate profits had fallen to 8.2 percent. Rental income, which is the payment to persons providing natural resources in the economy, also declined. It fell from 3.0 percent in 1950 to 0.5 percent in 1988. Net interest, the payment to the owners of financial capital, increased from 1.3 percent in 1950 to 9.9 percent in 1988.

In the next section we examine how a firm decides how many workers to hire. This decision, when made by millions of firms, is an important determinant of income earned in our economy.

> A more detailed discussion of the distribution of income is presented in *Speical Topic G: Income Distribution and Poverty.*

6.2 The Employment Decision of the Individual Firm

Suppose that Paul were to open a business selling pottery crocks, called Paul's Crock Shop. As the owner of the firm, Paul must decide how many pottery workers to hire. He will solve this problem by weighing the extra revenue and the extra costs generated by the employment of an additional worker. A wrong decision will result in relatively higher costs and less revenue, causing total profit to fall, whereas a correct decision will generate more revenue than cost, resulting in higher profit. Finding the solution to this problem will provide you with an important foundation for understanding the overall behavior of factor markets.

Weighing the Revenue Gained from Employment

The firm's demand for labor is a ***derived demand,*** derived from the demand for goods by households in the product market. A firm hires additional workers in order to produce more goods for sale. The sale of these goods adds to the firm's total revenue. The contribution that an additional worker makes to the firm's total revenue is called the ***marginal revenue product of labor.*** Since a firm will hire additional workers because of their contribution to the firm's total revenue, the marginal revenue product of labor is the ***firm's demand for labor.*** Note that in calculating the firm's demand for labor, we assume that all workers have the same physical and mental abilities (i.e., the labor force is homogeneous). All other conditions are assumed to be unchanged such as the amount of capital and the type of technology used in production.

Table 6.2 illustrates the information that Paul needs to derive the marginal revenue product of labor for his crock shop. Columns 1 to 3 are similar to Table 4.1, which was used in Chapter 4 to describe the marginal physical product of labor. As Paul hires additional workers (shown in column 1), the total output of crocks increases (column 2). The *marginal physical product of labor* (column 3) is measured as the change in total output per additional worker. For example, when Paul hires the first worker, total output increases by 100 crocks, which

Table 6.2
Firm's Demand for Labor

(1) Labor	(2) Total Output	(3) Marginal Physical Product of Labor	(4) Price of the Product	(5) Marginal Revenue Product of Labor
0	0	—	$10	—
1	100	100	10	$1,000
2	175	75	10	750
3	225	50	10	500
4	265	40	10	400
5	295	30	10	300
6	315	20	10	200
7	325	10	10	100

means that the marginal physical product of the first worker is 100. If Paul hires a second worker, the two workers together produce a total output of 175 crocks. The marginal physical product of the second worker is 75 crocks since the employment of this additional worker causes total output to increase from 100 to 175 crocks. The contribution of the third worker to total output is 50 crocks. The marginal physical product of labor decreases with the employment of additional workers in the short run because of the law of diminishing returns (discussed in Chapter 4). According to the *law of diminishing returns,* as the firm employs more workers, given the fixed amount of land and capital, eventually each extra worker will produce less additional output. The marginal physical product of labor falls because the additional workers have less than the optimum amount of fixed inputs with which to work.

Table 6.2 assumes that Paul sells each crock at a price of $10 (see column 4). In a purely competitive market, the marginal revenue product of labor (column 5) is calculated by multiplying the marginal physical product of labor (column 3) by the price of the product (column 4). For example, the marginal physical product of the first worker is 100 crocks. Since each crock is sold at a price of $10, the marginal revenue product of the first worker is $1,000. The second worker produces an additional 75 crocks which are sold for $10 each; therefore, the contribution of the second worker to the firm's total revenue is $750. Figure 6.2 illustrates the firm's demand for labor curve. Note that the firm's demand for labor is the same as its marginal revenue product of labor $(d_L = MRP_L)$ since the firm's willingness to hire an additional worker is based on that worker's contribution to the firm's total revenue. The marginal revenue product of the second worker is illustrated in this graph.

Weighing the Cost of Employment

Under conditions of pure competition, firms must pay their workers the market equilibrium wage rate. Why? Suppose that the market wage for pottery workers is $300 per week. If Paul

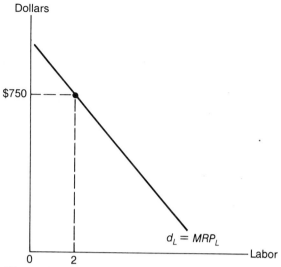

Figure 6.2. The Firm's Demand for Labor. The firm's demand for labor is equal to the marginal revenue product of labor (MRP_L) The MRP_L is the contribution of an additional worker to the firm's total revenue.

attempted to pay less than $300 per week, no workers would be willing to work for him since they would be able to find employment with other firms at the higher market wage. In addition, Paul could not afford to pay a wage higher than $300. The increase in production costs would force him to raise the price of his crocks above the market price, which in turn would cause households not to buy from Paul's Crock Shop.

Paul can hire all the pottery workers that he wants to hire at this market wage rate of $300 per week because his firm is small. Therefore, as we can see in Figure 6.3, from the viewpoint of the firm, the supply of labor is horizontal. The average cost of each worker is $300, since the firm must pay each worker the going market wage. The ***average cost of labor*** is the cost per worker, calculated by dividing the total cost of labor by the total number of workers employed. For example, if Paul hires two workers, the total cost of both workers is $600 and the average cost of labor is $300. The most important concept is the marginal cost of labor. The ***marginal cost of labor*** is the cost of hiring an *additional* worker, calculated as the change in total labor costs divided by the change in labor. Because the firm must pay each additional worker employed the going market wage (see Figure 6.3), the market wage rate is both the firm's average cost of labor and marginal cost of labor. In other words, given the market wage of $300, the average cost of labor is $300 (the cost per worker), which is identical to the marginal cost of labor of $300 (the cost per *additional* worker).

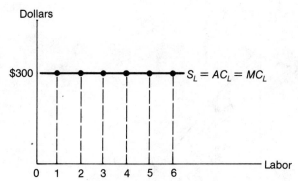

Figure 6.3. The Firm's Supply of Labor. The firm's supply of labor is equal to its AC_L and MC_L curves.

The Employment Decision

How many workers will the firm hire? Paul has to balance the extra revenue gained when he hires an additional worker against the extra cost paid. When Paul hires the first worker, this additional worker contributes $1,000 to total revenue and $300 to total cost (see columns 1 to 3 in Table 6.3). Therefore, the first worker adds $700 to total profit (see column 4). As long as the marginal revenue product of labor exceeds the marginal cost of labor, the firm will have the incentive to hire more workers. Total profit will increase as additional workers are hired, reaching a peak when the marginal revenue product of labor equals the marginal cost of labor. Paul will not hire an additional worker when the extra revenue is less than the extra cost. This occurs with the sixth worker, since the sixth worker adds only $200 to the firm's total revenue and $300 to total cost — total profit falls by $100. Therefore, the firm maximizes total profit by hiring five workers. Note that the firm wants to maximize *total* profit, not *marginal* profit

Table 6.3
Employment Decision by the Individual Firm

(1) Labor	(2) Marginal Revenue Product of Labor	(3) Marginal Cost of Labor	(4) Change in Total Profit
0	—	—	—
1	$1,000	$300	$700
2	750	300	450
3	500	300	200
4	400	300	100
5	**300**	**300**	**0**
6	200	300	−100
7	100	300	−200

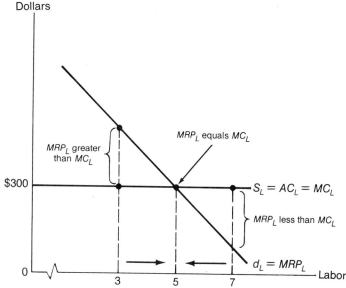

Figure 6.4. The Employment Decision of the Individual Firm. The firm will hire workers up to the level of employment at which $MRP_L = MC_L$.

(i.e., the change in total profit per additional worker). This behavior is called the $MRP_L = MC_L$ *rule* since the profit-maximizing level of employment is always that level of employment where the marginal revenue product of labor (MRP_L) equals the (MC_L) marginal cost of labor.

Figure 6.4 reviews the general principle discussed above by bringing together the marginal revenue product of labor and the marginal cost of labor curves. We can see that with the addition of the third worker, the marginal revenue product of labor exceeds the marginal cost of labor. Therefore, the firm will hire up to the fifth worker. If the firm hires more than five workers, the marginal revenue product of labor is less than the marginal cost of labor, which will cause the firm to reduce its work force back to the fifth worker.

We have just explored how an individual firm decides how many workers to employ, given the market wage rate. Our attention now turns to the overall behavior of the labor market. How is the wage rate determined and how many workers will be employed in an industry?

6.3 The Competitive Labor Market

There is wide variation in the amount of income people earn when they go to work. But money isn't everything in life . . . is it? For instance, some students may major in education, taking jobs after graduation in teaching despite the lower potential earnings. They may feel that the loss of potential income is adequately offset by higher expected job satisfaction. The purpose of this section and Section 6.4 is to explain the behavior of the overall labor market in determining employment and wages.

> Upon completing this chapter you may want to read *Special Topic C: The Economics of Higher Education,* which focuses on the market for college graduates.

Supply and Demand

Just as prices and output are determined by supply and demand conditions in the product market, wages and employment are determined by supply and demand conditions in the labor market. The wage rate and level of employment are established through the interaction of firms and households in the thousands of labor markets that exist in our economy.

Demand   In the preceding section we explored the employment decision made by Paul running Paul's Crock Shop. We noted that Paul's demand for labor was his firm's marginal revenue product of labor. The **market demand schedule** presented in Table 6.4 and the corresponding **market demand curve** presented in Figure 6.5 are derived by adding together the number of pottery workers demanded at each wage rate by all the firms in the market. The market demand for labor shows the amount of labor services demanded at various wage rates (in a specific time period), keeping all other influences constant. An increase in the wage will ration scarce labor services away from some firms since they are either not willing or not able to pay the higher wage. Conversely, a decrease in wage will increase the amount of labor services that firms are willing and able to buy. For example, when the wage is $4, firms plan to hire 800 thousand pottery workers (point *A*). If the wage rate were to increase to $7, firms would want to hire only 650 thousand pottery workers (point *D*).

Table 6.4
Market Demand for
Pottery Workers
(thousands)

Wage		Quantity Demanded
$4	A	800
5	B	750
6	C	700
7	D	650
8	E	600

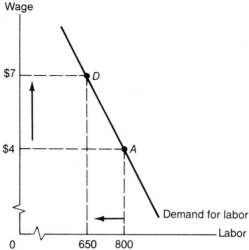

Figure 6.5. The Market Demand for Pottery Workers (thousands). An increase in the wage rate will reduce the quantity of labor demanded.

Supply *Market supply* refers to the quantity of labor services that households are willing and able to sell at various wages (in a specific period of time), with all other influences assumed to be fixed. The ***market supply schedule*** and ***market supply curve*** are illustrated in Table 6.5 and Figure 6.6. As the wage for pottery workers increases relative to the wages of workers in other industries, more people will attempt to find employment making crocks. In this example, a rise in the wage rate from $4 to $7 causes the quantity of pottery workers supplied to increase from 600 thousand to 750 thousand (a move from point *A* to point *D*).

Table 6.5
Market Supply of
Pottery Workers
(thousands)

Wage		Quantity Supplied
$4	A	600
5	B	650
6	C	700
7	D	750
8	E	800

167

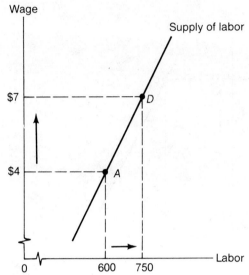

Figure 6.6. The Market Supply of Pottery Workers (thousands). An increase in the wage rate will increase the quantity of labor supplied.

Market Equilibrium

The *equilibrium wage* is defined as a position of stability toward which the *actual wage* (the current wage) moves. Once the actual wage reaches equilibrium, it will not change any further since it has achieved the equilibrium condition. The *equilibrium condition* is defined as the situation where buyers and sellers agree on the wage and quantity of labor services sold (i.e., where the quantity demanded equals the quantity supplied at a particular wage rate).

Table 6.6 illustrates the equilibrium wage and equilibrium quantity sold in the market for pottery workers. The equilibrium condition is met at a wage of $6 since 700 thousand people

Table 6.6
Market Equilibrium for Pottery Workers
(thousands)

Wage	Quantity Supplied	Quantity Demanded	Shortage or Surplus
$4	600	800	−200
5	650	750	−100
6	**700**	**700**	**0**
7	750	650	+100
8	800	600	+200

168

are seeking jobs as pottery workers, which is the number of pottery workers that firms plan to hire. How do changes in the actual wage of labor clear the market, eliminating both shortages and surpluses as they occur?

Case of a Shortage At wages below the equilibrium level, there is a *shortage* of pottery workers, because firms are seeking to buy more labor services than households are willing to sell. See Table 6.6 and Figure 6.7a, which illustrate the case of a shortage of labor. At a wage of $4, only 600 thousand people are seeking work in pottery (point *A* on the supply curve), but firms want to hire 800 thousand (point *B* on the demand curve). A shortage of 200 thousand pottery workers exists.

Note that at the wage of $4, households are content because the amount of labor services they offer are employed (600 thousand workers). Firms are not content because at the wage of $4, they had wanted to hire 800 thousand pottery workers. What happens as a result of this shortage? Firms bid the wage rate up, bringing into play the ***role of wages.***

See Table 6.6 and Figure 6.7a for an illustration of the process. We noted that at a wage of $4, there is a shortage of 200 thousand pottery workers (the distance between points *A* and *B*). This shortage will cause the actual market wage to increase to $6 (point *C*), signaling to households the need to increase the quantity of labor supplied by 100 thousand (from 600

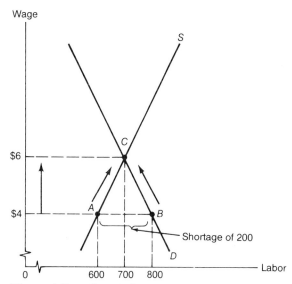

Figure 6.7a. Case of a Shortage of Pottery Workers (thousands). If the actual wage rate is below the equilibrium position, a shortage of labor will result. Firms will bid the wage rate up, causing an increase in the quantity of labor supplied and a decrease in the quantity of labor demanded until the shortage is eliminated.

thousand to 700 thousand). At the same time, some firms are rationed out of the market, decreasing the quantity of labor demanded by 100 thousand units (from 800 thousand to 700 thousand units). At the wage of $6, both decision makers are in agreement (i.e., the quantity supplied equals the quantity demanded at 700 thousand workers). Consequently, there is no reason for the wage rate to change any further. The actual wage will stabilize at $6, making it the equilibrium wage.

We may summarize how changes in the wage rate eliminate a shortage, using the notation developed in Chapter 3:

$$\text{shortage} \rightarrow \text{firms} \uparrow W \rightarrow \downarrow Q_d \text{ and } \uparrow Q_s \text{ until } Q_d = Q_s$$

The above translates as follows. A shortage causes firms to bid the wage up, which in turn causes the quantity demanded to decrease and the quantity supplied to increase until the quantity demanded equals the quantity supplied.

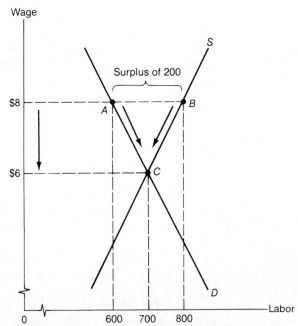

Figure 6.7b. Case of a Surplus of Pottery Workers (thousands). If the actual wage rate is above the equilibrium position, a surplus of labor will result and households will accept a lower wage rate. The drop in the wage rate will cause an increase in the quantity of labor demanded and a decrease in the quantity of labor supplied until the surplus is eliminated.

Case of a Surplus   If the actual wage lies above the equilibrium position, a *surplus* will occur. What is the role of wages in eliminating a surplus? We can keep the explanation very brief since the answer is a mirror image of the role of wages in eliminating a shortage discussed above. Suppose that the actual wage rate happened to be $8. As we can see in Table 6.6 and Figure 6.7b, more people want to work than firms want to hire. Consequently, households seeking employment will accept lower wages. As the actual wage falls from $8 to $6, firms will hire more workers (an increase in the quantity demanded by 100 thousand, from 600 thousand to 700 thousand). At the same time, this decrease in wage causes some households to want to work less, decreasing the quantity supplied by 100 thousand units, from 800 thousand to 700 thousand). Equilibrium is reached at a wage of $6, where 700 thousand workers are employed.

6.4 Changes in Labor Market Conditions

In the preceding section we assumed that supply and demand were unchanged. However, in reality, market conditions do change. For example, during the last decade there was an increase in the demand for computer programmers and accountants, while the demand for teachers, steel workers, and unskilled labor decreased. The purpose of this section is to explore the effects of such changes on the equilibrium wage and employment.

Nonwage Determinants of Supply and Demand

Many factors other than the wage rate affect the decision of households and firms in the labor market. In the following discussion we examine these nonwage determinants of the supply and demand for labor.

Supply   We noted that the movement from point *A* to point *D* up the supply curve in Figure 6.6 represented an increase in the quantity of labor supplied caused by an increase in the wage rate. Supply (the whole curve) has not changed. An increase in the supply of labor would be represented by an outward shift to the right in the supply curve, (not illustrated).

The factors that shift the supply curve are called ***nonwage determinants of the supply of labor*** or *shift factors*. What factors do we consider other than the wage rate when we choose to work at a particular occupation?

1. The *amount of education and training required* by the job is an important consideration. For example, relatively few persons are willing or able to become brain surgeons because of the tremendous investment that they would have to make in education in order to qualify as brain surgeons.

2. *Ability* is another factor. People differ in their innate abilities. For example, not everyone has the general intelligence, dexterity, and personality to become a brain

surgeon. Similarly, those who have the ability to be brain surgeons might not have the ability to be professional dancers.

3. *Job satisfaction* is also important. People seek to work at occupations that give them the most satisfaction in terms of such factors as self-fulfillment and companionship on the job.

4. *Expected future earnings* is another nonwage determinant of the supply of labor. If people expect to make higher earnings in a given occupation in the future (given the current wage), more persons will attempt to find employment in this market.

5. *Prestige* is a factor because society often identifies the "worth" of the individual in terms of his or her occupation. For example, a major league baseball player generally has more prestige than an unskilled worker.

6. *Location* is often an important consideration when people choose jobs. People tend to want to settle down near their parents and friends. They often also want to live in specific geographic areas, such as large urban centers or in places near the mountains or beaches of our nation.

7. *Job security* also affects the desirability of a given occupation independent of the wage rate. People tend to avoid taking jobs that are likely to be eliminated during their lifetime. For example, fewer high school students are planning to seek work in our steel mills.

8. Finally, a *change in population* will tend to shift the supply of labor curve. For example, an increase in the birth rate relative to the death rate will generally increase the number of people seeking employment.

Demand   There are also ***nonwage determinants of the demand for labor.*** They are called *demand shift factors* because a change in any of them would shift the demand curve. (Keep in mind that a change in the quantity demanded refers to a movement along a given demand curve, whereas a change in demand refers to a shift in the curve itself.)

Since the firm's demand for labor is its marginal revenue product of labor curve, the market demand for labor will shift given a change in anything that affects the contribution that each additional worker makes to total revenue. For example, an increase in the *price of the product* due to a higher demand for the good would increase the demand for labor since the output produced by each additional worker would be worth more. In addition, an increase in the amount of land, machinery, or other nonlabor inputs that *complement* labor in the production process would make each additional worker more productive. The marginal physical product of labor increases since workers have more resources with which to produce goods. This in turn would raise the demand for labor. Similarly, innovation affects the productivity of *substitute* inputs such as robotic machinery. The demand for labor will decrease if firms develop a new technology that makes machinery more productive relative to the productivity of labor, given the relative costs of these inputs.

Table 6.7
Case of an Increase in the Demand for Pottery
Workers (thousands)

Wage	Quantity Supplied	Quantity Demanded	New Quantity Demanded
$4	600	800	1,000
5	650	750	950
6	700	700	900
7	750	650	850
8	800	600	800
9	850	550	750

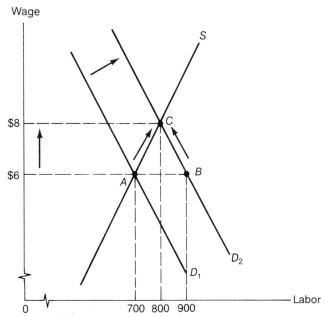

Figure 6.8. Case of an Increase in the Demand for Pottery
Workers (thousands). An increase in the demand for labor will create
a shortage at the initial equilibrium wage rate. Firms will bid the
wage rate up, which causes an increase in the quantity of labor
supplied and a decrease in the quantity of labor demanded until the
shortage is eliminated.

173

Case of an Increase in Demand

Suppose that the price of jogging shoes were to suddenly rise. What impact would this price increase have on the demand for workers in the jogging shoe industry? How are the wage and employment of these workers affected? See Table 6.7 and Figure 6.8 on the preceding page, which illustrate the impact of the resulting increase in the demand for labor (shown as an outward shift to the right in the demand curve from D_1 to D_2. Note that at the original equilibrium wage of $6, a shortage is created by the rise in demand. Firms are not satisfied at the wage of $6 because they are not able to hire the quantity of labor services that they had planned to hire. Households are planning to sell only 700 thousand units (point A) rather than the 900 thousand units (point B) demanded by firms. Therefore, there is a shortage of 200 thousand units of labor services.

As a result of this shortage, firms bid the wage rate up to the equilibrium position (point C), setting in motion the role of wages. As the actual wage rises it signals the need for an increased number of workers in the jogging shoe industry, causing the quantity of labor supplied by households to go up by 100 thousand workers. At the same time, the increase in the actual wage rate rations labor services away from some firms, causing a decrease in the quantity of labor demanded by 100 thousand). Therefore, as the actual wage changes, the two decision makers will come into agreement over the wage and quantity of labor to be sold. Once the actual wage reaches the new equilibrium wage of $8, both households and firms agree on a level of employment of 800 thousand workers. The shortage has been eliminated.

Long-Run Market Adjustment: The Role of Education, Training, and Migration

So far we have implicitly assumed the *short-run time period.* In the short run there is not sufficient time for households to migrate from one area of the country to another, or to move from one occupation to another. In addition, workers do not have enough time to acquire more education or new skills. As a result, the supply of labor is fixed for any occupation in a given area. On the other hand, in the *long-run time period,* households do have sufficient time to migrate, to find new occupations, and to acquire more education and new skills. Therefore, the labor supply curve can shift in the long run. What is the effect of such labor supply changes on wages and employment?

To illustrate long-run market behavior, let us assume that there are two separate labor markets for computer programmers. As Figure 6.9 illustrates, an increase in the demand for computer programmers in Los Angeles from D_1 to D_2 causes an increase in the wage they receive in this area from W_1 to W_2 in the short run. This increase in demand causes the wage paid in Los Angeles to be higher than the wage paid in Pittsburgh. Assuming no change in the demand for computer programmers in Pittsburgh, the long-term effect of such wage differentials is the migration of computer programmers from Pittsburgh to Los Angeles. The resulting in-migration experienced in Los Angeles causes the wage received to fall from W_2 to W_3, owing to the increase in supply from S_1 to S_2. At the same time, there is a decrease in the

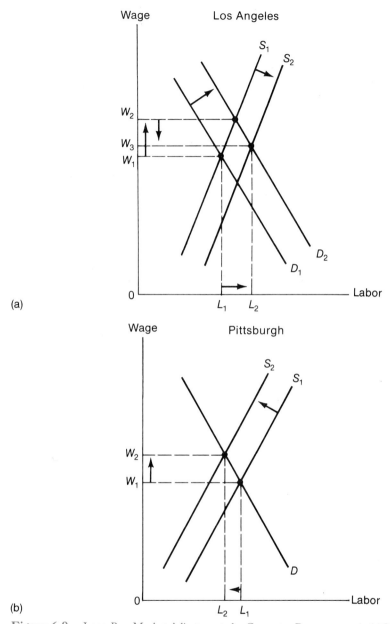

(a)

(b)

Figure 6.9. Long-Run Market Adjustments for Computer Programmers in (a) Los Angeles and (b) Pittsburgh. An increase in the demand for programmers in Los Angeles will cause the wage rate to rise in the short run. In the long run, programmers will migrate from Pittsburgh (the low-wage area) to Los Angeles (the high-wage area). In-migration causes wages to fall in Los Angeles at the same time out-migration causes wages to increase in Pittsburgh. Employment increases in Los Angeles and decreases in Pittsburgh.

175

supply of computer programmers in Pittsburgh from S_1 to S_2, which causes the wage of computer programmers to rise in Pittsburgh from W_1 to W_2. Employment in Pittsburgh would decrease from L_1 to L_2 while employment in Los Angeles would increase from L_1 to L_2.

In addition to geographic migration, workers have sufficient time in the long run to acquire more education and new skills. For example, many workers permanently laid off in the steel industry are going to college or seeking other forms of training.

Impediments to the Migration of Labor

Despite a 14-year low in the national unemployment rate, there are five states with recession-level unemployment according to the Department of Labor. While analysts indicate that people still move in search of better economic opportunities, there are no longer the streams of migration that occurred in the late 1970s and early 1980s as people left depressed areas in the Northeast and moved to the booming oil regions of the Southwest.

One of the major deterrents to migration is the relatively high cost of living in the regions experiencing labor shortages. According to Larry Long, chief of demographic analysis at the Bureau of the Census, "Many (Boston-area) jobs are going unfilled because people can't afford to move there to take them." Housing costs are a major consideration. Many people, for example, cannot afford to move from Houston, Texas (where the cost of a three-bedroom house averages $86,000) to Boston (where the cost of a three-bedroom house averages $296,000 in the suburb of Newton).

A change in family life-styles may also have reduced labor mobility. "It's more difficult for a family to move today because there are usually two earners, and it's rare that both lose their jobs at the same time," says Sar Levitan, the director of the Center for Social Policy Studies at George Washington University. More traditional obstacles to migration include family ties and the roots that unemployed workers have in their communities. Frequently, people who are laid off will stick it out in their home towns in the hope of getting their old jobs back. In addition, unemployed workers with obsolete skills face the difficulty of acquiring new skills to match those currently sought after by employers.

The migration of capital is a possible solution for some companies having difficulty in hiring a sufficient number of workers. "Such factors as the availability and the cost of labor — and to a lesser extent the cost of housing — are beginning to become the key factors in determining where (companies) go," says Gary Ciminero, chief economist at Fleet/Norstar Financial Group.

The above is a summary of an article, "The Jobless Aren't Migrating to Boom Areas" by Hilary Stout, which appeared in *The Wall Street Journal*, February 21, 1989, p. B1.

6.5 The Market for Other Factors of Production

Up to this point we have focused on the market for labor since this input is often the most important ingredient in the production process. As we saw earlier in Section 6.1, the income earned by labor accounts for three-fourths of our national income. The other one-fourth of national income is made up of interest, rent, and profit. The principles that guide the operation of the labor market also govern the behavior of the markets for other resources.

Interest

The interest rate is the payment to persons who provide firms with financial capital. ***Financial capital*** is the means of financing the purchase of ***real capital,*** the human-made inputs used in production. Firms take out loans to purchase buildings, machinery, and equipment, as well as to finance their inventories (unsold goods). To purchase real capital, firms obtain financial capital in the money market by borrowing from banks and selling stocks and bonds.

The basic properties of supply and demand analysis used to explore the labor market can be applied to examine the financial capital market. As we can see in Figure 6.10, the equilibrium

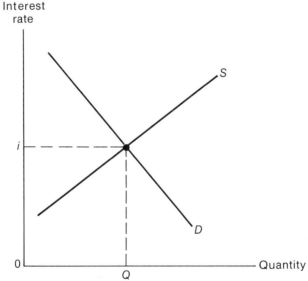

Figure 6.10. Financial Capital Market for Loanable Funds. The equilibrium interest rate and quantity of money lent are determined by supply and demand conditions in the financial capital market.

177

interest rate *(i)* is determined by the intersection of the supply and demand curves for *loanable funds.* The demand for loanable funds reflects the marginal revenue product of real capital. Firms borrow money to invest in machinery and other capital goods. Their willingness to borrow and invest depends on whether the anticipated return would cover the cost of obtaining funds (the interest rate). If a firm can invest in an asset that will earn a 10 percent return, it will do so only if it can borrow the necessary funds at an interest rate of 10 percent or less. It would be foolish to pay 12 percent to borrow funds that will earn a return of only 10 percent. As the rate of interest falls, the number of profitable investment opportunities will rise, which in turn will cause the quantity of loanable funds demanded by firms to increase.

On the other hand, the quantity of loanable funds supplied is positively related to the interest rate. As the interest rate rises, households will be induced to put more of their money into the loanable funds market (through savings accounts and the purchase of private bonds). The impact of the interest rate on the economy is discussed in more detail in Chapters 9, 10, and 11.

If the actual interest rate is above the equilibrium position, it will be forced back down to the equilibrium position because lenders will decrease the price at which they sell their loanable funds in order to eliminate the existing surplus. Similarly, a below-equilibrium interest rate will create a shortage in the financial capital market, causing firms that want to borrow money to bid the interest rate up to the market-clearing equilibrium position. Therefore, the interest rate plays the same role as the wage rate in eliminating shortages and surpluses in the factor market.

To illustrate the *role of the interest rate* further, assume that there is an increase in the demand for loanable funds in order to expand plant facilities in the manufacture of plastics. An increase in the demand for loanable funds is illustrated in Figure 6.11. The increase in demand from D_1 to D_2 creates a shortage at the initial equilibrium interest rate *(i)*. The firms wanting to borrow money are not satisfied since they cannot obtain the funds that they had planned to borrow at this interest rate. Consequently, they will bid the interest rate up from *i* to *i'*. The increase in the interest rate will *ration* buyers out of the market, decreasing the quantity of loans demanded. The increase in the interest rate will also *signal* to the suppliers of loanable funds the increased need for financial capital, increasing the quantity of loans supplied. The new equilibrium interest rate *(i')* is achieved when the quantity of loanable funds supplied equals the quantity demanded at Q'.

To simplify the discussion, we have examined a single hypothetical market for loanable funds. In reality there are many different types of financial markets, such as the markets for corporate bonds and U.S. securities. Therefore, there is not a single interest rate which we referred to in the foregoing analysis as "the" interest rate. Instead, there are numerous interest rates that tend to move together since they respond to the same basic market forces.

Rent

Rent is paid to the owners of such natural resources as land and minerals. The *role of rent* is similar to that of wages and interest. For example, an increase in the demand for land for

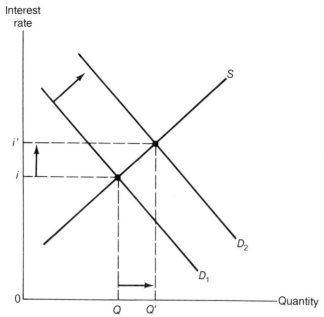

Figure 6.11. An Increase in the Demand for Loanable Funds. An increase in the demand for loans causes an increase in the equilibrium interest rate and the quantity of money lent.

housing due to urban sprawl will create a shortage of land parcels around the outer limits of the city. Persons wanting to build houses in the suburbs will bid the price of this land up, setting into play the role of rent. The resulting increase in rent will *ration* prospective buyers out of the land market, decreasing the quantity of land demanded. The higher rent payments will also *signal* the increased need for land for residential use. Land that was formerly used for farming will be converted into land for suburban housing.

Profit

We examined the *role of profit* in detail in Chapters 4 and 5. We noted that there are three types of profit: normal profit, economic profit, and monopoly profit. Normal profit was defined as the return necessary to cover the opportunity cost of the resources possessed by the persons who own the firm, including the time spent in the business, the market value of their buildings, land, and so on. In addition, normal profit is partially a measure of the opportunity cost of the risk that they take when they commit resources to business ventures that may fail. It is also a payment for entrepreneurial ability, referring to the special skills that are involved in the management of a business.

Economic profit, on the other hand, occurs when total revenue exceeds the total cost of production (including the opportunity cost of the owners' own resources). Therefore, economic profit is above-normal profit. In a competitive market, economic profit serves the vital function of enticing rival firms into the market. These firms attempt to imitate those who are doing well. This expansion causes the payments for all the resources used in the industry to increase since the demand for them is now higher. As a result, resources are channeled by market forces from declining and low-growth industries to those experiencing the greatest growth. Long-run equilibrium is reached when the owners of all resources receive a payment equal to the opportunity cost of their resources. Therefore, economic profit causes the competitive market mechanism to allocate economic resources to the uses most valued by the market economy.

As we saw in Chapter 5, if economic profit is received as a result of market power, it is not a reward to firms for good performance. This type of economic profit is called *monopoly profit* since it results from the control that monopolies and oligopolies exert over production. By restricting production, given significant barriers to entry, firms with market power can raise the price at which they sell their product above the level that would have prevailed in a competitive market. This creates above-normal profit that causes consumers to pay a higher price for less output in comparison to the competitive market. It also tends to redistribute income from consumers who buy the products to the owners of the monopolies and oligopolies.

Summary

Buyers and sellers interact to determine the price and the amount of inputs sold in a purely competitive market. Households supply inputs in the factor market in order to buy goods in the product market. Firms, on the other hand, demand inputs in order to produce goods for sale in the product market.

A firm will continue to hire additional workers as long as each extra employee adds more to total revenue than to total cost. The firm will maximize total profit by hiring that number of workers at which the marginal revenue product of the last worker equals the marginal cost of labor.

An increase in the demand for labor (with supply unchanged) creates a labor shortage at the initial equilibrium wage, while a decrease in supply (with demand unchanged) creates a surplus. Firms are upset by a shortage since they are not able to buy the amount of labor services that they had planned to purchase at the current market wage. This causes them to bid the current wage up in an attempt to buy more labor services. Similarly, households are upset by a surplus since they are attempting to sell more labor services than firms plan to buy. To sell additional labor services, households must accept a lower wage rate.

Changes in the wage rate serve to eliminate shortages and surpluses. For example, if a shortage occurs, the resulting increase in the actual wage will cause the quantity demanded to decrease as labor services are rationed away from certain firms. This increase in the current wage will also signal to households the need for additional labor services by firms, increasing the quantity supplied. Actual wage reaches equilibrium when firms and households agree on the quantity to be sold. Since both decision makers are in agreement, the market is cleared. Consequently, there is no tendency for the actual wage to change any further.

The basic principles of supply and demand analysis used to explain behavior in the labor market are also used to explore how buyers and sellers interact in the market for capital and natural resources. The role of interest and rent parallels the role that the wage rate plays in our economy.

Key Concepts

functional distribution of income
derived demand
marginal revenue product of labor
firm's demand for labor
average and marginal cost of labor
$MRP_L = MC_L$ rule
demand and supply schedules/curves
equilibrium and actual wages
equilibrium condition
changes in labor market conditions
nonwage determinants of the supply of labor and the demand for labor
short-run and long-run time periods in the labor market
role of education, training, and migration
financial and real capital
role of wages, interest, and rent

Self-Test Questions: True or False

T **F**   1. The contribution that an additional worker makes to the firm's total revenue is called the marginal revenue product of labor.

T **F**   2. From the viewpoint of the purely competitive firm, the average cost of labor is equal to the marginal cost of labor.

T **F**   3. If the marginal revenue product of the tenth worker is $450 and the marginal cost of the tenth worker is $300, the tenth worker adds $150 to the firm's total profit.

T **F**   4. The firm wants to hire workers up to the point where the marginal revenue product of labor exceeds the marginal cost of labor by the maximum amount possible.

Answer Questions 5 and 6 using the following table:

**Market for Dress Designers
(thousands)**

Wage	Quantity Supplied	Quantity Demanded
$10	250	600
12	325	523
14	390	390
16	435	235
18	520	100

T   F   5. If the actual wage is $18, there is a surplus of 220 thousand dress designers.

T   F   6. If the actual wage ($18) moves to the equilibrium wage, the quantity of labor supplied will decrease by 130 thousand workers.

T   F   7. Suppose that there are two labor market areas for plumbers, East Orange and Patterson. An increase in the demand for plumbers in Patterson would tend to cause a decrease in the supply of plumbers in East Orange in the long run. As a result, the wage paid to plumbers in East Orange would increase.

T   F   8. An increase in the demand for loanable funds would create a shortage at the initial equilibrium interest rate. This shortage of loanable funds would cause prospective borrowers to bid up the interest rate.

T   F   9. Rent, in its role as a rationing device, allocates natural resources among alternative uses.

T   F   10. An increase in the wage rate will decrease the demand for labor.

Answers to Self-Test Questions

1. *True.* The additional worker which the firm hires produces output that is sold by the firm at the market price, increasing the firm's total revenue. This contribution is called the marginal revenue product of labor.

2. *True.* The purely competitive firm must pay each worker the same wage. For example, suppose that the market wage is $6. Since the firm must pay each worker $6, the cost per worker (i.e., the average cost of labor) is $6. The cost per *additional* worker (i.e., the marginal cost of labor) is also $6, since each new worker costs the firm $6.

3. *True.* The tenth worker contributes $450 to the firm's total revenue and $300 to the firm's total cost. Therefore, total profit goes up by $150.

4. *False.* As long as the marginal revenue product of labor exceeds the marginal cost of labor, the firm will have the incentive to hire more workers since total profit will increase as additional workers are hired. Total profit reaches a peak when the marginal revenue product of labor equals the marginal cost of labor (the $MRP_L = MC_L$ rule). Note that the firm wants to maximize *total* profit, not *marginal* profit (i.e., the change in total profit per additional worker.)

5. *False.* There is a surplus of 420 thousand workers since at the wage of $18, the quantity supplied is 520 thousand workers and the quantity demanded is 100 thousand (see table).

6. *True.* The equilibrium wage illustrated in the table is $14 since at this wage rate, the quantity supplied equals the quantity demanded (with 390 thousand workers employed). If the actual wage of $18 moves to the equilibrium wage of $14, the quantity supplied decreases from 520 thousand to 390 thousand workers.

7. *True.* The increase in the demand for plumbers in Patterson would cause their wage to rise in the short run relative to the wages paid plumbers in East Orange. In the long run, plumbers would tend to migrate from East Orange to Patterson. This out-migration reduces the supply of plumbers in East Orange, causing the wage rate in East Orange to increase.

8. *True.* A shortage would be created at the initial interest rate, causing firms seeking financial capital to bid up the price of loanable funds.

9. *True.* Rent is the price of natural resources. An increase in rent will ration resources to persons who are willing and able to pay the higher price.

10. *False.* An increase in the wage rate will decrease the quantity of labor demanded (Q_d). The demand curve for labor (D_L) has not shifted.

Discussion Questions

1. Describe how households and firms interact in the product market and the factor market using the concepts of supply and demand. Illustrate your answer by drawing the circular flow diagram.

2. Discuss the factors that you consider important in choosing an occupation.

3. Describe the $MRP_L = MC_L$ rule. How would a firm alter its work force if the marginal revenue product of labor was less than the marginal cost of labor? Why?

4. Describe the role of wages in eliminating a shortage in the labor market in the short run.

5. Describe how the functional distribution of income has changed since 1950.

Problems

Answer questions 1 through 4 using the following information for a hat shop called The Mad Hattery. Assume that all resources except labor are fixed and that the competitive market wage is $200. Also assume that the market price for hats is $20.

Labor	Total Output	MPP_L	MRP_L
0	0	—	—
1	30		
2	50		
3	65		
4	75		
5	80		

1. Calculate the marginal physical product of labor and the marginal revenue product of labor.

2. How much would the second worker add to total profit? Why?

3. What would happen to total profit if the fifth worker were employed? Why?

4. How many workers would the hat shop employ? Why?

5. See the following figure, which illustrates the employment decision of an individual firm in a purely competitive market. Suppose that the firm initially hires L number of workers. Would this firm increase or decrease the number of workers hired? Why?

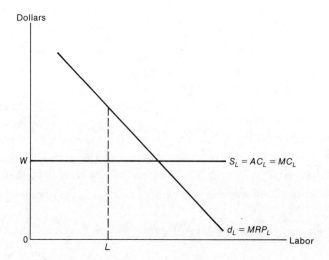

6. See the following figure, which represents the financial capital market for loanable funds. Describe the effect of a decrease in the demand for loans on the equilibrium interest rate and the quantity of money lent, using the graph to illustrate your answer.

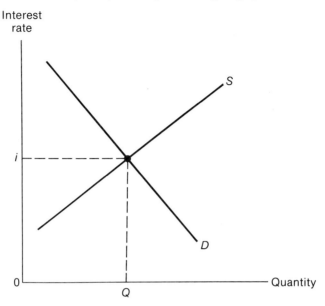

The Economic Role of Government/Public Finance

Objectives

Upon completion of this chapter, you should understand:

1. The economic functions of government.

2. The difference between pure private, pure public, and semipublic goods.

3. Why the market may fail to allocate resources efficiently.

4. The different sources of revenue for government and the various types of government expenditures.

5. The problems facing the government when it attempts to provide the optimal amount of goods.

Over the past forty years, we have witnessed increased government spending, taxes, and regulations. According to the Tax Foundation, in 1989 government spending at all levels surpassed $1.6 trillion, or over $6,600 for each man, woman, and child living in the United States. Also in 1989, the average worker spent 2 hours and 43 minutes of every eight-hour workday earning money to pay his or her taxes, which were needed to finance government spending. Where does this money go? What benefits are gained from government?

There is great debate over how much government should intervene in the economy. Our use of the automobile is a good example. The government has spent a great deal of money building the interstate highway system. In addition, there are many regulations concerning the use of our cars, such as the 55-mph speed limit. What are the benefits and costs of the 55-mph speed limit to travelers and to truckers?

The benefits of government intervention have been significant. For example, as a result of the 55-mph speed limit, there have been fewer accidents and fuel consumption has decreased. However, the lower speed limit has extended travel time, which has increased the cost of each trip. Currently, some states have passed legislation raising the speed limit to 65 mph, while others have maintained the 55-mph speed limit. Speed limits should be determined by the conditions and curvature of roads and the density of the area the road travels through.

Are we worse or better off as a result of government intervention? The purpose of this chapter is to examine the public sector in the United States. We begin by examining the reasons why government is needed. Next we look at the economic theory underlying the intervention of the government in the private market. The expenditure and tax structure of the public sector of the United States is then examined. Finally, we focus on the difficulty of determining the optimal amount of goods the government should provide, and we examine why government intervention does not always produce the desired result.

7.1 An Overview of the Functions of Government

There are essentially four functions of government. First, government maintains a *legal framework* that enables the private market system to operate. This includes the specification of property rights, enforcing contract laws, establishing standards for weights and measures, and declaring what constitutes money in our society.

The second function of government is to *redistribute income* to make it more equitable. Even if the private market is able to arrive at the most efficient allocation of resources, that level of output may not be distributed in the most equitable way. It is generally agreed that some income should be redistributed to the poor and to those not able to take care of themselves. As discussed in Chapter 1, determining a "fair" distribution is very difficult because each person has different perceptions of equity.

See *Special Topic G: Income Distribution and Poverty* for further discussion.

Third, the government may intervene in the private market to **stabilize the business cycle.** The government's struggle to eliminate unemployment and inflation is the subject of Chapters 8 through 12.

The fourth function of government is to **reallocate resources** when there is market failure. **Market failure** occurs when the market is not able to allocate resources efficiently. As we will discover in the next section, the private market cannot produce certain goods needed by society such as national defense, the criminal justice system, and lighthouses. Some goods are not produced by the private market in sufficient quantity — health care and education are examples. Likewise, the private market will allocate too many resources to goods whose production generates pollution, such as the production of paper which causes wood byproducts to spill into our rivers and streams. What is the role of government in redirecting resources to produce those goods in that amount most valued by society?

7.2 The Role of Government in Reallocating Resources

There are three cases of market failure in which government is needed to correct the misallocation of resources by the private market: (1) externalities, (2) public goods, and (3) monopoly.

Externalities

There are two types of externalities that cause the market to fail to allocate resources efficiently: external costs and external benefits.

The Case of External Costs   **External costs** occur when consumers or producers engage in actions that create pollution, imposing a cost on *third parties* (persons outside the market, where the first and second parties are the buyers and sellers). First, we look at the effects of external costs from *consumption* (e.g., smoking cigarettes) using a numerical example. We will then use graphical supply and demand analysis to analyze the situation where the private market fails to consider external costs created from *production* (e.g., the dumping of industrial waste into rivers by companies producing tires).

The consumption of cigarettes adversely affects nonsmokers. Unfortunately, persons who decide to smoke do not consider the impact on others. They weigh the personal cost of an extra carton of cigarettes (ignoring the effect on their own health) against the pleasure they expect to receive. As a result, the private market will produce too many goods that generate external costs through consumption. For example, assume the value of smoking an extra carton of cigarettes to George (his marginal private benefit) is $15 and the additional cost to George (his marginal private cost) is $10. Since the purchase of a carton of cigarettes results in a net benefit of $5 to George, the sale will be made. However, if there were external costs of $6 per additional carton owing to the smoke others have to breathe, the extra cost to society (the marginal social cost) would be \$16 (\$10 + \$6). This additional carton should not be consumed from society's viewpoint.

To illustrate why the private market misallocates resources when there are external costs from production, let's assume that companies producing automobile tires are dumping their industrial waste into rivers. How does this pollution impose a cost on communities that border the river downstream (i.e., the third parties)? Think of the opportunity costs of using the river to dispose of industrial waste. The communities downstream give up numerous alternative uses of the river. For example, the communities lose the river as a source of clean drinking water, recreation, water for bathing, as well as water used in other industries such as agriculture.

Why does the private market misallocate resources when production generates costs to third parties? For the explanation, see Figure 7.1 which illustrates the private market for automobile tires. The supply of tires, S, reflects the costs of production paid by the firm before any government intervention. Equilibrium occurs where the demand curve intersects the supply curve (point E). At point E, the market price is P and the equilibrium quantity is Q. Since external costs are not paid by the buyers and sellers in the market, market prices will not reflect the true costs of producing tires.

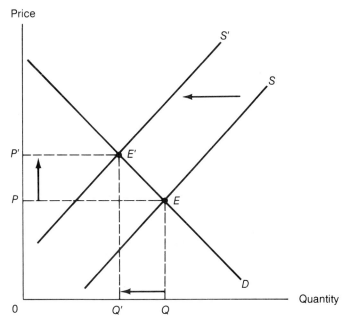

Figure 7.1.   The Effect of an External Cost on Equilibrium Price and Quantity in a Purely Competitive Market. In the presence of external costs, the market equilibrium price will be too low and equilibrium quantity too high.

189

Suppose that the government now forces firms in the tire industry to take the external costs they have created into account either through *regulation* or *taxation*. These firms would not be willing to supply as much as before, since their production costs are higher. They are now paying not only for such resources as labor and supplies, but also for the proper disposal of industrial waste. As Figure 7.1 indicates, the increased private cost imposed by government through regulation or taxation has decreased the supply curve for tires from S to S'. The new supply curve, S', intersects the demand curve at point E', creating a new equilibrium price (P') and equilibrium quantity (Q'). The social optimum level of production, Q', is achieved since *all* costs are now being considered (the original private costs plus the cost to third parties).

Note that without government intervention the private market will ignore external costs. As a result, too much will be produced (the difference between Q' and Q) at too low a price (the difference between P and P'). By ignoring external costs, the private market will allocate too many resources to industries that pollute. This **overallocation of resources** occurs because not all costs are being considered. Firms cannot individually volunteer to take external costs into account because that would put them at a competitive disadvantage. In addition, the firms may not even be aware of the true dimension of the problem they are creating.

The Case of External Benefits Resources may also be misallocated because of the presence of external benefits. **External benefits** occur when a market engages in an action that yields a benefit to third parties (persons outside the market). For example, when Beth is vaccinated against measles, she directly benefits from the reduced risk of getting that disease. Do others benefit? Yes. Since Beth is less likely to catch measles, there is a smaller chance that she will pass the disease to other people. Therefore, the reduced likelihood of her catching the disease becomes a benefit to others. The same is true for education. A person graduating from college benefits from the knowledge gained (e.g., the individual is able to get a higher paying and more interesting job). Society also gains from having a better educated population. College graduates contribute to technological advance, cultural development, and they should be better informed citizens.

Again let us first consider a numerical example, and then use supply and demand analysis to illustrate the effect of external benefits on the allocation of resources by the private market. When a person decides to purchase a flu shot, he or she will only consider the personal benefits received; benefits received by others will be ignored. Assume that the benefit of a flu shot to Manuel (his marginal private benefit) is $20. In addition, assume that the benefit of his flu shot to others is $10. The *overall* benefit of his flu shot to society (the marginal social benefit) is $30, calculated as the private benefit plus the external benefit. If the cost of the flu shot is $25 to Manuel (his marginal private cost), he will not purchase the flu shot because the marginal private cost ($25) exceeds the marginal private benefit ($20). Manuel's decision not to buy the flu shot is a detriment to society since the marginal social benefit of $30 exceeds the additional cost of $25.

How do external benefits affect the allocation of resources? See Figure 7.2 where the supply and demand curves for flu shots in the absence of any externalities are illustrated by S

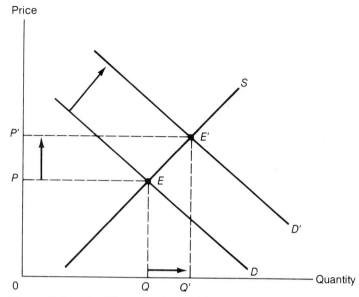

Figure 7.2. The Effect of an External Benefit on Equilibrium Price and Quantity in a Purely Competitive Market. In the presence of external benefits, the market equilibrium price and quantity will be too low.

and *D,* respectively. The demand curve *(D)* is the private market demand curve since it reflects only private benefits. Equilibrium occurs at point *E,* which is the purely private market solution, where the market price is *P* and quantity is *Q. D'* is drawn as society's demand for flu shots since it incorporates the external benefits (i.e., each level of output is valued more than *D* because of the external benefits). Society's demand curve intersects the supply curve at point *E',* which results in an equilibrium price of *P'* and quantity of *Q'.* This is the social optimum amount of flu shots since *all* benefits are being considered. If the externality is ignored, too little will be produced at too low a price. The private market will cause an ***underallocation of resources*** to health care because not all benefits are being considered. Government can correct this misallocation of resources by providing *subsidies* to persuade people to buy more goods that yield external benefits.

See *Special Topic D: Environmental Economics* for further discussion of the use of taxes and direct regulation. See *Special Topic B: The Economics of Health* and *Special Topic C: The Economics of Higher Education* for more discussion of the impact of external benefits.

Public Goods

Before we discuss the role of government in providing public goods as a method for correcting the misallocation of resources caused by market failure, let us describe what is meant by private goods.

Pure Private Goods   A *pure private good* has two characteristics. First, it is subject to the *exclusion principle*, which means that if you do not pay for the good, you are excluded from the benefits received in consuming the good. For example, if you walk into an ice cream store with only $1 in your pocket or purse and you put your $1 on the counter to purchase a fudge sundae that sells for $1.50, you are going to walk away from the store hungry.

The second characteristic of a pure private good is that the good is subject to *rival consumption,* which means that the good only benefits the person who consumes the good. For example, suppose that on your next trip to the ice cream store you remember to bring enough money to pay the $1.50 for the much-desired fudge sundae. After purchasing the sundae, you sit on a bench outside the store. The people walking by you do not benefit from your ice cream sundae. When you are finished enjoying the sundae, it is all gone. You throw the spoon and empty plastic dish into a trash can. Consumption is described as being *rival* in this example because the private market has decided how to ration output among rival (competing) consumers via the price mechanism. The ability of the private market to price individual units of the good has excluded others from enjoying the benefit of the good.

Pure Public Goods   A *pure public good* has characteristics that are opposite those of a pure private good. First, the exclusion principle cannot be applied in providing the pure public good. For example, suppose one of your friends has a "get-rich" scheme — he builds a lighthouse on his uncle's beachfront property. He then sits in the tower as the light shed across the water warns passing ships of the rocks that abound in the area. How is your friend going to collect money from the passing ships? He isn't. If he runs down from the tower and jumps into his rowboat to collect his money, all he is likely to get from the people on deck is a hearty wave. These happy souls who are able to benefit from the good without paying for it are called *free riders.* If society is to benefit from public goods, the goods must be provided by government through taxation (i.e., financed through compulsory charges).

The second characteristic of a pure public good is that it is subject to *nonrival consumption,* which means that, for a given amount of production, consumption of the good by one person need not reduce the amount of the good available for others to consume. For example, once the lighthouse is built, the light received by one ship does not detract from the light received by other ships that pass in the night. National defense and flood control projects are other examples of pure public goods. They must be financed through *taxation,* and they are *collectively consumed* by society.

Semipublic Goods   Most of the goods provided by government are semipublic goods, such as health care. A *semipublic good* also has two characteristics. First, it is a good that can be subjected to the exclusion principle, which means it can be produced for sale by the private market as well as by government. For example, there are both private and public hospitals, each of which bills the people they treat for services rendered.

The second characteristic of a semipublic good is that it generates significant external benefits. Health care provides benefits to persons other than those receiving medical treatment in part by reducing the spread of disease. Since the private market cannot voluntarily consider benefits received by persons outside the market, it will underallocate resources to health care. One option of government to correct this misallocation of resources is to *directly produce* public hospitals. An alternative to producing semipublic goods is the provision of government subsidy such as Medicare to the private market. This approach was already described in our discussion of external benefits in this section. Other examples of semipublic goods are schools, parks, museums, and waste disposal facilities.

Monopoly

The third case of market failure is monopoly. As we noted in Chapter 5, if the barriers to entry are very high, there may be only one firm in the market. Because the firm is producing a unique product, it will be able to restrict production in order to be able to charge a higher price (relative to the purely competitive market solution). Therefore, society will consume less of this good than it wants. The *underallocation* of resources caused by the lack of competition can be corrected by government in two ways. First, government can impose ***antitrust laws*** that are designed to make the market more competitive. By reducing the barriers to entry, government would permit more firms to enter the market, which in turn would cause production to increase to the social optimum.

Second, if the firm is a natural monopoly, then government would want the firm to remain as the sole producer in order for society to benefit from the existing economies of scale (i.e., technology is such that the average cost of production is lower because the firm is large). In this situation, government could write a law that makes this natural monopoly a ***public utility.*** By making the monopoly a public utility, government would have the authority to regulate the rate (price) charged by the firm. This would eliminate the incentive for the firm to restrict production because it would not be able to charge a higher price. Public policy in correcting the underallocation of resources caused by monopoly is treated in more detail in *Special Topic F: Government Regulation.* We now turn to the public finance portion of this chapter to examine the different types of government expenditures and taxes.

7.3 Government Expenditures and Taxes

In this section we first examine the different types of government expenditures. Next we discuss the size of the public sector. Then we look at the principles behind the different types of taxes and the breakdown of taxes by level of government. Finally, the question of tax incidence, or who pays taxes, is discussed.

The Breakdown of Government Expenditures

It is important to distinguish between two types of *government expenditures.* First, there are *government purchases* of goods and services, such as defense, health, education, and highways. Second, there are *government transfers.* This involves the redistribution of funds from one group to another through programs such as social security, welfare, and unemployment compensation. Table 7.1 shows the breakdown of expenditures for the federal government, and state and local governments.

At the federal level, national defense, with about $290 billion in expenditures, is the largest category of government outlays. If we add in the interest on money borrowed by the federal government (the national debt), veterans' benefits, and expenditures on international affairs, spending on defense-related programs is over $480 billion. This amounts to approximately 45 percent of the federal budget.

The second largest category is expenditures for social security benefits, our national pension program. This program required almost $220 billion or approximately 21 percent of the federal budget in 1988. Federal expenditures for all human resource programs (social security, income security or unemployment compensation, health and Medicare, and education) were over $500 billion, or approximately 47 percent of the federal budget.

At the state and local government level, expenditures for education represent the leading outlay, accounting for 29 percent of state and local budgets. Public welfare, ranking a distant second on the list, accounted for 11 percent of state and local expenditures.

Table 7.1
Federal Government Expenditures, 1988 (billions of dollars)

Type of Expenditure	Amount	Percent of Total
National defense	290.4	27.3
International affairs	10.5	1.0
General science, space, and technology	10.8	1.0
Natural resources and environment	14.6	1.4
Agriculture	17.2	1.6
Transportation	27.3	2.6
Education and training	31.9	3.0
Health	44.5	4.2
Medicare	78.9	7.4
Income security	129.3	12.2
Social security	219.3	20.6
Net interest	151.7	14.3
Other	37.6	3.5
Total	1,064.0	100

State and Local Government Expenditures, 1985 (billions of dollars)

Type of Expenditure	Amount	Percent of Total
Education	192.7	29.4
Highways	45.0	6.9
Public welfare	69.6	10.6
Health	13.7	2.1
Hospitals	36.0	5.5
Police protection	21.0	3.2
Fire protection	8.9	1.4
Sanitation	17.4	2.7
Housing and urban renewal	10.4	1.6
Interest on general debt	32.4	4.9
Utility and liquor stores	59.8	9.1
Employee retirement/unemployment comp.	44.2	6.7
Other	105.0	16.0
Total	656.1	100

Source: *Economic Report of the President,* January 1989; Statistical Abstract of the United States, 1989.

The Size of the Public Sector

In addition to examining the breakdown of government expenditures, it is interesting to look at the size of the public sector. One way to measure the size of the government is to determine the amount of government spending relative to total production. Figure 7.3 show that total government expenditures have grown since 1947. If transfers were taken out, we would see that government purchases of goods and services have stabilized over the last forty years at approximately 20 percent of total production (not shown).

The federal government's share of total government expenditures increased from approximately 35 percent in 1930 to around 68 percent by 1987. Note that the increase in federal expenditures is due to the growth in transfer payments (programs that redistribute funds from one income group to another such as welfare). Federal government purchases as a percentage of total government purchases have actually declined.

The Organization for Economic Cooperation and Development calculates a measure similar to Figure 7.3 for other countries. For 1986, government expenditures in the United States were approximately 29 percent of total output, which compares to 54 percent for Sweden, 39 percent for the United Kingdom, and 33 percent for Canada. Government expenditures of the United States, big as they are, still do not approach the relative size of those of many other countries.

Since the majority of government revenue comes from taxes, let us now examine the principles used in designing different taxes and the breakdown of tax revenue by level of government.

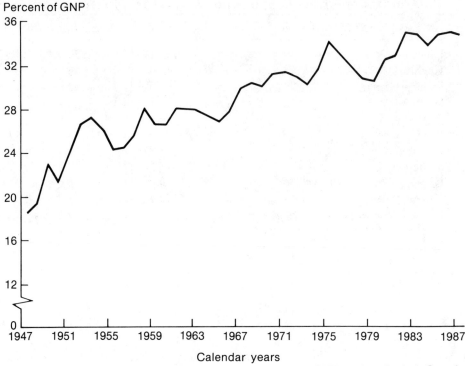

Percent of GNP

Figure 7.3.   Total Government Expenditures as a Percentage of GNP (total production). Over the past 40 years, total government outlays have generally risen to about 34 percent of GNP. (Source: *Economic Report of the President,* January 1989.)

Principles of Taxation

Two principles are used in deciding who should pay relatively more taxes. First, the **ability-to-pay principle** calls for *equal sacrifice* in taxation, which means that everyone should "hurt" the same when they pay taxes. Assuming that lower income families receive more pleasure from an additional dollar than higher income families, the ability-to-pay principle concludes that we should use a **progressive tax,** which means that persons in higher income brackets should pay a higher *percentage* of their income out in taxes than those in lower brackets. It differs from a **regressive tax** in which persons with higher incomes pay out a smaller percentage of their income in taxes compared to persons with lower incomes.

Second, there is the **benefit-received principle,** which states that people should pay taxes in proportion to the benefits they receive from government. For example, the interstate highway system has been partially financed through the gasoline tax based on the principle that motorists should pay taxes in proportion to the benefits received from highway use (measured in terms of mileage via gasoline consumption). This principle is difficult to apply for two reasons. First, some people benefit from public goods such as highways even though they do not use them. For example, parents benefit because their children are able to get home from college more easily because of the highway system. In addition, in some programs, such as welfare, if the recipients of the benefit were required to pay the taxes needed to support the program, there would be no program.

Breakdown of Taxes

The majority of government revenue comes from taxes. Other sources include the borrowing and printing of money (discussed in Chapter 11) and charges for services such as mail delivery and public higher education.

Tax revenue as a percentage of total output has increased dramatically over the past seventy years. Total taxes for federal, state, and local government were approximately 10 percent of total output in 1927. By the 1980s, taxes were over 25 percent of total output. The federal portion of total taxes for all levels of government was about 35 percent of total output in 1930. By 1987 it had grown to over 62 percent (which is down from the 68 percent peak reached in 1960). Table 7.2 illustrates the recent breakdown of these revenue sources for government.

Federal Taxes   The major source of revenue for the federal government is the personal income tax, which provides 44 percent of all federal budget receipts. The other major source of revenue is payroll taxes (social security contributions), which account for 37 percent of federal receipts. The corporate income (profit) tax is a minor source of federal revenue, contributing only 10 percent.

Personal Income Tax: In the United States, the personal income tax was designed as a progressive tax. As we noted earlier in this section, this means that persons with higher incomes pay out a larger percentage of their income in taxes compared to persons with lower incomes. In 1986 Congress passed a major tax reform act. One intention of the Tax Reform Act of 1986 was simplification of the tax schedule by reducing the number of marginal tax rates. Tax reform has also reduced the progressivity of the personal income tax by reducing the maximum marginal tax rates. Another result of the Tax Reform Act of 1986 was that some loopholes that allowed wealthy taxpayers to avoid taxes were closed. This increased the progressivity of the tax. Therefore, the true impact of this tax reform will not be known for some time. For additional information about the Tax Reform Act of 1986, see the boxed insert.

197

Payroll Taxes: Payroll taxes are also called social security taxes and are used to finance the social security system and Medicare (which provides health care for the elderly). In 1989, the payroll tax was 15.02 percent of each dollar earned up to $45,000 with the employer paying half. As Table 7.3 shows, this is a ***proportional tax*** for the first $45,000 of salaries and wages because persons with lower incomes (e.g., $35,000) pay out the same percentage of their income in taxes as persons with higher incomes (e.g., $45,000). After $45,000 all persons pay out the same maximum tax of $6,759 regardless of income. Therefore, the payroll tax becomes *regressive* because persons with more earnings (e.g., $100,000) pay out a smaller percentage of their income in taxes compared to persons with $45,000 in income or less.

Corporate Income Taxes: The Tax Reform Act of 1986 reduced the maximum tax rate on corporate profit from 46 percent to 34 percent on corporate incomes of $75,000 and above. In order to make up for the lower marginal tax rates on corporate income, investment and depreciation allowances were reduced. As a result, the amount of taxes which corporations pay is expected to increase. One quirk with the corporate income tax is the double taxation of

Table 7.2
Federal Government Revenue, 1988 (billions of dollars)

Source	Amount	Percent of Total
Personal income taxes	401.2	44
Payroll taxes	334.3	37
Corporate income taxes	94.5	10
Excise taxes	35.2	4
Miscellaneous receipts	43.5	5
Total	908.7	100

State and Local Government Revenues, 1986–1987 (billions of dollars)

Source	Amount	Percent of Total
Property taxes	121.2	18
Sales taxes	144.3	21
Personal income taxes	83.7	12
Corporation income taxes	22.7	3
All other taxes and charges	199.3	29
Revenue from federal government	115.0	17
Total state and local revenue	686.2	100

Source: *Economic Report of the President, 1989.*

The Tax Reform Act of 1986

A major overhaul of the federal tax laws occurred with the passage of the Tax Reform Act of 1986. Virtually every aspect of the personal and corporate income tax code was affected. The major simplification of this law was the reduction in the number of marginal tax rates. The old tax law consisted of 15 rates, ranging from 11 percent to 50 percent. What follows is an overview of some of the changes that affected individual taxpayers in 1988:

Single Taxpayers

Tax Rates: (on taxable income)	$0 –$17,850	15%
	$17,850–$43,150	28%
	$43,151–$89,560	33%
	above $89,560	28%

Joint Returns

	$0 –$ 29,750	15%
	$29,750–$ 71,900	28%
	$71,901–$149,250	33%
	above $149,250	28%

	Old Law		New Law
Standard deduction	$2,480	single taxpayers	$3,000
	$3,670	joint returns	$5,000
Personal exemption	$1,080		$1,950
State and local sales taxes	fully deductible		nondeductible
Charitable deductions	fully deductible		deductible for itemizers only

According to the new law, if you are a single taxpayer and have earnings up to $17,850, the marginal tax rate is 15 percent. If your income increases and you move into the next income bracket, the tax rate on the excess over $17,850 rises to 28 percent. The standard deduction is used by those who are unable to take itemized deductions. It is subtracted from total income to determine taxable income. Under the new law it has increased by 21 percent for single taxpayers, from $2,480 to $3,000. Individuals also get a personal exemption for each dependent claimed to lower their taxable income. The personal exemption has increased by almost 81 percent.

In addition to these changes it had become more difficult to deduct expenses such as medical, dental, and business expenses. Also, all unemployment insurance benefits are now treated as taxable income. Because of these changes, the amount of taxable income of individuals and families has changed. Some individuals found their taxable income lowered, and some found it increased.

Table 7.3

Income	Tax paid	Tax as Proportion of Income
$ 35,000	$5,257.00	15.02%
45,000	6,759.00	15.02
100,000	6,759.00	6.76

corporate profits. If profits are distributed to shareholders in the form of dividends, the shareholder must pay personal income tax on money received. This is in addition to the tax already paid on those profits. Therefore, corporate profits are being taxed twice. The incidence of the corporate profits tax remains uncertain.

State and Local Revenue   State and local governments raise the majority of their revenues from taxes. Sales taxes (e.g., general sales, motor fuel, and alcohol) are the largest source of tax revenue for states. Local governments rely primarily on property taxes. Personal income taxes also provide a significant amount of state and local revenue. In addition, currently about 17 percent of state and local revenue is received from the federal government in the form of *federal grants*. Federal grants are categorical, which means that they are designed to be used for specific purposes such as highways, medical care, and education.

Property Taxes: Property taxes can be levied on real estate, cars, boats, or any other property. It is difficult to determine whether the property tax is progressive or regressive because different areas assess the tax differently. To the extent that lower income people spend a larger percentage of income on housing than higher income people, property taxes are regressive.

Sales Taxes: Sales taxes are regressive, affecting lower income groups more than others. Persons with higher income save more. Therefore, their income is less subject to a sales tax. As Table 7.4 shows, if the sales tax is 6 percent, a family with income of $20,000 which spends all of its income will pay out $1,200 in sales tax. This $1,200 in sales tax is 6 percent of the family's income. Table 7.4 also indicates that a family with $100,000 in income which spends only half of its income ($50,000) will pay out $3,000 or 3 percent of its income in sales tax.

Table 7.4

Income	Spending	Sales Tax Paid	Sales Tax as a Percent of Income
$ 20,000	$20,000	$1,200	6%
100,000	50,000	3,000	3

We should note that a sales tax is generally not paid only by the household. To better understand why sales taxes are usually partially paid by the retailer, let's explore the impact of an excise tax (which is a sales tax on a specific good).

When a cigarette excise tax is levied on retailers, *both* households and retailers generally share in paying the tax. In Figure 7.4 equilibrium occurs at the intersection of demand curve D and supply curve S (point E) before the excise tax is imposed, resulting in a price of $8 per carton and a quantity of 80 cartons sold.

Assume that an excise tax of $2 per carton is now imposed on cigarettes. The supply curve will shift to the left from S to S' because retailers now attempt to receive $2 more for each carton sold. This $2 tax has the same effect on the supply curve as an increase in the cost of production. Retailers now want $10 to supply 80 cartons (see point A). Households, however, have decreased the amount they plan to buy at this higher price, creating a surplus. As a result,

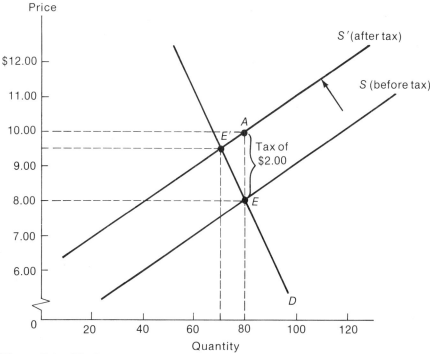

Figure 7.4. The Impact of an Excise Tax on Equilibrium Price and Quantity in a Purely Competitive Market. An excise tax of $2 will lead to a decrease in supply, causing equilibrium price to increase from $8 to $10 and equilibrium quantity to decrease from 80 to 70. The tax burden is shared by both the firm (which pays $0.50 of the tax) and the household (which pays $1.50 of the tax).

Problems in Financing the Social Security System

In 1980, Victor Fuchs wrote that the social security system was in trouble. Young workers were concerned that even though they were paying so much in taxes, there was no guarantee that they would collect benefits. The elderly were fearful that benefits might be cut, making it more difficult to buy food and pay the rent.

Fuchs notes that the basic problem is that the system was never intended to be a "save for retirement" plan, but was designed as a "pay as you go" system. Current workers do not pay into the system for their own retirement, but pay for the benefits of workers who have already retired. If the number of retired workers is small relative to the current work force, there is no problem. But if the number of retired persons grows more quickly than the size of the labor force, problems arise. Namely, more taxes will have to be collected to pay the increased benefits.

This is precisely what happened to the social security system. The program became the victim of the changes in the demographic characteristics of the United States. The two major factors contributing to this were the longer life expectancy and declining birth rates. With people living longer, more and more workers reached retirement. For example, Fuchs observes that between 1968 and 1977 the life expectancy of retiring males increased from 12.8 to 13.9 years. Because the birth rate declined, the increased number of retirees were not offset by more workers entering the labor force. In addition, the government enacted changes in the retirement program which allowed workers to retire earlier, at age 62. This also contributed to the budget imbalance.

It is not surprising that the problems of the social security system came about because a program designed for the 1930s was not able to cope with the demographic changes that occurred in the economy. What could the government do? Fuchs proposed a solution which, if applied immediately, would not have required an increase in taxes or a reduction in benefits. His proposal was simple. Given that people were living longer, raise the age of retirement by two months a year, so that by the year 2000 the earliest eligible age of retirement would be 65 years old. The former eligibility age of 65 would rise to 68 years. The change in retirement age would provide a financial boost to the system without causing any profound problem to households or firms.

NOTE: At the time of writing this edition, the social security system was generating a surplus because of new tax laws which postponed the retirement age, increased the payroll tax rate, and raised the ceiling of the maximum tax. Since the average age of the U.S. population is increasing, the social security system may once again face a financing problem.

Source: This is a summary of "How to Save Social Security" by Victor R. Fuchs, which appeared in *Newsweek* on October 27, 1980.

price falls to the new equilibrium point (E'), where market price is $9.50 and the quantity sold is 70 cartons. At E', consumers will be paying $1.50 more than they were paying before the imposition of the tax. This $1.50 is the part of the tax that has been passed on to consumers. Retailers pay the rest of the $2 tax (or $0.50). Note that the quantity of cigarettes consumed has decreased, which was probably a goal of government officials when they imposed this tax.

7.4 Determining the Optimal Amount of Public Goods

Should society purchase more defense, education, or health care? If health care is chosen, which illness should get the support: cancer, heart disease, amyotrophic lateral sclerosis, or another disease? How much should be spent on these programs? These are but a few of the questions the government must answer in determining how much to intervene in the private market.

Benefit-Cost Analysis

In trying to formalize the decision-making process, the public sector uses benefit-cost analysis to compare options. **Benefit-cost analysis** is an attempt to evaluate alternative courses of action when a common measure of inputs (costs) and outputs (benefits) exists. Society attempts to maximize benefits, subject to a given level of costs.

For example, assume that medicine X exists which costs $10 and provides a good day of health. With that good day of health assume that the person would work and earn $100. The *benefit-cost ratio* would be

$$\text{benefits/costs} = \frac{\$100}{\$10} = 10$$

Assume there were an alternative medicine Y which also provides a good day of health, available at $20. For medicine Y,

$$\text{benefits/costs} = \frac{\$100}{\$20} = 5$$

Using benefit-cost analysis, it is possible to choose a medicine on the basis of which medicine has the highest ratio. Given the two ratios above, it is clear that medicine X will provide greater benefit per dollar spent to the person. This simple example is essentially what benefit-cost analysis is all about. As long as the benefits are measurable in terms that are comparable to costs, this approach will work very well.

203

An Application of Benefit-Cost Analysis

Crime remains a problem that plagues our society. In order to determine the optimum amount of resources needed to prevent crime, the benefits and costs must be determined. Each dollar spent on crime prevention is one less dollar available for other goods and services. Crime prevention should be provided as long as the marginal (additional) social benefit from providing one more unit of protection is greater than the marginal social cost.

Not only is it necessary to decide how much money to spend on crime prevention, but it must also be determined where this money should be spent. For example, we could spend more money on police, or the court system, or jails. In order to determine where to allocate resources, it is useful to examine the benefits and costs as perceived by the person who may commit a crime. For example, the expected benefit of a robbery is primarily the money the person believes he or she will gain from committing the crime. On the other hand, the expected costs include the probability of being arrested and convicted, the expected sentence, and the monetary value of the time lost due to imprisonment. In addition, there may be psychological costs. Many people feel "guilty" if they do something that goes against their own values. If the expected cost is greater than the expected benefit, a rational person will not commit the crime. But if the expected benefit is greater than the expected cost, it is likely the crime will be committed.

Crime prevention may take a number of forms. It is clear that if the probability of being caught increased (e.g., by employing more police), the likelihood of being convicted was greater (e.g., more judges able to handle a growing caseload), or the expected sentence or penalty were to be larger (e.g., mandatory loss of license for one year for a drunken driving conviction), the expected costs to the criminal would be larger and fewer crimes would be committed. Another approach is to increase the opportunity cost of committing a crime by providing employment opportunities to the potential criminal. The larger the income of the person contemplating the commission of a crime, the greater the private cost of imprisonment because of higher foregone earnings.

Problems of Using Benefit-Cost Analysis

The problem with applying benefit-cost analysis to the public sector is that benefits and costs are not always easy to measure. In the previous example, it was assumed that all benefits and costs could be measured. However, this is not always possible. For example, the scenic beauty lost when an area is strip mined or the pain and suffering avoided by the use of the polio vaccine is difficult to evaluate in monetary terms. Benefit-cost analysis ignores things it cannot measure. This obviously leads to imprecise measures. Nevertheless, it is still possible to use the benefit-cost ratio as a crude guide if its shortcomings are explicitly stated.

Another important consideration is that benefits from health programs tend to occur far into the future. How are future costs and benefits compared to present ones? Which program would be more beneficial to society: program A, which yields benefits of $400 in the fifth year, or program B, which yields benefits of $200 in the fourth year and another $200 in the fifth year. The process that enables the decision maker to compare benefits received and costs incurred in different periods within a common time frame is called ***discounting.***

One dollar earned one year from today is not worth $1 today. Interest rates are used to value money over time. For example, if a person had $1 and was able to receive 10 percent annual interest, the dollar would be worth $1.10 one year from now. Therefore, $1.10 received one year from today would be worth $1.00 day. In Table 7.5, the *present value* of $1.00 received in different periods, discounted by different interest rates, is illustrated.

For example, at an interest rate of 6 percent, $1.00 received in year 50 would be worth $0.05 today (year 0). This is the same as saying that if $0.05 were invested at 6 percent interest, it would be worth $1.00 fifty years from now.

Returning to the example cited earlier, we see that program *B* would be preferable to program *A* because, even though the total value of the benefits is the same ($400), in program *B* half of these benefits are being received sooner and therefore are worth more. The present value of the two programs could be calculated from Table 7.5, assuming a discount rate of 6 percent. For program *A*, the present value would be $400 multiplied by 0.75 or $300. (0.75 is the value of $1 received five years from now.) For program *B*, the present value of benefits would be $308. (Verify this, using the information from Table 7.5.) Clearly, program *B* would be the preferable one.

It is important to discount future benefits, because with many public-sector programs most costs take place in the present while the majority of benefits occur many years into the future. For example, building a highway today will provide reduced travel time for future generations.

In addition, the choice of a discount rate will greatly influence whether a program is considered desirable. The higher the discount rate employed, the lower a dollar of future

Table 7.5
Present Value of $1 Received in Various Years at Different Discount Rates

Year	Discount Rate		
	6%	9%	12%
0	$1.00	$1.00	$1.00
1	0.94	0.92	0.89
2	0.89	0.84	0.80
3	0.84	0.77	0.71
4	0.79	0.71	0.64
5	0.75	0.65	0.57
10	0.56	0.42	0.32
50	0.05	0.01	0.004

benefits will be worth today (see Table 7.5). If the discounted benefits are smaller, the benefit-cost ratio is lower.

Given the problems discussed above, it should be clear that there are a great many difficulties involved in the calculation of benefit-cost ratios. Society is always faced with choosing between alternatives since resources are limited. Politicians must allocate expenditures among education, environment, health, or defense. Once they have picked the specific category (e.g., defense) they must then determine which programs to fund (e.g., missiles, aircraft carriers, tanks). Even though benefit-cost analysis can be extremely imprecise, it forces decision makers to list the alternatives to any given program and to examine the choices.

7.5 Government Failure

Throughout this chapter we have examined the role of government in reallocating resources when the private market fails to allocate resources efficiently. Although government may improve the allocation of resources, it also may fail to do so. Just like the home handyman whose "repairs" go awry, government failure may make matters worse.

X-Inefficiency

When the government decides to produce something, the profit motive is removed and much of the incentive to be efficient disappears. Therefore, it is not surprising to hear people complain about such government-produced services as the U.S. Postal Service.

Because of the lack of profit-motive incentives facing the public sector, government does not have to minimize the cost of producing goods and services in order to survive (as is the case of a firm in a competitive market). *X-inefficiency* refers to the less than optimal use of resources by government which occurs because of the lack of motivation. The absence of market discipline may cause poor management, poor organizational structure, or poor performance of employees.

Problems of Voting

The government must find a method of determining people's preferences. *Majority voting* is frequently used to make public choices. Unfortunately, the use of majority voting can sometimes yield a result that is not in the best interests of society, as Table 7.6 illustrates.

In Table 7.6a, the benefits and costs which five people expect from constructing a new school are presented in columns 2 and 3. Palmer expects to receive $450 of benefits from the school, which is greater than the expected cost facing him of $200. (For simplicity it is assumed that the expected costs are divided evenly among all five persons.) In column 4 the difference between each person's expected benefits and costs are given. For Palmer, since expected benefits exceed expected costs, there is a *net benefit* of $250. Since he receives a net benefit, he would vote for the new school, which is shown as a "For" vote in column 5. If

Table 7.6
Effects of Majority Voting

(1) Person	(2) Expected Benefit	(3) Expected Cost	(4) Net Benefit (+) or Net Cost (−)	(5) Vote on New School
(a) Example of a Situation Where Majority Voting Leads to a Solution in Which Society Benefits				
Palmer	$ 450	$ 200	$+250	For
Cliff	350	200	+150	For
Phoebe	250	200	+50	For
Daisy	150	200	−50	Against
Nina	50	200	−150	Against
Total	$1,250	$1,000	+250	
(b) Example of a Situation Where Majority Voting Leads to an Inefficient Allocation of Resources				
Palmer	$350	$ 200	$+150	For
Cliff	250	200	+50	For
Phoebe	225	200	+25	For
Daisy	50	200	−150	Against
Nina	25	200	−175	Against
Total	$900	$1,000	−100	

there was a *net cost,* the person would vote against the school. Given the information presented in Table 7.6a, it is clear that three of the five people (Palmer, Cliff, and Phoebe) would vote for the school and two (Daisy and Nina) against it. Therefore, according to majority voting, the school would be built. In this instance there is no problem because the project is beneficial to the community, since total benefits ($1,250) are greater than total costs ($1,000).

But what if the total costs were greater than the total benefits? Given majority voting as the decision-making tool, it is possible that the school will be built even though it fails by the benefit-cost criteria. This is exactly the situation illustrated in Table 7.6b. In this example, costs ($1,000) are greater than benefits ($900), which means that this project should not be pursued. Since Palmer, Cliff, and Phoebe receive net benefits, the majority will prevail and the project will be undertaken despite the objections of Daisy and Nina. Majority voting has led to a solution that is not using resources efficiently since voting does not enable one to express *intensity of preference.* In Table 7.4b, Phoebe's vote is given the same weight as Nina's, even though the magnitude of the net benefit to Phoebe is less than the net cost to Nina.

Furthermore, in order to attract as many votes as possible, political candidates will try to appeal to the broadest spectrum of voters. As such, many political candidates are as vague as possible about the issues, so that they will not offend any group. This may lead to voter apathy and explain why many people do not vote to express their preferences. They feel that their vote does not matter. Therefore, majority voting is an imperfect mechanism. This imprecision leads to allocation decisions that may not be in the public interest.

Summary

It is clear that there are a number of reasons for government intervention in the marketplace. The provision of a legal framework allows the private market to operate. Given the existence of a market economy, government intervention is necessary because the private market sometimes fails to allocate resources efficiently. Market failure occurs because of the existence of externalities, public goods, and monopoly. Therefore, the government will attempt to improve on market performance by reallocating resources. The government also has the functions of redistributing income, and stabilizing the economy.

To accomplish these goals the public sector provides goods and services directly. For the federal government, income security and defense are the two major expenditure items. For state and local governments, education is the largest expenditure category.

Taxes are the major source of revenue used to finance these expenditures. Many types of taxes have evolved. Different government jurisdictions rely on diverse types of taxes. The federal government depends primarily on the income tax, state governments generally utilize sales taxes, and local governments depend on the property tax. Most people believe that all taxes are borne by consumers. In fact, the study of tax incidence shows that both consumers and producers share the burden of taxation.

To determine the optimal amount of public goods, society's preferences must be known. Benefit-cost analysis is used by decision makers to compare alternatives. Unfortunately, it has many shortcomings.

Government intervention does not always have a beneficial impact on the private market. Causes of government failure include X-inefficiency and the problems associated with majority voting.

Key Concepts

legal framework
redistribute income
stabilize the business cycle
reallocation of resources
market failure

external costs and benefits
overallocation and underallocation of resources
pure private good
exclusion principle
rival consumption
pure public good
free riders
nonrival consumption
semipublic good
antitrust laws
public utility
government expenditures
ability-to-pay and benefit-received principles
progressive, regressive, and proportional taxes
benefit-cost analysis
discounting
government failure
X-inefficiency
problem of majority voting

Self-Test Questions: True or False

T F 1. The government should always allow the private market to allocate resources without interference.

T F 2. The difference between pure private and pure public goods is that pure private goods are characterized by external benefits.

T F 3. When external benefits are ignored, the private market overallocates resources.

T F 4. Government expenditures have increased over the past forty years and government purchases have remained relatively constant.

T F 5. If the excise tax on cigarettes were increased by $0.05, consumers would generally bear the full burden.

T F 6. If project *A* has a benefit-cost ratio less than 1, it should not be pursued.

T F 7. One dollar earned ten years from now is worth the same as $1 today.

T F 8. According to the theory of X-inefficiency, because governments are not subject to the competitive forces of the private market, there is little incentive for them to behave efficiently.

T F 9. The ability-to-pay principle calls for people to pay taxes in proportion to the benefits received from government.

T F 10. Majority voting, as a substitute for the private market, will always lead to an efficient allocation of resources.

Answers to Self-Test Questions

1. *False.* There are a number of situations in which the private market will fail to allocate resources efficiently and government intervention will be required. For example, if external costs are present and not taken into account, too many resources will be allocated to that good. In addition, the government may intervene to redistribute goods and services or stabilize the economy.

2. *False.* When Denise consumes a pure private good, she gets to determine who receives the benefit. Therefore, there are no external benefits.

3. *False.* When there are external benefits present, the benefits that accrue to society are greater than the benefits received by the individual. In this case, the market demand curve underestimates the true value of the good. Therefore, if external benefits are ignored, not enough will be produced. There will be an underallocation of resources to this good.

4. *True.* Government expenditures include transfer payments. When transfer payments are subtracted from government expenditures, the remainder is government purchases. Unlike government expenditures, which have been rising, government purchases have remained constant at about 20 percent of total production.

5. *False.* Although it is true that an increase in the excise tax will raise the price consumers pay for cigarettes, the burden will generally be shared by both consumers and producers.

6. *True.* The benefit-cost ratio is determined by dividing the dollar value of benefits by the dollar value of costs. If the benefit-cost ratio is less than 1, then costs must be greater than benefits. When costs are greater than benefits, it is not desirable to undertake this project.

7. *False.* One dollar earned ten years from now is worth less than $1 earned today. For example, in Table 7.5, if $1 were received ten years from today (year 0), at a discount rate of 6 percent, its present value would be $0.56. In other words, $0.56 saved for ten years at an interest rate of 6 percent would be worth $1 in ten years.

8. *True.* The theory of X-inefficiency states that producers who are not subject to the competitive forces of the market will lack the incentives to operate efficiently. Because of factors such as poor management and poorly motivated workers, internal efficiency may be difficult to attain. Governments are particularly vulnerable to this problem because they are operating outside a competitive market.

9. *False.* The ability-to-pay principle states that people should bear equal sacrifice in taxation. Therefore, persons with higher income should pay a higher proportion of their income out in taxes than persons with lower income.

10. *False.* Using majority voting can yield a solution that is not efficient. For example,

when a person determines whether to vote for or against a highway, he or she looks at the net benefit. If the net benefit is positive (negative), the person will vote for (against) the highway. Even if overall total benefits are less than total costs to society, a majority of the people voting may receive net benefits individually, resulting in their vote for the construction of the highway.

Discussion Questions

1. Discuss why there is a need for a public sector. Under what circumstances does the private market fail to allocate resources efficiently?

2. Distinguish between pure public goods and pure private goods. Why won't the private market provide pure public goods?

3. Describe the trend in government expenditures and government purchases over the past forty years. List the types of government expenditures made and taxes collected by federal, state, and local governments.

4. List some of the costs and benefits associated with the following types of public-sector projects:
   a. construction of a new highway
   b. increased military expenditures
   c. increased air pollution control

5. Explain why government intervention may not improve the allocation of resources.

Problems

1. Use a graph to illustrate the affect of each of the following on the private market equilibrium price and quantity:
   a. air pollution by a coal-burning electric utility
   b. the illegal dumping of hazardous wastes
   c. public education
   d. immunization from chicken pox

2. The table below illustrates the benefits and costs of three alternative government programs for 1990 (in billions of dollars):

	Benefits	Costs
Education	$25	$10
Pollution control	30	15
Crime prevention	12	5

a. Which program would the government choose if all the benefits and costs were to occur in 1990?

b. Would your answer to question 1 change if you discovered that the benefits for these three programs would be received 10 years from 1990, given that all costs occur in 1990? Why? Assuming a discount rate of 12 percent, calculate the present value of each program (use Table 7.5 in Section 7.4).

PART
THREE
Macroeconomics

CHAPTER

8

National Income Accounts/
The Business Cycle

Objectives

Upon completion of this chapter, you should understand:

1.   The problems of unemployment, inflation, and increasing economic growth.

2.   The various measures of total output and their limitations.

3.   How inflation and unemployment are measured.

4.   The different types of inflation and unemployment.

5.   The general properties of the business cycle.

6.   The recent history of the business cycle in the United States.

During the Great Depression, which lasted from 1929 to 1941, the unemployment rate rose to approximately 25 percent. People were literally starving because they could not afford to buy food. Men and women committed suicide because of their inability to provide for their families. The tremendous loss of output can never be regained. In short, the Great Depression had a devastating impact on the economy. The economy recovered from the depression as we entered World War II.

Throughout the 1950s and 1960s, economists believed that it was possible to have both low unemployment and low inflation. But in the 1970s and early 1980s both unemployment and inflation rose to post-World War II highs. Full employment and price stability no longer seemed to be compatible goals. In addition, the economy was no longer experiencing the previous robust rates of growth. However, since November 1982 the U.S. economy has recorded the longest peacetime economic expansion without a recurrence of high inflation.

In Parts I and II of this text, the primary focus has been on the behavior of the individual firm and household as buyers and sellers in a particular market. In Part III we study the behavior of the overall economy, with a focus on the causes of the business cycle, and policy options for reducing inflation and unemployment. We begin this chapter by defining macroeconomics. In the next section, national income accounting is discussed to examine the various measures of income used by economists. We then examine how the federal government measures inflation and unemployment. We conclude the chapter by discussing the cyclical behavior of economic activity since 1920.

8.1 What Is Macroeconomics?

In the study of microeconomic theory we used a "microscope" to study the behavior of buyers and sellers in a particular market. Macroeconomics deals with the whole economy. We will use a "telescope" to examine the behavior of aggregate demand and aggregate supply. *Aggregate demand* is *total* spending in all markets of the economy, and *aggregate supply* is the amount of all goods and services produced. Therefore, macroeconomics is the study of the overall behavior of consumers, businesses, and government. It is particularly concerned with the problems of unemployment, inflation, and increasing economic growth.

Unemployment

Unemployment occurs when people who are able and willing to work cannot find employment despite their active search for a job. We can use the production possibilities model, which was introduced in Chapter 2 (Section 2.2), to indicate part of the impact of unemployment on the economy.

The production possibilities curve represented in Figure 8.1, assumes that all resources are fully employed. The economy can choose among any of the points on the curve. For example, we might choose point *B*, where the country is producing many consumer goods and few capital goods. Or we might choose point *C*, where the opposite occurs — a lot of capital goods and few consumption goods are produced. If there is unemployment, the economy will not be able to attain any of the points on the curve. We will be forced to a point inside the curve, such as point *E*. It is clear that we will not be as well off as we would be if our resources

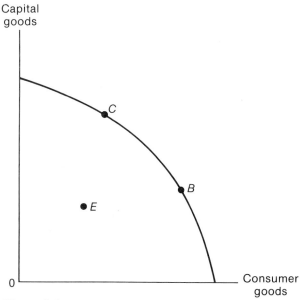

Figure 8.1. The Production Possibilities Model and Unemployment. Insufficient aggregate demand leads to unemployment, which is indicated by a point inside the production possibilities curve.

were fully employed. We are not producing as much output as we could produce to satisfy our wants. Therefore, one major concern with unemployment is the loss of production that occurs when resources are idle. In fact, once a workday of labor is lost, it can never be recovered.

A second concern is that unemployment is not equally shared, causing feelings of inequity. For example, during 1988 the unemployment rates varied widely among different groups in society. Table 8.1 shows that the unemployment rate varied from 32.7 percent for black male teenagers to 4.1 percent for white men 20 years and over. By industry, workers in construction and agriculture experienced the largest unemployment rate, while government workers were least affected.

A third concern with unemployment is that it causes families to lose income, forcing some of them into poverty. This can have a devastating impact on select communities. With increased unemployment, tax revenues fall, which can lead to lower public expenditures on police, schools, and so on. In addition, the human cost of unemployment is high. People who lose their jobs incur emotional trauma. They are unable to support their families, and their own feelings of personal worth may deteriorate. Asocial behavior may be triggered in the form of drug and alcohol abuse, spouse and child abuse, muggings, robbery, as well as suicide. Unemployment may also present a threat to the stability of the political system if the number of people out of work is large.

Table 8.1
Selected Unemployment Rates, Seasonally Adjusted

Selected Categories	Annual Average for 1988 (%)
Characteristic	
Total, all civilian workers	5.5
Both sexes, 16 to 19 years	15.3
Men, 20 years and over	4.8
Women, 20 years and over	4.9
White, total	4.7
Both sexes, 16 to 19 years	13.1
Men, 16 to 19 years	13.9
Women, 16 to 19 years	12.3
Men, 20 years and over	4.1
Women, 20 years and over	4.1
Black, total	11.7
Both sexes, 16 to 19 years	32.4
Men, 16 to 19 years	32.7
Women, 16 to 19 years	32.0
Men, 20 years and over	10.1
Women, 20 years and over	10.4
Hispanic origin, total	8.2
Married men, spouse present	3.3
Married women, spouse present	3.9
Women who maintain families	8.1
Full-time workers	5.2
Part-time workers	7.6
Unemployed 15 weeks and over	1.3
Industry	
Nonagricultural private wage and salary workers	5.5
Mining	7.9
Construction	10.6
Manufacturing	5.3
Durable goods	5.0
Nondurable goods	5.7
Transportation and public utilities	3.9
Wholesale and retail trade	6.2
Finance and service industries	4.5
Government workers	2.8
Agricultural wage and salary workers	10.6

Source: *Monthly Labor Review,* February 1989.

See *Special Topic G: Income Distribution and Poverty* for a more detailed discussion of the causes of poverty. Also, see the *Data Appendix* for additional statistics on unemployment and poverty.

Inflation

Inflation is defined as a *general rise in the prices* of goods and services. A change in one price relative to another is not inflation. For example, an increase in the demand due to increased preferences for McDonald's Big Macs will lead to an increase in the price for Big Macs. Big Macs will be more expensive relative to Burger King's Whoppers.

Inflation is an increase in the level (or average) of all prices, not one good's price change relative to another. One extreme example of inflation occurred in Germany after World War I. In 1923, German prices were 1 trillion times what they had been a year earlier. The German economy was in shambles. There was no longer any incentive to save money. Prices were changing so rapidly that people wanted to be paid at noon and then again at the end of the workday, so that they would be able to spend it immediately. If they waited, they would not be able to buy nearly as much.

This example illustrates why we are concerned with the consequence of inflation. The standard of living in a country depends in part on how much can be purchased with the money people earn. If prices are rising at a rate higher than the increase in money income, the purchasing power of money income will fall. Certain groups are affected more than others by rising prices. For example, those on fixed incomes will lose purchasing power when prices rise. Thus, there will be a redistribution of income away from those who live on a fixed income to those who can increase their money income by more than the inflation rate. Lenders of money (creditors) will lose if inflation is unforeseen since creditors are being paid back with dollars worth less than the ones they lent. Inflation may also provide a disincentive to save, since the money saved will not be able to buy as much in the future.

Growth

With increases in the size of the population, it is important for the economy to grow in its productive capability to meet the greater needs of society. The production model (described in Section 2.2 of Chapter 2) can be used to illustrate the effects of *growth* possibilities on the economy. See Figure 8.2.

In the figure, curve *AB* indicates the maximum combination of two goods that society can produce if it fully employs resources in the most efficient manner. Points *D, E,* and *F* are currently unattainable given the current technology and resources available since they are outside the initial curve *AB*. But if the amount of resources or technology were to change, it would become possible for the economy to produce more of both goods. For example, if this society were to defer current consumption in order to devote resources to the production of capital goods, the result would be an outward shift in the production possibilities curve to *CG*.

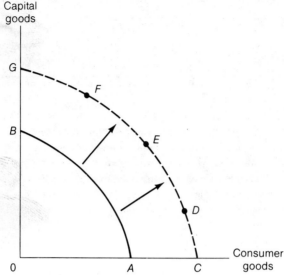

Figure 8.2. The Production Possibilities Model and Growth. If technology changes or society presently invests more resources in the production of capital goods, the production possibilities curve will shift outward in the future.

The increase in capital goods would expand resources available in the future, enabling society to produce more of both goods.

Decisions made today will have a profound impact on the future state of the economy. These decisions are not simple to make. Should resources be devoted to increased current production to meet today's needs, or should society defer current consumption so that more will be available in the future? Growth-oriented policies are examined in more detail in Chapter 12.

In the next section, we examine how the government measures total output for the economy.

8.2 National Income Accounting

National income accounting refers to the various measures of output and income used by economists to describe macroeconomic behavior.

Measuring Gross National Product

Gross national product (GNP) is the value of the final goods and services produced in the economy in a given period of time. We must be sure to count only expenditures on *final* goods (not the value of intermediate goods, which are already included). Expenditures on the *value added* by *intermediate* goods used in production (such as steel, plastic, and rubber used to produce a car) are included in the final price of the goods produced. If we were to count all expenditures, GNP would be overstated owing to *double counting.* In national income accounting, the term *final goods* does not refer just to *consumer* goods since capital goods produced during the current period are also included in the measure of GNP.

There are two approaches to measure GNP. It can be measured as the sum of all expenditures on final goods and services, called the **expenditure approach,** or the sum of all incomes earned in production, called the **income approach.** Since every dollar that is spent by one person becomes a dollar of income for the recipient, total spending will equal total income.

The circular flow diagram represented by Figure 8.3 illustrates the flows between households and firms. In the product market (upper loop), households buy goods and services from producers who receive dollars for them. The factor market (lower loop) measures the flow of income. Households supply factors of production to producers in order to receive income. The value of production being measured in the economy should be the same regardless of the approach employed. Total expenditures in the product market should equal total income earned in production in the factor market. See Section 2.3 of Chapter 2 and Section 6.1 of Chapter 6 for a more detailed discussion of the circular flow model.

Expenditure Approach   According to the expenditure approach, GNP measures the flow of *currently* produced *final* goods and services in the economy by summing expenditures on these goods and services. Only spending on goods and services produced in the United States is included in our measure of GNP. Spending is broken up into four categories. First,

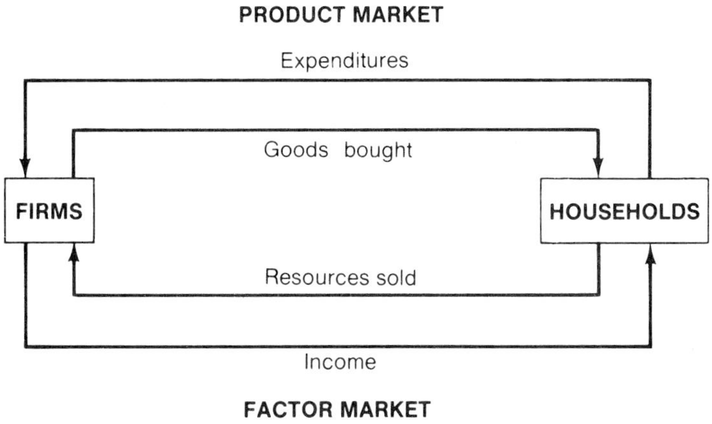

PRODUCT MARKET

FACTOR MARKET

Figure 8.3.   The Circular Flow Diagram. In the product market (upper loop), households spend income to buy goods and services from firms. In the factor market (lower loop), households sell factors of production to firms in order to receive income.

personal consumption expenditures *(C)* are the expenditures on goods and services by households. Goods may be *durable,* which usually means they have an expected life of more than one year (e.g., cars and refrigerators). *Nondurable* goods have an expected life of one year or less (e.g., milk, beef). Expenditures on all *services* such as medical care and legal representation are also included.

Second, **gross private domestic investment** *(I)* is the technical term used for spending on real capital. It consists of three components: spending on new construction, equipment, and inventories. Larger inventories include materials not yet used in production which were bought by firms, and increases in the stock of produced goods not yet sold by the firm. For example, suppose that cars worth $100 million for sale to households are produced in 1990 but only $95 million are sold. Since GNP is a measure of production value we should include all $100 million, of which $95 million is consumption expenditure. The unsold cars will appear as a $5 million increase in inventory, which is a form of investment spending.

Third, **government purchases of goods and services** *(G)* are included. Transfers (e.g., social security payments, welfare payments) are excluded because they are merely a redistribution of income among individuals and do not directly involve an increase in the production of goods and services.

Finally, **net exports** *(X_N)* are a part of our GNP. Goods produced in the United States but sold in foreign countries, called exports, are included, and imported goods are subtracted from total spending to measure domestic production. The equation for GNP then becomes

$$GNP = C + I + G + X_N$$

Care must be taken to ensure that the accounts measure only current production. Therefore, expenditures on secondhand sales and financial transactions must be excluded. For example, the sale of a used car produced in 1987 should not be included in GNP for 1990. Only if work was done to enhance the value of the used car in 1990 should it be included. Also, financial transactions that involve simply the transfer of assets from one person to another should be excluded. For example, if Erica purchases 100 shares of Chrysler previously owned by Palmer, a transfer of ownership of those 100 shares has taken place, but no new current production has occurred.

Income Approach According to the income approach, GNP measures the income earned by U.S. households in current production. Recall from Chapter 6 that there are four types of income: wages (earned by labor), rents (earned by owners of natural resources), interest (earned by people who lend money), and profits (earned by the owners of firms). GNP is equal to the sum of all these sources of income. In addition, there are two nonincome components needed as accounting adjustments. These two nonincome components are depreciation (which is the value of capital worn out in current production) and indirect business taxes (which are taxes on goods such as sales or excise taxes).

In Table 8.2 the expenditure and income approaches are illustrated for 1988. As we can see, consumption accounted for 66 percent of total expenditures, and wages accounted for 66 percent of total income.

> See the *Data Appendix* for more comprehensive statistics on our national income accounts.

Limitations of GNP Accounting

Although economists use GNP as an indicator of economic success, it has some serious flaws. Many productive activities are not included in GNP. These can be divided into two broad categories: *market versus nonmarket* and *legal versus illegal transactions.* If activities do not go through normal market channels, they do not appear in the government's measure of GNP. For example, many informal cash transactions between persons are not reported. Barter transactions (where one good or service is traded for another good) are also not included. Many economists refer to this as the underground economy. This type of activity has been growing over the years, partially because it enables people to escape taxation. For example, suppose that Luke helps Holly, an accountant, paint her house. In return, Holly helps Luke with his taxes. If Luke had paid Holly, she would have to pay income taxes. The same is true for Luke.

Homemaker services are another nonmarket activity that is excluded. All of the time spent cleaning a house and caring for children are not activities for which a parent receives monetary payment; therefore, they are excluded. If a single parent were to hire a person to perform these same functions, they would be included. If the parent proceeded to marry the person who

Table 8.2
Income and Expenditure Approaches (billions of 1988 dollars)

Expenditure Approach	Amount	Percent	Income Approach	Amount	Percent
Consumption	$3,227	66	Wages	$3,230	66
Investment	766	16	Rent	20	0.5
Government	964	20	Profits	324	7
Net exports	−94	−2	Interest	392	8
GNP	4,863	100	Indirect business		
			taxes	390	8
			Depreciation	506	10
			Adjustment	1	0
			GNP	4,863	100

Source: U.S. Department of Commerce, *Survey of Current Business,* February 1989 (Washington, D.C.: U.S. Government Printing Office).

The Underground Economy

In making economic decisions, households, businesses, and government officials all rely on information concerning the current and expected performance of the economy. The most widely recognized barometer of economic performance is the measure of gross national product (GNP). In principle, GNP represents the value of all final goods and services produced for a given time period.

In practice, however, not all economic activity is accounted for in GNP. Empirical evidence suggests that a significant portion of economic activity takes place in a sector that has been alternatively referred to as the "shadow," "hidden," "irregular," or "underground" economy, where goods and services — some legal, some not — are produced but not reported.

Interest in understanding and estimating the size of the underground economy has increased recently, due in part to the current political environment in which budget deficits and tax reform have dominated the news. High budget deficits have led legislators to search for untapped sources of revenue.

What is the underground economy? The underground economy conjures up a variety of images. Often, people first think of illegal activities, such as selling drugs, gambling, or loan-sharking. They might also think of income earned in perfectly legal activities but not reported, for example, income earned moonlighting "off the books" to avoid taxes or to supplement social security or unemployment benefits without facing a reduction in benefits. More generally, the underground economy incorporates all unmeasured economic activity. Thus it includes other activities as well, such as bartering goods and services: the dentist wires braces for the electrician's child, and in return the electrician wires the dentist's house. It even includes activities like growing your own food or doing your own repairs.

How big is the underground economy? For some very obvious reasons, it is impossible to come up with a direct estimate of the size of the underground economy. By definition, participants in the underground economy are actively trying to avoid detection, so there is no simple and direct place to look for information about its size. This makes the underground economy inherently difficult to measure.

The various estimates differ considerably, ranging from 5 to 25 percent of reported GNP in recent years. Most of the estimates, however, suggest its size is quite large and lies in the more narrow range of 5 to 15 percent of reported GNP. At the beginning of 1987, that amounted to between $200 and $650 billion.

The above is an excerpt of an article "The Underground Economy: A Troubling Issue for Policymakers" by Joel F. Houston, which appeared in *Business Review,* Federal Reserve Bank of Philadelphia, September/October 1987, pp. 3–11.

performed these same jobs, that income would no longer be reported, and GNP would fall. Other examples include home repairs, lawn care, and fixing cars.

In addition, external costs are not included in the calculation of GNP. An external cost occurs when someone other than the buyer and seller in a particular market is forced to bear a part of the cost of their transaction (see Chapter 7, Section 7.2). For example, in the production of electricity, a power plant may emit a pollutant that affects the health of the population surrounding the plant. The cost that the people are forced to bear in the form of reduced health is not included in the estimate of GNP. But if the firm were to buy pollution abatement devices, their cost would be included.

There are also many resources spent in the production of illegal activities. Billions of dollars of illegal goods and services are produced each year including prostitution, drugs, and gambling.

In addition to these excluded items, other things that affect economic well-being are not a part of GNP such as the distribution of income. Changes in product quality are also impossible to discern from GNP figures. Finally, GNP does not show the value that we receive from increased leisure, better health, lower crime, and enjoyment of scenic beauty.

Other Measures of Income

There are a number of other related accounts used by economists. These alternative measures of income are summarized in Table 8.3.

Table 8.3
National Income Accounts

	1988 Totals[a] (billions)
Gross national product (GNP)	$4,863
Subtract: Depreciation	506
Net national product (NNP)	4,357
Subtract: Indirect business taxes	389
Other adjustments	3
National income (NI)	3,965
Subtract: Corporate profits	324
Contributions to social security	445
Add: Transfer payments	555
Other adjustments	312
Personal income (PI)	4,063
Subtract: Personal taxes	590
Disposable income (DI)	3,473

[a] Numbers do not add exactly, due to rounding.

Source: U.S. Department of Commerce, *Survey of Current Business,* February 1989 (Washington, D.C.: U.S. Government Printing Office).

Net national product (NNP) is the total output available for use. Depreciation (also called capital consumption allowance) is deducted from GNP to get NNP. GNP can give an exaggerated picture of output. When automobiles are produced, the machines used in the process experience wear and will not be as productive next year. In order to produce at the same level in the next period, worn out capital must be replaced.

National income (NI) is a measure of income *earned* and is calculated as NNP minus indirect business taxes. Indirect business taxes such as sales or excise taxes are excluded because these taxes are not earned in the private market.

A third measure used when economists want to examine spending patterns is called personal income. In order to understand the relationship between spending and income, we must distinguish between income earned and income received. *Personal income (PI)* is a measure of income *received.* It is equal to *NI* minus income earned but not received plus income received but not currently earned. Some income earned is not received, such as retained earnings and social security contributions. Retained earnings are corporate profits that are kept by the firm and not distributed to shareholders. Social security contributions are the payments to the social security system. In addition, some income not earned in current production is received, such as welfare payments, unemployment compensation, pensions from businesses, and social security benefits.

Finally, to calculate the amount of income that people have at their disposal to spend or to save, personal taxes (income, property, and inheritance taxes) must be deducted from *PI*. *Disposable income (DI)* equals *PI* minus personal taxes.

8.3 Measuring Changes in the Level of Prices

This section examines how the Bureau of Labor Statistics (within the Department of Labor) measures changes in the average price level for the national economy. As mentioned in Section 8.1 of this chapter, inflation is a change in the *level* of prices (not a change in *relative* prices, such as an increase in the price of apples relative to the price of oranges). The best known measure of inflation is the *consumer price index (CPI)* since it is used to estimate the change in prices which households pay for the goods and services they typically buy. Another important, broader, price index is the *implicit price deflator* which measures the level of prices for GNP (the market value of all the final goods and services produced in our economy).

The Consumer Price Index

The consumer price index measures how prices for a market basket of goods and services purchased by a typical urban family change from one month to the next. The consumer price index includes the prices of food, clothing, shelter, fuels, transportation, health care, and other items purchased by households for day-to-day living. These items were chosen on the basis of the past buying habits of urban consumers. Data collectors obtain prices in 91 locations. This survey of prices is then reported to the Bureau of Labor Statistics, which combines the local data to compute a U.S. city average. Separate indices are published for regions and 27 metropolitan areas.

The consumer price index is not an exact measure of inflation. It measures how prices for a *fixed* market basket of goods and services change from one period to another. The composition of items in this hypothetical basket cannot be altered to reflect current changes in the mix of goods and services actually consumed by households. The consumer price index does not measure the switching among different goods and services that households frequently practice when there is a change in relative prices. For example, when the price of beef increases, most households will buy more chicken or fish instead of beef. In addition, the index fails to adjust for changes in the quality of existing goods and services as well as the introduction of new products such as personal computers, video recorders, compact discs, and pocket televisions.

Calculation of the Consumer Price Index and the Measurement of Inflation

Assume that the hypothetical market basket of goods and services cost consumers $10,000 in 1967 and $40,000 in 1990. Given these differences in the cost of the basket, how do we calculate a consumer price index? The first step is to choose the **base year,** the year against which we will compare the level of prices in all other time periods. Any year may be chosen. A year in which the economy is stable is preferable to one in which there is a recession or high inflation. In this example, 1967 will be used as the base year. The 1990 consumer price index expresses the market value of the basket of goods and services for 1990 as a percentage of the market value of the basket in 1967 (the base year). Assuming the cost of the hypothetical basket to be $40,000 in 1990, the price index for 1990 is 400, calculated as:

$$\frac{1990 \text{ market basket cost}}{1967 \text{ market basket cost}} \times 100 = \frac{\$40,000}{\$10,000} \times 100 = 400$$

Note that the price index of the base year will always be 100 because that year's price level is 100 percent of itself. We calculate the price index for the base year (1967) as:

$$\frac{1967 \text{ market basket cost}}{1967 \text{ market basket cost}} \times 100 = \frac{\$10,000}{\$10,000} \times 100 = 100$$

How is the consumer price index used to measure inflation? We estimate that the level of consumer prices has increased by 300 percent from 1967 to 1990 by subtracting the consumer price index of 400 in 1990 from the base year index (1967) of 100. This means that goods costing $10 in 1967 cost consumers $40 in 1990. In addition to using the price index to measure the change in the level of consumer prices from the base year to the current year, it is used monthly to estimate the annual rate of inflation. The *annual* inflation rate is calculated as the monthly percentage change in the consumer price index, projected over the course of 12 months. Figure 8.4 shows that, in comparison to the 1950s and 1960s, the inflation rate

227

Percent change

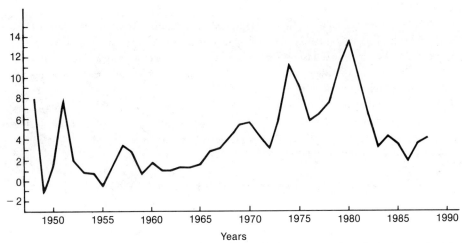

Figure 8.4. Average Annual Rates of Inflation. The inflation rate rose abruptly during much of the 1970s and early 1980s, then fell sharply during the 1983–1988 period. (Source: Percent changes in CPI, Year to Year 1948–1987, *Economic Report of the President,* January 1989; 1988 calculated from Monthly Labor Review, March 1989.)

increased abruptly during much of the 1970s and early 1980s. The inflation rate fell sharply during the 1983–1988 period. Reasons for the changes in the inflation rate during the 1970–1988 period will be discussed in Chapter 12.

Using the Implicit Price Deflator to Calculate Real GNP

Nominal (or current) GNP is the *money* value of goods and services sold at current prices. Nominal GNP is not a good measure of the physical amount of output produced since it does not control for changes in the level of prices. For example, an increase in the level of prices could cause nominal GNP to rise despite the fact that the production of goods has stayed the same (or even declined!). Economists calculate ***real GNP*** to measure the physical amount of goods and services produced.

The implicit price deflator is used to compute real GNP. As we mentioned in the introduction to this section, the implicit price deflator is a broader measure of the level of prices than the consumer price index since it estimates the prices of all goods produced in the market (not just consumer goods). Real GNP is calculated by dividing nominal GNP by the implicit price deflator (using 1982 as the base year), multiplying the result by 100. For example, nominal GNP was $4,486 billion in 1987. Real GNP for 1987 measured in *constant 1982 dollars* was $3,818 billion, calculated as:

$$\text{(nominal GNP in 1987)/(implicit price deflator for 1987)} \times 100 =$$
$$(\$4,486 \text{ billion}/117.5) \times 100 = \$3,818 \text{ billion}$$

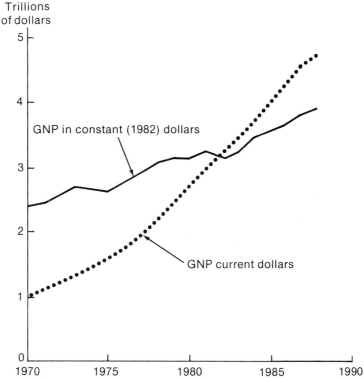

Figure 8.5. Nominal and Real GNP from 1970 to 1988. Because of inflation, nominal GNP overstates the growth in real output (shown by real GNP). (Source: 1970–1986, *Statistical Abstract of the U.S.*, 1988; 1987–1988, *Economic Report of the President*, January 1989.)

Movements in real GNP measure changes in the level of output. Figure 8.5 illustrates the growth of real and nominal GNP in the United States from 1970 to 1988. Note that, while real GNP fell during 1973–1975 and 1979–1982, nominal GNP rose because of inflation.

See the *Data Appendix* for more comprehensive statistics on the CPI and inflation.

Types of Inflation

There are several causes of inflation. Just as individual prices might rise because of shifts in either demand or supply curves, aggregate prices can rise because of shifts in either aggregate demand (total spending) or aggregate supply (total production). **Demand-pull inflation** occurs when aggregate demand is greater than full-employment output. When the economy is at full employment, an increase in aggregate demand will have the effect of pulling up the general level of prices because no new output can be produced to meet the resulting excess demand. As a result, buyers will be bidding against each other, forcing up the level of prices.

Demand-pull inflation is not the only type of inflation. A second type is called *cost-push inflation,* where average prices increase as a result of increases in input costs such as oil and labor. Chapters 9, 10, and 11 deal with demand-pull inflation and its consequences. Cost-push inflation is discussed in Chapter 12. Another major concern to be examined in all of these chapters is the problem of unemployment.

8.4 Measuring Unemployment

As mentioned earlier, unemployment can be devastating. The social costs of unemployment are high. There are the monetary costs in terms of the lost income and the nonmonetary costs (e.g., psychological costs and antisocial behavior) to the people who have lost their jobs and to their families. In this section we discuss how to measure unemployment, and we distinguish the different types of unemployment.

The Unemployment Rate

The federal government conducts a survey each month to determine the number of persons, 16 years or older, who are unemployed. The results of this survey are used to calculate the *unemployment rate*, which measures the percent of people in the labor force who are able and willing to work but cannot find employment despite their active search for a job. As can be seen in Figure 8.6, the unemployment rate has varied widely over the past sixty years from a high of 25 percent during the Great Depression (1929–41) to a low of approximately 1.5 percent during World War II (1941–45).

Many economists feel that the reported unemployment rate does not accurately reflect the true number of people unemployed. First, people working part-time because they cannot find full-time employment are not counted as "part"-unemployed; they are treated as being fully employed. Second, people working in jobs for which they are overqualified are treated as fully employed rather than underemployed. Finally, anyone who has quit looking for work is not counted as being a part of the labor force. Some people stop looking due to the frustration of not being able to find work rather than the desire not to work.

Types of Unemployment

There are four types of unemployment. *Frictional unemployment* occurs when people who are looking for a *better* job or who have entered the labor force for the first time (such as college graduates) are easily able to find employment. Frictional unemployment is not considered to be a problem to the economy since mobility is needed for economic growth. Imagine what would happen if people stayed at the first job they took.

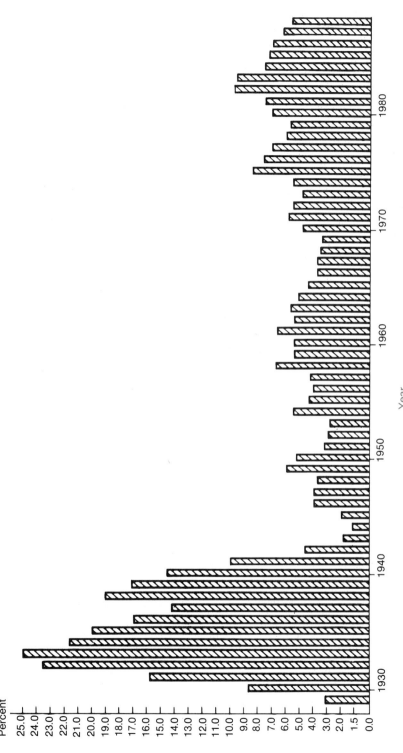

Figure 8.6. Annual Unemployment Rates for the Past 60 Years. Unemployment peaked during the Great Depression at about 25 percent, varying between approximately 1 percent and 10 percent in the following years. (From U.S. Department of Labor.)

Second, ***structural unemployment*** exists when people are out of work because of a mismatch in the composition of the supply and demand for labor. There are three major reasons for structural unemployment. First, some people are unemployed because they lack the education and skills required for job openings (e.g., a mismatch occurs when high school dropouts look for work in a market that requires college-level computer programming skills). Second, some people fail to find jobs because they reside in the wrong geographic locations (e.g., in ghettos or coal-mining regions where the local economy is depressed). Finally, people who face discrimination in the job market (e.g., minorities and women) have a more difficult time becoming employed because some firms will not hire them based on personal characteristics unrelated to the job. They also lack equal access to information concerning job openings and training opportunities.

Third, there is ***seasonal unemployment*** caused by people who are periodically laid off because of changes in the seasons. For example, auto workers are temporarily unemployed each fall as the auto producers retool to produce new car models.

Finally, there is ***cyclical unemployment*** which is caused by insufficient demand which creates the recessionary phase of the business cycle. When overall business activity declines due to decreases in aggregate demand below full-employment supply, unemployment will increase.

When economists define ***full employment***, they mean that 95 percent of the labor force is employed. This allows for 5 percent frictional and structural unemployment which are excluded since our major concern is cyclical unemployment.

8.5 Introduction to the Business Cycle

This section describes the various phases of the business cycle and the economic performance of the United States.

The Nature of the Business Cycle

Business cycles are divided into four parts. See Figure 8.7. The ***expansion*** phase occurs when spending is growing. The ***peak*** takes place when money GNP is highest relative to full employment. A *recession* or *depression* happens when there is a ***contraction*** in the economy caused by a decrease in spending. Finally, the ***trough*** or bottom of the business cycle is the lowest point of business activity relative to how much could be produced.

The difference between depression and recession is a matter of degree, where *recession* is much less severe in terms of the degree of unemployment and excess plant capacity. While the U.S. Department of Commerce uses two consecutive quarters of negative economic growth as an indicator of a possible recession, the official designation of what constitutes a recession is left up to the subjective judgment of the National Bureau of Economic Research (NBER).

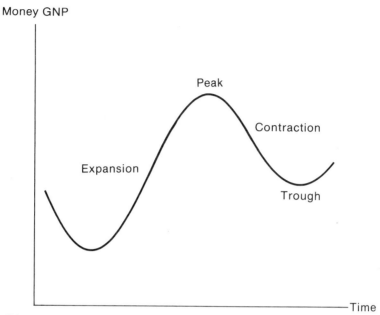

Figure 8.7. The Pattern of the Typical Business Cycle. An increase in total spending causes output to expand to the peak, where output is highest relative to potential output. A decrease in spending causes output to contract until it reaches a trough.

The NBER has devoted many years to the study of business cycles by an in-depth analysis of a great deal of economic data. They use three different measures to help predict where the economy is currently heading. The index of *leading indicators* includes such variables as the change in inventories, new construction, and a stock market index. These variables reflect upswings and downswings in the economy before GNP actually shows the change. For example, before production actually increases, inventories will decrease, indicating that not enough is currently being produced. Therefore, if the index assumes an upward movement, that would indicate GNP will rise, and vice versa. Second are *coincident indicators* which move with the general activity of the economy. Examples are current GNP and the unemployment rate. Finally, there are *lagging indicators,* which reflect changes after the economy has turned up or down and are used to confirm whatever signal the leading indicators gave. An example of this is business spending on new plant and equipment. Businesses tend to revise their plans after they have evidence that the economy is headed in a given direction.

See the *Data Appendix* at the end of this book for examples of some of these data.

The U.S. Business Cycle, 1920–1989

The economic performance of the United States is illustrated in Figure 8.8, developed by the Ameritrust Corporation. The growth trend in the economy is indicated by the horizontal axis. It is assumed that the potential growth in GNP is 4 percent. Whenever the level of output of the economy (represented by the shaded area) is below the horizontal trend line, the economy is growing at a rate less than 4 percent per year, and whenever above the horizontal line, GNP is growing more than 4 percent a year. The line that is not shaded indicates changes in the level of prices representing inflation.

The belief prior to the 1920s was that if the economy was left alone, it would arrive naturally at full employment. After World War I (1919) the economy was generally booming. Rapid expansion was generated by the development of new products such as the car and the telephone and generally favorable expectations about the economy. Industrial production fell abruptly in the summer of 1929, signalling the start of the Great Depression. Unemployment reached 25 percent in the early 1930s. There was no social safety net to catch those people hurt by the fall in the economy.

The economy made a major recovery during World War II owing to the huge increase in military spending. As a result of the Great Depression, a revolution in economic thinking spread (called the Keynesian revolution). More government involvement was believed necessary to soften future downturns. For example, the Federal Deposit Insurance Corporation (FDIC) was established to insure bank accounts against bank failures. Unemployment compensation and social security were also implemented during this period to lessen the impact of the depressed economy.

After World War II, as the economy converted to peacetime production, there was a slight recession. It did not last long, as demand increased in the United States because of the Korean War (1950–1953).

A recession occurred after the Korean War. However, in the mid-1960s, the Kennedy tax cuts stimulated the economy. This was the first time the government deliberately attempted to move GNP toward full employment. Increased military expenditures in the late 1960s because of the greater involvement in the war in Vietnam pushed unemployment to under 4 percent. The war grew in size and expenditures increased, but there was no corresponding increase in taxes to finance the military effort. Instead, the government opted for increased borrowing. As a result of this increased demand, inflation rose significantly. Inflation was considered the major economic problem during the late 1960s and early 1970s. This led the Nixon administration to impose wage and price controls in 1971. Government expenditures did not rise as rapidly because of the decreased spending on the Vietnam War. The result was a recession. But because of increases in the price of food and energy, decreases in productivity, and inflationary expectations built up in the 1960s, prices continued to rise. This condition is called stagflation because unemployment and inflation are rising at the same time. Specifically, unemployment was greater than 10 percent and inflation was above 12 percent. The economy hit a trough in 1975, followed by a period of growth. But high inflation remained a problem. By 1980, inflation was again above 12 percent. In the early 1980s, high interest rates reduced

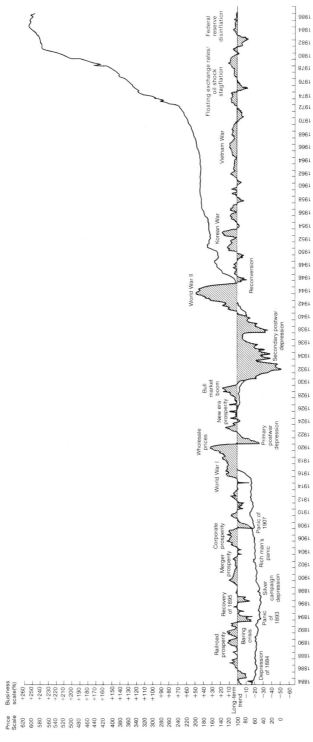

Figure 8.8. The Business Cycle in the American Economy from 1884 to 1986. The cycle of business activity in the United States is associated with major historical events. (From The Ameritrust Corporation.)

investment and consumer spending, resulting in one of the largest downturns in modern U.S. economic history. This recession lasted into 1983, during which inflation was a modest 5 percent, but unemployment was still approximately 10 percent.

The expansion that began in 1983 continued into 1989. Unfortunately, this period of expansion may be ending. At the time of writing, fears of recession have resurfaced as the inflation rate rose slightly, growth slowed, and unemployment increased.

Summary

Macroeconomics involves the study of aggregate economic behavior. The major issues of importance are unemployment, inflation, and growth. GNP is the value of final output produced in the economy in a given period of time and can be measured by using either the expenditure or the income approach. GNP provides only a rough measure of production because it does not include nonmarket and illegal transactions. In addition, GNP falls short as a measure of well-being. For example, it cannot describe the distribution of income, and it cannot measure the value of leisure.

The consumer price index is the most commonly used measure of inflation. Price indexes are important because they enable us to distinguish between real and nominal changes in GNP. Inflation may be caused by pressures on the demand or supply side.

There are four types of unemployment. Frictional unemployment occurs when people first enter the labor force or are between jobs. Those who are structurally unemployed are unable to find jobs because their skills are no longer in demand. Seasonal unemployment exists because some types of production processes require the temporary layoff of labor. Finally, cyclical unemployment occurs when people are unable to find work owing to insufficient aggregate demand.

Key Concepts

aggregate demand/aggregate supply
inflation
gross national product (GNP)
expenditure and income approaches
personal consumption expenditures
gross private domestic investment
government purchases of goods and services
net exports
market versus nonmarket transactions
legal versus illegal transactions
net national product (NNP)

national income (NI)
personal income (PI)
disposable income (DI)
consumer price index (CPI)
implicit price deflator
base year
nominal or current GNP
real GNP
demand-pull inflation
cost-push inflation
unemployment rate
frictional, structural, seasonal, and cyclical unemployment
full employment
expansion/peak/contraction/trough

Self-Test Questions: True or False

T   F   1. Macroeconomics involves the study of aggregate demand and supply.

T   F   2. An example of inflation is an increase in the cost of crude oil, causing only the price of gasoline to rise.

T   F   3. Gross national product is the market value of *all* goods and services produced in a given period of time.

T   F   4. Gross national product does include the capital goods that are worn out in the production of current output.

T   F   5. The consumer price index fails to take into account how consumers change their spending in response to changes in prices.

T   F   6. An increase in nominal GNP always indicates that output has increased.

T   F   7. If nominal GNP is valued at $150 million in 1980 and the price index for 1980 is 150 (base year = 1970), real GNP is $100 million.

T   F   8. Demand-pull inflation is caused by excess aggregate demand at full-employment output.

T   F   9. The unemployment rate is a measure of all people out of work.

T   F   10. When someone is unable to find employment because of a lack of demand for people with that particular skill, he or she is said to be cyclically unemployed.

Answers to Self-Test Questions

1. ***True.*** Macroeconomics deals with the aggregate demand and supply of goods and services. It is concerned with what motivates spending and savings decisions and

how changes in spending affect GNP. In contrast, microeconomics deals with the study of the individual consumer and producer, and their interaction in the marketplace.

2. *False.* When one price goes up in the marketplace, that is a normal occurrence reflecting the changes in demand or supply that caused it. Inflation occurs when there is a general rise in prices. If the increase in the cost of oil were to cause prices in general to rise, this would be an example of inflation originating on the supply side.

3. *False.* To avoid double counting, GNP does not include the value of *all* goods and services. Only the value of *final* goods and services produced is included. Final goods are made up of expenditures on all finished goods. If the cost of the thread and material is included in GNP together with the price of the dress they made, the thread and material will have been included in GNP twice.

4. *True.* GNP does include the value of capital goods used up in the production of current output. In order to calculate the net increase in output, depreciation must be deducted from GNP. The resulting figure is called Net National Product (NNP).

5. *True.* When prices rise, the consumer price index will increase. But when these prices increase, consumers will shift to less expensive products. For example, when the price of Coke goes up, people will substitute Pepsi or other cola alternatives. The calculation of the CPI falsely assumes that consumers will continue to buy the same amount of Coke.

6. *False.* When nominal GNP rises, it is possible for real GNP to increase, decrease, or remain the same. For example, assume nominal GNP is $4,000 billion this year. If the level of prices rises next year while the level of real GNP remains the same, nominal GNP will increase.

7. *True.* To calculate real GNP, nominal GNP must be divided by the price index $\times$ 100. In this example, nominal GNP of $150 million is divided by 150, because a price index of 150 indicates that prices have increased 50 percent above their original level in the base year. The result is a real GNP of $100 million.

8. *True.* Demand-pull inflation occurs when aggregate demand exceeds full-employment output. Since output cannot increase, prices will rise.

9. *False.* The unemployment rate is calculated by looking at those persons who are in the labor force. The labor force includes people who are unable to find jobs but are still searching. If a person is no longer looking for employment, he or she is no longer counted as part of the labor force and is not included in the unemployment rate.

10. *False.* People who are out of work because of a lack of demand for their skills are structurally unemployed. Cyclical unemployment refers to those people who cannot find employment because of inadequate aggregate demand.

Discussion Questions

1. What are the three major problems with which macroeconomics attempts to deal?

2. Describe the two approaches for measuring GNP. Discuss the alternative measures of income (e.g., NNP, NI).

3. Explain why GNP is not a "perfect" measure of the market value of final goods and services produced. Why is GNP not considered a good measure of well-being?

4. Differentiate between the four types of unemployment. Why is the unemployment rate an imperfect measure of the percentage of people out of work?

5. Discuss the four parts of the business cycle. Using the *Data Appendix* located at the end of the text, examine figures on GNP, unemployment, and consumer prices. Chart the series to see how they relate to the business cycle shown in Figure 8.8.

Problems

The country of Tricknaut reports the following figures for the cost of a market basket for the last five years.

	Money Value of Market Basket
1987	$ 400
1988	750
1989	1,450
1990	2,560
1991	3,500

1. Assuming the base year is 1988, compute the price index for each year.

2. Using the price indexes from your answer to question 1, determine the real value of the market basket for each year. Compare the change in the real value of output to the change in the money value of output.

CHAPTER

9

An Introduction to the Keynesian Model

Objectives

Upon completion of this chapter, you should understand:

1. The components of aggregate demand and how changes in spending affect production.

2. How excess or insufficient demand causes inflation and unemployment.

3. The difference between the classical and the Keynesian models.

Approximately fifty years ago our country went through one of the most trying times it has ever experienced — the Great Depression. The depression, which lasted from 1929 to 1941, called into question the conventional wisdom of that era called classical economics. While classical economists acknowledged that temporary setbacks could occur, they believed that the price system would automatically bring the economy back to full employment. The severity of the Great Depression led John Maynard Keynes, a British economist, to develop a theory to explain this breakdown of the private market economy. The swiftness of the adoption of his theory by other economists, and the seemingly radical departure from classical economics, caused this new theory to be called the Keynesian revolution.

The purpose of this chapter is to examine the forces that affect employment, production, and prices. We begin by examining the Keynesian model of income determination and the component parts of aggregate demand. We then discuss how unemployment and inflation are explained by the Keynesian model. We conclude the chapter by examining the assumptions and conclusions of the classical model in light of the information shed by the Keynesian revolution.

9.1 The Behavior of Consumption, Savings, and Investment

According to the **Keynesian model,** a change in *aggregate demand* (or total spending) is the primary cause of the business cycle. In this chapter we are assuming that there is no government or international trade in order to simplify our description of the Keynesian model. This narrows our focus down to households (that consume or save) and firms (that invest). **Total consumption,** which is spending by households, is the largest component of the overall demand for goods and services. It is important to study the behavior of consumer spending because changes in consumption have a major impact on the business cycle.

Induced Consumption and Induced Savings

Consumption   Clearly, the most important determinant of how much a household plans to spend on consumer goods such as refrigerators, food, and clothing is the level of disposable income. In the examples that follow, disposable income equals GNP because we are initially assuming that there is no government. An increase in GNP will *induce* households to spend more. Likewise, if GNP falls, households will be expected to reduce their spending. The relationship of consumer spending to changes in income is called **induced consumption.** See Table 9.1 which uses hypothetical numbers to describe the Keynesian model. When income changes from $3,800 billion to $3,900 billion (an increase of $100 billion), consumption rises from $3,480 billion to $3,560 billion (an increase of $80 billion). The fraction of additional income that households plan to spend is called the **marginal propensity to consume (MPC).**

241

We calculate it as

$$MPC = \frac{\text{change in consumption}}{\text{change in income}} = \$+80/\$+100 = 0.8$$

An *MPC* of 0.8 means that for every $1 increase in income, consumption will increase by 80 cents.

Savings The amount of income that is received by households but is not spent is called *savings.* For example, in Table 9.1, when income is $3,900 billion, households plan to spend $3,560 billion, leaving $340 billion in savings (see column 3). Thus, the relationship between consumption and savings is expressed as

$$S = GNP - C$$

We noted that if income rose from $3,800 billion to $3,900 billion, households would increase spending from $3,480 billion to $3,560 billion. This increase would also induce households to raise their savings from $320 billion to $340 billion (see column 3, Table 9.1). The fraction that households save out of additional income is called the *marginal propensity to save (MPS).* It is calculated as

$$MPS = \frac{\text{change in savings}}{\text{change in income}} = \$+20/\$+100 = 0.2$$

Table 9.1
Income, Consumption, and
Savings (billions of dollars)

(1) GNP	(2) Consumption (C)	(3) Savings (S)
$ 0	$ 440	$−440
.	.	.
.	.	.
.	.	.
3,800	3,480	320
3,900	3,560	340
4,000	3,640	360
4,100	3,720	380
4,200	3,800	400
4,300	3,880	420

It follows that if people are spending 80 cents out of each additional dollar earned, the remaining 20 cents is saved.

Just as higher income induces households to save more, lower income causes them to save less. If their income were to fall low enough, households might even spend more than they earn (see Table 9.1). In the first row, when the income level is $0 billion, consumption is $440 billion and there is a negative amount of savings of $440 billion. How can people spend more than they are currently earning? They *dissave* (i.e., draw on past savings).

Autonomous Consumption and Autonomous Savings

In addition to the effect of income, there are other influences on the behavior of households in their decision to spend or save. *Autonomous consumption* is the amount of consumer spending that is not related to GNP. It picks up the effects of all nonincome influences on consumption. We can see in Table 9.1 that households would plan to spend $440 billion if GNP were zero; therefore, autonomous consumption is $440 billion. Likewise, *autonomous saving* is the amount of consumer saving that is not related to GNP. Changes in any nonincome influence will lead to a change in consumer spending and saving independent of the level of income.

An important determinant of consumption is wealth. A decrease in wealth would be expected to lead to a decrease in spending. For example, on October 19, 1987, when the stock market crashed, households that saw their wealth decline postponed the purchase of expensive items such as luxury cars and condominiums. Another factor is the interest rate charged for consumer credit. If interest rates rise, it becomes more expensive to finance consumer purchases; therefore, increases in the interest rate will tend to reduce consumption regardless of the level of income. The age of the stock of durable goods will also influence consumption spending. As cars break down and refrigerators wear out with the passage of time, they will have to be replaced, causing an increase in autonomous consumption.

In addition to the *objective* factors discussed previously, there are three types of *subjective* influences on consumption. First, there are psychological drives such as precaution, foresight, pride in saving money, and greed. For example, many people attain great pride from saving more than others. Second, peer or social pressure ("keeping up with the Joneses") is a common influence on spending. Often, we will spend more than we had originally anticipated in order to keep pace with purchases made by our friends or neighbors. Finally, there are consumer expectations. These include expectations about future income and prices. If real income is anticipated to be lower in the future, savings will increase in the present in order to help maintain consumption spending in the future. Likewise, many students spend more than their current income. They borrow money now (dissave) in the anticipation of greater future incomes upon graduation. Expectations concerning changes in the level of prices also affect consumer behavior. For example, if prices are expected to be higher in the future, households will want to increase current purchases to try to "beat inflation."

If any of the autonomous factors change, the entire consumption and savings schedule will change. The impact of changes in autonomous consumption and autonomous savings on the economy will be examined in Section 9.4.

243

Determinants of Planned Investment

The other major category of spending in the private sector is **planned investment.** Planned investment is the intended expenditure by firms for acquiring new plant and equipment and for building up inventories. These expenditures differ from **unplanned investment (an unintended change in inventories).** The amount that firms actually spend on investment is equal to their planned expenditures on plant, equipment, and inventories plus any unintended change in inventories. For example, suppose that firms had planned to invest $200 billion. If their sales are $50 billion below the level expected, they will find their inventories (unsold goods) rise $50 billion above the planned level. Therefore, **actual investment** is $250 billion, equal to planned investment of $200 billion plus the unintended change in inventories (unplanned investment) of $50 billion.

The primary determinant of whether or not a firm will decide to build a new building, order more equipment, or build up its inventories is its profit expectations. If the firm sees the potential to sell more in the future, it is likely to invest more now. On the other hand, if expectations are bleak, the firm will want to cut back its expenditures on new plant and equipment.

A major factor influencing a firm's profit expectations is the cost of financing investment. If there is an increase in the interest rate, the firm will not be willing to spend as much on investment. Alternatively, if the costs of financing investment decrease, the firm will want to increase its spending on new plant and equipment to take advantage of additional profitable opportunities. To simplify this discussion, we assume there is only **autonomous investment,** which means that all planned investment is independent of income and is related only to changes in nonincome determinants such as the interest rate. In column 4 of Table 9.2, planned investment (I_P) is equal to $340 billion at all levels of GNP.

The purpose of the following section is to examine how expenditures by consumers and investors affect production. For simplicity, government expenditures and taxes are not considered in this chapter. Their impact on the economy will be studied in Chapter 10.

9.2 Equilibrium GNP

Equilibrium GNP is the only level of income that the economy will be able to sustain. Market conditions will force actual (current) GNP toward the equilibrium level. Once the actual level of GNP stabilizes at equilibrium, it will remain there until there is a change in autonomous spending. Two conditions are necessary for equilibrium: (1) aggregate demand must equal aggregate supply, and (2) savings must equal planned investment.

Condition One: Aggregate Demand Equals Aggregate Supply

Equilibrium occurs at that level of GNP where **aggregate demand $(C + I_P)$ equals aggregate supply** (GNP). As Table 9.2 indicates, equilibrium GNP is $3,900 billion because

Table 9.2
Determination of Equilibrium Level of Income (billions of dollars)

(1) Aggregate Supply (GNP)	(2) Consumption (C)	(3) Savings (S)	(4) Planned Investment (I_P)	(5) Aggregate Demand (C + I_P)	(6) Unplanned Investment	(7) Direction of Change in GNP
$3,600	$3,320	$280	$340	$3,660	$-60	Increase
3,700	3,400	300	340	3,740	-40	Increase
3,800	3,480	320	340	3,820	$-20	Increase
3,900	3,560	340	340	3,900	0	Equilibrium
4,000	3,640	360	340	3,980	20	Decrease
4,100	3,720	380	340	4,060	40	Decrease
4,200	3,800	400	340	4,140	60	Decrease
4,300	3,880	420	340	4,220	80	Decrease

aggregate demand (column 5) is equal to aggregate supply (column 1) at this level of production. There is no excess demand or excess supply. All that is currently being produced is bought. As a result, inventories do not change — unplanned investment (the unintended change in inventories) is equal to zero (see column 6). Once GNP has reached $3,900 billion, it will stabilize there.

Why will the current level of GNP gravitate to the equilibrium position? To understand this concept better, let us consider GNP levels in Table 9.2 which are greater or less than equilibrium GNP.

Actual GNP Greater Than Equilibrium   If aggregate supply is $4,100 billion, aggregate demand is $4,060 billion. In column 6, unplanned investment (or unintended change in inventories) is equal to $40 billion, or the difference between the amount supplied ($4,100 billion) and the amount demanded ($4,060 billion). The excess inventories will cause firms to reduce production. Producers will continue to cut back production until aggregate supply is equal to aggregate demand, which causes unplanned investment to be zero.

Actual GNP Less Than Equilibrium   If aggregate supply is $3,700 billion in Table 9.2, aggregate demand is $3,740 billion, which is greater by $40 billion than the amount being supplied. How will this excess demand be satisfied? Since current output is not adequate to satisfy demand, inventories will fall below their desired level. In column 6, unplanned investment (or unintended change in inventories) is equal to $\$-40$ billion or the difference between what is being supplied (\$3,700 billion) and the amount demanded (\$3,740 billion). Producers will see their inventories falling below their desired stock and will increase production until aggregate demand is exactly equal to aggregate supply, which causes actual inventories to equal the planned level.

Condition Two: Leakages Equal Injections

Another way we can describe the equilibrium level of GNP is called the **leakages-injection equality.** With an economy that excludes government, leakages, which represent income not spent, must always equal injections, which represents planned spending injected from business. In other words, **savings equals planned investment.** At the equilibrium GNP of \$3,900 billion in Table 9.2, savings (in column 3) are \$340 billion. Thus, savings are exactly equal to planned investment (in column 4) of \$340 billion (i.e., leakages equal injections), which is not true at any other level of production. Therefore, planned investment injects \$340 billion into spending, replacing the \$340 billion not spent by households (savings). At the equilibrium GNP of \$3,900 billion, unplanned investment is zero, indicating that firms are investing exactly the amount they intended to invest. Given this second equilibrium condition, what would happen if actual GNP were greater than or less than the equilibrium position?

Actual GNP Greater Than Equilibrium If GNP were \$4,100 billion (Table 9.2), households would save \$380 billion. At the \$4,100 billion level of production, planned investment would be \$340 billion. If savings (income not spent) are greater than planned investment, the amount supplied exceeds the amount demanded and too much will be produced. Firms will be forced to accept a buildup of unplanned inventories of \$40 billion. As a result, producers will decrease production. Only at equilibrium will planned investment equal savings.

Actual GNP Less Than Equilibrium At a level of production of \$3,700 billion, which is below equilibrium, savings are \$300 billion and actual investment is also \$300 billion (planned investment of \$340 billion plus unplanned investment of \$-40 billion). In this case the amount demanded exceeds the amount supplied because savings (income not spent) are less than planned investment (creation of capital). Firms would increase production to meet this excess demand.

9.3 Impact of Changes in Autonomous Demand: The Income Multiplier

The basic structure of the Keynesian model has been examined with an emphasis on the forces that determine the equilibrium level of GNP. We will now analyze the impact of a change in autonomous demand on equilibrium GNP.

Changes in Autonomous Investment

What would happen to the investment plans of firms if the interest rate were to change? If the interest rate were to fall, more projects would become profitable because the cost of financing the purchase of new capital would be lower. As a result, planned investment would increase, causing aggregate demand to rise. Since current equilibrium income would no longer be sufficient to meet this increased demand, GNP would grow.

Assume that as a result of a drop in the interest rate, planned investment rises from $340 billion to $400 billion (see Table 9.3). Table 9.3 reproduces Table 9.2 with one exception: planned investment is now $400 billion. When the interest rate was higher, planned investment was $340 billion, resulting in an equilibrium GNP of $3,900 billion. With the increase in planned investment to $400 billion, the initial equilibrium GNP of $3,900 billion is not sufficient since aggregate demand is $3,960 billion. Total demand exceeds total supply by $60 billion. Firms will step up production. The level of GNP at which aggregate demand is equal to aggregate supply is $4,200 billion. At the $4,200 billion level, planned investment equals savings, which results in no unintended change in inventories. Thus, this $60 billion increase in planned investment led to a $300 billion increase in equilibrium GNP.

Table 9.3
Impact of a $60 Increase in Planned Investment on Equilibrium Income (billions of dollars)

(1) Aggregate Supply (GNP)	(2) Consumption (C)	(3) Savings (S)	(4) New Planned Investment ($I_{p'}$)	(5) New Aggregate Demand (C + $I_{p'}$)
$3,800	$3,480	$320	**$400**	**$3,880**
3,900	3,560	340	**400**	**3,960**
4,000	3,640	360	**400**	**4,040**
4,100	3,720	380	**400**	**4,120**
4,200	3,800	400	**400**	**4,200**
4,300	3,880	420	**400**	**4,280**

In addition to an increase or decrease in the interest rate causing planned investment to fall or rise, any of the other nonincome determinants of planned investment mentioned previously could also cause a change. For example, if expectations about future profit worsened, planned investment would decline, which in turn would result in a decrease in equilibrium GNP by an amount greater than the initial decrease in autonomous investment.

Changes in Autonomous Consumption

Suppose that the economy were expected to slide into a recession. Workers fearing that they would be laid off in the future would now spend less at all levels of income. The reduction in autonomous consumption causes aggregate demand to decrease. This would cause GNP to fall as producers cut back their output in response to the unexpected buildup of their inventories.

Table 9.4 illustrates the lower level of autonomous consumption (column 2), the increase in autonomous savings (column 3), and the resulting decrease in aggregate demand (column 5). With the original consumption schedule, equilibrium income is $3,900 billion (see Table 9.2). With the decrease in autonomous consumption by $20 billion, the equilibrium level of income will fall from $3,900 billion to $3,800 billion. Why? At the initial equilibrium level of $3,900 billion, households are planning to buy $20 billion less than firms had planned to sell. As a result, there is a $20 billion buildup of unwanted inventories. Firms respond by cutting back production. At the equilibrium level, aggregate demand is exactly equal to aggregate supply and planned investment equals savings.

The Income Multiplier

Why did GNP change by five times the change in autonomous spending? The phenomenon is known as the income multiplier.

Table 9.4
Impact of a $20 Decrease in Autonomous Consumption on Equilibrium Income (billions of dollars)

(1) Aggregate Supply (GNP)	(2) New Consumption (C')	(3) New Savings (S')	(4) Original Level of Planned Investment (I_p)	(5) New Aggregate Demand (C' + I_p)
$3,800	$3,460	$340	$340	$3,800
3,900	3,540	360	340	3,880
4,000	3,620	380	340	3,960
4,100	3,700	400	340	4,040
4,200	3,780	420	340	4,120
4,300	3,860	440	340	4,200

The Inner Workings of the Multiplier Process An initial change in planned investment leads to an immediate increase in output (see Table 9.5). If producers place additional
orders for machinery for $60 billion, output will go up by $60 billion in the first round of the
income multiplier process. But the process does not end there. The $60 billion of production
becomes income for the owners of the resources used to produce the new machinery. This
increased income will *induce* these resource owners to spend more money on consumer goods.
For example, the workers earning additional income may buy more clothes. The amount of
additional spending depends on the marginal propensity to consume *(MPC)*. In the preceding
examples, the *MPC* was 0.8, which means that for each additional dollar earned, 80 cents
will be spent (with the remaining 20 cents being put into savings). If income rises by $60
billion in the first round, consumption will increase by $48 billion in the second round, since
households spend 80 percent of their additional income. Again the process is not complete,
since the increased spending of $48 billion on clothes will become additional income for the
workers producing this clothing. They, in turn, will spend 80 percent of $48 billion, or $38.4
billion in the third round. The successive rounds, in which spending creates income which in
turn is spent, become smaller and smaller.

The end result of the income multiplier process is a total increase of $300 billion in GNP.
Note that the two equilibrium conditions are met since the resulting $300 billion change in
total demand (consumption plus investment) equals the $300 billion increase in total supply
(GNP). Also, the $60 billion rise in planned investment equals the $60 billion change in
savings by households.

The Algebraic Definition of the Multiplier The overall impact of the income
multiplier process is calculated by multiplying the ***income multiplier*** by the change in

Table 9.5
Income Multiplier Process (billions of dollars)

	Change in Investment	Change in Consumption	Change in Income	Change in Savings
First round	$+60.00	0	$+ 60.00	0
Second round	0	$+ 48.00	+ 48.00	$+12.00
Third round	0	+ 38.40	+ 38.40	+ 9.60
Fourth round	0	+ 30.72	+ 30.72	+ 7.68
Fifth round	0	+ 24.58	+ 24.58	+ 6.14
All other rounds	0	+ 98.30	+ 98.30	+24.58
TOTALS	$+60.00	$+240.00	$+300.00	$+60.00

Note: Change in total demand = change in total supply = $+300.00; change in planned investment = change
in savings = $+60.00.

249

autonomous expenditures. We noted that the multiplier is directly related to the MPC, which means that it is inversely related to the MPS. The income multiplier in this simplified model is the reciprocal of the marginal propensity to save, or

$$\text{income multiplier} = \frac{1}{MPS}$$

Since $MPC + MPS = 1$, it follows that $MPS = 1 - MPC$. Therefore, the income multiplier can also be expressed as

$$\text{income multiplier} = 1/(1 - MPC)$$

In the example above, the MPC is 0.8 or $\frac{4}{5}$ and the MPS is 0.2 or $\frac{1}{5}$, so that

$$\text{income multiplier} = \frac{1}{1 - \frac{4}{5}} = \frac{1}{\frac{1}{5}} = 5$$

Given an income multiplier of 5, if autonomous investment were to increase by $60 billion, equilibrium GNP would rise by 5 times that amount, or $300 billion (the result described earlier).

The income multiplier can also be utilized to calculate the change in equilibrium GNP resulting from a drop in autonomous consumption spending as

$$\text{change in GNP} = \frac{1}{MPS} \text{ (change in autonomous } C)$$
$$= 5 \times \$-20 = \$-100$$

Remember in Table 9.2 equilibrium GNP was $3,900 billion. Assume that autonomous consumption falls by $20 billion. The multiplier indicates that when autonomous consumption decreases by $20 billion at every level of income, equilibrium GNP will fall by $100 billion (from $3,900 to $3,800 billion).

9.4 Recessionary Gap, Inflationary Gap, and Stabilization Policy

One of Keynes's main criticisms of the classical model was its belief that the economy would achieve full-employment equilibrium automatically. The purpose of this section is to explain the Keynesian position that there is nothing inherent in the private market that would cause GNP to stabilize at the full-employment level.

What Happens When Housing Expenditures Increase?

As the economy moved out of the recent recession and interest rates fell, the housing industry became revitalized. The National Association of Home Builders estimated that when one average house is built, the total economic impact is $148,000.

The reason for this impact is the effect of the multiplier. Many industries depend directly on the activity of the housing industry. Using a technique called input–output analysis, the University of Maryland's Interindustry Forecasting Project estimated the impact of an increase in housing sales on other industries. The most obvious beneficiary is the builder. Assuming that 1.44 million new housing units were started, 1,176,600 jobs would be created. This would involve over $38 billion in sales. This construction would require almost $12 billion in lumber for plywood and cabinets and would increase employment by 130,400 jobs.

Related industries that would benefit include transportation and trade (moving materials from production points to users); stone, clay, glass (concrete, brick, cement); fabricated metals (doors, storm windows, siding, plumbing fixtures); business services (lawyers, architects); nonelectrical equipment (furnaces, water heaters, gas stoves); primary metals; electrical machinery (washers, lighting equipment); and plastic products (pipe, moldings). All told, the impact on these industries would be over $75 billion, creating more than 1.7 million jobs.

Finally, Kleinfeld notes that other industries, not related to construction, also feel the "ripple effect" of a housing industry boom. For example, when houses are built in suburban areas, people may need a second car for transportation. Therefore, the automobile industry benefits. Other examples include new homeowners' demand for lawn care products, curtains, and all the other things needed to settle into their new houses.

Source: This is a summary of "Who Gains When Housing Prospers?" by N. R. Kleinfeld, which appeared in the Business Section of the *Sunday New York Times* on April 17, 1983.

Full Employment

"Full employment" does not mean that all people are working to their limits (e.g., people including young children working seven days a week, fifty-two weeks a year). Full employment is defined as the employment of all persons 16 years or older who are able and willing to work in the labor market under existing conditions minus the level of frictional and structural unemployment. Full employment is defined as 95 percent employment of the labor force, which allows for a 5 percent level of frictional and structural unemployment. With due consideration of the preferences for leisure, the economic goal is to maximize the production of these goods and services by achieving "full employment." The problems in reaching this goal will be discussed next.

Recessionary Gap

In the introduction to this chapter, we noted that classical economists concluded that the economy would stabilize at *full-employment GNP,* which is the amount of output the economy could produce if there were 95 percent employment of the labor force. The Keynesian revolution argued that this conclusion was not true. Why? Assume that the economy would achieve full employment when $4,200 billion of goods and services were produced (see Table 9.2). What would happen if the firms in the economy actually produced $4,200 billion worth of goods and services? Note that total demand is only $4,140 billion when GNP is $4,200 billion. Firms would find that they had produced $60 billion of goods and services more than consumers and investors wanted to buy. This insufficient spending by households and firms would result in a buildup of unwanted inventories of $60 billion at the $4,200 billion full-employment level of GNP. Consequently, firms would cut back production and lay off workers until they were producing that level of output which people would be willing and able to buy. Note that GNP would stabilize at $3,900 billion since, at this level, firms would be able to sell their total production (aggregate supply equals aggregate demand).

Therefore, people would not automatically buy the amount of goods and services that could be produced at full employment. If demand is insufficient, firms will adjust production downward until they are producing the amount of goods they could sell. This would cause the economy to stabilize below the full-employment level of output.

The amount by which total demand falls short of full-employment GNP is called the ***recessionary gap.*** There is a recessionary gap of $60 billion because total spending is only $4,140 billion at the full-employment level of production ($4,200 billion). The difference between equilibrium GNP and full-employment GNP is called the ***income gap.*** It represents one of the costs of unemployment from the viewpoint of society (i.e., the amount of output lost). In this example, equilibrium GNP is $3,900 billion and full-employment GNP is $4,200 billion, which means there is an income gap of $300 billion.

Inflationary Gap

We just demonstrated that insufficient demand would cause GNP to stabilize below full employment. Households and firms might also attempt to buy more goods and services than the economy could produce at full employment. The amount by which aggregate demand exceeds full-employment supply is called an ***inflationary gap.***

See Table 9.2 again. Assume that the full-employment level of GNP is $3,700 billion (rather than $4,200 billion as in the previous discussion). At the $3,700 billion level of production, aggregate demand stands at $3,740 billion (see column 5). There is an inflationary gap of $40 billion, since total demand exceeds the amount of goods and services that the economy can produce by $40 billion at full employment. This excess demand creates shortages that cannot be eliminated by an increase in production since GNP has reached the full-employment ceiling. The result will be a rise in the overall price level. The resulting rise in prices is called *demand-pull inflation* (see Chapter 8, Section 8.3).

Note that the actual level of GNP has stabilized at $3,900 billion (the same level as in the previous discussion). The difference between the equilibrium GNP and the full-employment GNP of $3,700 billion results in an *income* gap of $200 billion. Since the economy can produce only $3,700 billion worth of goods and services in real terms (i.e., in terms of the number of goods and services such as houses and cars), this $200 billion income gap represents nominal income. As noted in Chapter 8, real income is the purchasing power of nominal income after accounting for the effects of inflation. When people try to spend this $3,900 billion in nominal income to buy the $3,700 billion of goods and services that can actually be produced at full employment, the excess demand causes inflation.

Introduction to Stabilization Policy

Keynes felt that both recessionary and inflationary gaps could be corrected through government action. The federal government could boost aggregate demand when demand was insufficient to sustain full employment, and it could reduce aggregate demand when spending exceeded the level needed for full-employment output. In the next chapter we examine how the government can directly influence aggregate demand through the use of taxation and government spending (fiscal policy).

9.5 Classical Economics and the Keynesian Revolution

The *classical model* argued that there is a tendency for the economy to stabilize automatically at full employment. It concluded that since the economy was self-correcting, there was essentially no need for goverment to intervene to promote full employment.

Flexibility of Prices and Wages

Classical economists argued that the flexibility of prices and wages would ensure restoration of full employment. If spending was not great enough to sustain the full-employment level of production, product prices would fall. This would encourage people to buy more. These lower prices would also lead to lower production and to lower demand for the labor needed to produce this output. In response to competition among unemployed workers looking for jobs, the wage rate would fall, thus making the job seekers more attractive to potential employers. The classical economists believed that this chain of events would continue until all those who were willing and able to work were working, bringing the economy back to full employment.

Say's Law

A basic argument of the classical economists was that production created a level of income sufficient to purchase the goods produced. For example, if $100 of goods were produced, this would result in $100 of income to the owners of the resources employed, giving them the purchasing power needed to buy the $100 worth of goods. In other words, supply created its own demand, known as *Say's law*. The classical economists concluded that everything produced would be purchased, resulting in full employment.

The Role of the Interest Rate

But what if households did not spend all their income? What if they saved some? Classical economists concluded that this would not be a problem as long as someone else immediately spent the income that households saved. For example, businesses frequently invest by borrowing funds to finance expenditures on new buildings and machinery, and to build up their inventories. Funds are made available for investment when households buy stocks and bonds, or when households deposit a part of their income into banks, which in turn make business loans. Classical economists argued that as long as savings equaled investment, full employment would result.

According to the classical model, the interest rate would ensure that savings would equal investment. For example, if households saved more income than firms were willing to borrow, there would be an excess supply of funds available for loans. The expected result when there is a surplus of a good is that its price will fall. As we noted in Section 6.5 of Chapter 6, the price of loanable funds is the interest rate. Therefore, the excess of savings over investment should cause the interest rate to fall. With a fall in interest rates, firms would be willing to borrow more for investment purposes, and households would be likely to save less. This process would continue until savings again equaled investment, which theoretically would restore full employment.

The Keynesian Revolution

The beauty of the classical approach was its simplicity. It did not, however, accurately explain reality in the 1930s. Its primary assumptions and thus its conclusions seemed historically invalid. Owing to the length and severity of the Great Depression, which could not happen according to the classical model, there was a reexamination of the traditional classical theory. It seemed apparent that the economy had indeed stabilized below full employment. John Maynard Keynes, a British economist, led the attack on classical economic theory in his book, *The General Theory of Employment, Interest, and Money,* published in 1936. He raised many questions critical of the classical model.

Keynes pointed out that prices and wages were not flexible downward owing to the influences of labor unions, firms with market power, and government policies such as minimum wage laws. In addition, Keynes argued that the effect of the interest rate is not sufficiently strong to link the savings of households and the investment plans of firms at full employment. He noted that savings and investment decisions are made by different groups for different reasons. For example, households are motivated to save in order to buy expensive durable goods (such as houses or cars) in the future, and to build up a fund for possible emergencies. Firms, on the other hand, want to invest in order to make profits. Although the decisions made by both groups are affected by the interest rate, Keynes argued that the interest rate's influence was not powerful enough to cause households to save the exact amount that firms desire to borrow. Therefore, changes in the interest rate could not force GNP to stabilize at full employment.

In other words, Keynes felt that equilibrium of the economy was possible at less than full employment because of insufficient spending. This was his most damaging criticism of the classical model. He argued that the economy could reach an equilibrium (stabilize) below full employment. According to Keynes, there was nothing inherent in the operation of a private market economy to guarantee that people would want to buy the full-employment level of output. As we will note in Chapter 11, there has been a revival of classical economic thought which has led to development of alternative models to examine macroeconomic problems.

Summary

Prior to the 1930s classical economics was the prevailing school of thought. The classical model argued that there was a tendency for the economy to reach equilibrium at full employment. During the 1930s, the economy in the United States remained in the grips of a severe depression and showed no movement toward full employment. The Keynesian revolution attempted to explain how the economy could be in equilibrium at less than full employment.

In this chapter we examined two components of aggregate demand: consumption and investment. Consumption (household spending) is determined by income and autonomous factors. Actual investment is made up of planned business spending for capital goods and unintended changes in inventories.

Equilibrium GNP is attained when aggregate demand equals aggregate supply and when savings equals planned investment. When there are variations in autonomous consumption or investment, aggregate demand will increase or decrease, causing GNP to change. For example, when autonomous planned investment (I_P) or consumption (C) increase, GNP will rise by an amount greater than the original increase in C or I_P due to the effect of the income multiplier.

The Keynesian model argues that changes in aggregate demand are the primary cause of the business cycle. When aggregate demand is not sufficient to sustain full employment, GNP will fall, stabilizing at a level less than full employment. The amount that aggregate demand falls short of full-employment GNP is called the recessionary gap. Alternatively, when aggregate demand is greater than full-employment GNP, an inflationary gap will exist causing prices to rise.

Key Concepts

Keynesian model
total consumption
induced consumption
marginal propensity to consume (MPC)
savings
marginal propensity to save (MPS)
dissave
autonomous consumption, savings, and investment
planned and actual investment
unplanned investment
unintended changes in inventories
equilibrium GNP
aggregate demand equals aggregate supply
leakages-injection equality
savings equals planned investment
income multiplier
inflationary and recessionary gaps
income gap
classical model

Self-Test Questions: True or False

T   F   1. Classical economists believed that if aggregate demand was not sufficient to achieve full employment, goverment intervention was needed to correct the imbalance.

T   F   2. Keynes believed that equilibrium GNP can occur at less than the full-employment level.

Answer Questions 3 to 7 using the following table (values are in billions of dollars):

GNP	Consumption	Savings	Planned Investment
$ 300	$350	$−50	$25
400	425	−25	25
500	500	0	25
600	575	25	25
700	650	50	25
800	725	75	25
900	800	100	25
1,000	875	125	25

T F 3. The marginal propensity to consume is $\frac{3}{4}$.

T F 4. The equilibrium level of output is $500 billion.

T F 5. If aggregate supply is $800 billion, aggregate supply exceeds aggregate demand and output will fall.

T F 6. If planned investment were to increase by $25 billion to $50 billion, equilibrium income would rise to $700 billion.

T F 7. The income multiplier is $\frac{1}{4}$.

T F 8. An inflationary gap occurs when aggregate demand exceeds full-employment supply.

T F 9. An increase in income will induce an increase in consumption expenditures.

T F 10. The income multiplier will be larger the more people save out of each additional dollar earned.

Answers to Self-Test Questions

1. *False.* The classical model argued that there was no need for government intervention, asserting that the market economy was self-correcting.

2. *True.* Prior to Keynesian economic analysis, the common notion was that full employment was the position to which the economy would always naturally return. Keynes argued that it was possible for aggregate demand to equal aggregate supply at less than full employment; thus, GNP could stabilize below full employment.

3. *True.* The marginal propensity to consume is equal to the change in consumption divided by the change in income (GNP). When income rises by $100 billion, consumption increases by $75 billion or $\frac{75}{100}$ or $\frac{3}{4}$.

4. *False.* Equilibrium output occurs at that level of GNP at which aggregate demand equals aggregate supply (output) or where planned investment equals savings. In this problem, equilibrium is $600 billion.

5. *True.* If aggregate supply is greater than demand, inventories will build up. This is a sign that too much is being produced and as a result output will fall. When output is equal to $800 billion, aggregate demand is equal to $750 billion. The unintended increase in inventories is equal to $50 billion. As a result, output will fall to the equilibrium level of $600 billion.

6. *True.* Equilibrium income occurs where planned investment equals savings. At a level of output of $700 billion, savings is equal to $50 billion which is the same as the new level of planned investment. Also, when output equals $700 billion, aggregate demand will equal supply.

7. *False.* The income multiplier is equal to the reciprocal of the *MPS* or $1/MPS$. In this example, the $MPC = \frac{3}{4}$, which means that the MPS equals $\frac{1}{4}$ since the *MPS* is equal to 1 minus the *MPC*. Therefore, the income multiplier is $1/(\frac{1}{4})$ or 4.

8. *True.* Excess aggregate demand occurs whenever households and firms attempt to buy more goods and services than the economy can produce at full employment. This excess demand is called an inflationary gap.

9. *True.* The relationship of consumer spending to changes in income is called induced consumption. As income increases, consumption spending will increase.

10. *False.* The more people save out of each additional dollar earned, the less they spend. Therefore, the income multiplier will be smaller. Another way to look at this result is by examining the income multiplier formula. Recall that the income multiplier is equal to $1/MPS$. As the *MPS* increases, the income multiplier will decrease.

Discussion Questions

1. Explain how the income multiplier process works. Why does a change in autonomous spending lead to an even greater change in equilibrium GNP?

2. How would each of the following affect equilibrium GNP?
   a. an increase in the rate of interest
   b. consumers expect higher prices in the future
   c. an increase in profit expectations by firms

3. Outline the major differences between the classical and Keynesian models.

4. Explain why actual GNP moves to the equilibrium position when there is an unintended change in inventories.

5. Define the term *inflationary gap* and describe its impact.

Problems

For the country of Trogey, total planned consumption equals GNP at $300 billion. It is also known that the marginal propensity to consume is four-fifths and autonomous investment equals $40 billion.

1. Develop a table such as Table 9.2 in this chapter, which illustrates the Keynesian model without government (billions of dollars). Note that questions 2 through 5 refer to this table.

GNP	C	I_P
300		
400		
500		
600		
700		
800		

2. Determine the equilibrium level of GNP for Trogey.

3. Indicate why this level of GNP is the equilibrium level, citing how this level of output fulfills the equilibrium conditions.

4. Suppose that autonomous investment increases to $60 billion. Using the following table, calculate the new equilibrium level of income.

GNP	C	I_P
300		
400		
500		
600		
700		
800		

5. Compute the income multiplier. Use it to determine the change in equilibrium GNP that would result from a $15 billion decrease in planned investment.

Appendix

Graphic Analysis of the Keynesian Income Determination Model

In this appendix we examine the Keynesian model graphically, focusing on equilibrium income and inflationary/recessionary gaps.

Properties of the Aggregate Supply, Consumption, and Aggregate Demand Curves

To begin our discussion of the graphic approach, see Figure 9.1. The 45-degree line in Figure 9.1 represents *aggregate supply (AS)*, based on the assumption that firms will produce the

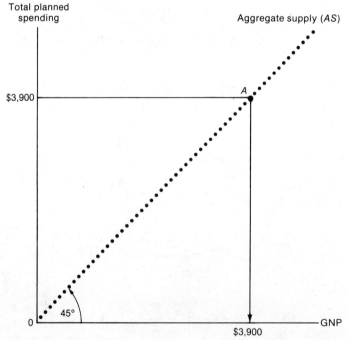

Figure 9.1.   *The Aggregate Supply Curve (AS).* The 45-degree line represents aggregate supply based on the assumption that firms produce the amount of goods and services that people plan to buy. At point *A*, firms will produce the $3,900 billion worth of goods that people plan to buy.

amount of goods and services that people plan to buy. For example, at point A people want to buy $3,900 billion worth of goods (indicated on the vertical axis). This results in $3,900 billion worth of goods being produced (indicated on the horizontal axis). Thus, the 45-degree line is the locus of points where GNP (aggregate supply) equals planned spending.

The consumption curve (C) is illustrated in Figure 9.2. This curve represents the amount of goods and services that households would plan to buy at each level of income. For example, if GNP were $3,900 billion, consumers would plan to spend $3,560 billion (see Table 9.6). This is illustrated by point A in Figure 9.2, where the $3,560 billion in consumption is measured by the vertical distance from the horizontal axis measuring $3,900 billion in income to the point on the consumption curve. The vertical difference between the aggregate supply curve (which measures GNP) and the consumption curve is the amount of savings by households (since savings is calculated as GNP minus consumption). Households plan to save $340 billion if GNP is $3,900 billion, measured by the line AB in Figure 9.2.

Note that autonomous consumption (C_o) (defined as consumer spending not related to income) is measured by the intercept of the consumption curve since the intercept indicates the point on the graph where GNP is zero. As Table 9.6 and Figure 9.2 indicate, autonomous consumption is $440 billion. Also note that as GNP increases, households plan to spend a fraction of this additional income according to the marginal propensity to consume (MPC). The marginal propensity to consume is the slope of the consumption curve, calculated as the change in consumption divided by the change in GNP. In this example, we have an MPC of 4/5 (see Table 9.6).

Having described the consumption curve, it is a simple matter to draw the aggregate demand curve, since as Table 9.7 indicates, aggregate demand (column 5) exceeds consumption (column 2) by $340 billion in planned investment (column 4) at each level of GNP.

Table 9.6
Income, Consumption, and
Savings (billions of dollars)

(1) GNP	(2) Consumption (C)	(3) Savings (S)
$ 0	$ 440	$−440
.	.	.
.	.	.
.	.	.
3,800	3,480	320
3,900	3,560	340
4,000	3,640	360
4,100	3,720	380
4,200	3,800	400
4,300	3,880	420

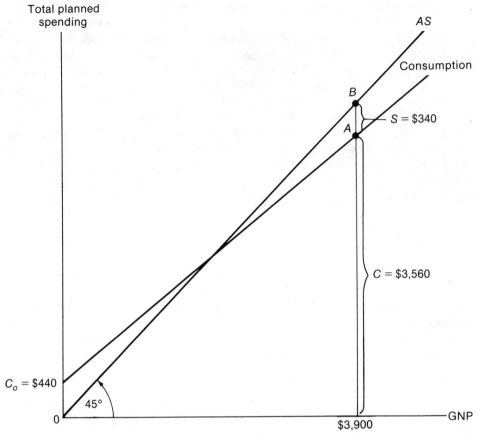

Figure 9.2. The Consumption Curve *(C)*. The consumption curve represents the amount of goods and services that households would plan to buy at each level of income. For example, at point *A* if GNP were $3,900 billion, households would plan to spend $3,560 billion *(C)*. Households plan to save *(S)* $340 billion (line *AB*) if GNP is $3,900 billion. Note that autonomous consumption *(C_o)* is $440 billion.

Figure 9.3 illustrates the aggregate demand curve, which is labeled consumption plus planned investment $(C + I_P)$. What does point *B* on this curve represent? It shows that if GNP were $3,900 billion, households would plan to spend $3,560 billion and firms would plan to invest $340 billion, giving us $3,900 billion in aggregate demand *(AD)*.

Equilibrium Conditions Reviewed Graphically

Note that the $3,900 billion (Y_E) in GNP cited above was selected to illustrate equilibrium. Actual GNP will stabilize at $3,900 billion since at this level of income, aggregate supply

262

Table 9.7
Determination of Equilibrium Level of Income (billions of dollars)

(1) Aggregate Supply (GNP)	(2) Consumption (C)	(3) Savings (S)	(4) Planned Investment (I_P)	(5) Aggregate Demand (C + I_P)	(6) Unplanned Investment or Unintended Change in Inventories
$3,600	$3,320	$280	$340	$3,660	$-60
3,700	3,400	300	340	3,740	-40
3,800	3,480	320	340	3,820	-20
3,900	3,560	340	340	3,900	0
4,000	3,640	360	340	3,980	20
4,100	3,720	380	340	4,060	40
4,200	3,800	400	340	4,140	60
4,300	3,880	420	340	4,220	80

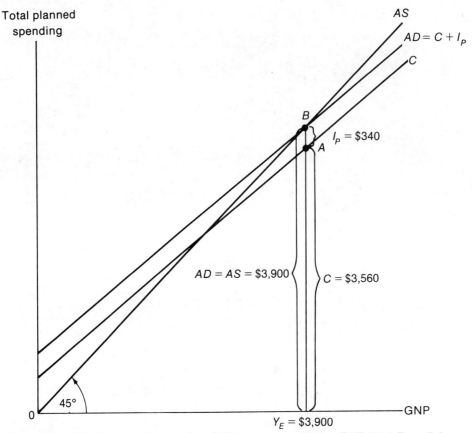

Figure 9.3. The Aggregate Demand Curve *(C + I_P)* and equilibrium GNP *(Y_E)*. Point *B* shows that if GNP were $3,900 billion, households would plan to spend $3,560 billion *(C)* and firms would plan to invest $340 billion *(I_P)*, giving us $3,900 billion in aggregate demand *(AD)*. GNP is in equilibrium *(Y_E)* when aggregate demand *(AD)* equals aggregate supply *(AS)*.

equals aggregate demand, fulfilling the first equilibrium condition discussed in Chapter 9. In other words,

$$\text{GNP} = C + I_P = \$3,900 \text{ billion}$$

Also note that the second equilibrium condition is met since at this level of GNP households plan to save $340 billion (see Figure 9.2), which exactly matches the investment plans of firms (see Figure 9.3). There is no unplanned investment since firms are maintaining the amount of inventories they desire for normal business purposes. In other words, the leakages equal the injections. This may be summarized as follows:

$$S = I_P = \$340 \text{ billion}$$

Unfortunately, GNP may stabilize either below or above the full-employment level of GNP, creating the problems of unemployment or inflation respectively.

Recessionary or Inflationary Gaps

Suppose that full-employment GNP is $4,200 billion (Y_{FE}). As Table 9.7 indicates, at this level of full employment there would be a recessionary gap of $60 billion since this is the amount by which aggregate demand ($4,140 billion) is less than full-employment supply ($4,200 billion). This recessionary gap is illustrated by Figure 9.4.

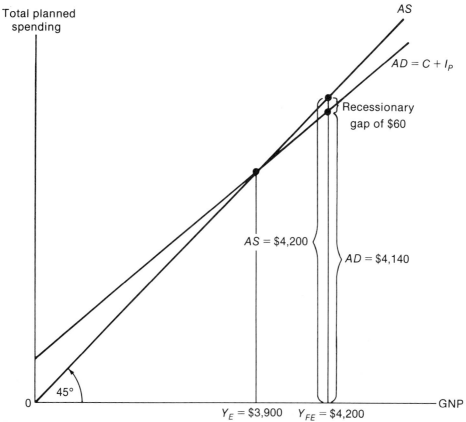

Figure 9.4. A Recessionary Gap. Assuming that full-employment GNP (Y_{FE}) is $4,200 billion, there will be a recessionary gap of $60 billion since this is the amount by which aggregate demand *(AD)* of $4,140 billion is less than full-employment supply *(AS)* of $4,200 billion.

265

Why wouldn't firms produce the full-employment level of output? If actual GNP were at the full-employment level, firms would discover that their inventories would exceed the planned level by $60 billion. They would be forced to lay off workers in order to reduce production to the level that people planned to buy. This will occur when actual GNP falls to $3,900 billion (Y_E), where aggregate demand equals aggregate supply. At this equilibrium level of GNP, there is no unplanned investment (excess inventories) since savings equals planned investment. The recessionary gap has created cyclical unemployment since it has caused GNP to stabilize below the full-employment level.

What problem would be created if the full-employment level of GNP happened to be $3,700 billion (Y_{FE}) instead of $4,200 billion? As Table 9.7 and Figure 9.5 indicate, there

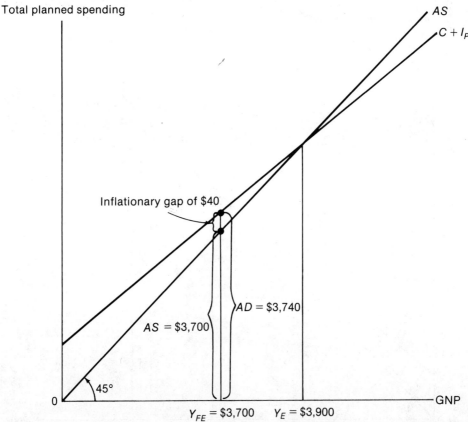

Figure 9.5. An Inflationary Gap. Assuming that full-employment GNP (Y_{FE}) is $3,700 billion, there will be an inflationary gap of $40 billion since this is the amount by which aggregate demand (AD) of $3,740 billion is greater than full-employment supply (Y_{FE}) of $3,700 billion.

would be an inflationary gap of $40 billion, the amount by which aggregate demand exceeds full-employment supply. As a result, the economy is overheated. Consumers and investors are attempting to buy more goods and services than firms can produce given the full-employment ceiling. The depletion of inventories below the planned level causes unrelieved shortages in the amount of $40 billion, creating demand-pull inflation.

CHAPTER

10

The Keynesian Model with Government/Fiscal Policy

Objectives

Upon completion of this chapter, you should understand:

1. How government spending and taxation affect aggregate demand.

2. How the federal budget affects equilibrium GNP.

3. How inflation and unemployment may be reduced by discretionary fiscal policy and automatic stabilizers.

4. Issues concerning the current federal budget deficit and the national debt.

5. Problems in implementing fiscal policy.

In the United States the federal government formally adopted the goal of reducing unemployment through passage of the Employment Act of 1946. The law was the direct result of the Great Depression. The impact of the depression was felt throughout the economy. During the depression (1929 – 1941) GNP fell from $103 billion to a low of $56 billion owing to a drop in aggregate demand. In 1933, one out of every four people in the labor force was unemployed.

As we noted in Section 9.4 of Chapter 9, Keynes developed an economic model to explain why GNP might stabilize below or above the full-employment level. He felt that the federal government could eliminate the problems of unemployment and inflation by using government spending or taxation as tools to bring aggregate demand in line with the full-production capabilities of the economy.

The purpose of this chapter is to examine the impact of the federal budget on the macroeconomy and to discuss how the federal government can use its budget to eliminate recessionary and inflationary gaps. First, we define the new elements added when government is included in the Keynesian model. Second, we examine the equilibrium conditions when government is included in the model. Next, we discuss the difference between discretionary fiscal policy and automatic stabilizers, and we examine the federal budget deficit and the national debt. The chapter concludes with an evaluation of fiscal policy.

10.1 The Effect of Government Purchases, Taxes, and Transfers on Aggregate Demand

The inclusion of government in the Keynesian model (described in Chapter 9) adds government purchases, taxes, and transfers as new elements. *Government purchases (G) of goods and services* such as military aircraft and health care services are now added to the model as a new component of aggregate demand. To simplify the discussion we initially assume that the federal government purchases $140 billion of goods and services at each level of GNP (see Table 10.1, column 5). Therefore, government purchases are assumed to be *autonomous* (i.e., independent of GNP).

In addition to government purchases, government **taxes** and **transfers** also affect aggregate demand indirectly by altering the disposable income of households (defined as income earned plus transfers minus taxes), which in turn affects consumer spending. Remember, transfer payments are not included in goverment purchases because they represent a transfer of money from one group to another (e.g., social security, unemployment, and veterans benefits). As such, transfers do not directly affect the production of goods and services. (See Chapter 7,

Table 10.1
Determination of Equilibrium Income with Government Purchases and Net Taxes (billions of dollars)

(1) Aggregate Supply (GNP)	(2) Consumption (C)	(3) Savings and Net Taxes (S + T)	(4) Planned Investment (I_P)	(5) Government Purchases (G)	(6) Aggregate Demand (C + I_P + G)
$3,800	$3,400	$400	$340	$140	$3,880
3,900	3,480	420	340	140	3,960
4,000	3,560	440	340	140	4,040
4,100	3,640	460	340	140	4,120
4,200	3,720	480	340	140	4,200
4,300	3,800	500	340	140	4,280

Section 7.3, for a detailed discussion of different types of government purchases, taxes, and transfers.) Note that, to simplify the discussion, taxes and transfers are also assumed to be *independent of GNP*. In addition, we also assume that taxes and transfers affect only consumption (i.e., they do not affect planned investment). We are initially assuming that taxes are $200 billion and that transfers total $100 billion. *Net taxes (T)* are $100 billion, calculated as the difference between taxes and transfers. In other words,

$$\text{Net Taxes} = \text{Taxes} - \text{Transfers}$$
$$\$100 \text{ billion} = \$200 \text{ billion} - \$100 \text{ billion}$$

Net taxes is a new leakage in the Keynesian model. Remember that leakages are the income that is received by households but is not spent. With government, leakages are the income that is saved or is used to pay taxes, calculated as the difference betwen GNP and consumption or,

$$\text{Leakages} = \text{GNP} - C = S + T$$

The leakages of savings *(S)* and net taxes *(T)* are illustrated in column 3 of Table 10.1

The inclusion of government also introduces government purchases *(G)* as a new injection into the Keynesian model. Table 10.1 represents our two injections—planned investment of $340 billion (column 4) and government purchases of $140 billion (column 5). Therefore, our total injections are $480 billion, calculated as planned investment *(I_P)* plus government purchases *(G)* or,

$$\text{Injections} = I_P + G$$

Having described the new elements that government adds to the Keynesian model, we are now able to examine the conditions that cause GNP to stabilize at equilibrium. This will be easy to do since the overall equilibrium conditions with government are the same as those described in Section 9.2 of Chapter 9.

10.2 Equilibrium Conditions with Government

As we noted in the previous chapter, equilibrium occurs at that level of GNP where *aggregate supply equals aggregate demand*. In the Keynesian model with government, aggregate demand is equal to consumption plus planned investment plus government purchases. Therefore, equilibrium GNP is $4,200 billion in Table 10.1 since at this level of production GNP is equal to aggregate demand of $4,200 billion.

$$\text{Aggregate Supply} = \text{Aggregate Demand}$$
$$\text{GNP} = C + I_P + G = \$4,200 \text{ billion}$$

If actual GNP is at a level where aggregate demand is greater than aggregate supply, it signifies that too little is being produced. One way to meet this excess demand is from existing inventories. When inventories fall below their desired levels, firms will increase their output to make up for the inadequate supply. Output will increase until aggregate demand is exactly equal to aggregate supply. When GNP reaches $4,200 billion, equilibrium is reached. On the other hand, if actual GNP is at a level where aggregate demand is less than aggregate supply, too much is being produced. Inventories are above desired levels, and firms will decrease their output. Output will decrease until aggregate demand is exactly equal to aggregate supply.

The second equilibrium condition is where *leakages equal injections*. Remember that leakages are reductions in consumption due to savings or taxes, and injections are additions to spending from business (planned investment) and government (government purchases). At the equilibrium GNP of $4,200 billion in Table 10.1, leakages are equal to injections of $480 billion or,

$$\text{Leakages} = \text{Injections}$$
$$S + T = I_P + G = \$480 \text{ billion}$$

If leakages are less than injections, the amount demanded exceeds the amount of goods supplied. Firms will increase production to meet the excess demand until leakages equal injections at the equilibrium GNP of $4,200 billion. On the other hand, if leakages are greater than injections, the amount supplied will exceed the amount demanded and too much will be produced. Firms will decrease production until leakages equal injections.

10.3 Fiscal Policy

In the previous chapter we concluded that consumers and investors may plan to spend too little or too much relative to the full-employment production capabilities of the economy, causing the problems of unemployment or inflation. Many economists believe that the federal government has an obligation to promote policies that would cause GNP to stabilize at full employment. They advocate the use of ***discretionary fiscal policy,*** which is the attempt by the federal government to manage aggregate demand by changing government purchases, taxes, or transfers in order to close recessionary and inflationary gaps.

Increasing Government Purchases to Eliminate a Recessionary Gap

As we noted in Section 9.4 in Chapter 9, a recessionary gap is the amount by which demand falls short of full-employment GNP. Remember that full-empolyment GNP is defined as the amount of goods the economy could produce if only 5 percent of the labor force were unemployed. Assume that full-employment GNP is $4,300 billion. As Table 10.1 indicates, if full-employment GNP is $4,300 billion (column 1), then aggregate demand is $4,280 billion (column 6), which means that there is a recessionary gap of $20 billion. The $100 billion difference between equilibrium GNP ($4,200 billion) and full-employment GNP ($4,300 billion) is the income gap.

How much would the federal government have to increase its purchases to cause GNP to stabilize at full employment? If government purchases were to be increased by the amount of the recessionary gap ($20 billion), GNP would rise by $100 billion because of the multiplier effect, bringing GNP to the full-employment equilibrium of $4,300 billion. Note that the value of the income multiplier (see Section 9.3) has not been affected by the inclusion of government in the model since net taxes and government purchases are assumed to be autonomous (i.e., independent of GNP). The multiplier is still calculated as $1/MPS$, which in this example is $1/(1/5)$ or 5. In other words,

$$\text{change in equilibrium GNP} = (1/MPS) \times (\text{change in autonomous government purchases})$$
$$= 5 \times \$20 \text{ billion}$$
$$= \$100 \text{ billion}$$

Table 10.2 (compared to Table 10.1) illustrates the impact of this $20 billion increase in government purchases from $140 billion to $160 billion. We can see that the full-employment level of output of $4,300 billion (column 1) now equals aggregate demand (column 6). Therefore, equilibrium GNP has stabilized at the full-employment level, eliminating cyclical unemployment. Also, note that Table 10.2 shows that the $500 billion of leakages into savings and net taxes (column 3) now equals the injections of planned investment plus government purchases (column 4 plus column 5) at the full-employment level of GNP, satisfying the second equilibrium condition. We can summarize how an increase in goverment

Table 10.2
Increasing Government Purchases by $20 to Eliminate a Recessionary
Gap of $20 (billions of dollars)

(1) Aggregate Supply (GNP)	(2) Consumption (C)	(3) Savings and Net Taxes (S + T)	(4) Planned Investment (I_P)	(5) New Government Purchases (G')	(6) New Aggregate Demand (C + I_P + G')
$3,800	$3,400	$400	$340	**$160**	**$3,900**
3,900	3,480	420	340	**160**	**3,980**
4,000	3,560	440	340	**160**	**4,060**
4,100	3,640	460	340	**160**	**4,140**
4,200	3,720	480	340	**160**	**4,220**
4,300	3,800	500	340	**160**	**4,300**

purchases can eliminate a recessionary gap as follows:

↑ Autonomous Government Purchases → ↑ GNP to full employment

Decreasing Net Taxes to Eliminate a Recessionary Gap

Since changes in taxes and transfers influence consumption, they are an alternative fiscal policy tool that the federal government can use to reduce unemployment caused by insufficient spending. Transfers have the opposite effect of taxes. For example, both a decrease in taxes and an increase in transfers will cause an increase in disposable income. This increase in disposable income will cause an increase in autonomous consumption because households raise their spending plans at each level of GNP.

To illustrate the use of net taxes as an alternative fiscal policy tool, let us return to the original example in Table 10.1 where equilibrium GNP is $4,200 billion. Assume again that the full-employment level of GNP is $4,300 billion, resulting in a recessionary gap of $20 billion. We concluded that an increase in autonomous government purchases by $20 billion would cause equilibrium GNP to rise to the full-employment level. Note that an increase in autonomous consumption by $20 billion would have the same effect. The only complicating factor is that we must now calculate how much the federal government would have to decrease taxes to achieve a $20 billion increase in autonomous consumption. To achieve our objective of raising autonomous consumption by $20 billion, we must raise disposable income by $25 billion since only four-fifths of this increase in income will be spent by households (as determined by our marginal propensity to consume of 0.8). Note that one-fifth of this increase in income or $5 billion will be saved. Therefore, a $25 billion decrease in taxes is needed to raise disposable income by $25 billion in order to increase consumption by $20 billion at each level of GNP. This $20 billion increase in autonomous consumption sets off rounds of spending in the private sector that ultimately results in a $100 billion increase in GNP. The income multiplier of 5 multiplied by the increase in autonomous consumption spending of $20 equals the change in equilibrium income of $100 billion.

$$\text{Change in GNP} = 1/MPS \times \text{change in autonomous consumption}$$
$$= 5 \times \$20 \text{ billion}$$
$$= \$100 \text{ billion}$$

As we can see in Table 10.3, GNP has stabilized at the full-employment level of income. Aggregate demand now equals aggregate supply at the full-employment GNP of $4,300 billion. In addition, our leakages of $480 billion equal injections at full employment. At $4,300 billion in GNP, savings plus net taxes matches planned investment plus government purchases ($480 billion). Note that an increase in transfers would have the same effect on income as a decrease in taxes. We may summarize this process as follows:

$$\downarrow \text{Taxes} \rightarrow \uparrow \text{Disposable Income} \rightarrow \uparrow \text{Autonomous Consumption}$$
$$\rightarrow \uparrow \text{GNP to full employment}$$

Note that there is an important difference between a change in government purchases and a change in taxes or transfers. A $25 billion decrease in taxes (or an increase in transfers) does not lead to a $25 billion increase in spending. When taxes fall or transfers increase, households will spend a fraction of the change in disposable income according to the marginal propensity to consume. They will also save a fraction according to the marginal propensity to save. For example, if disposable income rose by $25 billion and the marginal propensity to consume were 0.8, consumption would increase by $20 billion and the rest ($5 billion) would be put

Table 10.3
Decreasing Taxes by $25 to Eliminate a Recessionary Gap of $20 (billions of dollars)

(1) Aggregate Supply (GNP)	(2) New Consumption (C')	(3) New Savings and New Net Taxes (S' + T')	(4) Planned Investment (I_P)	(5) Government Purchases (G)	(6) New Aggregate Demand (C' + I_P + G)
$3,800	$3,420	$380	$340	$140	$3,900
3,900	3,500	400	340	140	3,980
4,000	3,580	420	340	140	4,060
4,100	3,660	440	340	140	4,140
4,200	3,740	460	340	140	4,220
4,300	3,820	480	340	140	4,300

into savings. Therefore, a $25 billion decrease in taxes or increase in transfers will not have the same effect on equilibrium GNP as a $25 billion increase in government purchases. The increase in transfers or decrease in taxes must work its way into the system indirectly, whereas an increase in government purchases will have an immediate effect on spending in the *first round* of the income multiplier process. For example, when government increases purchases by $20 billion, output will go up by $20 billion in the first round. But it takes a $25 billion decrease in taxes (or an increase in transfers) to increase consumer spending by $20 billion in the first round.

The Use of Fiscal Policy to Reduce an Inflationary Gap

How can fiscal policy be used to eliminate demand-pull inflation? The federal government can use fiscal policy to eliminate an inflationary gap in a fashion similar to that used to get rid of a recessionary gap. To simplify the discussion, we will avoid a numerical example, concentrating instead on the overall mechanism of change. The following analysis is a mirror image (upside-down) of the previous discussion concerning the recessionary gap and fiscal policy.

Remember, an inflationary gap is the amount by which aggregate demand exceeds full-employment supply. The result of an inflationary gap is a general rise in prices (demand-pull inflation). People are not able to purchase the amount of goods that they had planned to buy because the labor force is fully employed.

The federal government could reduce this excess demand through a decrease in its purchases of goods and services by the amount of the inflationary gap. The income multiplier would cause equilibrium GNP to fall by an even greater amount until the inflationary gap had been eliminated. This chain of events can be summarized as follows:

$$\downarrow \text{Autonomous Government Purchases} \rightarrow \downarrow \text{GNP to full employment}$$

Tax and transfer policy tools can also be used to eliminate the excess demand of an inflationary gap. Assume that the government decides to use an increase in taxes as the means of reducing consumption. Remember how the change in taxes works its way into the economy. When taxes are increased, disposable income will drop. With this decrease in disposable income, consumption will fall at each level of GNP. This decline in autonomous consumption spending by households causes equilibrium GNP to fall by a multiple amount, eliminating the inflationary gap. The same result would occur if transfers were reduced. This process can be summarized as follows:

$$\uparrow \text{Taxes} \rightarrow \downarrow \text{Disposable Income} \rightarrow \downarrow \text{Autonomous Consumption}$$
$$\rightarrow \downarrow \text{GNP to full employment}$$

In the examples above, government purchases, taxes, or transfers were changed. In the real world it is more likely that some combination of the three would be used. In any case, the

275

policy choice is the result of deliberate action taken by the Congress and the Executive Branch of the federal government to fight unemployment or inflation. In the next section we examine how automatic changes in government taxes and transfers help to reduce the business cycle.

10.4 Automatic Stabilizers

Some spending and taxation programs are called *automatic stabilizers* since they have an *automatic stabilizing* effect on GNP, reducing the peaks and troughs of the business cycle described in Section 8.5 of Chapter 8. For example, let us explore the impact of the progressive personal income tax structure in the United States. As income begins to fall during a recessionary period (owing to a decrease in spending), the amount of taxes paid will also decline since families affected by the recession fall into lower tax brackets. The automatic decline in taxes paid (given no change in the tax rate structure) causes disposable income not to fall by as much as it would have fallen without the progressive income tax. Consequently, spending will not fall by as much as it might have if the percentage of tax revenue collected remained the same no matter what level of income was earned. As a result, the decline in GNP is not as great as it would have been without the personal income tax.

Another type of automatic stabilizer is unemployment compensation. As the economy enters a recession, workers who lose their jobs automatically become eligible for unemployment compensation. These unemployment benefits keep disposable income from falling as much as gross income. Therefore, since aggregate spending will not fall by as much as the drop in aggregate pretax income, the decline in GNP will not be as great as it would have been without unemployment compensation. As a result, unemployment compensation has a stabilizing influence on the business cycle.

Automatic stabilizers may also reduce demand-pull inflation. For example, given the personal income tax, as incomes rise, so do the taxes that most Americans pay (without a change in the tax rate structure). Therefore, their disposable income will not rise as much. As a result, spending will not increase as much, and inflationary pressures will be less than would otherwise be the case. Note that automatic stabilizers are too weak to eliminate the business cycle; therefore, there is still need for discretionary fiscal policy.

Although the manner in which automatic stabilizers function may appear sound, they have sometimes conflicted with current economic policy. For example, when GNP is rising toward full employment, tax revenues will increase automatically. The increase in taxes will reduce aggregate demand because income will be lower. This reduced spending will have the effect of a drag on the economy since aggregate demand will be less than it might have been if taxes had not increased. As a result, the rate of increase in GNP may be slower. In the next section we examine the overall impact of the budget of the federal government on the economy.

10.5 The Federal Budget Deficit and the National Debt

Many people are concerned that the government is spending beyond its means. In this section we examine some of the issues surrounding the federal budget deficit and the national debt.

Budget Positions

There are three ways that the government can raise money to finance government expenditures on government purchases and transfers. First, the government can raise funds through taxation to pay for the programs it desires to undertake. Second, the government can borrow money by selling U.S. Treasury bonds (also called U.S. securities). By borrowing money, the government can spend more than it is currently bringing in through taxation. (This topic is discussed in detail in Appendix B of this chapter.) Finally, some governments have used the printing press to fund public programs. Printing money when needed seems, on the surface, to be a "painless" method and has been used frequently by developing countries. In reality, however, this may not be true. If printing more money causes excess demand, the effect will be inflationary. As a result of this inflationary pressure, rising prices act as a hidden "tax" in that they reduce purchasing power.

When government spending is greater than tax revenue, a ***deficit budget*** is created. The government will have to borrow money to make up the difference. During periods of recession or depression, a deficit will have the desired effect of stimulating the economy by increasing aggregate demand. However, when aggregate demand is greater than full-employment output (demand-pull inflation), a deficit will make the situation worse by increasing demand even further.

When tax revenue is greater than government spending, a ***surplus budget*** is generated. The government is taking more purchasing power out of the economy than it is putting in the economy. During periods of inflation, a budget surplus may help to dampen price increases by reducing spending. During periods of less than full employment, a budget surplus may retard recovery by suppressing aggregate demand.

Budget Philosophies

There are three philosophies concerning the federal budget. First, some people feel that the federal government should balance its budget each year (making tax revenue equal to government spending). The philosophy behind the need for an ***annually balanced budget*** is that "fiscal integrity" should be maintained. The belief is that, except under extraordinary circumstances, the government should limit its spending to the money it raises. Proponents of the annually balanced budget mistakenly believe that this approach has a neutral impact on GNP. The effect on GNP, however, is not neutral. An annually balanced budget is *procyclical,* which means that an attempt to balance the budget "pushes" the economy further in the direction it was headed in, causing the business cycle to become more extreme.

For example, in a recessionary period when income is falling, tax revenue (given existing tax rates) tends to fall. Tax revenue will decrease because there is less income earned on which to collect taxes. At the same time there is an increase in certain transfer payments such as unemployment compensation. The decrease in tax revenue together with the increase in government transfers creates a budget deficit. To balance the budget, the government could lower spending or increase the tax rate. Either policy would result in a decrease in aggregate demand, causing equilibrium GNP to fall even further, making the recession worse.

On the other hand, during periods of demand-pull inflation, spending and income are rising. Tax revenue will increase because there is more income to tax (given existing tax rates) and certain transfer payments such as unemployment compensation will decrease. An increase in tax revenue and a decrease in transfers would create a budget surplus. To balance the budget the government could increase spending or it could reduce tax rates. Either policy would result in an increase in spending, which would intensify the business cycle by contributing to demand-pull inflation.

Second, there are those who argue for a *cyclically balanced budget.* They believe the budget should be used to stabilize the economy with the goal of equating expenditures to taxes over the course of the business cycle (rather than annually). During periods of contraction, deficits should be incurred to stimulate spending. During periods of expansion, a surplus should be generated to reduce demand-pull inflation. This surplus should then be used to retire the deficits incurred during the last recession. The desired result would be a balanced budget over the course of the business cycle. Unfortunately, the cyclically balanced budget does not work out this neatly because the business cycle is not uniform in either magnitude or timing. In other words, the upswings in the economy rarely are equal to the downswings.

The third philosophy is that we should be more concerned with using the federal budget to balance the economy (i.e., reduce the business cycle) than with balancing the federal budget. This approach is called *functional finance.* It is the Keynesian policy prescription of using the federal government budget to eliminate recessionary and inflationary gaps (described in Section 10.3 of this chapter).

Controversy Over the Current Federal Deficits and the National Debt

During the 1980s there were a series of tax reductions accompanied by large increases in federal spending. The result was growing federal deficits. To finance these budget deficits the federal government has accumulated a huge *national (public) debt.* The debt is created when the federal government borrows money from households, financial institutions, and other sources. The government issues U.S. securities (e.g., savings bonds, Treasury bills) and pays interest for the money borrowed. When these bonds expire, the government sells new bonds to refinance the debt.

Deficits in the 1980s were at record high levels. Prior to 1980, there were only two years in which the federal deficit was greater than $70 billion. As we can see in Table 10.4, the

Table 10.4
The Federal Government Deficit, National Debt (both in billions of
dollars), and the National Debt as a Percent of GNP, 1930–1988
(average annual data for 1930–1939 through 1970–1979)

Year	Deficit	Gross Federal Debt	National Debt as a Percent of GNP
1930–1939	$ −2.4	$ 27.9	———
1940–1949	−17.8	182.7	97
1950–1959	−1.8	269.5	70
1960–1969	−5.7	323.8	48
1970–1979	−35.6	566.1	36
1980	−73.8	908.5	34
1981	−78.9	994.3	33
1982	−127.9	1,136.8	36
1983	−207.8	1,371.2	41
1984	−185.3	1,564.1	42
1985	−212.3	1,817.0	46
1986	−221.2	2,120.1	51
1987	−149.5	2,345.6	53
1988	−155.1	2,800.8	54

Source: *Economic Report of the President,* January 1989.

federal deficit (column 2) increased sharply from $73.8 billion in 1980 to $155.1 billion in 1988. In addition to enormous deficits, the national debt has grown substantially. As Table 10.4 shows, the national debt rose abruptly from $908.5 billion in 1980 to $2,800.8 in 1988. The national debt as a percentage of GNP (column 4) increased from 34 percent in 1980 to 54 percent in 1988, after having fallen for decades. Finally, in 1980 interest payments were 12.7 percent of total federal spending (not shown). The tremendous increase in the national debt during the early 1980s caused interest payments to swell to 14 percent of total federal spending by 1988. Figures 10.1a and b show the size of the deficit and debt, respectively, as a percentage of GNP for the period 1790–1988.

Many were concerned about the speed and the magnitude of the increases in the federal deficit and the national debt during the 1980s. This concern changed to fear on October 19, 1987 — helping to precipitate the stock market crash. In addition to the destabilizing effect on our financial markets, many economists are troubled that the size of the present deficit has tied the hands of policymakers and may prevent the federal government from using fiscal policy should the economy fall into a recession.

The current talk tends to favor an annually balanced budget. During the 99th session of Congress, an amendment to the Constitution was introduced that would require the federal government to balance its budget (see the boxed discussion). The bill failed to pass in the

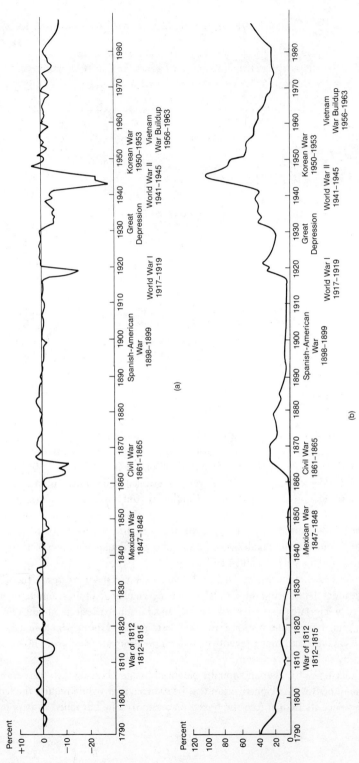

Figure 10.1. The Federal Budget Surplus or Deficit and the National Debt from 1789 to 1988. (a) The Unified Federal Budget Surplus or Deficit as a Percentage of GNP. The United States has run a deficit regularly since 1950, with major deficits associated with wars. (b) The National Debt as a Percentage of GNP. The national debt has been at its highest levels during the Great Depression and periods of war. (From Federal Reserve Bank of Atlanta, *Economic Review*, August 1982; *Economic Report of the President*, January, 1989.)

House of Representatives but is likely to be introduced again. In addition, in late September 1987, in an attempt to control the growing deficits, Congress passed the Gramm-Rudman-Hollings deficit reduction law. This legislation calls for a balanced budget by fiscal year 1993 by mandating a deficit reduction timetable.

See *Appendix B: The Debate Over the National Debt* for a more complete discussion of this controversy.

A Balanced Budget Amendment

Section 1. Prior to each fiscal year, the Congress shall adopt a statement of receipts and outlays for that year in which total outlays are no greater than total receipts. . . . Whenever three-fifths of the whole number of both Houses shall deem it necessary, Congress in such statement may provide for a specific excess of outlays over receipts by a vote directed solely to that subject. The Congress and the President shall, pursuant to legislation or through exercise of their powers under the first and second articles, ensure that actual outlays do not exceed the outlays set forth in such statement.

Section 2. Total receipts for any fiscal year set forth in the statement adopted pursuant to this article shall not increase by a rate greater than the rate of increase in national income . . . unless a majority of the whole number of both Houses of Congress shall have passed a bill directed solely to approving specific additional receipts and such bill has become law. . . .

Section 6. On and after the date this article takes effect, the amount of Federal public debt limit as of such date shall become permanent and there shall be no increase in such amount unless three-fifths of the whole number of both Houses of Congress shall have passed a bill approving such increase and such bill has become law.

The above are selected sections of the Balanced Budget Amendment introduced to Congress in 1983.

10.6 Problems in Implementing Fiscal Policy

There exists a major problem impeding the effectiveness of fiscal policy. It can be categorized in terms of the time lags involved in the recognition of the problem, and the administration and operation of fiscal policy. Because of these lags, the economy may stay depressed or suffer from the effects of inflation longer than would be the case if fiscal policy were employed at the outset of the problem. These lags can also cause fiscal policy to miss its target, causing a destabilizing effect on the economy.

Recognition Lag

The *recognition lag* refers to the time it takes policymakers to realize that the economy is either heading downward into a recession or is approaching an inflationary period of excess demand. It is not a simple task to predict the direction of the economy at any given point in time.

Economists use complex computerized simulation models of the economy to predict the direction in which the economy is headed. Some of the well-known models are produced by the University of Pennsylvania's Wharton School of Business, the Chase Manhattan Bank, and the Federal Reserve Bank of St. Louis.

Economists also use a series of economic indicators to predict the actual performance of the overall economy. They include stock prices, the money supply, housing starts, and new orders for durable goods. If the composite (overall) measure of these indexes were to show economic activity declining, this would be an indication that a recession was imminent. Clearly, there can never be certainty as to the direction in which the economy is headed.

Administrative Lag

Once the government has recognized that a problem exists, the next step is to choose the appropriate policy. The amount of time it takes to get legislation through Congress and approved by the Executive Branch is called the *administrative lag.* It can take months or years to get the approval necessary to implement a plan, and it is possible that business activity might reverse before the policy is enacted.

There are a number of issues that policymakers must address when allocating expenditures. Policymakers have to choose among the many projects that might fulfill the policy objective, such as changes in expenditures on defense, education, and health care. They must also consider the following problems. How quickly will they be able to implement the program? How flexible is the program (can it be administered in large or small doses, if necessary)? Does it favor or harm any particular group? Once these issues have been dealt with, the decision makers can determine the appropriate policy. Again, this may involve a long period of time since the questions listed above are very difficult to answer.

Operational Lag

Finally, after all of the foregoing obstacles have been surmounted, there is the operational lag. The *operational lag* is the time it takes for the policy to have the desired effect once the program has been implemented. For example, once a tax cut has been enacted, the operational lag refers to the period of time that the tax cut takes to eliminate a recessionary gap. As noted in Chapter 9, the income multiplier involves numerous rounds of spending and income creation, which might take several years.

Summary

Keynes felt that through the use of fiscal policy, the federal government could improve the performance of the economy. By changing the level of government purchases, taxes, or transfers, it would be possible to close recessionary and inflationary gaps by bringing aggregate demand to full-employment GNP. In addition to the effect of discretionary fiscal policy, automatic stabilizers can smooth the business cycle by automatically changing spending levels.

When government spending is greater than tax revenues, deficits are created. The money borrowed to finance the deficit becomes part of the national debt. If tax revenue is greater than government spending, a surplus exists. Many people believe that an annually balanced budget is the best approach because it maintains "fiscal integrity." Unfortunately, an annually balanced budget will intensify the business cycle. An alternative approach is the cyclically balanced budget.

There are many problems in implementing fiscal policy. The overall time lags consist of the following: (1) the time it takes for policymakers to realize that the economy is approaching a recession or an inflationary period, (2) the speed with which the appropriate policy is chosen, and (3) how long the policy takes to have its desired effect once it is implemented.

Key Concepts

taxes
transfers
net taxes
discretionary fiscal policy
automatic stabilizers
deficit budget
surplus budget
annually balanced budget
cyclically balanced budget
functional finance
national (public) debt
recognition lag
administrative lag
operational lag

Self-Test Questions: True or False

T   F   1. If there is an inflationary gap, the government should increase government purchases.

T   F   2. An increase in transfers will have the same effect on GNP as a decrease in taxes.

T   F   3. A $1 billion increase in taxes will have the same impact on the economy as a $1 billion decrease in government purchases.

T   F   4. Contrary to popular belief, an annually balanced budget will not have a neutral effect on GNP.

T   F   5. A deficit will result when tax revenue is greater than government spending.

Answer Questions 6 to 8 using the table below:

T   F   6. The equilibrium level of GNP is $900 billion.

T   F   7. If full-employment GNP is at $800 billion, the federal government could eliminate the inflationary gap by reducing government purchases by $75 billion.

T   F   8. If taxes were increased by $100 billion, equilibrium GNP would fall to $800 billion.

T   F   9. The operational lag refers to the time it takes for government to change taxes, transfers, or government purchases.

T   F   10. Formal action by Congress and the Executive Branch is required in order for automatic stabilizers to take effect.

GNP	Consumption	Savings and Net Taxes	Planned Investment	Government Purchases	Aggregate Demand
$ 400	$425	$−25	$50	$100	$ 575
500	500	0	50	100	650
600	575	25	50	100	725
700	650	50	50	100	800
800	725	75	50	100	875
900	800	100	50	100	950
1,000	875	125	50	100	1,025
1,100	950	150	50	100	1,100

Answers to Self-Test Questions

1. *False.* An inflationary gap exists when aggregate demand is greater than full-employment output. Increasing government purchases would aggravate the situation. The appropriate remedy would be to decrease government purchases.

2. **True.** Transfers are negative taxes. Transfers and taxes affect aggregate demand by changing the amount of disposable income. For example, an increase in transfers and a decrease in taxes will increase disposable income by the same amount. By increasing disposable income, consumption expenditures will rise at each level of GNP.

3. **False.** A $1 billion decrease in government purchases will decrease autonomous aggregate demand by $1 billion. Autonomous consumption will fall by less than $1 billion since a part of the $1 billion tax increase is paid out of savings. For example, if the MPC were $\frac{3}{4}$, autonomous consumption (and aggregate demand) would fall by $750 million.

4. **True.** An annually balanced budget will exert a procyclical effect on GNP. For example, when the economy is in a recession, a deficit will be generated due to the automatic decline in tax revenue. The only way to balance the budget is for government spending to fall or tax rates to rise. Either of these approaches will depress aggregate demand and further reduce GNP.

5. **False.** A deficit will result when government spending is greater than tax revenue. A surplus will be generated when tax revenue exceeds government spending.

6. **False.** Equilibrium GNP is $1,100 billion. Equilibrium occurs when aggregate demand equals aggregate supply. Aggregate demand is the summation of consumption, planned investment, and government purchases. At a GNP of $1,100 billion, aggregate demand is equal to $1,100 billion. Also, at equilibrium GNP, leakages ($150 billion) equal injections ($150 billion). At a lower level of GNP, too little is produced to satisfy demand.

7. **True.** If full-employment GNP was $800 billion, the income gap would be the difference between the equilibrium level ($1,100 billion) and the full-employment level ($800 billion) or $300 billion. Given a MPC of $\frac{3}{4}$, the income multiplier would be 4 and government purchases would have to fall by $75 billion to eliminate the inflationary gap.

8. **True.** If taxes were increased by $100 billion, disposable income would fall by $100 billion. With an MPC of $\frac{3}{4}$, consumption would decrease by $75 billion ($100 billion $\times \frac{3}{4}$). Given an MPC of $\frac{3}{4}$, the income multiplier would be 4 and GNP would decrease by $300 billion (or 4 $\times$ $75 billion) to $800 billion.

9. **False.** The operational lag refers to the time it takes for the policy to have its desired effect once it has been administered. The administrative lag refers to the time it takes for the policy to be implemented.

10. **False.** Automatic stabilizers take effect without any formal action taken by Congress and the Executive Branch. Discretionary fiscal policy (e.g., tax cuts and new government spending programs) needs formal action.

Discussion Questions

1. Explain why a $1 billion decrease in taxes will not have the same impact on equilibrium GNP as a $1 billion increase in government purchases.
2. How would each of the following affect equilibrium GNP:
   a. decrease in taxes
   b. decrease in government purchases
   c. simultaneous increase in taxes and transfers by the same amount
3. Outline how automatic stabilizers operate to reduce the business cycle.
4. Explain the three types of budget philosophies.
5. Explain the three problems impeding the effectiveness of fiscal policy.

Problems

The country of Trogey has established a government with the power to spend and tax. Assume that consumption equals $930 billion when GNP is $1,000 billion, the *MPC* is nine-tenths, and autonomous investment is $40 billion. In addition, assume that government purchases amount to $60 billion.

1. Develop a table such as Table 10.1 in Chapter 10, which illustrates the Keynesian model with government (billions of dollars). Note that questions 2 through 4 refer to this table.

GNP	C	Savings and Net Taxes	I_p	G	$C + I_p + G$
1,000					
1,100					
1,200					
1,300					
1,400					
1,500					

2. Determine the equilibrium level of aggregate GNP.
3. Indicate why this level of GNP is the equilibrium level, citing how it fulfills the equilibrium conditions.
4. Suppose that government purchases were to increase by $10 billion. Compute the new equilibrium level of GNP using the table developed in answer to question 1.

| Appendices |

A: Graphic Analysis of the Keynesian Model with Government/Fiscal Policy

The Keynesian model with government can also be presented graphically. In this appendix we use graphs to examine equilibrium income and how fiscal policy can eliminate inflationary and recessionary gaps. To simplify the use of graphs, we will focus on aggregate demand and aggregate supply (ignoring leakages and injections described in detail in the main body of this chapter). Note that you should review the appendix to Chapter 9 before reading this appendix.

Properties of the Graph

Figure 10.2 presents the basic tools necessary to analyze the Keynesian model graphically when government is included. The values shown in Figure 10.2 correspond to the values in Table 10.5 (which reproduces the table used in Section 10.1). Figure 10.2 illustrates the aggregate demand $(C + I_P + G)$ with government. It has a slope of $\frac{4}{5}$ which is the same as the slope of the consumption function because both net taxes and government purchases are autonomous. Also drawn in Figure 10.2 is the 45-degree line which again represents aggregate supply. Remember that this represents aggregate supply, because we assume that firms will produce the amount of goods and services that people plan to buy. Point A shows that if aggregate demand were $4,200 billion, aggregate supply would equal $4,200 billion.

Equilibrium Reviewed Graphically

Note that the $4,200 billion in GNP cited above was selected to illustrate equilibrium GNP (symbolized by Y_E in Figure 10.2). Actual GNP will stabilize at $4,200 billion since at this level of income, aggregate supply equals aggregate demand. In other words,

$$GNP = C + I_P + G = \$4,200 \text{ billion}$$

Unfortunately, GNP may stabilize either below or above the full-employment level of GNP, creating the problems of unemployment or inflation, respectively. Fiscal policy can be used to eliminate recessionary and inflationary gaps.

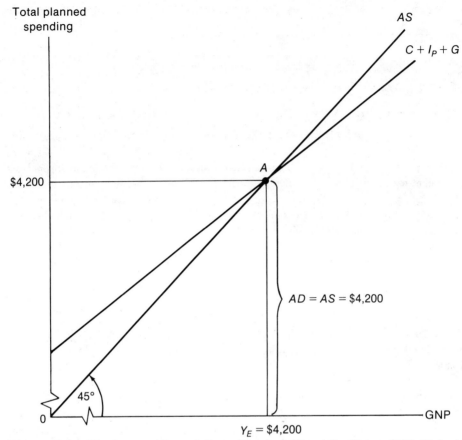

Figure 10.2. The Aggregate Demand Curve $(C + I_P + G)$ and Equilibrium GNP (Y_E) with Government. Point A represents equilibrium GNP (Y_E) since aggregate demand (AD) is equal to aggregate supply (AS) of $4,200 billion.

Table 10.5
Determination of Equilibrium Income with Government Purchases and Net Taxes (billions of dollars)

(1) Aggregate Supply (GNP)	(2) Consumption (C)	(3) Savings and Net Taxes (S + T)	(4) Planned Investment (I_P)	(5) Government Purchases (G)	(6) Aggregate Demand $(C + I_P + G)$
$3,800	$3,400	$400	$340	$140	$3,880
3,900	3,480	420	340	140	3,960
4,000	3,560	440	340	140	4,040
4,100	3,640	460	340	140	4,120
4,200	3,720	480	340	140	4,200
4,300	3,800	500	340	140	4,280

Using Fiscal Policy to Reduce Unemployment

Assume that with the full employment of our labor force, our economy could produce a maximum of $4,300 billion in goods. We can see in Table 10.5 that at this full-employment GNP, aggregate demand is $20 billion less than aggregate supply. This recessionary gap of $20 billion is illustrated in Figure 10.3.

How much would the federal government have to increase its purchases to bring equilibrium GNP (Y_E) to full employment GNP (Y_{FE})? As indicated in Table 10.6, government

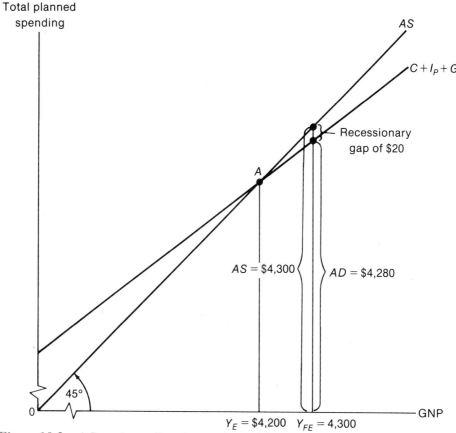

Figure 10.3. A Recessionary Gap. Assume that at full employment (Y_{FE}), our economy could produce a maximum of $4,300 billion in goods. We can see that, at this full-employment GNP, aggregate demand *(AD)* is $4,280 billion, which is less than aggregate supply *(AS)* of $4,300 billion. The amount by which aggregate demand is less than full-employment supply represents a recessionary gap of $20 billion.

Table 10.6
Increasing Government Purchases by $20 to Eliminate a Recessionary
Gap of $20 (billions of dollars)

(1) Aggregate Supply (GNP)	(2) Consumption (C)	(3) Savings and Net Taxes (S + T)	(4) Planned Investment (I_P)	(5) New Government Purchases (G')	(6) New Aggregate Demand (C + I_P + G')
$3,800	$3,400	$400	$340	$160	$3,900
3,900	3,480	420	340	160	3,980
4,000	3,560	440	340	160	4,060
4,100	3,640	460	340	160	4,140
4,200	3,720	480	340	160	4,220
4,300	3,800	500	340	160	4,300

purchases would have to be increased by the amount of the recessionary gap ($20 billion) from $140 billion to $160 billion. Equilibrium GNP would rise by five times the increase in government purchases ($100 billion) to the full-employment equilibrium of $4,300 billion.

Figure 10.4 illustrates the impact of the $20 billion increase in government purchases as a parallel upward shift in the aggregate demand curve from $(C + I_P + G)$ to $(C + I_P + G')$. At each level of GNP the government plans to buy an additional $20 billion of goods. Note that this increase in autonomous spending has caused equilibrium income to increase from Y_E to Y'_E. The recessionary gap has been eliminated. At point B, aggregate demand now equals aggregate supply at the full-employment level of output of $4,300 billion; therefore, equilibrium income equals full-employment GNP $(Y'_E = Y_{FE})$.

Fiscal policy can also eliminate the $20 billion recessionary gap by decreasing taxes or increasing transfers in an amount sufficient to increase autonomous consumption by $20 billion (described in Section 10.3 of this chapter). Note that the graphic analysis of this policy choice is the same as that used to illustrate the impact of a $20 billion increase in government purchases. The only difference is that the aggregate demand curve would be shifted upward by an increase in autonomous consumption rather than an increase in government purchases (see Figure 10.4).

Overview of the Use of Fiscal Policy to Fight Inflation

Just as fiscal policy can eliminate a recessionary gap to reduce unemployment, it can also be used to eliminate an inflationary gap. The federal government could correct this situation by reducing this excess demand through a decrease in government purchases of goods and

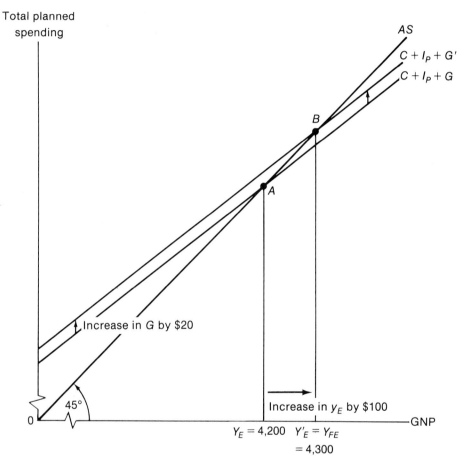

Figure 10.4. The Impact of an Increase in Government Purchases. The impact of the $20 billion increase in government purchases is shown by a parallel upward shift in the aggregate demand curve from $(C + I_P + G)$ to $(C + I_P + G')$. If government purchases were increased by the amount of the recessionary gap, $20 billion, equilibrium GNP (Y_E) would rise by $100 billion to the full-employment equilibrium of $4,300 billion (Y_{FE}).

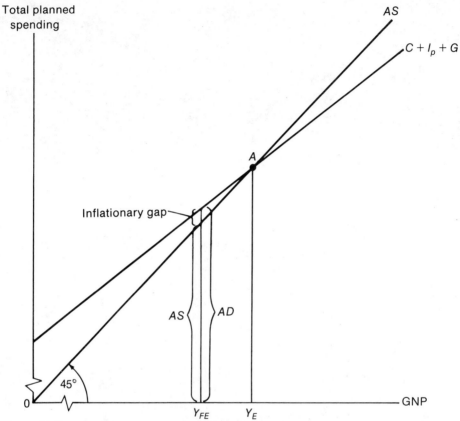

Figure 10.5. An Inflationary Gap. Assuming that full-employment GNP is Y_{FE}, there will be an inflationary gap, since aggregate demand *(AD)* is greater than full-employment supply *(AS)*.

services, an increase in taxes, or a decrease in transfers. Figure 10.5 illustrates an inflationary gap. Note that equilibrium occurs at point *A* which means that equilibrium GNP (Y_E) is greater than full-employment GNP (Y_{FE}). If autonomous spending were to be decreased through fiscal policy, equilibrium GNP would fall to full-employment GNP. This is illustrated by Figure 10.6. The aggregate demand curve has shifted downward from $(C + I_P + G)$ to $(C' + I_P + G')$ causing equilibrium GNP to move to the full-employment level $(Y'_E = Y_{FE})$.

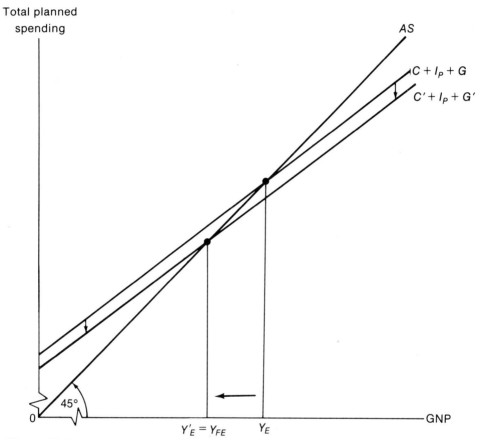

Figure 10.6. The Impact of a Decrease in Autonomous Spending. If autonomous spending were to be decreased through an increase in taxes, decrease in transfers, or decrease in government purchases, equilibrium GNP (Y_E) would fall to full-employment GNP (Y_{FE}). The aggregate demand curve would shift downward from $(C + I_P + G)$ to $(C' + I_P + G')$, causing equilibrium GNP to move to the full-employment level $(Y'_E = Y_{FE})$.

B: The Debate Over the National Debt

The national debt is a concern of many people. The following discussion examines the benefits and costs of this debt.

Pros: Benefits of the Deficit and National Debt

One argument in favor of the national debt is that the bulk of the national debt has arisen to finance wars (primarily World War II as indicated in Figure 10.1 in Section 10.5 of this chapter). Most people would agree that these are circumstances in which the debt incurred was justified.

Another benefit of the national debt is our ability to use fiscal policy to stimulate the economy during periods of recession by creating budget deficits (which add to the national debt). To increase aggregate demand, the federal government could increase government purchases and transfers or decrease taxes. The increase in aggregate demand will lead to an increase in GNP to full employment via the income multiplier process. The budget deficit will be financed by more federal borrowing through the sale of U.S. securities, which will increase the size of the national debt. In the period 1929–1932 President Hoover tried to balance the budget by raising taxes while the economy was in the Great Depression. This increase in taxes made the situation worse. If deficits had been incurred to stimulate spending, the depression would not have been as severe or have lasted as long.

Finally, the bonds issued by the U.S. government are among the safest type of savings. People regularly purchase bonds through payroll deduction plans and give them as gifts.

Cons: Costs of the Deficit and National Debt

As we noted in Section 10.5 of this chapter, the rapid increase in the federal debt from 34 percent of GNP in 1980 to 54 percent by 1988 has had a destabilizing effect on the stock market. Whether or not the *fear* of the increase in the national debt can be justified, it did help to rock our financial markets. We also noted in Section 10.5 of this chapter that the burden of interest payments on the debt increased sharply from 12.7 percent of federal spending in 1980 to 14 percent of federal spending in 1988, and that the current size of our federal debt may preclude the use of fiscal policy to reduce a recessionary gap in the future. We now turn to other arguments against the national debt.

First, deficit financing by the federal government can lead to an increase in the demand for loanable funds, causing the interest rate to rise. As the interest rate increases, some private investment may no longer be profitable because of the added cost of borrowing. As a result, some private investment may not be undertaken. This is referred to as "crowding out." In certain instances, public projects may be undertaken that may not be as desirable for society as the private investment it is replacing. In this case, the size of the debt and its influence on the interest rate are exerting a cost on society by excluding the more desirable private projects. The crowding-out effect may create a lower rate of capital formation which will leave a smaller capital stock to future generations.

Second, deficit spending and the subsequent borrowing needed to finance it can be inflationary if it occurs at the wrong time. By increasing spending when the economy is at full employment, the tendency will be for the general level of prices to rise.

A third argument against deficit financing is that it may cause wasteful government spending. When politicians do not have to depend solely on tax revenues, they may be more agreeable to excessive spending. Politically, borrowing money and paying it off in the future is more acceptable than increasing taxes now. By borrowing now and paying for it in the future, the burden is placed on future generations, which have to pay for goods benefiting current citizens. We should note that many of the goods purchased are capital goods that benefit future generations as well. For example, we currently benefit from spending that occurred to build the interstate highway system. Hopefully, in deciding whether to borrow money to finance a project or program, the public decision makers choose only those projects that have expected future returns at least equal to expected future interest payments.

Fourth, another concern is the potential impact of the national debt on the distribution of income. Income is redistributed from the taxpaying public to bondholders to the extent that the interest of the national debt is financed through taxation. If government bondholders are primarily high-income persons, the bondholders will get a return that is financed from the general population. This results in a redistribution from the general population to high-income bond owners. A related concern is the amount of debt held by foreigners. In the third quarter of 1988, foreigners held $334 billion in bonds, which translates into 13 percent of the national debt.

Finally, some people fear that the country will go bankrupt. The fallacy that most people fall into is that they liken their own family budget situation to that of the government. They see that the government is not living within its means, and they compare that situation to the person who is living beyond his or her earnings and is having difficulty paying off debts. If people believe in the ability of the U.S. government to repay its obligations, then there is no threat of bankruptcy. Because of the ability of the federal government to print money, and the confidence the public places in it, the federal government can borrow money with ease. In fact, the debt is never repaid in its entirety since the federal government is easily able to rollover the debt. That is, while some people are cashing in their government securities, the government turns around and sells bonds to others.

CHAPTER

11

Money, Banking, and Monetary Policy

Objectives

Upon completion of this chapter, you should understand:

1.   The three functions of money and the different definitions of our money supply.

2.   The structure and functions of the Federal Reserve Banking System.

3.   How the banking system creates money.

4.   How the Federal Reserve uses monetary policy tools to reduce unemployment and inflation.

5.   The effectiveness of monetary policy.

6.   The difference between the monetarist and Keynesian models.

Throughout history, many objects have been used as money. For example, on Fiji, whale teeth served as money; in the Philippines, rice was used; in Barbados, sugar; and in Virginia in the 1600s, tobacco was accepted as money. Our fascination with money has not diminished over the years. Its importance to most people stems from the desire to possess money so as to be able to buy the necessities and extras they want. Many people misunderstand what money is and why it is important. Some still believe that the dollar is valuable because it is backed by gold, when in fact the only reason that the dollar has value is because people are commonly willing to accept it as money.

In this chapter we are concerned with the role money plays in modern society. We first examine the functions of money. Next, we discuss the structure of the U.S. banking system and how banks create money. Third, we describe how the Federal Reserve attempts to control the supply of money in order to eliminate recessionary and inflationary gaps. Our discussion of the impact of monetary policy on income, employment, and prices will be initially developed from the Keynesian perspective. We conclude the chapter with an examination of an alternative approach called monetarism.

11.1 Money

What makes something money? In order for an object to be considered money, it must be commonly accepted. For example, individuals, stores, and banks are willing to take the object in exchange for goods and services because they are confident that others will accept it as money. One reason for this common acceptance is that the government declares that the object is money. For example, on each dollar in the United States the sentence in the upper left-hand corner proclaims "This note is legal tender for all debts, public and private." In addition, through responsible management of the economy and the resulting faith that people place in the stability of the government, we have confidence that the dollar will have a stable value. What are the functions of money?

Functions of Money

There are three functions that must be fulfilled for something to serve as money. It must be accepted as (1) a medium of exchange, (2) a standard unit of value, and (3) a store of value. Money functions as a ***medium of exchange*** when someone purchases or sells an item with money. Economies in which money is not used to conduct transactions are called ***barter*** economies. The use of money frees up time for more productive activity. For example, if a student were willing to type term papers for others in a barter economy, how would this student be paid? The student would have to locate someone who wanted a paper typed and was willing to trade something that the student desired. A person with woodworking skills might offer to build shelves in exchange for the typed paper. A person who cooked well might offer five dinners. The time spent in searching for the ***coincidence of wants*** required for a barter exchange would be better spent in a productive activity. With money we can buy from

297

anyone because they accept the money to purchase whatever they desire. Over time, societies have adopted a variety of commodities as money, as we noted in the introduction to this chapter. The common characteristics of commodities used as money are as follows: they are durable, portable, divisible, and limited in supply.

A second function of money is that it serves as a ***standard unit of value***. When money is used to express the prices of all our transactions, it acts as a standard unit of value. For example, in a department or grocery store, money enables the manager to put price tags on items to indicate their value.

Finally, money serves as a ***store of value***. Money can be saved so that it can be spent in the future. Money in the United States is easily saved since banks are willing to repay depositors. Deposit $1 in a bank today and you can easily withdraw $1 in one year.

The Money Supply

The ***money supply*** is defined in a variety of ways. The definition most economists consider the best, officially called ***M1***, includes those assets that can be used directly as a medium of exchange: (1) coins, (2) paper money or Federal Reserve Notes, and (3) demand deposits. Most coins in circulation are called token money since their face value is greater than the metal from which they are made. Our coins and paper money are minted by the U.S. Treasury and are subsequently issued by the central bank of the United States, the Federal Reserve, to replace old money as it wears out. The U.S. Treasury destroys old money by shredding or burning it. Together, coins and paper money are referred to as ***currency*** and make up approximately 25 percent of the money supply. Currency in the United States is based on an ***inconvertible money standard***, which means that it cannot freely be converted into gold or silver through government. Therefore, the value of currency is based on its purchasing power — what can be bought with it.

Demand deposits (or deposits in checking accounts) make up about 75 percent of the money supply. Why are demand deposits regarded as money? Demand deposits are a promise by the bank to pay the bearer upon demand (i.e., presentation of a check). They are considered to be money because they are an acceptable form of payment in transactions. Most checking accounts earn no interest, but M1 also includes interest-bearing checking deposits in *NOW* (Negotiable Order of Withdrawal) accounts in both commercial banks and thrift institutions.

M2 is a broader measure of money, incorporating some assets that, although not directly "spendable," can easily be converted for transactions. These assets are less *liquid* than demand deposits, which means that they are not as easy to convert into currency. They are called ***near-money***. M2 contains, in addition to the components of M1, savings deposits, time deposits of less than $100,000, and money-market mutual funds (where small savers are able to pool their money with others to purchase short-term bonds). Finally, ***L*** is the broadest measure of liquid assets, adding to M2 large-denomination time deposits, Treasury bills, and U.S. savings bonds. These securities are part of savings but can be transformed quickly into spending money. For the period ending December 1988, M1 totaled $789 billion, M2 totaled $3,067 billion, and L totaled over $4,600 billion. Note that currency held *in bank vaults* is not a part of our money supply because it is not in circulation, being used as money. We would be double counting if we included the currency inside of bank vaults in our definition of money since demand deposits are already representing that currency. Throughout the remainder of this chapter, the term *money* will always refer to the M1 definition.

See the *Data Appendix* for more comprehensive statistics on the U.S. money supply.

11.2 The Banking System

Since most of our money supply is in the form of demand deposits, we need a clear understanding of our banking system and how it affects us. We will discover in the following sections that banks and some other types of financial institutions have a unique ability to create and destroy money.

Banks

Banks are privately owned, profit-maximizing firms. Traditionally, there have been two types of banking institutions: commercial banks and thrift institutions (e.g., savings and loan associations, mutual savings banks, and credit unions). Both accept deposits, keep some deposits on hand, and lend the rest out to individual, corporate, and government borrowers. The major difference between commercial banks and thrift institutions was in the types of loans issued. Historically, only commercial banks were able to issue demand deposits. Other institutions were restricted to savings and time deposits against which checks could not be written. As will be discussed later, recent legislation has blurred this traditional distinction since commercial banks and thrift institutions are now offering similar services. Even so, commercial banks still issue the majority of demand deposits.

The structure of the banking industry in the United States is unique. In other countries, the banking industry tends to be dominated by a relatively small number of large banks, each with a large number of regional branch offices. In the United States, however, the banking industry contains many relatively small localized units. There are about 15,000 independent commercial banks in the United States and many thousands more thrift institutions as well. As we will soon discuss, legislature passed in 1980 has altered the complexion of the U.S. banking system.

The Federal Reserve System

The *Federal Reserve Banking System* (called *the Fed*) is the central bank of the United States. The Fed was created by the Federal Reserve Act of 1913, which was enacted after the Bank Panic of 1907. A large number of banks failed in 1907, amid the chaos of a collapsing monetary system. The major function of the Fed is to control the money supply. The Fed also acts as a clearinghouse for checks issued by commercial banks. For example, assume that while on vacation you write a check from your bank in Philadelphia to a merchant in Florida, who deposits it in a Miami bank. How does the Miami bank get the money? It would be costly if the bank in Miami had to collect directly from each bank from which it receives checks. In reality, these transactions occur quickly because the Fed assists in the transfer of funds from the Philadelphia bank to the bank in Miami. Another function of the Fed is to issue new paper money to replace old, worn out bills. It also acts as the bank for the federal government in its budget transactions. Finally, the Fed regulates commercial banking operations for safety by conducting periodic bank examinations.

As Figure 11.1 shows, the United States is divided into twelve Federal Reserve Districts, each having its own Federal Reserve District Bank. Each of the Federal Reserve District banks is owned by its member banks, since the initial financial capital required to establish the district banks came from the member banks. Even though the Fed is owned by member banks, it is responsible to Congress and is chartered to act in the best interests of the public.

The actions of these district banks are coordinated by a seven-member *Board of Governors* in Washington, D.C., where the Fed is headquartered. The members of the Board of Governors are appointed by the president of the United States, subject to approval by the Senate. They each serve fourteen-year terms which are staggered so that one member is replaced every two years. Now that we have examined our banking system, we are in a position to understand the sweeping impact of legislation passed in 1980.

The Depository Institutions Deregulation and Monetary Control Act of 1980

Regulation of the banking industry changed dramatically with the passage of the *Depository Institutions Deregulation and Monetary Control Act of 1980 (DIDMCA)*. One effect of this act was to increase the power of the Fed. Prior to its enactment, less than half of all commercial banks were members of the Fed, although these member banks held more than 70 percent of all demand deposits. Members of the Fed were required to hold more currency on reserve at the Fed than banks which were not members. With interest rates rising during the 1970s, banks became more and more reluctant to keep currency on deposit with the Fed since the opportunity cost was so high. Currency that they were not permitted to lend was not earning a return. As interest rates increased, the cost to banks of the potential return lost on idle funds increased. This induced banks to leave the Fed, causing the power of the Fed to diminish. The DIDMCA of 1980 requires *all* commercial banks that issue demand deposits to keep the same level of currency on deposit at the Fed or at member banks even if they themselves are not members of the Fed. By forcing all banks to keep the same deposits, the Fed now has greater control over the money supply (to be discussed in Section 11.4).

In addition, the DIDMCA of 1980 permitted interest payments on demand deposits and set in motion the elimination of ceilings on interest rates offered by savings accounts. Finally, banks were allowed to expand the size of operation through branch banking into contiguous

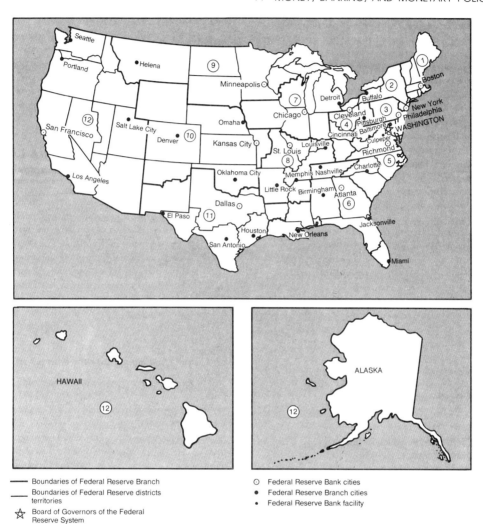

Figure 11.1. The Federal Reserve System: Boundaries of Federal Reserve Districts and Their Branch Territories. The Federal Reserve System is divided into 12 regional branches. (From Board of Governors of the Federal Reserve System, *Federal Reserve Bulletin,* Washington, D.C.: Publication Services.)

counties. The main motivation for the removal of interest rate regulations and expansion of bank services into rival areas was to increase competition and therefore to make the money market operate more efficiently. Additional legislation was passed to make savings and loan institutions (S&Ls) more competitive in attracting funds. Unfortunately, this led to the collapse of many S&Ls, as the following boxed insert describes.

What Caused the Current Crisis in the Savings and Loan Industry?

As inflation heated up in the 1970s, competition for deposits intensified. Interest rates that savings and loan institutions (S&Ls) were permitted to pay hit the legal limit as the interest rates offered by other financial institutions surged past it. This caused currency to be pulled out of S&Ls as depositors looked for higher returns.

In response, Congress passed the Garn-St. Germaine bill in 1982 which allowed S&Ls to offer more financial services and to pay higher interest rates. In a separate action, Congress increased the insurance limit by the Federal Deposit Insurance Corporation on savings per account from $40,000 to $100,000.

S&Ls began to expand their operations in the Southwest in response to the oil boom of the early 1980s. They provided the funds to finance many high-risk projects such as the construction of apartments and office buildings. In addition, during the mid-1980s many S&Ls were taken over by dishonest management. In 1986, the Texas economy collapsed as a result of the sharp decrease in oil prices. Many of the loans that the S&Ls financed went into default. The record default rate drove many S&Ls into insolvency, putting tremendous financial pressure on the federal insurance agencies.

NOTE: Federal legislation passed August 1989 created the Resolution Trust Corp. to bail out ailing S&Ls. The cost of this mammoth cleanup is expected to be $166 billion over the next ten years.

The above is a summary of an article, "How $100B Slid Down the Drain," which appeared in *USA Today,* February 13, 1989, p. 3B (no author cited).

11.3 How Banks Create Money

As mentioned in Section 11.2, banks are profit maximizers like other businesses. Banks want to make as many loans as they safely can in order to earn interest. Our main interest in this section is how banks create money through this lending process.

Goldsmith Banks and the Creation of Money

Early banks existed because it was difficult and risky to carry around large amounts of gold. People paid to leave their gold with goldsmiths and others with sturdy vaults in exchange for a receipt that could be traded for merchandise or exchanged for the gold that was originally deposited. These "goldsmith banks" were the foundation of our modern banking system, and they provide a good example of how banks in general can create money.

Assume that the goldsmith bank held all the gold placed on deposit in its vault. This type of banking system has no effect on the supply of money. Customers have simply traded in one type of money (gold) for another type (the gold deposit receipt). But if the goldsmith were to lend out some of the gold left on deposit, the supply of money would rise. For example, assume that the goldsmith bank had $1,000 worth of gold placed on deposit. The banker realized that, based on past experience, it was likely that the gold would not all be withdrawn at the same time. In fact, the bank would probably have other deposits coming in to offset any withdrawals that occurred. Because of this, the bank would not need to hold the entire original deposit. The bank could earn extra income by keeping only a fraction of the original deposit in the vault and lending out the rest. Over time banks found that lending gold was so lucrative that banks paid customers interest to attract more deposits. As a result, banks gradually evolved from safekeeping institutions (to which depositors paid a fee) to lending institutions (which paid interest to depositors to attract funds that could be loaned out at a profit).

Note that this lending process increases the supply of money. If the goldsmith bank lends out $400 of the $1,000 in gold deposits, it is injecting $400 of additional money back into the economy. In addition to the $1,000 of gold receipt deposits (a type of money) still held by bank customers, there is now an extra $400 of gold in the system. Modern commercial banks are able to create money in a similar way.

The Commercial Banking System and the Money Multiplier

Before we can explain how modern banks create money, we must define a few terms. The currency held by commercial banks is called **total reserves**. Total reserves are not part of our money supply since (as we noted in Section 11.1) currency held in bank vaults is not in circulation being used as money. These banks are required to keep a certain *percentage* of their total reserves at the Federal Reserve Bank or vault cash, which is called the **reserve requirement** (r). The currency kept on deposit at the Fed, which the banks are not permitted to lend, are called **required reserves** (total reserves multiplied by the reserve requirement). Banks are free to lend out the remaining portion, called **excess reserves** (total reserves minus required reserves), to consumers, businesses, and the government. Figure 11.2 and Table 11.1 illustrate the process.

For example, assume that $100 not previously in circulation is deposited in bank *A* (column 2). Assuming a reserve requirement of 20 percent, bank *A* has required reserves of $20 (column 3), which leaves this bank with $80 in excess reserves. Bank *A* would now be able to lend out this $80 in excess reserves (column 4). It is through this lending process that the creation of money takes place. Why? Note that the $80 in excess reserves is not money. This $80 of currency inside the bank vault only becomes money when it is placed into circulation through the lending process.

Now assume that bank *A* lends the $80 (newly created money) to Joe, who then buys a camera. The camera dealer deposits the $80 in his or her checking account in bank *B*. Bank *B* also has to maintain a 20 percent reserve and would therefore keep $16 ($80 multiplied by

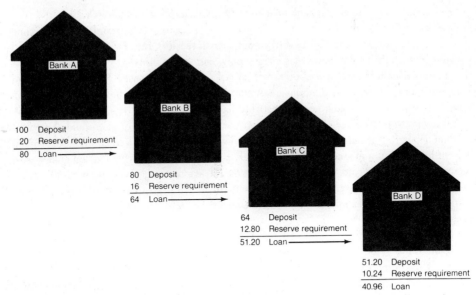

Figure 11.2.   Banks and the Creation of Money. Because of fractional reserve banking, when $100 is deposited into the banking system, the money supply will increase by more than $100. (From American Enterprise *Teaching Notes.*)

Table 11.1
Expansion of the Money Supply When $100 of
New Deposits Are Injected into the Banking
System

(1) Bank	(2) New Deposits	(3) Required Reserves[a]	(4) Amount Banks Can Lend
A	$100.00	$ 20.00	$ 80.00
B	80.00	16.00	64.00
C	64.00	12.80	51.20
D	51.20	10.24	40.96
	.	.	.
	.	.	.
	.	.	.
TOTAL	$500.00	$100.00	$400.00

[a] Reserve requirement is 20 percent.

0.20) as required reserves. This would leave $64 ($80 minus $16) as excess reserves which bank B would then lend. When the $64 of idle currency (excess reserves) is put into circulation through this lending process, $64 of money is created. As Figure 11.2 illustrates, this process continues as deposits are made in banks C and D. But this is not the end of the story. This process would continue as long as excess reserves were created by new deposits. The amount that each bank has available to lend out is diminishing (20 percent of each deposit is held as required reserves). Note that the banking system can expand the amount of loans it makes by many times the initial excess reserves.

Algebraically, it is simple to calculate the resulting change in the money supply when there is a change in initial excess reserves (bank A) given the reserve requirement (r). The potential *money multiplier* is $(\frac{1}{r})$. In the example above it was assumed that banks were holding 20 percent, or $\frac{1}{5}$, in required reserves. Therefore, the money multiplier would be calculated as

$$\left(\frac{1}{r}\right) = (1/\tfrac{1}{5}) = 5$$

With a potential money multiplier of 5, the money supply will increase by a maximum of five times the amount of the initial excess reserves. When $100 is deposited in bank A (see column 2), the potential increase in the money supply is $400 (column 4) based on the initial excess reserves *(ER)* created ($80). This is calculated by using the following equation:

$$\text{change in money supply} = \frac{1}{r} \times \text{initial } ER$$
$$= 5 \times \$80$$
$$= \$400$$

This process also works in reverse. If there is a decrease in excess reserves, the money supply will fall by a multiple amount. For example, if $100 were removed from the banking system, the money supply would decrease by $400, which is five times the loss in excess reserves of $80.

There are a variety of reasons why the actual increase in the money supply is normally less than the potential increase. First, people receiving funds must deposit them into their bank accounts. In the example above, if the camera dealer had held the $80 received from Joe as cash rather than depositing it in bank B, no more loanable excess reserves would have been created and the expansion process would have ended prematurely.

Second, banks must be willing to make loans rather than holding excess reserves. During periods of low interest rates, banks tend to hold more excess reserves since they do not feel the interest rate adequately covers the costs of the loan. During the Great Depression of the 1930s, the interest rate was very low (less than 1 percent) and the risk of default on loans was high. As a result, banks were reluctant to lend money.

Finally, people must be willing to borrow from the bank. There may be funds available, but no new money will be created if people are not willing to borrow it. This tends to occur more during periods of recession since households facing layoff and firms with excess inventories are reluctant to borrow.

11.4 Monetary Policy

The purpose of this section is to explain how the Fed attempts to control the money supply in order to stabilize GNP at full employment, eliminating unemployment or inflation.

Tools of Monetary Policy

There are three major quantitative tools that the Fed uses to influence the money supply: (1) open market operations, (2) the reserve requirement, and (3) the discount rate.

Open Market Operations   By buying or selling U.S. securities (bonds) in the open market, the Fed can change bank reserves and thereby tighten or loosen the money supply. This buying and selling of U.S. securities by the Fed is called *open market operations*. Open market operations is the most frequently used monetary policy tool.

The *Federal Open Market Committee (FOMC)* is responsible for determining open market policy. The committee is composed of twelve members — the seven-member Board of Governors (described in Section 11.2) and five presidents selected from the twelve regional Federal Reserve District banks. The committee meets approximately once a month and tries to keep the meetings as confidential as possible so that no one has an advantage in financial markets when policy is implemented. The buying and selling of U.S. securities is carried out by the Federal Reserve Bank of New York since New York City is the financial center of the United States.

If the FOMC decides that it will be desirable to increase the money supply, it will buy bonds in the open market. If it *buys* $100 in government securities, the people selling the bonds will probably deposit the $100 received in a bank, thus increasing reserves. This is a fresh injection of funds into the banking system by the Fed. Given additional excess reserves, commercial banks will generally make more loans, which will lead to an increase in the money supply. The potential increase in the money supply depends on the size of the money multiplier.

The *sale* of U.S. securities has the opposite effect. By selling bonds, the Fed is paid with checks from commercial banks, which decreases the banks' excess reserves. This reduction in excess reserves will force banks to cut back on their lending, which in turn will cause the money supply to contract.

The Reserve Requirement   Legislation passed in the 1930s gave the Fed the power to change the percent of reserves that member banks were not permitted to lend. With the passing of the DIDMCA of 1980, *all* commercial banks issuing demand deposits (including nonmembers) have to comply with the reserve requirement set by the Fed. Earlier, we assumed that there is only one reserve requirement. In reality, there are different reserve requirements, depending on the type of deposit and amount deposited in banks.

When the Fed alters the reserve requirement, it is varying the amount that banks may lend by adjusting the amount of excess reserves banks hold. For example, assume that the Fed lowers the reserve requirement on demand deposits from 20 percent to 10 percent. The result of the decrease in the reserve requirement would be increased excess reserves and a larger potential money multiplier. If bank A is holding $1,000 in demand deposits, it previously was required to hold 20 percent or $200 in reserves. With the decrease in the reserve requirement from 20 percent to 10 percent, its required reserves would fall from $200 to $100. This would result in a $100 increase in excess reserves that the bank could lend from $800 to $900.

In addition, if the reserve requirement were decreased from 20 percent to 10 percent, the potential money multiplier would rise from 5 to 10. The original potential money multiplier equals $(1/r)$ which is $(1/\frac{1}{5})$ or 5. The new potential money multiplier equals $(1/\frac{1}{10})$ or 10. With the original reserve requirement of 20 percent, the money supply could rise by $4,000 ($5 \times 800). When the reserve requirement decreased to 10 percent, the money supply would be able to expand by $9,000 ($10 \times 900).

As a regulatory tool, the reserve requirement is not used with great frequency. The reserve requirement is considered a blunt instrument because a slight change in the reserve requirement can have a great impact on the money supply. In addition, if the Fed were to change the reserve requirement frequently, it could wreak havoc with each bank's long-term planning in deciding how much currency to lend.

The Discount Rate   The discount rate is the third major monetary policy tool. When banks borrow reserves from the Fed, these loans are called "discounts." The ***discount rate*** is the interest rate paid by banks for these loans. By varying this rate, the Fed affects the willingness of banks to borrow from the Fed, which changes the amount of excess reserves in the banking system. The change in excess reserves will affect the ability of banks to lend money, which in turn causes the money supply to rise or fall.

Originally, the Fed was intended to be the "lender of last resort." For example, if member banks' reserves fell below their required amount, they could temporarily borrow funds from the Fed to cover the shortage. As things have turned out, commercial banks have been reluctant to borrow from the Fed since it might make the Fed look more carefully into their dealings. Banks prefer to borrow from other banks or to sell securities. Therefore, this tool is also not often employed and is not very effective. By borrowing from other banks, there is no change in total reserves in the banking system as there would be if banks were to borrow from the Fed. The *federal funds rate* is the interest rate banks pay other banks when they borrow money from each other.

The primary reason that the Fed varies the discount rate is to indicate a change in Federal Reserve policy. If the Fed wanted to tighten credit, it would announce a rise in the discount rate. The announced rise in the discount rate would be a signal to banks that the Fed was tightening credit. As a result, banks might begin cutting back their loans in response to the anticipated change. If the Fed were to reduce the discount rate, it would have the opposite effect. It would signal a loosening of credit conditions. Given these three monetary policy tools, how does a change in the supply of money affect the rest of the economy?

Eliminating Recessionary and Inflationary Gaps

Keynesians believe that changes in the money supply indirectly affect equilibrium GNP through variations in the interest rate. These changes in the interest rate alter the level of planned autonomous investment and consumption. We will now examine how monetary policy might be used to influence aggregate demand to reduce recessionary and inflationary gaps.

Recessionary Gap   Given a recessionary gap, the goal of policymakers is to raise total demand to full-employment GNP in order to eliminate unemployment. In order to stimulate spending, monetary authorities would want to lower interest rates to make credit easier to obtain. To achieve the desired increase in the money supply, more excess reserves must be made available to banks. As noted above, this could be accomplished by the Fed buying U.S. securities in the open market, lowering the reserve requirement, and lowering the discount rate. The increase in the money supply will cause interest rates to fall, which in turn brings about an increase in planned autonomous investment as well as autonomous consumption $(I_0 + C_0)$. Consequently, aggregate demand will rise, increasing GNP to full employment. This process is summarized by the following notation:

$$\uparrow ER \rightarrow \uparrow M \rightarrow \downarrow i \rightarrow \uparrow I_0 + C_0 \rightarrow \uparrow AD \rightarrow \uparrow \text{GNP to full employment}$$

Excess reserves increase ($\uparrow ER$), which increases the money supply ($\uparrow M$). This increase in the money supply will cause interest rates to fall ($\downarrow i$), leading to increased planned autonomous investment and consumption ($\uparrow I_0 + C_0$), which leads to greater aggregate demand ($\uparrow AD$) and an increase in GNP ($\uparrow$ GNP) to full employment.

Inflationary Gap   When an inflationary gap exists, policymakers must find ways to decrease aggregate demand so that inflation is reduced. To discourage spending, monetary authorities would want to raise interest rates to make credit more difficult to obtain. To attain the necessary decrease in the money supply, excess reserves must be reduced. We noted that selling U.S. securities in the open market by the Fed, raising the reserve requirement, and increasing the discount rate will accomplish this. The reduction in the money supply will cause interest rates to rise, which in turn brings about a decline in planned autonomous investment as well as autonomous consumption. Consequently, aggregate demand will fall, reducing equilibrium GNP to full employment. This process is summarized as follows:

$$\downarrow ER \rightarrow \downarrow M \rightarrow \uparrow i \rightarrow \downarrow I_0 + C_0 \rightarrow \downarrow AD \rightarrow \downarrow \text{GNP to full employment}$$

11.5 Evaluation of Monetary Policy

Chapter 10 examined how fiscal policy can be used to stabilize GNP at full employment. Now we've seen that monetary policy can be used to achieve the same end. Is there any reason to prefer one policy over the other?

Advantages of Monetary Policy

There are three advantages of monetary policy. First, decisions on monetary policy by the Board of Governors can be reached and applied rapidly. Second, it is easy to change the amount of the dose if needs dictate. Fiscal policy, on the other hand, takes considerable time to apply, and it is very difficult to vary the size of the spending or tax change once the budget is enacted. Finally, some economists argue that monetary policy is more impersonal. They state that the market, not the Fed, determines who is affected by the change in monetary policy. For example, when the Fed decreases the supply of money and drives the interest rate up, it does not choose who will receive loans and who will not. Those firms that can afford the higher interest rates will still be able to borrow money. On the other hand, fiscal policy is not as impersonal. An increase in defense spending will benefit certain manufacturers and specific regions of the United States.

Disadvantages of Monetary Policy

However, there are also a number of disadvantages of monetary policy. First, the Fed's attempt to reduce the business cycle might backfire and have a destabilizing effect on the economy. For example, the Fed might pursue a low-interest policy to stimulate aggregate demand and output. This low-interest policy might fuel inflation, which would later require higher interest rates to dampen the expansion and hold down inflation. Fiscal policy, however, suffers from the same problem. An increase in spending or lower taxes might be required to increase aggregate demand to reduce unemployment, which could lead to inflation, requiring a subsequent reduction in spending or higher taxes.

Second, the effectiveness of monetary policy in changing aggregate demand is questionable. Some economists argue that investment is not very sensitive to changes in the interest rate. For example, we would expect a drop in interest rates to cause investment spending to rise. But in a recession, planned investment is likely to decrease regardless of the rate of interest because of the slump in sales.

Third, tight monetary policy harms certain types of firms more than others. For example, small firms depend more on borrowing than large firms. Also, the construction industry is very sensitive to changes in the interest rate. A change of a few percentage points in interest rates has a major impact on monthly payment of mortgages. For example, a $50,000, 25-year mortgage at 9 percent will require a monthly payment of $420.00. If the interest rate were 12 percent, all other things remaining the same, the monthly payment would be $527.00. If interest rates rise, the effective demand for new housing will fall. Other interest-sensitive industries include automobiles, major appliances, and home renovation. In addition, older firms with established lines of credit have an easier time obtaining loans than newer firms.

Fourth, there is a possible conflict between the Federal Reserve and the Executive Branch of the federal government. Since the members of the Board of Governors of the Federal Reserve Bank are appointed for fourteen-year terms which do not coincide with the election of the president, there have been periods during which the Fed undertook actions in opposition to the stated policy of the president. This can make coordinating fiscal and monetary policy difficult. But the separation of power is important because it provides for a system of "checks and balances" — no *one* group holds all power. It is hoped that this system leads to policy that is in the best interest of society.

Finally, there can be conflict between domestic and international policies. Programs that are desirable for the United States may clash with international economic events. For example, during an inflationary period, the Fed might pursue a policy that was designed to increase interest rates. If interest rates were to rise above the level that prevailed in other countries, it is likely that foreign investors would shift their funds to the United States to take advantage of the higher interest rates. This would increase bank reserves in this country, thus enabling banks to lend more money. The Fed might have to undertake further measures to tighten credit, which would raise interest rates and start the process all over again.

It is not always clear when and how much of each type of policy to employ. During a recessionary period, aggregate demand is very difficult to stimulate through loose monetary policy. Fiscal policy can directly force an increase in aggregate demand through increased government purchases, lower taxes, or increased transfer payments. Monetary policy is more effective in reducing inflationary gaps. In general, some combination of fiscal and monetary policy is needed to stabilize the economy. Because of the many limitations described in this chapter and in Chapter 10, it is difficult to design a foolproof stabilization policy to fine-tune the economy into a position of full employment with stable prices.

11.6 Monetarism

Up to this point the focus has been on the Keynesian perspective of how the money supply affects income, employment, and prices. An alternative view of the role of money in our economy is called **monetarism**. The emphasis of the new classical school is on long-run economic growth rather than short-run stability. As we note in the appendix, the proponents of monetarism believe that any policy measures designed to achieve short-run stability will actually have a destabilizing effect on the economy.

What Is Monetarism?

The classical school of thought believes that there is a direct relationship between the money supply and the price level. The classical approach is based on the **equation of exchange**:

$$MV = PQ$$

In this equation, MV represents the total spending for goods and services or what is purchased in a given period of time. Total spending is equal to the money supply (M), multiplied by the number of times each unit of money is spent, which is called the *velocity of circulation of money* (V). On the right-hand side, PQ represents the value of production or what is sold in a given period. The value of production is determined by multiplying the prices of all goods and services (P) by the quantity of all goods and services produced (Q). MV and PQ are equal to each other since what is purchased is always equal to what is sold.

The classicists argued that the quantity of goods and services produced (Q) is determined by the amount of resources available, such as the supply of labor and capital. In addition, they assumed that the economy would always be at full employment in the long run. If GNP were to fall below full employment, market forces would act to bring the economy back to full employment. Because of these assumptions, Q is treated as a constant.

The velocity of money is determined by institutional characteristics such as payment habits, the structure of the banking industry, and frequency of wage payments. Since these influences do not often change, velocity is assumed to be stable. Therefore, if both Q and V are constant, changes in the money supply affect only the price level. An increase in the money supply results in increased demand. Since the economy is already at full employment and velocity is constant, the only change that will occur is an increase in prices. This theory is called the *quantity theory of money*. For example, if M equals \$1,000, V equals 4, P is \$2, and Q totals 2,000, the equation of exchange is

$$MV = PQ$$
$$\$1,000\ (4) = \$2\ (2,000)$$
$$\$4,000 = \$4,000$$

If the money supply increases to \$1,500, the following change would occur:

$$MV = PQ$$
$$\$1,500\ (4) = \$3\ (2,000)$$
$$\$6,000 = \$6,000$$

The only variable that would change is the price level because both the velocity of money and output remain constant. A 50 percent increase in the money supply has led to increased spending and a 50 percent increase in the price level. The monetarists, therefore, argued that the money supply should be carefully controlled because growth in the money supply will lead to a rise in prices.

Modern monetarists propose that money be allowed to grow at a rate equal to the growth of full-employment output. In this way the increase in the money supply would provide just enough additional spending power for the new goods and services produced. The intended result is that the economy will enjoy full employment and stable prices over the long run.

See the appendix to this chapter for a detailed discussion of the difference between the Keynesian and monetarist philosophies.

Barter Exchange: A Case Study

P.O.W. camps during World War II provide a good example of how a simple economy works. Radford's observations were based on camps which held between 1,200 and 2,500 people, housed in buildings holding approximately 200 people. There was trading between groups living within each building. Each prisoner received parcels from the Red Cross, consisting of such items as jam, butter, sugar, and cigarettes. Private parcels of all sorts of articles were received, but were not equally distributed. Trading became the means by which the prisoners were able to maximize individual satisfaction.

Simple barter exchange, such as a nonsmoker trading cigarettes for anything else, were the first exchanges. Thereafter, exchanges became more complex. As the volume of trade grew, the relative values of goods were well known and expressed in terms of cigarettes, which became the standard of value. People wandered the camp calling their offers — "cheese for seven" (cigarettes). This was replaced by a board that listed offers, which were crossed out when consummated.

Cigarettes were the normal currency and fulfilled the roles of money. They were homogeneous, fairly durable, and convenient for trading. The more popular brands of cigarettes were rarely traded, and those that were machine-made were universally acceptable. Home-made cigarettes were carefully examined. Some people would use less tobacco to make these cigarettes, decreasing their value.

Because of the changes in the supply of cigarettes there was a great deal of economic instability. Generally, prices for goods varied directly with changes in the supply of money (cigarettes). For example, in August 1944, the supplies of cigarettes and rations were cut in half. When the steady inflow of cigarettes stopped, the stock of cigarettes fell, prices fell, trading declined, and barter prevailed.

Source: This is a summary of "The Economic Organization of a P.O.W. Camp" by R. A. Radford, which appeared in *Economica* in 1945.

Summary

Many things can serve as money. The key to an item's success as money is that it must be commonly accepted. There are three functions of money: (1) medium of exchange, (2) standard unit of value, and (3) store of value. Economists use a number of different definitions of money, but the most common is M1, which defines money as currency plus demand deposits.

The supply of money is largely determined by the banking system. Since banks can lend out a part of their reserves, the banking system is able to create money. The banking system can increase the money supply by many times the original deposit via the money multiplier. The amount of money created is influenced by the Federal Reserve. The Federal Reserve is the central bank of the United States. Through the use of open market operations, the reserve requirement, and the discount rate, the Fed can vary the quantity of excess reserves banks hold. The Fed's most frequently used weapon is open market operations, which is the buying and selling of U.S. securities in the open market. When the FOMC buys U.S. securities, it is injecting excess reserves into the banking system. When it sells bonds, excess reserves will fall. Under the Keynesian approach, the Fed manages excess reserves, which influences loans, and therefore the money supply. The resulting change in the interest rate will then cause investment and consumer spending to change, leading to a movement in equilibrium GNP toward full employment.

Advantages of monetary policy include the ease, quickness, and impersonal nature of its application. The major disadvantage is that it is not certain that a change in the money supply will have a significant effect on investment and consumption, especially during a recession.

Monetarists believe that monetary policy is the only effective tool. Monetarism is based on the equation of exchange. Assuming that velocity is predictable, changes in the money supply will have a direct effect on price. Monetarists frown on the use of discretionary policy because they believe it is impossible to fine-tune the economy. Finally, monetarism stresses long-run growth as a goal rather than short-run stabilization.

Key Concepts

medium of exchange
barter
coincidence of wants
standard unit of value
store of value
money supply
currency
inconvertible money standard
demand deposits
M1, M2, and L definitions of money
near-money
Federal Reserve Banking System (the Fed)
Board of Governors
DIDMCA of 1980
reserve requirement
total, required, and excess reserves
money multiplier
open market operations
Federal Open Market Committee (FOMC)
discount rate

monetarism
equation of exchange
velocity of circulation of money
quantity theory of money

Self-Test Questions: True or False

T F 1. Money is serving its role as a store of value when something is purchased with money.

T F 2. M1 is the most commonly accepted definition of money because it includes all types of money and near-money.

T F 3. The main purpose of the DIDMCA of 1980 was to decrease competition in banking.

T F 4. The value of the dollar is assured because it is backed by gold.

T F 5. The banking system is able to create money because it can lend out a part of its reserves.

T F 6. If the reserve requirement is 10 percent, a $10 million increase in initial excess reserves will lead to a $100 million potential increase in the supply of money.

T F 7. The most frequently used tool of monetary policy by the Fed is open market operations.

T F 8. According to the Keynesian approach, if the Fed wanted to stimulate investment in order to increase GNP, the Fed could lower the discount rate, lower the reserve requirement, or sell bonds in the open market.

T F 9. An advantage of monetary policy is that a decrease in interest rates will cause investment spending to fall by a significant amount.

T F 10. Assume that $M = \$2,000$, $V = 3$, $P = \$6$, and $Q = 1,000$. If the money supply increases to $3,000, then according to the quantity theory of money, the price level will rise to $9.

Answers to Self-Test Questions

1. *False.* When money is used to purchase a good or service, it fulfills its role as a medium of exchange. Money is acting as a store of value when it is saved.

2. *False.* While it is true that M1 is the most commonly accepted definition of money, the reason given is false. M1 is the most narrow definition of money. It is made up of currency, demand deposits, and savings deposits on which checks can be drawn. Near-monies, which are less liquid than demand deposits, are only included in M2 and L.

3. ***False.*** The main purpose of the DIDMCA of 1980 was to increase competition among banks and to allow them to compete more effectively against other financial institutions. In addition, the DIDMCA of 1980 gave the Fed more power over the control of the money supply.

4. ***False.*** The value of the dollar is not based on gold. Its value is measured by how many goods and services we can purchase with the dollar. The dollar is commonly accepted because of the confidence people place in the stability of the economy of the United States.

5. ***True.*** Banks hold only a fraction of reserves and can lend out the rest. Through the lending of reserves, the banking system is able to create money. If a 100 percent reserves system were used, the banking system would not be able to make loans, and therefore banks would have no impact on the money supply.

6. ***True.*** If the reserve requirement is 10 percent, the money multiplier will equal $(1/r)$ or $(1/\frac{1}{10})$ or 10. The money multiplier shows the potential increase in the money supply when there is an increase in initial excess reserves. Therefore, if excess reserves initially increase by $10 million, the total increase in the money supply will be 10 times this increase in excess reserves or $100 million.

7. ***True.*** Open market operations are the most frequently used tool the Fed has at its disposal. It is used on a daily basis. The other major weapons, the discount rate and the reserve requirement, are used with much less frequency.

8. ***False.*** For investment to increase, the interest rate would have to fall. To achieve this result, the Fed would embark on a program to increase the money supply. Lowering the discount rate and lowering the reserve requirement would have the desired effect. But by selling bonds in the open market, the Fed would actually be decreasing excess reserves and therefore decrease the money supply. Consequently, if the Fed wanted to increase the money supply, it would have to *buy* bonds rather than *sell* bonds.

9. ***False.*** Although it is true that investment is inversely related to the interest rate, it is not clear that a decrease in the interest rate may significantly affect investment. Because investment demand decreases in a recession, only a large decrease in the interest rate will have any significant effect. In fact, business conditions might be so bad that firms would not be willing to borrow money even if the interest rate were close to zero.

10. ***True.*** According to the equation of exchange, MV equals PQ. Proponents of the quantity theory of money assume that V and Q (at full employment) are stable. Therefore, if the money supply increases, there will be more money for spending, and since no more can be produced, the price level will be directly affected. If the money supply increases to $3,000, MV will become $9,000 ($3,000 multiplied by 3). Since PQ must also equal $9,000 and Q remains 1,000, the price level must rise to $9.

Discussion Questions

1. Describe the three functions of money.

2. Explain how the money multiplier works. Why does a $1 change in initial excess reserves lead to an even greater change in the money supply in the overall banking system?

3. Describe how each of the following would change the money supply:

   a. an increase in the discount rate
   b. an increase in the reserve requirement
   c. the Fed's sale of U.S. securities in the open market

4. Outline the advantages and disadvantages of monetary policy.

5. Why do monetarists believe that any change in prices is directly related to a change in the money supply?

Problems

The First Metropolitan National Bank has just received a demand deposit of $100,000 from a person who sold a bond to the Federal Reserve Bank.

1. Assuming a reserve requirement of 25 percent, what is the maximum amount this bank will be able to lend based on this single demand deposit?

2. What is the maximum amount of money the banking system will be able to potentially create?

3. What factors might prevent the banking system from expanding the money supply by this potential amount?

4. How would your answers to problems 1 and 2 change if the reserve requirement were reduced to 10 percent?

Appendix

The Debate Between Keynesians and Monetarists

There are two major differences between the Keynesian and modern monetarist approaches. First, Keynesians believe that government intervention is needed to stabilize the economy at full employment. Without government intervention, they feel the economy will be doomed to erratic fluctuations that will hamper the functioning of the private market. On the other hand, monetarists believe that the market system is capable of dealing with fluctuations and that in the long run, the economy will maintain a stable course if it is free of interference. In fact, monetarists would argue that it is government intervention and actions taken by the Fed over the past forty years that has caused much of the instability in our economy.

The second major difference concerns the role that monetary and fiscal policy should play. Keynesians have argued that fiscal policy is the more effective tool to manage aggregate demand because it has an immediate effect on the economy. They argue that monetary policy is not as effective because it does not have a strong effect on aggregate demand. For example, changes in the money supply will alter the interest rate, which affects the level of consumption and investment spending. Because of this indirect linkage to aggregate demand, Keynesians maintain that monetary policy is less effective and less predictable. Moreover, Keynesians feel that consumption and investment are not sensitive to changes in the interest rate during recessionary periods.

Monetarists contend that monetary policy is not desirable as a discretionary policy tool because it can produce short-run instability. They argue that the impact of monetary changes on GNP is both strong and predictable in the long run. In the monetarist model, velocity is assumed to be stable. Therefore, they believe that changes in the money supply have a direct impact on the value of output (PQ). Historically, there has been a close relationship between M and the value of output (PQ).

This relationship has led monetarists to conclude that changes in M cause changes in PQ. Because of this, Milton Friedman, a leading advocate of the monetarist position, has proposed that money be allowed to grow at a rate equal to the growth of full-employment output (Q). For example, if output is increasing at a rate of 4 percent per year, Friedman would suggest a steady growth in the money supply of 4 percent annually. In this way the increase in the money supply would provide just enough additional spending power for the new goods and services produced. By doing so, he and other monetarists believe that full employment will be achieved and that prices will remain stable over the long run. However, Keynesians downgrade the role of money because they maintain that the velocity of money varies with the interest rate.

An even stronger statement is made by economists who advocate the theory of rational expectations. According to the *theory of rational expectations,* countercyclical policy will have no impact on real income. They believe that, over time, people are able to correctly anticipate policy changes. As a result, such policy changes will have little or no impact on real output. For example, if policymakers are committed to increasing aggregate demand during a recessionary gap, banks, unions, and corporations will expect this and adapt. In an attempt to increase real GNP the federal government may be expected to use deficit financing to stimulate aggregate demand. Anticipating these moves, unions will push for higher wages for its members, firms will raise prices anticipating the increase in demand, and banks will demand higher interest rates because of the expected rise in prices. Therefore, the policy will be ineffective because the reactions of these economic agents diminish the effect of the policy.

Rational expectationists believe that decision makers learn from previous experience and are not likely to make the same mistake over and over. As a result, their errors are believed to be random, contrary to the Keynesian belief in a deviation in actual output from full-employment output (i.e., the business cycle). Consequently, believers in the theory of rational expectations contend that the Fed should pursue a policy of constant growth in the money supply.

Monetarists also disagree with Keynesians about the strength of fiscal policy. They contend that changes in government spending are typically offset by opposite changes in private spending. Why might private spending change? We argued earlier (Chapter 10) that a $100 increase in government spending caused a $100 increase in aggregate demand. But the monetarists ask, where does the government get the extra $100 to spend? If the government *increases taxes* by $100, the contractionary impact of the tax increase will largely offset the effect of the spending increase. The government will spend more, but consumers, with lower after-tax incomes, will spend less. Moreover, if the government *borrows* the $100, a similar effect will occur. By entering the financial markets to borrow the $100, the government increases the demand for loanable funds. As the demand rises, the price of these funds (the rate of interest) will be driven up. If the rate of interest rises, private investment spending will be stifled. This is called the *crowding-out hypothesis*. The increase in government spending is likely to "crowd out" either private consumption or private investment. Monetarists argue, changes in government spending are offset by changes in private spending and therefore have no net impact on aggregate demand. Given these differences, where does the current debate between Keynesians and monetarists stand?

The news media characterize economists as continually bickering and unable to arrive at any type of consensus on macroeconomic policy. Over the years, most Keynesians and monetarists have modified their positions and have come to recognize that both monetary and fiscal policy have an impact on output and inflation. This is not to say that there is full accord on fiscal and monetary policy. There is still the underlying difference over the desirability of government intervention. The normative argument regarding the benefits and costs of market intervention will never disappear. In addition, the emphasis of monetarists on long-run results continues, whereas Keynesians still look at short-run fluctuations and how they may be dealt with to improve long-run performance. What has caused Keynesians and monetarists to alter their positions?

The reason is that a number of the assumptions that the monetarists have made have been refuted, or at least some doubt has been cast over them. First, monetarists have argued that as long as velocity is predictable, keying the change in M to the rate of growth in output will result in a stable economy. But the velocity of money does not appear to be stable over the short run or long run.

The second assumption of the monetarists that has been challenged is their belief that velocity and interest rates are unrelated. Recent evidence suggests that interest rates are very important in the determination of how much money to hold and how intensely it is used. As a result, further doubt has been cast over the assumption of a stable velocity. Therefore, the use of the 4 percent rule for money growth could result in instability.

For these two reasons, the usefulness of the quantity theory of money has been questioned. Nevertheless, there exists a relationship between the money supply and aggregate output, particularly in the long run. Monetarists claim that the existence of the relationship is what is important and they recommend a long-run view. Keynesians criticize this, stating that what is important are the underlying factors causing M and PQ to be related, and they believe that short-run stabilization is possible.

These criticisms are not meant to say that the Keynesians have been correct all along. Keynesians have also altered their view on the usefulness of monetary policy and have changed the degree to which they believe that monetary policy is important. They clearly recognize that long-run changes in output are related to changes in the money supply.

Does monetarism work? We cannot really say, since monetarism as described above has never been tried. Both Keynesians and monetarists agree that it is difficult to stabilize the economy. However, there still is basic disagreement over the role of government in our economy, with no sign of resolution in the near future.

CHAPTER

12

The Aggregate Supply/ Aggregate Demand Model

Objectives

Upon completion of this chapter you should understand:

1. The general properties of the aggregate supply/aggregate demand model.

2. How to use the aggregate supply/aggregate demand model to analyze the causes of four major macroeconomic problems.

3. The policy options available to eliminate depression/recession, demand-pull inflation, and stagflation.

John Maynard Keynes developed the Keynesian model approximately sixty years ago in an attempt to explain the Great Depression, which lasted from 1929 to 1941. This severe breakdown of the private market worldwide was caused by forces operating on the demand side of the economy. To be able to focus more clearly on the impact of spending on the economy, Keynes assumed away production problems.

During the 1970s and early 1980s, however, it became clear that disturbances on the supply side of the economy were creating a new problem — stagflation — in which both unemployment and the level of prices were rising at the same time. To explain this new phenomenon, economists had to develop a new theory, which is called the aggregate supply/aggregate demand model.

While we do not ignore aggregate demand, the purpose of this chapter is to examine difficulties on the supply side of the market which have caused unemployment and inflation. First, we describe the aggregate supply/aggregate demand model, showing how it can be used to determine the equilibrium level of prices and output (real GNP). We then use this model to analyze the causes of four major macroeconomic problems which our economy has experienced since 1929, as well as to examine policy options for tackling these problems.

12.1 An Overview of the Aggregate Supply/ Aggregate Demand Model

We will begin our discussion of the model by examining the basic properties of the aggregate demand and aggregate supply curves.

Aggregate Demand

The aggregate demand *(AD)* curve, illustrated by Figure 12.1, represents the amount of output (real GNP) that consumers, investors, and the government would plan to buy at various price levels. The vertical axis represents the *level of prices*, measured by an index of the average of prices for all goods produced in the economy. An upward movement along the vertical axis represents inflation (defined as a rise in the general level of prices). The horizontal axis measures the amount of goods demanded (real GNP) in all the markets of our economy.

The aggregate demand *(AD)* curve indicates that the quantity of goods demanded decreases in the overall economy as the level of prices increases. Figure 12.1 shows that the rise in the price index from P_1 to P_2 causes the quantity of goods demanded to decrease from Q_1 to Q_2.

Note that we cannot use the *micro*economic demand model described in Chapter 3 to develop a *macro*economic demand curve for the overall economy. Why? A movement up the vertical axis does not represent an increase in the price of a particular good relative to the price of other goods (as is the case in drawing a microeconomic demand curve). An increase in the general level of prices represents inflation rather than a change in *relative prices*. Therefore,

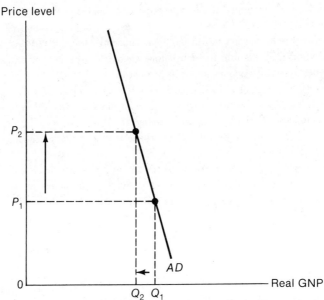

Figure 12.1. The Aggregate Demand *(AD)* Curve. The rise in the level of prices from P_1 to P_2 causes the quantity of goods demanded to decrease from Q_1 to Q_2.

we cannot explain the decrease in the amount of goods demanded in the *overall* economy in terms of households substituting cheaper goods for goods that have become relatively more expensive (e.g., households buying grapefruit instead of oranges because of an increase in the price of oranges). Why then does the *AD* curve slope downward? There are three major reasons.

Real Cash Balances Effect First, persons who save and deposit their unspent income into savings accounts lose out to inflation because the nominal (money) interest they receive from these accounts is usually less than the inflation rate. For example, if the nominal interest rate were 5 percent as the price level increased by 7 percent, households would lose 2 percent in the real value of their cash balances held in their savings accounts. In addition, to the extent people hold cash balances in checking accounts which yield no interest return at all, they lose even more purchasing power to inflation. As the real value of cash balances falls (no matter in what form they are held), people plan to buy fewer goods. This process can be summarized as follows:

↑ Price Level → ↓ Real Value of Cash Balances → ↓ Amount of Goods Demanded

The Interest Rate Effect   Second, an increase in the level of prices causes each dollar of loanable funds supplied to be worth less at each rate of interest. Therefore, inflation decreases the real supply of loanable funds, which in turn drives up the equilibrium level of interest (see Section 6.5 of Chapter 6). Since consumers and investors borrow less money as the interest rate for loans increases, the quantity of goods that they plan to purchase falls. This chain of events can be summarized as follows:

$\uparrow$ Price Level $\rightarrow$ $\downarrow$ Real Supply of Loanable Funds $\rightarrow$ $\uparrow$ Interest Rate
$\rightarrow$ $\downarrow$ Borrowing $\rightarrow$ $\downarrow$ Amount of Goods Demanded

The International Trade Effect   Finally, an increase in the general level of prices of goods produced in the United States relative to the prices of foreign-produced goods causes people in the United States to plan to buy more imported goods and fewer domestically produced goods. The resulting impact on the quantity of goods demanded on the AD curve for the United States can be summarized as follows:

$\uparrow$ Price Level $\rightarrow$ $\uparrow$ Price of U.S. Goods Relative to Foreign-Produced Goods
$\rightarrow$ $\downarrow$ Amount of U.S. Goods Demanded as More Goods Are Imported

Aggregate Supply

The aggregate supply *(AS)* curve shows the amount of output (real GNP) that firms would plan to produce in relation to the general level of prices. How can we interpret the shape of the *AS* curve illustrated by Figure 12.2? The ***horizontal range*** of the *AS* curve (0 to Q_1) represents the situation in which the economy is experiencing significant unemployment — most companies are operating at less than full capacity. Note that full-employment GNP is represented by Q_{FE}. An increase in planned output is possible without any change in the level of prices (i.e., there is no inflation because the price level remains.

However, when the ***intermediate range*** of the *AS* curve is reached, a further increase in production from Q_1 to Q_{FE} results in a rise in the level of prices because more and more firms begin to experience *bottlenecks* (critical shortages of key resources). The resulting increase in production costs causes these firms to raise the prices of their products.

As the ***vertical range*** of the *AS* curve indicates, a further increase in production is not physically possible once full employment is reached. (This occurs at Q_{FE}). The price level can rise, but the amount of goods produced remains fixed at Q_{FE} because we have hit the full-employment ceiling. A more detailed explanation of the underlying properties of the *AS* curve will be given in Section 12.2, which analyzes major macroeconomic problems.

The Equilibrium Level of Prices and Output

The overall economy achieves an equilibrium (stable) level of prices and output when the amount of goods that people plan to purchase equals the amount of goods firms plan to produce. Figure 12.3 illustrates the equilibrium level of prices (P_E) and the equilibrium level of output (Q_E), which occurs where the AS and AD curves intersect. In the next section we will examine how changes in aggregate demand or aggregate supply may cause unwanted changes in our equilibrium level of prices and output.

12.2 Using the Aggregate Supply/Aggregate Demand Model to Analyze Macroeconomic Problems

Having explored the properties of the aggregate supply/aggregate demand curves and equilibrium, we will now use the model to explain the causes of four major macroeconomic problems: depression/recession, premature inflation, demand-pull inflation, and stagflation.

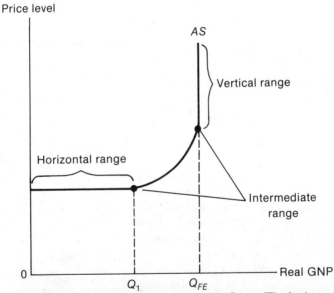

Figure 12.2. The Aggregate Supply *(AS)* Curve. The horizontal range (0 to Q_1) represents the situation in which the economy is experiencing significant unemployment. An increase in planned output (real GNP) is possible without any change in the level of prices. Within the intermediate range, an increase in production from Q_1 to Q_{FE} results in a rise in the level of prices because more and more firms begin to experience bottlenecks. When the vertical range is reached, the price level can rise, but the amount of goods produced remains fixed at Q_{FE} because we have hit the full-employment ceiling.

Depression/Recession

The economy is in a **depression** when there is extremely high unemployment. Because total spending is very low, most firms are operating at far below full capacity. The most recent such economic disaster, called the Great Depression, began in late 1929. The stock market crashed in October of that year, signaling the end of the long period of prosperity called the "Roaring Twenties." During the 1929–1933 period, unemployment shot up from 3 percent to 25 percent while real GNP fell 30 percent, led by an 84 percent drop in real gross investment and a 49 percent decrease in real personal consumption expenditures for durable goods.

As Figure 12.4 indicates, total spending had been high prior to the Great Depression, illustrated by AD_1 with the overall output (Q_1) near the full-employment level, and the price level at P_1. The sudden drop in aggregate demand caused production to fall sharply. Most firms were forced to operate at far less than full capacity, illustrated in Figure 12.4 by the plunge of aggregate demand into the horizontal range of the AS curve (from AD_1 to AD_2). With the inventories of firms swollen far in excess of the planned levels, massive layoffs occurred. Our economy experienced a rare phenomenon, called *deflation*. The price level actually tumbled downward. As Figure 12.4 indicates, the drop in total spending from AD_1 to AD_2 caused the level of prices to fall from P_1 to P_2 as output fell from Q_1 to Q_2.

Economic recovery from the Great Depression began in 1941 (which was the start of World War II). The rise in defense spending caused an overall increase in aggregate demand.

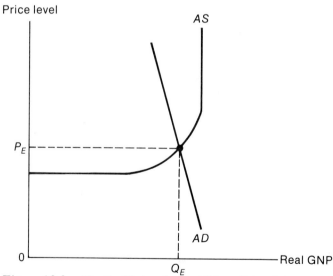

Figure 12.3. The Equilibrium Level of Prices (P_E) and the Equilibrium Level of Output (Q_E). The overall economy achieves a stable level of prices and output when the amount of goods that people plan to purchase equals the amount of goods firms plan to produce, which occurs where the AS and AD curves intersect.

325

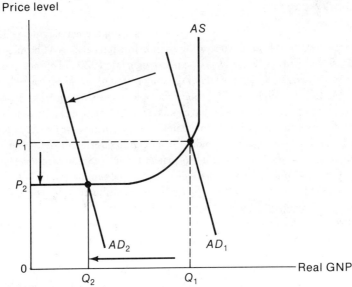

Price level

Figure 12.4.   The Great Depression. The drop in total spending from
AD_1 to AD_2 caused the level of prices to fall from P_1 to P_2 as output fell from
Q_1 to Q_2.

Figure 12.5 shows the *initial* phase of the recovery period, with aggregate demand increasing within the horizontal portion of the AS curve. We can see that the increase in aggregate demand (from AD_2 to AD_3) caused an increase in production (from Q_2 to Q_3) with no change in the level of prices (prices remained at P_2).

Because of the high degree of underutilized plant facilities during the initial phase of recovery, firms increased production by hiring more workers without large expenditures for new capital. These firms were able to use old factories and machines that had previously been idle. Even if the firms had to buy new capital, the cost was low because of the sluggish demand for new buildings and equipment. In addition, wages remained low because of high unemployment.

As we noted in Chapter 8 (section 8.5), the difference between depression and recession is a matter of degree, where **recession** is much less severe in terms of the degree of unemployment and excess plant capacity. While the U.S. Department of Commerce uses two consecutive quarters of negative economic growth as an indicator of a possible recession, the official designation of what constitutes a recession is left up to the subjective judgment of the National Bureau of Economic Research (NBER). According to the NBER, the United States has had seven recessions since the end of World War II (the three most recent occurring in the years 1969–1970, 1973–1975, and 1981–1982).

The stock market crash of October 19, 1987, caused many people to fear that our economy was headed into another recession. Some even feared that the crash was the har-

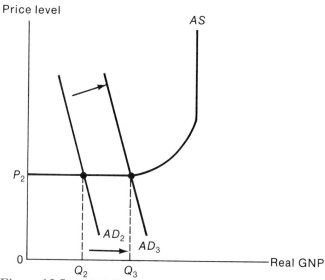

Figure 12.5. Initial Recovery from the Great Depression. An increase in aggregate demand (from AD_2 to AD_3) within the horizontal range caused an increase in production (from Q_2 to Q_3) with no change in the level of prices. (Prices remained at P_2.)

binger of another great depression. See the appendix at the end of this chapter for an analysis of the stock market crash, its economic implications, and an overview of the policy response to the crash according to the Council of Economic Advisers.

Premature Inflation

An increase in total spending within the intermediate range of the AS curve causes inflation to occur *before* full-employment GNP (Q_{FE}) is reached, which is sometimes called *premature inflation*. As Figure 12.6 illustrates, an increase in aggregate demand from AD_1 to AD_2 causes the price level to rise from P_1 to P_2 as output increases from Q_1 to Q_{FE}. Note that this increase in production causes unemployment to fall as GNP approaches full employment.

This inverse relationship between unemployment and inflation is called the *Phillips curve tradeoff* after A. W. Phillips, the British economist who discovered it. As Figure 12.7 indicates, the Phillips curve shows a tradeoff between the goal of reducing unemployment and our desire to stabilize the level of prices. If the economy is located at point *A*, unemployment is high and inflation is low. An increase in aggregate demand will move us to point *B*, reducing unemployment at the cost of a higher rate of inflation. (Note that because our aggregate supply/aggregate demand model is a static rather than a dynamic model, we can use it only to show a change in the level of prices. We cannot use it to show changes in the rate of inflation illustrated by the Phillips curve.)

Why does an increase in aggregate demand within the intermediate zone of the *AS* curve cause the level of prices to increase before full-employment GNP is reached (see Figure 12.6)?

327

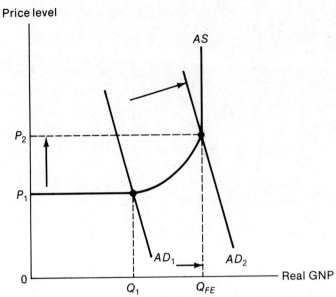

Figure 12.6. Premature Inflation. An increase in total spending from AD_1 to AD_2 within the intermediate range of the AS curve causes inflation to occur before full-employment GNP (Q_{FE}) is reached, illustrated by a rise in the price level from P_1 to P_2.

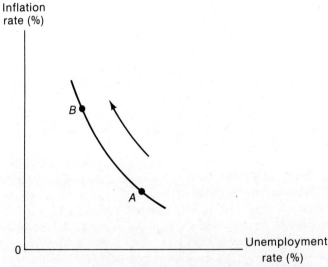

Figure 12.7. Phillips Curve Tradeoff. At point A on the Phillips curve, unemployment is high and inflation is low. An increase in aggregate demand will move us to point B, reducing unemployment at the cost of a higher rate of inflation.

As we noted in the previous section, an increase in production within the intermediate zone will cause bottlenecks to begin to appear in certain industries and some geographic areas of the economy. **Bottlenecks**, critical shortages of essential resources, are frequently caused by structural problems in the labor market. People do not easily acquire the necessary education and skills that are in high demand, nor do they readily move from economically depressed areas to regions in the country that are experiencing rapid economic growth. Therefore, as total spending for goods rises in the overall economy, shortages occur in the market for workers with the skills and education required by expanding industries located in high-growth areas of our nation. Rising wages coupled with the fact that certain industries reach full capacity before others cause the firms experiencing these bottlenecks to raise their prices, which in turn contributes to a general rise in the level of prices.

Demand-Pull Inflation

An increase in aggregate demand within the vertical segment of the *AS* curve results in demand-pull inflation. **Demand-pull inflation** is inflation that occurs because people are attempting to buy more goods than the economy is able to produce at full employment, represented by Q_{FE} in Figure 12.8. As this figure illustrates, an increase in aggregate demand

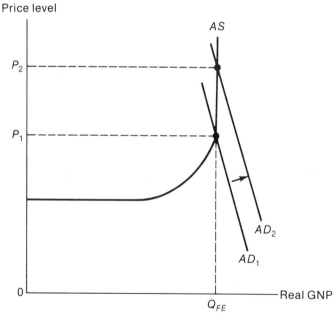

Figure 12.8. Demand-Pull Inflation. An increase in aggregate demand from AD_1 to AD_2 within the vertical segment of the *AS* curve results in demand-pull inflation, illustrated by a rise in the price level from P_1 to P_2, while the amount of goods produced remains fixed at Q_{FE}.

from AD_1 to AD_2 will cause the price level to rise from P_1 to P_2 while the amount of goods produced remains fixed at Q_{FE}.

As we noted earlier in this section, the United States recovered from the Great Depression because of the sharp increase in defense spending during World War II (1941 – 1945). Federal government expenditures for national defense jumped from 2 percent of GNP in 1940 to 41 percent of GNP by 1944. This huge increase in defense spending caused the unemployment rate to drop to 1.2 percent by 1944. The increase in aggregate demand also caused demand-pull inflation, which the federal government suppressed with wage-price controls (discussed in the next section).

The United States also experienced significant demand-pull inflation during the 1966 – 1969 period. The inflationary pressure began when President Johnson escalated the military effort in Vietnam without attempting to finance the war by raising taxes. He was assured by his advisers that victory would come quickly, and therefore the expansion of military spending would be short-lived. But the prolonged and intense nature of the war forced aggregate demand to exceed full-employment supply, causing the inflation rate to rise from 1.7 percent in 1965 to 5.4 percent in 1969.

Stagflation

As Figure 12.9 illustrates, an unusual phenomenon occurred in the 1970s and early 1980s. Both unemployment and the level of prices increased at the same time, seemingly in defiance of the Phillips curve tradeoff described earlier in this section. During the 1970s, the average annual unemployment rate for the civilian labor force was 6.8 percent, while the average

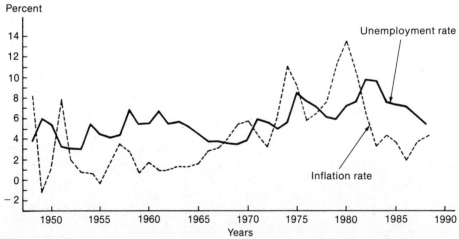

Figure 12.9. Average Annual Rates of Civilian Unemployment and Inflation. Both unemployment and the level of prices increased during the 1970s and early 1980s. The inflation rate fell abruptly during the 1981 – 1982 recession, accompanied by a decrease in unemployment. Source: *Economic Report of the President,* 1989 (Tables B-39, B-62); 1988 calculated from *Monthly Labor Review,* April 1989 (Tables 8, 30).

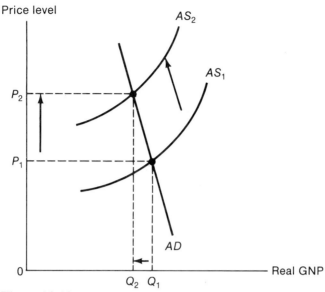

Figure 12.10. Stagflation — Both Unemployment and the Level of Prices Increased at the Same Time. An increase in the general level of production costs reduces aggregate supply from AS_1 to AS_2, causing the level of prices to increase from P_1 to P_2 and the level of output to fall from Q_1 to Q_2 (resulting in higher unemployment).

annual inflation rate stood at 7.1 percent; both figures were up sharply from the average annual rates experienced during the 1950s and 1960s, 4.7 percent and 2.2 percent, respectively. As Figure 12.9 indicates, inflation fell abruptly during the 1981–1982 recession (to be discussed in the next section).

When we face an increase in both unemployment and the price level at the same time, the economy is suffering from **stagflation**, with "stag" referring to stagnation (i.e., high unemployment) and "flation" referring to inflation. Stagflation is caused by **cost-push inflation** in which an increase in the general level of production costs reduces aggregate supply. See Figure 12.10, which focuses on the intermediate range of the aggregate supply curve. As the figure indicates, the decrease in aggregate supply from AS_1 to AS_2 caused the level of prices to increase from P_1 to P_2 and the level of output to fall from Q_1 to Q_2 (resulting in higher unemployment). A number of factors may contribute to cost-push inflation.

Wage-Push/Profit-Push Inflation   A primary reason for stagflation is the development of an inflationary psychology. The term **inflationary psychology** refers to an expectation of continued high inflation in the future. As we noted earlier in this section, the United States experienced significant demand-pull inflation during the 1966–1969 Vietnam War buildup. This triggered an inflationary psychology in our economy which lasted until the 1981–1982 recession.

331

Welcome Back to the Stagflation of the 1970s?

As an increasing number of economists are predicting that a recession will occur in late 1989 or 1990, there is talk about another danger — stagflation. "It is becoming increasingly hard to ignore the signs of impending stagflation. Real activity is finally showing some signs of cooling off, while both wage and price (profit) inflation are doing quite the opposite."

At Smith Barney, Harris Upham and Company, Michael J. Held stated that "in the late 1970s and early 1980s, the Fed was forced to make more aggressive policy moves, given delayed policy reactions to accelerating inflation and external forces (i.e., oil). This time around, the Fed has acted early and seems to have anticipated an acceleration of inflation. It clearly hasn't tightened sufficiently to create a recession."

Alexander P. Paris at Barrington Research Associates is also optimistic. He believes that "stagflation" is "too strong a word to describe the likely economic environment. So far, we envision only a slowing of economic growth, not stagnation, and something much less than double-digit inflation."

The above is a summary of an article, "The Talk of Stagflation: Hot Issue or Hot Air?" by Henry F. Myers, that appeared in *The Wall Street Journal,* April 24, 1989, p. 1.

How does the inflationary psychology actually create inflation? The expectation of continued high inflation tends to cause unions with market power to make excessive wage demands in an attempt to maintain the purchasing power of their nominal (money) income. A wage demand is considered excessive only to the extent that the wage increase exceeds the growth in labor productivity (i.e., output produced per hour of labor). For example, if wages were increased 7 percent while labor productivity rose by only 3 percent, then the wage increase would have an inflationary impact of 4 percent. In general, corporations with significant power in the product market are able to meet the demands of these unions by passing excessive wages off onto consumers in the form of higher prices. This behavior results in *wage-push inflation*, which causes a *wage-price spiral*. In other words, an expected increase in prices causes a wage hike which, in turn, causes prices to increase, and so on.

In addition, corporations with market power will also raise the prices of their products in anticipation of inflation, treating the expected erosion in the value of the dollars they receive as a cost of business. Their motivation is the same as that of unions. They attempt to prevent their real income (profit) from being decreased by inflation. The result is *profit-push inflation*, a self-fulfilling prophecy in which firms increase the prices of their products in anticipation of inflation, causing a *price-price spiral*.

An Increase in the Cost of Natural Resources   An increase in the cost of natural resources will also decrease aggregate supply. For example, the Organization of Petroleum

Exporting Countries (OPEC) succeeded in raising the international price of oil 1,312 percent during the 1973–1980 period (from $2.50 per barrel to $35.29 per barrel). The international price of oil increased because of the success of OPEC in forming a formal cartel agreement in which major oil-producing nations agreed to restrict oil production in order to charge a higher price. (As we will note in the last section of this chapter, the subsequent failure of OPEC to maintain the cartel agreement during the 1980s resulted in a decline in oil prices, which in turn helped significantly to reduce cost-push inflation during this decade.)

How does a sudden increase in the cost of resources such as oil contribute to the problem of stagflation? At the microeconomic level, the resulting increased production costs force firms to reduce production, causing layoffs at the same time that the prices of their products have to be raised. This causes a decline in aggregate supply (illustrated by Figure 12.10).

A Decrease in the Growth of Labor Productivity   We noted earlier in this section that ***labor productivity*** is a measure of the amount of output produced per hour of labor. A decrease in the growth of labor productivity increases the average cost of production because each worker produces fewer goods, given the wage rate. The resulting decrease in the supply of goods causes workers to be laid off while the price of these goods increases.

A possible cause of a decline in the growth of labor productivity is a decrease in the investment rate caused by a decrease in the rate of saving by households. During a period of high inflation, households develop a "buy-now psychology." People attempt to "beat inflation" by purchasing consumer goods before the expected price increase occurs. As a result, the rate of saving decreases, making less money available to firms to fund investment (such as the construction of new factories). Labor productivity in this case falls because workers have less capital with which to work. This phenomenon was one of the major factors that contributed to the problem of stagflation during the 1970s and early 1980s.

A second possible cause of a fall in labor productivity is a decrease in work incentives. Critics of "big" government claim that the public sector has reduced work incentives. They cite high taxes that reduce the private benefits gained from work as well as government regulations, which they believe interfere with the ability of management to manage and the ability of workers to work. They also blame social programs (such as welfare, unemployment compensation, and food stamps) for blunting the cutting edge of poverty which they feel is necessary to force some people to seek employment. Others claim there has been a loss of work incentives because of the evolution of large corporations. They argue that business is being conducted more and more by salaried managers. Because these managers are not owners of the businesses, their income is not tied directly to profit or loss. As a result, salaried managers (as well as the workers they supervise) are not directly rewarded for doing well or punished for doing poorly.

We have just examined the four major macroeconomic problems that our economy has experienced at one time or another since 1929. One of the powers of economics is to help solve social problems. We will now turn our attention to this end, examining the policy options we have at our disposal to reduce unemployment and inflation.

12.3 Policy Options

How can the aggregate supply/aggregate demand model be used to examine policy options for reducing depression/recession, demand-pull inflation, and stagflation?

Policy Options for Managing Aggregate Demand

Aggregate demand can be increased or decreased through the use of monetary and/or fiscal policy in order to reduce unemployment caused by insufficient spending or inflation caused by excess spending.

Policies to Stimulate Aggregate Demand to Reduce Depression/Recession

Before we review how authorities can eliminate unemployment caused by insufficient spending, let us briefly examine a potential policy dilemma. In the previous section, we noted that an increase in aggregate demand within the horizontal range of the AS curve will stimulate production, causing a reduction in unemployment without a rise in the price level (see Figure 12.5). However, once production reaches the intermediate range of the AS curve, a further increase in aggregate demand reduces unemployment at the cost of an increase in the price level (see Figure 12.6). Therefore, the Phillips curve tradeoff presents us with a policy dilemma. We must choose between two evils — which is worse, unemployment or inflation? In making this choice, we want to be certain to avoid the development of an inflationary psychology. As we noted in the previous section, the expectation of continued high inflation causes an increase in both unemployment and the level of prices at the same time (i.e., stagflation). Let us now review how monetary policy and fiscal policy can be used to increase aggregate demand in order to eliminate a recession/depression.

We noted in Chapter 11 that *monetary policy* refers to the efforts of the Federal Reserve Bank (our central banking system) to manage the money supply in an effort to reduce inflation or unemployment. We also noted that the most important monetary policy tool is *open market operations*, the buying and selling of U.S. securities (bonds) by the Federal Reserve. Recovery from a depression or recession can be initiated through loose monetary policy in which the Federal Reserve buys U.S. securities from the general public. When the Federal Reserve buys U.S. securities, it gives the general public currency (which is money) in exchange for U.S. securities (which are not money). The people who receive money from the central bank tend to deposit their currency in banks. These new deposits of currency increase the ability of banks to make loans. As banks increase the amount of funds they lend to their customers, the overall money supply increases, which in turn decreases the interest rate. The reduction in the interest rate encourages consumers to borrow more to purchase such durable goods as new houses, cars, and refrigerators. Likewise, a drop in the interest rate gives firms the incentive to borrow more money to buy new factories and equipment. Therefore, monetary policy can decrease unemployment by stimulating production through an increase in aggregate demand.

Fiscal policy refers to the use of the federal government's budget to manage overall spending in the economy. The federal government could initiate an increase in aggregate demand to help us recover from a depression or recession by decreasing taxes or increasing transfer payments. The decrease in taxes or increase in transfers would give households more disposable income to spend, which in turn would raise consumption at each level of GNP. Likewise, the federal government could stimulate an increase in aggregate demand by increasing government purchases of goods and services. Proponents of fiscal policy argue that the federal government should incur budget deficits during periods of high unemployment by increasing government spending (government purchases plus transfers) and decreasing taxes.

Policies to Reduce Aggregate Demand to Eliminate Demand-Pull Inflation

The opposite use of the monetary and fiscal policy tools described above can be employed to reduce excess spending which has created demand-pull inflation. As Figure 12.11 demonstrates, a decrease in aggregate demand (from AD_1 to AD_2) causes a decrease in the level of prices (from P_1 to P_2) and a drop in production (from Q_{FE} to Q_2).

A reduction in aggregate demand can be initiated through tight monetary policy in which the Federal Reserve sells U.S. securities to the general public. By selling these bonds, the Federal Reserve takes currency out of circulation, which decreases the ability of banks to make loans. As banks begin to lend less money, the overall money supply decreases, which in turn

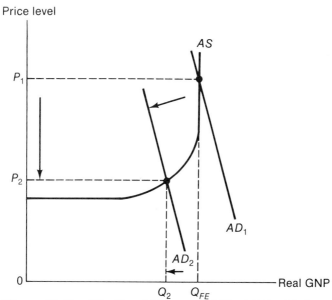

Figure 12.11. The Use of Monetary and Fiscal Policy Tools to Reduce Excess Spending which has Created Demand-Pull Inflation. A decrease in aggregate demand (from AD_1 to AD_2) causes a decrease in the level of prices (from P_1 to P_2) and a drop in production (from Q_{FE} to Q_2).

causes the interest rate to increase. The increase in the interest rate discourages consumers and investors from borrowing. Therefore, monetary policy can cause a reduction in the level of prices by decreasing consumption and investment.

The federal government could use fiscal policy to reduce aggregate demand to eliminate demand-pull inflation. How? An increase in taxes or a decrease in transfers would give households less disposable income to spend, which in turn would reduce consumption at each level of GNP. The federal government could also reduce aggregate demand by decreasing government purchases of goods and services. According to proponents of fiscal policy, the federal government should create budget surpluses during periods of high inflation by decreasing government spending (government purchases plus transfers) and increasing taxes.

Policy Options for Increasing Aggregate Supply

We noted in Section 12.2 that stagflation is caused by a decrease in aggregate supply, which in turn causes an increase in both unemployment and the level of prices (see Figure 12.10). Therefore, policies designed to increase aggregate supply would reduce the problem of stagflation. As Figure 12.12 indicates, an increase in aggregate supply from AS_1 to AS_2 causes the

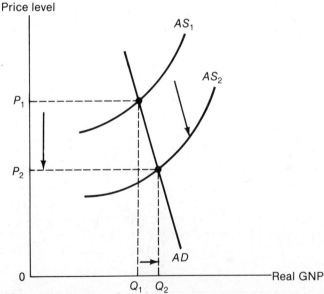

Figure 12.12. Policies to Increase Aggregate Supply Would Reduce the Problem of Stagflation. An increase in aggregate supply from AS_1 to AS_2 causes the level of prices to decrease from P_1 to P_2, while the level of output increases from Q_1 to Q_2 (causing lower unemployment).

level of prices to decrease from P_1 to P_2, while the level of output increases from Q_1 to Q_2 (causing lower unemployment). There are a number of policy options for increasing the AS curve.

Policies to Break the Inflationary Psychology A primary cause of stagflation is the development of an inflationary psychology (described in Section 12.2). Monetary and fiscal policies can break the expectation of continued high inflation by reducing overall spending. How can a reduction in overall spending cause an increase in aggregate supply? As Figure 12.11 indicates, the decrease in aggregate demand from AD_1 to AD_2 would force the price level to fall from P_1 to P_2 as output decreases from Q_{FE} to Q_2. If the resulting recession lasts long enough, people will eventually expect a lower rate of inflation in the future. Once the inflationary psychology is broken, unions will reduce their excessive wage demands and companies will moderate the price increases they had been making in anticipation of high rates of inflation. Both wage-push and price-push inflation will be reduced. The reduced costs will cause increased production, causing firms to hire more workers. As Figure 12.12 indicated, the resulting increase in aggregate supply (from AS_1 to AS_2) would cause the level of prices to fall (from P_1 to P_2) and production to increase (from Q_1 to Q_2).

An alternative approach that might be used to break the inflationary psychology is the imposition of ***wage-price controls***. Under *wage controls,* workers are prevented from receiving wage increases in excess of a certain percentage prescribed by the federal government (unless the wage hike can be justified in terms of advances in labor productivity). *Price controls,* on the other hand, force firms to rescind price increases that exceed the price target established by law (unless the price increases can be justified on the basis of higher production costs).

Wage-price controls can reduce wage-push and price-push inflation if they succeed in preventing powerful groups from increasing their relative shares of real income. If these groups are not permitted to increase their wages and product prices in step with *anticipated* inflation, people will no longer expect inflation to be high in the future. Once the inflationary psychology is broken, the self-fulfilling prophecy will cease, ending the need for the controls.

On the other hand, many economists believe that these controls cannot work because they would prevent prices and wages from performing their signaling and rationing functions. According to their argument, government interference with the pricing mechanism would cause the market to operate inefficiently. They claim that this would drive up production costs, causing a decrease in aggregate supply, which would lead to an increase in both unemployment and the level of prices (see Figure 12.10).

We have had wage-price controls primarily in times of war — World War I (1915–1920), World War II (1941–1945), and the Korean War (1950–1953). Wage-price controls were also established once when the nation was at peace. President Nixon imposed wage-price controls from 1971 to 1974 in an attempt to break the inflationary psychology, even though he was strongly opposed to such government regulation.

Other Policy Options for Increasing Aggregate Supply   A number of other policy options exist to decrease stagflation. First, attempts might be made to reduce *structural unemployment*, defined in Chapter 8 as unemployment caused by a mismatch in the composition of supply and demand conditions in the labor market. Government could reduce structural unemployment by channeling more resources into manpower programs designed to provide remedial education, training, job counseling, and job placement. Additional efforts might be made to increase the mobility of the labor force and to reduce discrimination. The resulting reduction in bottlenecks in the labor market would increase the aggregate supply curve, causing a reduction in stagflation (see Figure 12.12).

Second, a number of programs might be adopted to raise labor productivity. Government might increase its subsidies to research and development by awarding more grants to researchers in our colleges and universities. In addition, a decrease in taxes on savings and investment might encourage the purchase of new capital.

Third, efforts might be made to make the private market work more effectively. Industries that lack meaningful competition might be made more competitive through the enforcement of stronger antitrust legislation. In addition, industries hindered by outmoded government regulations might be given relief through the elimination of such regulations.

Note that deregulation and tax-reduction policies were the cornerstones of Reaganomics. When President Reagan took office in 1980, he vowed to continue the deregulation efforts initiated by the Carter administration (which had deregulated the airline and trucking industries). Reagan accelerated the deregulation of oil prices, eliminated "excessive" health and safety laws affecting the workplace, and reduced "unnecessary" environmental safeguards. He also led the way for the tax cuts of 1982 and 1983, and the Tax Reform Act of 1986 (see Chapter 7). In addition, Reagan made substantial reductions in federal expenditures for social welfare, while increasing the national defense budget.

Programs to reduce structural unemployment are discussed in *Special Topic G: Income Distribution and Poverty*. Policies that might help make the private market work more effectively by enacting antitrust legislation or by reducing outmoded government regulations are discussed in *Special Topic F: Government Regulation*.

A Concluding Comment

To end the expectation of continued high inflation, our central bank put a very tight rein on our money supply during the early 1980s. Restrictive monetary policy caused the prime rate to hit a historic high of almost 19 percent in 1981. Note that the annual prime rate (the rate of interest that banks charge their most creditworthy customers) had averaged about 8 percent during the 1970s. The Federal Reserve engineered the 1981–1982 recession to break the inflationary psychology that had plagued our economy for over a decade. This policy worked. As we can see in Table 12.1, the resulting increase in unemployment to 9.7 percent in 1982

Table 12.1
Civilian Unemployment Rate and
the Inflation Rate, 1980–1988
(percent)

Year	Unemployment	Inflation
1980	7.1	13.5
1981	7.6	10.4
1982	9.7	6.1
1983	9.6	3.2
1984	7.5	4.3
1985	7.2	3.6
1986	7.0	1.9
1987	6.2	3.7
1988	5.5	4.1

Source: *Economic Report of the President,* 1989
(Tables B-39, B-62); 1988 calculated from *Monthly
Labor Review,* April 1989 (Tables 8, 30).

was accompanied by a decrease in inflation to 6.1 percent in that same year (a sharp departure from the double digit inflation experienced during the 1980–1981 period). The inflationary psychology was also dampened by lower farm prices as well as by a decrease in the price of oil. Oil prices fell dramatically during the 1980s because of OPEC's failure to maintain the cartel agreement (described in the previous section) as well as an increase in the production of oil by nations operating outside the cartel. An easing of credit conditions by the Federal Reserve after the 1981–1982 recession has aided the longest peacetime expansion of real output in the history of the U.S. economy. As Figure 12.9 and Table 12.1 indicate, both inflation and unemployment decreased during this economic upturn. Unfortunately, this period of expansion may be ending. At the time of writing, there is uncertainty concerning the ability of the Federal Reserve to maintain this expansion. Many economists fear that tight monetary policy may be needed to reduce inflationary pressures. Such action could cause the economy to fall into another recession.

Summary

We investigated the problems of unemployment and inflation in our economy using the newly developed aggregate supply/aggregate demand model which permitted us to examine problems on the supply side of the economy. The aggregate demand curve represents the amount of output that consumers, investors, and the government would plan to buy at various price levels. The aggregate demand curve slopes downward because of the impact of inflation on real cash balances, the interest rate, and international trade. The aggregate supply curve, on the other hand, shows the amount of output that firms would plan to produce in relation to the general level of prices.

The model was used to analyze the causes of four major macroeconomic problems. First, the economy will experience depression/recession if aggregate demand falls into the horizontal range of the aggregate supply curve. The sharp drop in spending creates significant unemployment, with most companies operating at less than full capacity. Second, premature inflation occurs if aggregate demand increases within the intermediate range of the aggregate supply curve because bottlenecks begin to appear in certain industries and some geographic areas of the economy. The inverse relationship between unemployment and inflation which occurs within the intermediate range of the aggregate supply curve is called the Phillips curve tradeoff. Third, demand-pull inflation is created if aggregate demand increases in the vertical range of the aggregate supply curve because a further increase in production is not physically possible once full employment is reached. Fourth, stagflation is caused by cost-push inflation in which an increase in the general level of production costs reduces aggregate supply. The decrease in aggregate supply causes an increase in both unemployment and the price level at the same time. A primary reason for stagflation is the development of an inflationary psychology, which triggers wage-push and profit-push inflation. An increase in the cost of natural resources and a decrease in the growth of labor productivity will also decrease aggregate supply.

We then examined policy options to reduce unemployment and inflation. First, aggregate demand can be increased or decreased through the use of monetary and/or fiscal policy in order to reduce unemployment caused by insufficient spending, or inflation caused by excess spending. Second, we explored policies designed to increase aggregate supply in order to reduce the problem of stagflation. An increase in aggregate supply causes the level of prices to decrease while the level of output increases (causing lower unemployment). The following options for increasing the aggregate supply curve were discussed: policies to break the inflationary psychology, manpower programs, programs to raise overall labor productivity, and efforts to make the private market work more effectively.

Key Concepts

level of prices/relative prices
real cash balances, interest rate, and international trade effects
horizontal, intermediate, and vertical ranges
depression/recession
premature inflation
Phillips curve tradeoff
bottlenecks
demand-pull inflation
stagflation
cost-push inflation

inflationary psychology
wage-push/profit-push inflation
labor productivity
monetary/fiscal policy
open market operations
wage-price controls
structural unemployment

Self-Test Questions: True or False

T F 1. The aggregate demand curve for the overall economy was constructed by adding together the individual demand curves found in each of the markets of the economy.

T F 2. When aggregate demand increases within the horizontal range of the aggregate supply curve, the level of prices rises because more and more firms begin to experience bottlenecks.

T F 3. Stagflation is caused by cost-push inflation in which an increase in the general level of production costs decreases aggregate supply.

T F 4. A possible cause of a decline in the growth of labor productivity is a decrease in the investment rate caused by a decrease in the rate of saving by households.

T F 5. Recovery from a depression or recession can be initiated through loose monetary policy in which our central bank, the Federal Reserve, buys U.S. securities (bonds) from the general public.

T F 6. Policies designed to decrease aggregate supply would reduce the problem of stagflation.

T F 7. Some argue that wage-price controls should be used to break the inflationary psychology.

T F 8. Profit-push inflation occurs when unions attempt to gain excess wage increases to prevent their real income from being eroded by anticipated inflation.

T F 9. Some economists argue that restrictive monetary and fiscal policy should be used to reduce total spending in order to break the inflationary psychology.

T F 10. A decrease in the growth of labor productivity contributes to stagflation by reducing aggregate supply.

Answers to Self-Test Questions

1. *False.* A movement up the vertical axis of the aggregate demand curve represents an increase in the general level of prices — not an increase in the price of a particular good relative to the price of other goods. Therefore, we cannot explain the decrease in the amount of goods demanded in the *overall* economy in terms of households

substituting cheaper goods for goods that have become relatively more expensive (e.g., households buying grapefruit instead of oranges because of an increase in the price of oranges).

2. *False.* When aggregate demand increases within the horizontal range of the aggregate supply curve, the level of prices remains the same because the economy is experiencing significant unemployment with most companies operating at less than full capacity. The increase in aggregate demand does not cause an increase in production costs. Bottlenecks begin to appear when aggregate demand increases within the intermediate range of the aggregate supply curve, which causes premature inflation.

3. *True.* The decrease in aggregate supply caused by an increase in production costs raises the level of prices (inflation) at the same time that the level of output falls (resulting in higher unemployment).

4. *True.* During a period of high inflation, people attempt to "beat inflation" by purchasing consumer goods before the expected price increase occurs. As a result, the rate of saving decreases, making less money available to firms to fund investment. Labor productivity falls because workers have less capital with which to work.

5. *True.* The Federal Reserve gives the general public currency (which is money) in exchange for U.S. securities (which are not money). The people who receive money from the central bank tend to deposit their currency in banks, which increases the ability of banks to make loans. As a result, the overall money supply increases, which in turn decreases the interest rate, encouraging consumers and investors to borrow more to purchase more goods. This causes an increase in aggregate demand, which stimulates production, causing a decrease in unemployment.

6. *False.* An *in*crease in aggregate supply would cause the level of prices to decrease while the level of output increases (causing lower unemployment).

7. *True.* Wage-price controls can reduce wage-push and profit-push inflation if they succeed in preventing powerful groups from increasing their relative shares of real income. If these groups are not permitted to increase their wages and product prices in step with anticipated inflation, people will no longer expect inflation to be high in the future.

8. *False.* The statement describes wage-push inflation. Profit-push inflation occurs when firms raise the price of their products to protect their real profit in anticipation of inflation.

9. *True.* They argue that the creation of a recession will reduce current inflation, which in turn will cause people not to expect higher inflation in the future.

10. *True.* A decrease in the growth of labor productivity contributes to stagflation by increasing the costs of production which, in turn, reduces aggregate supply. The

resulting decrease in aggregate supply causes production to decline (contributing to unemployment) and the level of prices to increase (contributing to inflation).

Discussion Questions

1. Describe the vertical range of the aggregate supply curve.
2. Why does an increase in aggregate demand within the intermediate range of the aggregate supply curve cause premature inflation?
3. What is meant by the term *inflationary psychology*?
4. Describe the real cash balances effect.

Problems

1. Using the *AS/AD* graph to illustrate your answer, describe how the inflationary psychology causes stagflation.
2. Using the *AS/AD* graph to illustrate your answer, describe how the Federal Reserve Bank could use monetary policy to break the inflationary psychology.
3. Describe how fiscal policy could be used to eliminate a depression. Use the *AS/AD* graph to illustrate your answer.

Appendix

The Stock Market Crash of 1987 and Its Impact on the Economy in 1988

The following material concerning the stock market crash of October 19, 1987 was excerpted from *The Annual Report of the Council of Economic Advisers,* which was published in the *Economic Report of the President,* Washington, D.C.: 1988 (pages 39 to 43) and 1989 (pages 271 to 274).

THE BREAK IN THE STOCK MARKET

As the third quarter ended (1987), preliminary evidence suggested — and data later confirmed — that the U.S. economy was growing strongly. The unemployment rate continued to edge down, reaching its lowest level since late 1979, and the index of leading indicators pointed to sustained economic growth. However, the outlook for further substantial improvement in the Federal deficit was clouded by an apparent deadlock between the Congress and the Administration over the budget for fiscal 1988, which began October 1. In financial markets, the Federal Reserve had tightened monetary policy in September. Interest rates, both short- and long-term, rose further in the first weeks of October.

In mid-October the stock market posted a string of large declines, culminating in a 1-day plunge of unprecedented magnitude. The stock market had soared more than 40 percent in value from the start of the year through its August peak, but, by the close of business on October 16, nearly half of that gain had been erased. And the following Monday, October 19, after stock markets elsewhere in the world had posted sharp declines, the Dow Jones Industrial Average lost 22.6 percent in a single day. Trading volume was enormous, the markets were chaotic, many stocks opened very late, and the word "panic" aptly described the atmosphere. It was a worldwide phenomenon with potentially worldwide consequences.

On that one day, the total value of the stock market dropped by roughly half a trillion dollars. The next day, again amid an enormous volume of transactions, market conditions worsened. Trading in many stocks and index futures halted for a time, but the market managed to recover and closed higher. In subsequent days and weeks, investors remained nervous, but they drew reassurance from the Federal Reserve's prompt provision of liquidity and the large number of corporations announcing stock buy-backs. During the remainder of the year, the market settled into a trading range that left the Dow at the end of 1987 quite close to its year-earlier level.

A wide range of explanations for the crash has been offered, and many factors may have contributed. However, no political or economic event occurred between the market's close on Friday and on Monday that appears capable of explaining such a huge revaluation of the net worth of U.S. corporations. To an extent, the stock market appeared to be reacting simply to itself; in increasingly heavy trading on the preceding Wednesday, Thursday, and Friday, the Dow had lost a total of 261 points, and on October 19, as more individuals and institutions became aware of the deepening plunge in stocks that day and tried to sell, the decline cumulated.

A survey regarding the factors that had propelled stock prices downward was included in *The Report of the Presidential Task Force on Market Mechanisms*, which reviewed the stock market break. A majority of the market participants and other interested parties that responded to the survey viewed technical and psychological factors, especially "sheer panic," as the cause of the intense selling pressure on October 19. By contrast, fundamental factors, such as rising interest rates, overvaluation of the market, and the large trade and budget deficits, were described as the primary cause of the preceding week's decline.

Some commonly watched measures of stock values lend support to the proposition that stocks were overvalued before mid-October. Dividend yields on stocks were well below their postwar average, while price/earnings ratios had soared to highs attained only briefly in recent decades. Since the beginning of 1987, stock prices had skyrocketed amid reports of escalating corporate earnings and robust economic growth. But while stock prices were soaring, bond prices were dropping, creating an unusual divergence between the two markets. In a sense, on October 19 the stock market caught up with the bond market.

Rising interest rates certainly were a factor in the stock market's decline. As noted above, rates had risen sharply in the weeks preceding the crash, and one major bank announced another half percentage point hike in its prime rate on the Thursday before the plunge. Moreover, the outlook for even higher interest rates had been bolstered by the lack of improvement in the monthly U.S. trade figures. The slower-than-expected turnaround in the trade deficit implied to some that further adjustments — either to exchange rates or to foreign or domestic fiscal or monetary policies — would be necessary to stimulate U.S. exports and reduce U.S. import growth.

Several additional factors may have played a role in the market's decline. In particular, publication of the large trade deficits appeared to strengthen the position of those supporting protectionist trade legislation, the passage of which would seriously impair the ability of U.S. firms to do business abroad and would signal the abandonment of a longstanding U.S. commitment to an open trading system. There also were other indications that international economic policy cooperation might be endangered. In addition, the House Ways and Means Committee had just approved a tax package containing several items adversely affecting business, including a measure that would increase the cost of corporate takeovers.

THE ECONOMY IN 1988: THE IMPACT OF
THE STOCK MARKET CRASH

It is now evident, more than 1 year later, that the stock market crash had little noticeable impact on U.S. economic activity. At a rudimentary level, little effect might have been expected because the stock market is not a particularly accurate predictor of economic activity. During the postwar period before 1987, about twice as many declines as recessions occurred in the stock market. Although by this measure the odds of recession in 1988 were 50 – 50, many economic forecasters were convinced that the magnitude of the decline, the largest since the crash in 1929, raised the probability of recession. On a more fundamental level, little effect should have been expected because economic activity was strong at the time of the crash and because Federal Government policies and institutions prevented the crash from escalating into a recession.

Changes in stock prices can affect real output growth through two main channels. One is personal consumption expenditures. Consumers generally are thought to take a long view, spending not according to their current income but according to their expected lifetime consumable resources, including both human and nonhuman wealth components. Human wealth is the present discounted value of expected future after-tax labor income, and nonhuman wealth is the consumer's expectation of the long-run or permanent value of his or her current net financial and tangible assets. A drop in the value of corporate equity holdings that is expected to be permanent, all else being constant, will lower consumption, while a transitory drop will not affect consumption.

At the end of the third quarter of 1987, nonhuman wealth of consumers amounted to $15.1 trillion, with corporate equities outside of pension funds worth about $2.7 trillion or 18 percent. At the end of the fourth quarter of 1987, holdings of corporate equities by households had fallen by about $650 billion, most of which reflected capital losses. A common estimate of the marginal propensity to consume real permanent nonhuman wealth is about 4 cents for every dollar of nonhuman wealth; which implies that real personal consumption expenditures should have fallen about $25 billion or about 1 percent before other factors are considered. Real personal consumption expenditures during the fourth quarter of 1987 fell by about one-half of this amount, and have grown at an annual average rate of 3.8 percent during the first three quarters of 1988. The personal saving rate rose 2 percentage points in the fourth quarter of 1987, and has averaged almost 1 percentage point higher in 1988 than in 1987. In the aggregate, therefore, apparently consumers initially believed that only part of the stock market decline was permanent. Indeed, improvement in the overall stock price indexes during 1988 indicates that they were correct.

A second channel through which the stock market can affect real output is business investment. The stock market provides an up-to-the-minute estimate of the value of thousands of publicly traded firms. When the profits of a firm are expected to rise faster than in the past, the share price of the firm will also rise to reflect the greater expected value of the firm. At times, the stock market's valuation of a firm will differ from the replacement cost of the firm — what it would cost to rebuild or replace the firm, hire equally competent personnel, and rebuild the firm's goodwill. Modern theories of investment posit that, in general, a new firm will be started or new investments will be undertaken by an existing firm when the firm's market value is greater than its replacement cost. Declines in stock prices, all other things being constant, depress investment.

Business investment did not fall in the fourth quarter of 1987, and continued to grow rapidly in 1988, suggesting that the impact of the stock market crash was small. During the first three quarters of 1988, real business fixed investment rose an average of 8.8 percent at an annual rate, unchanged from 1987. The reason why business investment did not collapse is that the stock market recovered some of its losses during the year and the decline in interest rates after the crash lowered the replacement cost of capital and offset some of the initial decline in stock prices.

The response of the economy to the 1987 crash, compared with its response after the 1929 crash, highlights the benefits that can be achieved when the Federal Government follows a proper course. Two differences of major importance emerge for the short-term adjustment of the economy, one affecting the exchange rate and one affecting the general conduct of monetary policy. In addition, differences in trade policy and taxation occurred in the periods following the two declines, as did differences in institutional arrangements affecting the financial system, built-in stabilizers, and other devices that reduce the risk of a severe contraction.

Immediately following both stock market crashes, the Federal Reserve acted to increase bank reserves. Major differences in monetary policy came later. A slowing in the decline of economic activity, visible in industrial production and personal income by the spring of 1930, was turned around by restrictive monetary actions. In 1929–33 the Federal Reserve allowed the money stock to fall by almost one-third, adding an extreme deflationary burden to any remaining effect of the crash. Attempts by money holders to shift from bank deposits to currency drained reserves from the banking system. By failing to offset the sequence of reserve drains, the Federal Reserve permitted large numbers of banks to fail, with severe effects on confidence and anticipations. In marked contrast, the Federal Reserve in 1988 first absorbed the additional reserves it had provided in timely response to the October crash, and through 1988 held money growth within its pre-announced growth range.

In 1929 the United States was on a gold standard, with exchange rates fixed against foreign currencies and gold. Under that regime, the deflationary effect of the crash and monetary restriction fell mainly on U.S. markets for goods and labor. Prices and wages had to fall. Because money wages adjust slowly, a decline in prices raised real wages and lowered employment. Adjustment to the deflationary impulse was achieved by a downward adjustment of U.S. output and spending and by reductions in employment. In 1987, in contrast, the U.S. dollar was allowed to respond flexibly to market forces. Flexible adjustment in the real value of the dollar facilitated the adjustment of costs of production, and of the relative prices of domestic and foreign goods and assets, buffering the effects of the stock market crash and other events on U.S. markets for goods and labor.

Trade policy also differed following the 1929 and 1987 stock market crashes. Unlike today's emphasis on free trade, the United States in 1930 intensified protectionist policies with the passage of the Smoot-Hawley Act. International trade collapsed as foreign countries retaliated with their own protectionist measures, lowering world efficiency and incomes. In contrast, the United States and Canada in 1988 completed negotiation of the Free-Trade Agreement, committing both countries to the elimination of most remaining barriers to trade. This step and the

President's rejection of strongly protectionist measures gave assurance that the United States did not intend to repeat the mistaken trade policies of the interwar period.

Another difference in the aftermath of the 1929 and 1987 stock market crashes can be found in tax policy. In 1932 President Hoover requested and received a large tax increase to balance the growing Federal Government budget deficit. This policy was, of course, the wrong one to request during a recession. In late 1987 the Administration and the Congress achieved modest reductions in the budget deficit for fiscal 1988 and 1989 from their projected baselines, but the last phase of the personal income tax reductions embodied in the Tax Reform Act of 1986 was allowed to take effect. Although partially offset by increases in corporate taxes, the personal income tax cut helped to limit any possible damage from the crash to real output.

PART
FOUR
Special Topics

Comparative Economic Systems

A.1   The U.S. Economy
A.2   The Soviet Economy
A.3   Other Economic Systems

Objectives

Upon completion of this special topic you should understand:

1. How the Soviet Union solves the three basic economic problems.
2. The major institutional similarities and differences among the Western market economies and the economies of the Soviet Union, China, and Yugoslavia.

What would your life be like if you had been born and raised in a different nation? While we really can't answer such a question, it is fun to speculate. The purpose of this special topic is to explore the diversity of economic systems found in our world. As a starting point, we will review the United States' solution to the three basic economic problems described in Section 2.4 of Chapter 2. Next, we will examine how the Soviet economy solves the three basic economic problems. Then, by comparing the basic characteristics of these two economic systems, we will describe the differences and similarities of several Western market economies as well as the economies of China and Yugoslavia.

A.1 The U.S. Economy

The purely private market system is rooted in private property, which is defined as assets such as land, houses, and factories owned by individuals (the opposite of public property, assets

351

owned by society through government). The right to the ownership of property by individuals is granted by government through the enforcement of contracts (an agreement between two or more parties). In addition, the private enterprise system operates principally through self-interest. This means that persons are motivated to help themselves. While self-interest involves "greed," it is also consistent with "altruism" because many people gain satisfaction by helping others.

Acting out of self-interest, households are assumed to want to maximize total satisfaction. This means that households want to buy that combination of goods in the product market and to sell that combination of inputs in the factor market which makes them as happy as possible. On the other hand, firms are assumed to want to maximize total profit.

The Purely Private Market Solution to the Three Basic Economic Problems

The way in which a particular economy produces and distributes goods depends on its solutions to the three basic economic problems: (1) what to produce and in what quantity, (2) how to produce, and (3) for whom to produce.

What to Produce and in What Quantity In a purely private market economy, the pattern of spending by consumers (dollar votes) plays an important role in allocating economic resources in the purely competitive market economy. This is because purchases by consumers generate revenue for firms. But decisions concerning what to produce and in what quantity also are based on the costs of production. Revenue and costs combine to form the decisive factor that motivates firms in the market economy. The decisive factor is the *expectation of profit*.

How to Produce Given the quantity of output, purely competitive firms will choose that method of production which minimizes total costs given the relative costs of the various inputs that may be used in the production process. By minimizing the cost of production, firms are maximizing total profit because profit is the difference between the revenue that firms receive from sales and the costs they pay out. The adoption of the technology that minimizes the total cost of production is called economic efficiency.

For Whom to Produce Who should benefit from the goods produced by the economy? In addition to seeking economic efficiency, the economy wants to achieve allocative efficiency, which means it wants goods to be produced in that combination that maximizes the total satisfaction of consumers. In a purely private market, the solution is largely determined by the distribution of income and wealth. The distribution of income is determined in the factor market, where households earn income by selling their factors of production (labor, capital, and natural resources). Wealth is a stock of assets accumulated over time, often being passed from one generation to the next through inheritance.

The Economic Role of Government in the United States

The United States is not a purely private market economy; instead, it is a mixed economy in which there is a private enterprise system plus a role for government. Whereas individuals act out of self-interest, government acts in the collective interest of all members of society. In general, we believe that people acting out of self-interest will behave in a manner that benefits society. For example, people go to work to earn income for their families. The goods they help to produce benefit others in the economy. But decisions made on the basis of self-interest are not always in the interest of the group. Government is needed to provide certain goods and services that either will not be provided by the private market (e.g., national defense) or, if provided by the private market, will not be provided in sufficient quantity (e.g., education and health care). In addition, government has a number of other roles that cannot be performed adequately by the private market (e.g., enforcing contracts, decreasing pollution, and decreasing unemployment and inflation). The functions of government in a mixed economy are discussed in Chapter 7 and in Chapters 10 through 12. The next section examines how the Soviet economy solves the three basic economic problems.

A.2 The Soviet Economy

What are the basic institutions of the Soviet economy? In the Soviet economy there is extensive *state ownership of capital.* While households own personal property in the Soviet economy, the government owns and operates factories, machinery and equipment, and other forms of large-scale capital. Most production decisions in the Soviet Union are made through *central planning,* in which the government devises an overall master plan for running the economy. The Soviet authorities strive to channel the self-interest motivation of individuals into work that they perceive to be in the collective interest. Because the Soviet system tries to solve its economic problems under the discipline of a comprehensive plan, it has been termed a **command economy.**

The Soviet Economy's Solution to the Three Basic Economic Problems

Given the institutional differences between the U.S. and the Soviet economies, how does the Soviet Union attempt to solve the three basic economic problems?

What to Produce and in What Quantity In the Soviet Union, the **Council of Ministers** sets the overall targets concerning what to produce and in what quantity. The council determines such strategic goals as the overall division between capital and consumer goods, luxury goods and necessities, agricultural products and nonfarm goods, and military and civilian goods. Within these individual categories, the specific quantities to be produced are determined by **Gosplan**, the state planning agency. In the Soviet Union, state planning substitutes for the profit motive in guiding resources in production.

How to Produce Gosplan sets production quotas for each specific industry in order to achieve the overall goals of the Council of Ministers. These quotas are a part of the *Central Plan*, which is a blueprint for the overall economy created by Gosplan. The central plan is initially established for a five-year period and is revised each year by Gosplan to adjust for previous failures and successes in production. Soviet enterprises are held accountable by the government, and bonuses are paid annually on the basis of success in achieving the objectives of the plan.

Implementation of the Plan: How is the central plan carried out? The Gosplanners send the annual plan to the state factory managers for initial review. These factory managers negotiate with officials in higher planning levels over the preliminary plans for their own plants. Next, the revised plans are sent back to the Gosplanners to be integrated into a comprehensive master plan. The comprehensive plan is then broken out and sent to the individual enterprises. Prices and production targets are set by the plan. The blueprint also specifies the amount of planned profit or loss which firms are expected to make. Note that the Soviets deliberately plan losses for some firms producing goods considered vital necessities for consumers; the firms receive public subsidy to maintain production.

What happens when there is a major problem in the implementation of the central plan? For example, what if steel production falls far short of its planned level of output? Steel is a major input used by many industries. Without an adequate supply of steel, many factories throughout the Soviet Union would be forced to fall short of their own production targets.

The Gosplanners use two techniques for handling such bottlenecks. First, they stockpile large reserves of essential inputs, creating a *buffer stock* to reduce the damage from shortages. For example, if steel production fails to meet the expected quota in a particular year, the Gosplanners will draw on their reserve of steel to minimize the damage to the other components of the central plan. Second, the Soviets have established the *priority principle*, in which they change their production priorities to minimize overall losses caused by a failure in the plan. For example, given a disappointing level of steel output, they may decide to reduce the number of automobiles produced in order to maintain the production of tractors.

Monitoring the Plan: Monitoring the success of the annual plan is the responsibility of *Gosbank*, the state banking system. At the beginning of the year, Gosbank will lend the individual production plants the money needed to meet their planned expenses in terms of meeting payroll, buying machinery, and purchasing all the other inputs required by the production process. Since factories sell output at planned prices, Gosbank knows which enterprises are on track by the enterprise bank balances.

The amount of money Gosbank lends to plants is based on expected average performance in terms of the planned production costs minus the anticipated revenue received from the sale of the products. If the plant fails, either in terms of experiencing above-normal costs or below-average revenue, it will record a profit that is below (or a loss that is above) the planned level. Such failure will require the managers to borrow more money from the state banking system. This will be a signal to Gosbank that something is wrong at the plant. The Gosplanners will then investigate the production problem in order to try to correct it.

354

On the other hand, if the relationship between revenue and cost is better than planned, this signals to Gosbank that the plant has been successful. As a reward for good performance, some of the excess money will be plowed back into the operation, perhaps to buy new equipment for the plant. Managers and workers are also given bonuses in the form of higher pay and additional vacation time. A large part of the money, however, will go back to the state as a form of taxation to help finance other goals designated by the Council of Ministers, including subsidies to enterprises that are planned to lose money.

Role of Profit: The role of profit in a command economy is distinctly different from the role of profit in a market economy. In a market economy, profit *directs* the decisions of firms concerning what and how to produce. This has not been true in the command economy. Such direction in the Soviet Union is provided by decisions made primarily by the Council of Ministers, Gosplan, and Gosbank. In the Soviet Union, profits have served an accounting function rather than an allocative function.

For Whom to Produce   As we noted in the previous section, the decision concerning who gets the benefits of the goods produced by the private market economy depends largely on the distribution of income and wealth. The Soviet economy's solution to the "for whom" problem is similar to that of the private market in that households that earn higher income in the Soviet Union tend to get more benefits from production.

But there are also important differences between the two systems. First, the Soviet economy determines the type and amounts of consumer goods that are made available for households to purchase by establishing production targets. By rewarding managers for production rather than for goods actually sold, Soviet firms tend to produce low-quality consumer goods. Therefore, planners' preferences may not match consumer preferences even if the plan is made with the best intentions.

Second, the Soviet government attempts to modify the amount of goods that specific groups in the nation can consume in two basic ways. It tends to reduce prices on certain necessities while raising prices on luxuries in order to subsidize lower income groups while taxing higher income groups.

Third, the Soviet economy, by eliminating the private ownership of capital, has reduced extreme variations in the amount of wealth held by households. The result has been a reduction in the inequality of the distribution of wealth among Soviet citizens compared to the distribution that exists in the United States.

Glasnost/Perestroika: The Gorbachev Reform Proposal   Upon taking power in 1985 as Communist party chairman and general secretary, Mikhail Gorbachev announced a revolutionary new policy of ***glasnost*** or "openness" which, if effective, would open the Soviet society to greater human rights and social freedom. At the economic level, Gorbachev has proposed ***perestroika*** or "restructure," a policy geared to restructure central planning to include a more significant role for market forces and profit incentives. Perestroika proposes that plant managers are to make decisions based more on profitability, with salaries tied to goods actually sold rather than goods produced. The policy, if effective, would increase the power of managers to fire workers who are not performing well on the job. In addition, small private business would be legalized, and state enterprises would be made to depend more heavily on self-financing, with the possibility of bankruptcy if firms failed to meet the expectations of the plan. If successful, the increased reliance on markets would be expected to increase incentives for efficiency while making the Soviet economy more responsive to consumer demands.

A.3 Other Economic Systems

In comparing the economy of the United States to that of the Soviet Union, we noted a number of critical differences. First, the United States relies predominantly on the private ownership of capital whereas most capital in the Soviet Union is owned by the state. Second, the U.S. economy is decentralized, with economic decisions being made by a vast array of markets rather than through a centralized plan made by government. Third, the U.S. economy is based on the philosophy that households and firms motivated by self-interest to seek material wants will benefit society at large by achieving economic and allocative efficiency. The U.S. economy is also based on the belief that problems which do emerge (such as a maldistribution of income, pollution, and an inadequate amount of private health care) can be corrected through government. The Soviet philosophy, on the other hand, relies more on moral incentives. Moral incentives refer to the use of government to persuade people to act in the collective interest of the group (i.e., to motivate people to act for the good of society). The purpose of this section is to examine the similarities and differences among other economies in terms of these three elements.

Western Market Economies

Like the United States, Canada as well as Western European countries and Japan rely primarily on private ownership of capital, decentralized market decision making, and material incentives. They do differ, however, in the relative degree of reliance on these three elements. For example, Great Britain has much more government ownership of industry than the United States. Sweden, which may rely more than the United States on the private ownership of capital (more than 90 percent of Swedish industry is privately owned), has perhaps the most comprehensive welfare program in the world. The term *welfare* in this context refers to the use of government to intervene in the market system for the purpose of bettering the well-being (welfare) of society. For example, the Swedish government offers subsidies to private firms that retain workers when their production drops and offers public jobs to fight unemployment when necessary. Sweden also has extensive public day care centers and free education including college. In addition, Sweden has more extensive public health care service, benefits for the unemployed, and retirement pensions than are found in the United States. The tradeoff, of course, is the higher tax burden paid by the Swedes.

In the post-World War II period, France (a predominantly private market economy) developed a unique planning system. The French system, called ***indicative planning***, was a planning apparatus established through voluntary compliance of private industry rather than by government decree. In order to coordinate economic activity (without the coercive planning apparatus of the Soviet Union), the French developed a national economic plan agreed on by representatives of government, industry, and labor. Through a process of negotiations, French planners provided an interchange of information between industries in an attempt to reveal potential shortages and surpluses before they arose. We should note that French indicative planning gradually fell into disuse during the economic difficulties of the 1970s.

Finally, the Japanese economy is similar to that of the United States in its reliance on the private ownership of capital and a system of markets. A major difference is that the Japanese government engages in long-term economic planning through the Ministry for International Trade and Industry (MITI) in an attempt to make its large export industries more competitive in world markets. Japan must export a large volume of goods in order to earn the foreign currencies needed to import many major natural resources that are not found domestically. To compete more effectively in world markets, the Japanese government also encourages the formation of "super" cartels (an arrangement in which companies are permitted to agree on production targets and pricing policies). One reason why the Japanese cartels have been effective in penetrating world markets is that they have been able to reduce the prices of the goods they export by raising the prices of the goods they sell domestically.

Another difference compared to the United States is in management style. The large Japanese corporations have a longstanding tradition of treating their employees as though they were "family." To instill company loyalty and strong work incentives, these Japanese manufacturers give their employees guaranteed lifetime jobs and a significant decision-making role in production. Their employees work in teams to design production techniques and to control the quality of the goods they produce. In addition, these companies reward excellence by giving bonuses not just to managers, as in the practice of many U.S. firms, but to *all* employees. These year-end bonuses are significant and give every employee a stake in the efficiency of the firm.

China and Yugoslavia

The Chinese and Yugoslav economies are like the economy of the Soviet Union in that most capital is owned by the state rather than by households. There are, however, differences in terms of the degree of central planning. Yugoslavia gives the workers of each firm the authority to choose managers to run the business (rather than to have state-appointed managers as in the Soviet Union). Under the system of ***workers' self-management***, each firm can choose within limits what and how much to produce as well as how to produce. The success or failure of firms in the Yugoslav economy depends on whether they produce products that consumers want and on how efficiently these goods are produced. Each firm can decide how much of its profit to invest in capital expansion and how much to pay its labor force. While the state owns major large-scale industry, it relies on markets to coordinate and motivate decision making.

Until recently, the economy of the People's Republic of China was based on the Soviet model, with an emphasis on state ownership of industry, centralized planning, and moral incentives. Chinese planning has always been more decentralized than the Soviet Union, with more authority given to provincial and local governments because of China's immense population size and its early stage of industrial development. After the communist takeover in 1949, China was closed to the West. It wasn't until the late 1970s (after Chairman Mao's death in 1976) that China began to welcome Western trade, technology, tourism, and foreign investment. In the early 1980s the Chinese decentralized farming, creating much smaller production units while establishing a two-tier system in agriculture to improve work incentives. Once farmers meet a quota of farm goods sold to the state at government prices, they are allowed to produce crops for sale at whatever price the market will bear. In 1984, the Chinese government announced that it would extend the agricultural experiment by allowing market forces to operate in other sectors of its economy. Therefore, the Chinese economy (while far removed from that of the United States) has recently become even less centralized than the Soviet Union, with a greater reliance on markets and material incentives.

Summary

The U.S. economy relies predominantly on the private ownership of capital, whereas most capital in the Soviet Union is owned by the state. The U.S. economy is decentralized, with economic decisions being made by a vast array of markets rather than through a centralized plan made by government. It is based on the philosophy that households and firms motivated by self-interest to seek material wants will benefit society at large by achieving economic and allocative efficiency. It is also based on the belief that problems which do emerge can be corrected through government. The Soviet philosophy, on the other hand, relies more on moral incentives, the use of government to persuade people to act in the collective interest.

The role of profit in a market economy is distinctly different from the role of profit in a command economy. In the United States, profit directs the decisions of firms concerning what and how to produce. Such direction in the Soviet Union is provided by decisions made primarily by the Council of Ministers, Gosplan, and Gosbank. In the Soviet Union, profits have served an accounting rather than an allocative function. The Soviet economy's solution to the "for whom" problem is similar to that of the private market in that households that earn higher income in the Soviet Union tend to get more benefits from production. We noted that there are also important differences between the two systems.

Like the United States, Canada, Japan, and Western European countries rely primarily on private ownership of capital, decentralized market decision making, and material incentives. They do differ in the relative degree of reliance on these three elements.

The Chinese and Yugoslav economies are like the economy of the Soviet Union in that most capital is owned by the state rather than by households. There are differences in terms of the degree of central planning. These differences will narrow if Mikhail Gorbachev's revolutionary policies of glasnost and perestroika are effective.

Key Concepts

command economy
Council of Ministers
Gosplan
Central Plan
buffer stock
priority principle
Gosbank
glasnost
perestroika
indicative planning
workers' self-management

Discussion Questions

1. Discuss how the Soviet Union solves the three basic economic problems.

2. Describe the Gorbachev reform proposal. How do the proposed changes in the Soviet economy parallel reforms that have occurred in the People's Republic of China?

3. What are the similarities and differences between the U.S. and Japanese economies?

4. If you were responsible for building a new economy, how would you do it? Describe the type of ownership of capital, the decision-making mechanism to be used for allocating resources to produce and distribute goods, as well as the incentive system you would use to achieve success.

The Economics of Health

Objectives

Upon completion of this special topic, you should understand:

1. Why the price of health care has increased faster than the overall consumer price index.
2. What distinguishes the health care market from other markets.
3. Alternative methods to promote health.

We all want to live long, healthy lives. Unfortunately, because of accidents and many different diseases, some people die early in their lives while others become disabled. Without a doubt, the health care industry has contributed to an increase in the overall level of health in the United States. But the question remains, what amount of resources should be devoted to health care services? Should we spend more on conquering diseases such as cancer, heart disease, and AIDS? Or maybe it is possible that too many resources are being devoted to health care services.

We begin with a description of the health care industry. We then describe the unique characteristics of the private market for health care services and why this market fails to operate efficiently. Finally, we explore the various public policy alternatives to improve health care.

360

B.1 The Health Care Industry

The health care industry consists of hospital services; services by physicians, dentists, and nurses; the pharmaceutical industry; and medical research. In 1987, the average cost per day for hospital care was about $460. Total expenditures on health care for the year 1986 totaled $458 billion or almost 11 percent of current GNP, up from 7.4 percent of GNP or $75 billion in 1970. Per capita spending on health care rose from $349 in 1970 to $1,837 in 1986, an increase of 526 percent. The government's share of these expenditures also rose dramatically, from $25 billion (33 percent of total expenditures) in 1970 to $180 billion (39 percent of total expenditures) in 1986.

The Price of Medical Care

The rising price of medical care is very disturbing to many households. The medical price index has been rising at a more rapid rate than the general level of prices measured by the consumer price index.

One reason why medical care prices have risen is because of a huge increase in the demand for health care. This is represented in Figure B.1. When demand increases, the demand curve shifts to the right to D', resulting in a higher price (P_2) with a larger quantity supplied (Q_2). Three factors contributing to the increase in demand are (1) the increased availability of health insurance and the practice of defense medicine (the increased use of tests by physicians to document the patient's condition in the event of a lawsuit) (2) the growth in population due to increased life expectancy in the United States, and (3) the change in the age distribution of the population. There are more citizens 65 years old and older than ever before, and they require more medical care than do younger people.

Variations in Health Levels

Even though the people of the United States enjoy one of the highest standards of living on earth, statistics indicate that Americans are not living any longer than their counterparts in other industrialized countries. Life expectancy for males (from birth) is about the same in Italy, Spain, Canada, Denmark, Norway, Israel, Japan, and the United States. In addition, persons in less developed countries such as Costa Rica, Panama, Venezuela, Greece, and Sri Lanka who survive to age 60 have about the same life expectancy as U.S. citizens.

Another interesting fact is the variation in health levels among groups within the United States. For example, there are significant differences in health levels between males and females, and blacks and whites. See Table B.1. In 1985, the life expectancy at birth was approximately 72 years for white males and 79 for white females. For black males and black females, the figures are 65 years and 74 years, respectively. The difference between males and

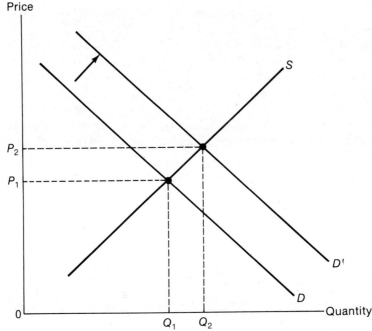

Figure B.1. The Impact of an Increase in Demand for Health Services. An increase in the demand for health services (from *D* to *D'*) causes an increase in equilibrium price (from P_1 to P_2) and quantity (from Q_1 to Q_2).

females of either race is about 7 years, and the difference between whites and blacks of either sex is approximately 5 years.

Many health researchers believe that differences in life expectancy are partially due to the problem of access. Not everyone has the same opportunity to buy medical care services. For example, rural dwellers do not have as many physicians available as the urban population. Also, many are not able to afford all the care they want.

The Allocation of Resources

How should we allocate scarce resources to satisfy human wants when health care is just one of many goods and services possible? Because of limited resources, underutilization of resources, and inefficiencies in production, it is not possible to produce enough goods and services to satisfy everyone. Also, why do some persons smoke, drink, eat too much, or live stressful lives, knowing that it may shorten their lives? For some people, the benefits of "fast living" far outweigh the costs of poor health. Economists are concerned with the allocation of scarce resources which may conflict with some health professional's desire to provide the best care possible regardless of cost. The government has intervened in the market for health

Table B.1
Selected Life Table Values: 1939–1985[a]

Average Expectation of Life (years)

Age and Sex	White					Black				
	1939–1941	1949–1951	1959–1961	1969–1971	1985	1939–1941	1949–1951	1959–1961	1969–1971	1985
At birth										
Male	62.8	66.3	67.6	67.9	71.9	52.3	58.9	61.5	61.0	65.3
Female	67.3	72.0	74.2	75.5	78.7	55.5	62.7	66.5	69.1	73.5
Age 20										
Male	47.8	49.5	50.3	50.2	53.3	39.7	43.7	45.8	44.4	47.4
Female	51.4	54.6	56.3	57.2	59.8	42.1	46.8	50.1	51.9	55.3
Age 40										
Male	30.0	31.2	31.7	31.9	34.7	25.2	27.3	28.7	28.3	30.2
Female	33.3	35.6	37.1	38.1	40.4	27.3	29.8	32.2	33.9	36.6
Age 50										
Male	22.0	22.8	23.2	23.3	25.8	19.2	20.3	21.3	21.2	22.5
Female	24.7	26.8	28.1	29.1	31.1	21.0	22.7	24.3	26.0	27.9
Age 65										
Male	12.1	12.8	13.0	13.0	14.6	12.2	12.8	12.8	12.9	13.3
Female	13.6	15.0	15.9	16.9	18.7	14.0	14.5	15.1	16.0	17.0

[a] Prior to 1960, excludes Alaska and Hawaii. Beginning 1970, excludes deaths of nonresidents of the United States. See *Historical Statistics, Colonial Times to 1970,* series B 116–125, and *Statistical Abstract of the United States, 1988.*

services to try to improve on the private market solution. Whether or not we are producing the optimal amount of medical care in an efficient and equitable manner is a question that needs to be examined.

B.2 Characteristics of the Market for Health Care Services

The health care industry possesses characteristics that make it unique.

The Demand Side

A variety of characteristics distinguish the demand for health services from the demand for other services. First, unlike that for most other goods, the demand for many health care services is irregular and unpredictable. This is because illness is very difficult to predict for the individual and, in many instances, occurs randomly.

Second, illness is costly in itself. When a person is ill, he or she will forgo work. Therefore, illness may cause a person to lose pay in addition to the cost of treatment.

Third, most of us carry some form of ***private health insurance*** in which the insurance company agrees to pay a portion of our bill. That portion is referred to as ***coinsurance*** and can range from 100 percent (the insurance company pays everything) to, more typically, 80 percent.

In 1986, families paid only 29 percent of the costs of medical care directly. The remaining portion (71 percent) was paid for by insurance companies and government. Many persons routinely receive health insurance as one of their fringe benefits from their employer. This reflects the increasingly popular notion that "need," not ability or willingness to pay, should be the criterion for providing medical care. It is primarily this idea that was responsible for the federal government's expenditures on such programs as Medicare and Medicaid, loans to students for medical school, and research funds. The poor depend on Medicaid and the elderly on Medicare to help pay their medical costs. As a result, most people purchase more health care than if they had to pay the entire cost out of pocket.

A fourth characteristic of the demand for health care is the *uncertainty* facing the consumer with regard to the quality of care. Most consumers are aware of an information gap that exists between the physician and themselves. Highly technical information is difficult for most people to understand, and as a result, their decisions may suffer from the lack of full information. In most cases we cannot pretest the service; therefore, trust plays a very important role in this market. Have you checked the credentials of your physician? Where did he or she go to school? Where did the physician do his or her residency? Is the physician board certified (indicating additional education and passing an examination in a specialized area)? Has he or she ever been convicted of malpractice?

The uncertainty regarding the outcome of the service provided by medical practitioners also hinders the decision-making process. For example, suppose you go to a doctor for an upper respiratory infection. Is there any guarantee that the treatment provided will make you better? In many cases the exact nature of the illness may not be apparent. In addition, there may be no prescribable medication available. When a person purchases medical care, he or she pays a *fee for service*, not performance, which is the real measure of output. There is no guarantee that the patient will get better from the treatment. Nevertheless, most people willingly accept the idea of paying for a course of action they hope will work. Most people are not nearly as tolerant when they purchase a car or hire an attorney. Many attorney's fees are contingent on the successful outcome of a litigation. One attempt to reduce the excessive use of health care providers is the creation of ***health maintenance organizations (HMOs)***, where people pay a fixed fee per year regardless of the number of visits. HMOs give physicians an incentive to keep the person well and away from their offices. Why? A healthy person makes fewer visits and is therefore more "profitable" to the HMO.

Finally, the health care industry produces *external benefits*. Remember that external benefits occur when a consumer engages in an action that yields a benefit to third parties (see Chapter 7, Section 7.2). When a person is inoculated for the flu or polio, he or she is not the only one who receives benefits. Others in society benefit since they now have a reduced probability of getting that disease. In Chapter 7 we saw that in the presence of external benefits, the market fails to allocate enough resources to the production of the good, which means that less than the optimal amount will be produced. As a result, government intervention may be desirable to ensure that enough people receive sufficient health care.

The Supply Side

There are also a wide variety of characteristics that distinguish the supply of health care services from the supply of other services. One major difference between the medical care industry and many other markets is the lack of competition. The restrictions include (1) licensing, (2) limitations on medical school admissions, (3) restraints on advertising, and (4) the lack of the profit motive by most hospitals.

Licensing tries to ensure that high-quality care will be available from practitioners. To become a medical doctor, a person must graduate from an accredited medical school, pass a comprehensive examination, and work as an intern in a hospital. Although it is difficult to measure to what extent these restrictions have increased the quality of care, it is true that licensing restricts the number of persons practicing medicine.

Another barrier to entry is that only schools that have been accredited by the American Medical Association (AMA) can offer medical education. Without that accreditation, a person could not be licensed to practice medicine. The AMA is made up of physicians who are in the position to regulate the supply of new doctors. There is an excess demand for education in medical schools in the United States.

Licensing also does not allow anyone but a medical doctor to perform many of the routine examinations and tests required in most office visits. It has been demonstrated that registered nurses with some additional training or physician's assistants (needing only two years of medical education) can perform many of the routine activities performed by a doctor. If these persons were used more extensively than they are now, the supply of medical services would be greater, causing the price of health care to be lower. Current resistance by physicians is preventing any widespread change in the way nurses are currently employed.

A second distinguishing characteristic on the supply side is that much of the cost of the education of medical doctors is borne by the public sector. As we noted earlier, because of external benefits, the market fails to allocate enough resources to medical care. By providing subsidies, the government lowers the cost of education to medical students. As a result, more people are willing to purchase medical education. In 1986 public expenditures on medical research and medical facilities construction were more than $10 billion.

Third, advertising and price competition have been prohibited by the AMA until the past few years, making it more difficult to obtain information about differences in price or quality. The physician is supposed to be divorced from the profit motive. The physician is relied on as an expert whose advice is to be determined solely by medical need and not financial consideration. Yet the practice of most physicians is a private business with a profit motive probably as strong as that of General Motors.

Finally, the hospital is the focal point of this industry since this is where many of the services are provided. Developing a model explaining the behavior of the hospital has proven to be a formidable task. Over 80 percent of all hospitals are run as not-for-profit institutions, maximizing some objective other than profit (e.g., serving as many patients as possible for a given level of costs or quality of care).

B.3 Alternative Investments in Health Care and Public Policy

Many things affect the general level of health in the United States. For example, income, education, diet, occupation, and life-style are related to differences in health status. An examination of the most frequent causes of death for different age groups will shed some light on policy alternatives. See Table B.2. For males from 15 to 24 violence (accidents, homicide, and suicide) is the largest cause of death. For males from 55 to 64, heart disease and cancer are the leading killers. In setting policy to deal with health care, it is important to examine the determinants of death because different causes will require different policy prescriptions.

Heart disease is believed to be closely related to hereditary factors and life-style. The relationship between obesity and heart disease is still controversial, yet statistics clearly show reduced life expectancy associated with long-term obesity. Many nutritionists believe that government standards should be set so that diet guidelines will be available. Many argue that

Table B.2
Deaths by Different Causes for White and Nonwhite Males by Age Groups (Rates per 100,000 population)

Cause of Death	Ages 15–24		Ages 35–44		Ages 55–64	
	White Males	NW Males	White Males	NW Males	White Males	NW Males
Motor accidents	59.1	31.9	29.3	33.8	20.9	31.5
Other accidents	20.9	20.6	21.0	45.3	28.7	57.6
Suicide	22.0	11.2	23.7	16.5	28.8	13.4
Cancer	6.8	6.4	38.5	74.4	504.5	841.7
Homicide	11.1	61.5	11.8	78.1	6.3	40.6
Influenza and pneumonia	0.7	1.1	2.7	15.7	21.0	51.8
Heart disease	3.8	8.3	61.6	153.0	738.7	1,100.9
Cirrhosis of liver	0.2	0.3	11.8	38.7	48.2	64.1
Stroke	0.8	1.2	5.9	26.0	54.3	159.0
All causes	138.8	163.9	235.1	616.0	1,625.5	2,658.3

Source: *Vital Statistics of the United States*, 1984, Table 1–9, "Death Rates for 72 Selected Causes by 10-Year Age Groups."

food labels should be more informative, specifying what is contained in the food such as cholesterol levels, amount of sugar, salt, and amount and type of preservatives.

In addition to diet, the medical profession is giving more importance to the impact of stress on health. Stress comes from many things, such as competition in the marketplace for goods or jobs. Stressful behavior early in life may have far-reaching consequences later on. It has been hypothesized that there may be a direct relationship between stress and heart disease.

The impact of a program designed to improve diet and life-style is shown in Figure B.2. Under this approach, people would not need to purchase as much medical care. As a result, the demand for medical care decreases to D'. Equilibrium price and quantity would fall to P_2 and Q_2.

People with higher levels of education and income utilize health care services more frequently. Many argue that the government should provide some form of **national health insurance** so that those with lower incomes will be able to get medical care when they need it. This type of insurance has been proposed to deal with the problems of inaccessibility due to high prices. Currently, Medicare and Medicaid provide health insurance for the elderly and

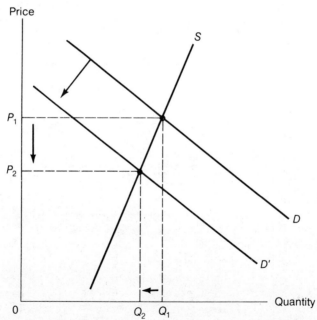

Figure B.2. The Impact of a Decrease in the Demand for Medical Care. When the demand for medical care falls, the equilibrium price and quantity of medical care will fall.

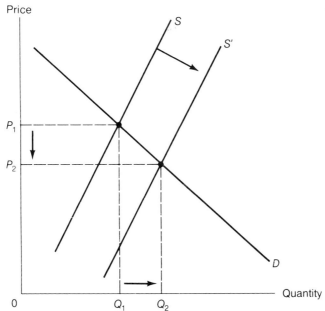

Figure B.3.   The Impact of an Increase in the Supply of Medical Care. When the supply of medical care increases, equilibrium price will decrease and the quantity of health services will increase.

some of the poor, respectively. Most other people depend on private insurers such as Blue Cross/Blue Shield. In 1988, Massachusetts became the first state to pass a statewide health care law that provided health insurance for those unable to pay for it.

An alternative solution has been the provision of direct subsidies to hospitals and medical students to increase the supply of health care. See Figure B.3 which illustrates the effect of an increase in supply on the health care market. The original equilibrium price is P_1 and equilibrium quantity is Q_1. With an increase in the supply of health care providers, the supply curve shifts outward to the right *(S')*. The equilibrium price of health care falls to P_2, with a corresponding increase in equilibrium quantity to Q_2.

Investment in hospitals and doctors is not the whole answer. It is very difficult to change people's living habits, yet this is one area where a great impact may result. Government subsidy to increase public awareness about the transmission of different diseases could lead people to change their habits in order to live healthier lives. For example, former Surgeon General C. Everett Koop was actively engaged in a campaign to advertise the ill effects of cigarette smoking as well as the risk factors associated with the spread of AIDS.

369

Summary

A major concern of the public sector is how much to invest in health. Expenditures on health care services have grown tremendously over the past forty years. Yet the overall level of health in the United States indicates that Americans are not living any longer than their counterparts in less prosperous countries. It is clear that factors other than medical care influence health. These include hereditary conditions, diet, and life-style.

Government intervention in the health care industry has occurred because this market is unique. On the demand side the unpredictability of illness, lost pay in addition to the cost of treatment, health insurance, uncertainty regarding the quality of health care, and external benefits distinguish this sector from the rest of the economy. In particular, health insurance has led to a huge increase in the price of health care because of soaring demand.

On the supply side, barriers to entry have restricted the supply of health care, resulting in higher prices. In addition, the subsidy of a significant portion of the costs of education by the public sector and the restraint of advertising and price competition distinguish this sector on the supply side.

Key Concepts

private health insurance
coinsurance
fee for service
health maintenance organizations (HMOs)
national health insurance

Discussion Questions

1. Distinguish the health care industry from other industries by examining the characteristics on the demand and supply sides.

2. Attempt to list the costs and benefits for the following programs:
   a. prenatal health care for the poor
   b. antismoking campaign
   c. free checkups for everyone

   Feel free to make assumptions about these programs.

3. Given the importance of diet in health, should the government try to alter people's eating habits? How might the government accomplish this?

The Economics of Higher Education

Objectives

Upon completion of this special topic, you should understand:

1.   The costs and benefits of higher education from the viewpoint of both students and society.

2.   How students and society decide how much to invest in higher education.

3.   How to use supply and demand analysis to determine the optimal allocation of resources to higher education as well as to determine who should pay for higher education.

4.   The boom-bust cycle of the labor market for college graduates.

How do students and society decide how much to invest in higher education? Who should pay the costs of going to college? How have market conditions for college graduates changed over the last couple of decades? To answer these questions, we begin by identifying the costs and benefits of higher education to students and society. Next, we examine the investment process to determine the optimal amount of education. We then describe the "boom-bust cycle" of the market for college graduates, concluding with a survey of annual starting salaries.

C.1 The Costs of Higher Education

How expensive is a college education? This section reviews the costs of higher education from the viewpoints of the student and society at large.

Private Costs

What are the **total private costs of higher education**? First, students must pay the *direct costs,* which include primarily payments for tuition and fees, books, and supplies. The annual tuition and fees charged by four-year universities were estimated to average $1,590 and $8,060 for the 1987 academic year at public and private institutions, respectively. Students and parents generally perceive these costs to be the most significant expenditures for higher education because they are paid "out of pocket." Thus, they are more obvious.

But these direct costs are generally less than the opportunity costs of student time, measured by the earnings that the student forgoes while attending college. This opportunity cost is substantial. It can be measured as the income that the college student could have earned with a high school education. The mean earnings of people 18 to 24 years of age with a high school degree in 1986 was $14,159 for males and $11,480 for females (year-round, full-time workers).

In addition, the student often faces *psychic costs.* Such costs may include the frustration of taking exams, writing term papers, learning new ideas, and adjusting to college life in general. Although these costs may be large, there is no known way to estimate them in terms of money.

There may also be *indirect costs,* which are the additional living costs that a person incurs because he or she is a student. Since certain basic living expenses would exist anyway, it would not be correct to calculate the full room and board charges of colleges as an educational expense. Only if the cost of rent or food is greater than the student would spend outside school would this *additional* living expense be considered a cost of education.

Costs to Society

The **total cost of higher education to society** is equal to the private costs just discussed (since students are a part of society) plus the *institutional costs* of operating colleges and universities minus tuition and fees. Tuition and fees are subtracted from the total cost to society to avoid "double counting," since they are a part of private costs and are used to finance institutional expenditures. The bulk of institutional costs are expenditures for faculty, administrators, and staff. Other institutional expenditures include the cost of acquiring and maintaining campus buildings and equipment.

C.2 The Benefits of Higher Education

Students and their families as well as taxpayers invest in the education produced by our colleges and universities. What are the benefits of higher education to students and society?

Private Benefits

The ***total private benefits of higher education*** can be divided into two major categories. First, there are ***immediate consumption benefits*** defined as the increased satisfaction that the person may enjoy while being a student. Second, there are ***long-run investment benefits*** that the student receives over a lifetime after graduation.

Immediate Consumption Benefits

While attending college a person may experience a feeling of achievement and upward mobility, the status attached to being a college student, as well as the possible "joy of learning." In addition, there are the pleasures offered by the campus life-style (e.g., meeting people of similar interests, going to parties, plays, and sporting events). The value of these benefits, although significant to the person's satisfaction, is very difficult to estimate.

Long-Run Investment Benefits

Higher education creates human capital in the form of the increased knowledge, skills, and new values that are instilled in the student while he or she attends college. This human capital generates benefits over the lifetime of the college graduate. These investment benefits include both monetary and nonmonetary components.

The *monetary benefits* are measured by the earnings that a college graduate receives in excess of the amount he or she would have received with only a high school degree. The mean earnings of four-year male college graduates was $13,779 more than male with only a high school degree in 1986 (year-round, full-time workers). The differential was $7,541 for females.

In addition, there are potential *nonmonetary benefits,* such as increased job satisfaction, lower risk of involuntary unemployment, flexible working hours, prestige in the community, greater social and cultural awareness, and the increased ability to solve problems.

Benefits to Society

Higher education produces external benefits for all members of society. The ***external benefits*** of higher education are benefits received by people who are outside the market for a college degree (see Section 7.2 of Chapter 7). These benefits include technological progress, cultural development, solutions to complex social problems, and continued economic growth, all of which depend heavily on the knowledge and creative abilities fostered by experiences gained in college. The ***total benefits of higher education to society*** are equal to the private benefits (because students are members of society) plus the *external benefits* gained by all of us, even if we do not attend college (described in Chapter 7, Section 7.2).

C.3 The Investment Decision

The decision to invest in higher education is based on consideration of the costs and benefits involved. The amount of education produced depends on the decisions to invest in higher education made by both students and society. The purpose of this section is to describe the principle for determining the optimal level of higher education as well as to answer the question: Who should pay the costs of college education?

The Optimal Amount of Education

Students will purchase education up to the point where the extra cost they have to pay to go to college is equal to the extra benefit they expect to receive personally from the investment. The amount of education provided by the private market will be less than optimal from society's viewpoint since students do not consider the "external" benefits to other persons when they decide to go to college. Since households are not willing to pay voluntarily for the external benefits received by others, the private market solution to the question, "How much college education should be produced?" will result in an underallocation of resources to higher education. The *optimal amount of education* from society's viewpoint reflects consideration of all the benefits received by students as well as the external benefits to others. See Section 7.2 of Chapter 7 for the graphic analysis of this discussion (Figure 7.2).

Who Should Pay?

If society wants to increase the level of education to the social optimum, it must *subsidize* households by an amount equal to the value of the external benefits. Such subsidy may be provided through low-interest student loans, tuition waivers, scholarships, and direct taxpayer expenditures for colleges and universities. Public subsidies, by reducing the private cost of the investment, encourage households to purchase more education than they would otherwise undertake. Therefore, the total cost of higher education should be divided between households and government (via taxpayers) in proportion to the benefits received by students and society at large.

Tuition and fees account for only a small portion of the funds raised to finance institutional costs. In the 1986 fiscal year, tuition and fees covered only 15 percent of the total current funds reserves of public colleges and universities, whereas government paid 59 percent. Even for private colleges and universities, tuition and fees were a minor source of revenue, paying only 39 percent of the total in the 1986 fiscal year, with government covering 13 percent of the expenditures. Other important sources of funding, especially for private colleges and universities, include private gifts and grants, the revenue generated through the operation of auxiliary enterprises (such as university hospitals, bookstores, and sporting events), and endowment earnings.

The preceding discussion was concerned with investment in higher education. The purpose of the next section is to examine the operation of the labor market for college graduates.

C.4 The Labor Market for College Graduates

How have market conditions changed over the last several decades for college graduates? What is the job outlook for persons currently graduating from college? Before turning to the answers to these questions, it will be helpful to review the principles governing labor markets in general, which we examined in Chapter 6.

The Operation of the Labor Market Reviewed

The employment and wages of college graduates are determined by supply and demand conditions. The following discussion reviews how changes in supply and demand affect the job market conditions for college graduates.

Changes in Supply   Figure C.1 illustrates the shift in the supply curve from S_L to S'_L, which shows the *long-run* market response when there is an increase in the number of persons graduating from college. This long-run increase in market supply depends on the costs and benefits that households consider in deciding how much to invest in a college education. For example, if the earnings of college graduates were *expected* to increase, more persons would be induced to invest in higher education. As we can see in Figure C.1, the resulting increase in the supply of college graduates would boost employment and decrease the wages actually received by college graduates.

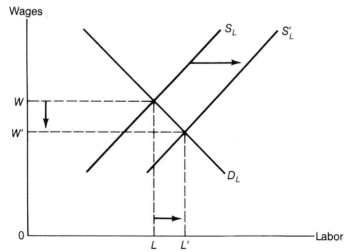

Figure C.1.   The Labor Market for College Graduates. An increase in the supply of college graduates decreases the wage rate while increasing employment.

375

Changes in Demand   A change in any of the "nonwage" determinants of the demand for labor would result in a shift in the demand curve for college graduates in the long run. As we can see in Figure C.2, if there were growth in industries that normally employ college-educated people, the demand for college graduates would shift outward from D_L to D_L'. This increase in demand would cause both the wages and employment of college graduates to increase.

Changes in Market Conditions: The Boom-Bust Cycle

During the 1960s, the college job market experienced a "boom" period due to the growth of industries with heavy manpower requirements for college graduates. As a result, the rise in the demand for college graduates outstripped the increase in supply. This situation is illustrated in Figure C.3. The earnings of college graduates rose from W to W', while the level of employment increased from L to L'.

This "boom" period of the 1960s was followed by a "bust" during the 1970s and early 1980s. The high expectations created during the boom period induced many people to attend college. From 1956 to 1969, the percentage of 18 and 19 year olds enrolled in college jumped from 29 percent to 44 percent. As Figure C.4 indicates, during the bust period, the rapid growth in the number of persons graduating from college outstripped the relatively sluggish growth in demand for college graduates. As a result of this uneven growth, the earnings of college graduates fell relative to the earnings of noncollege graduates.

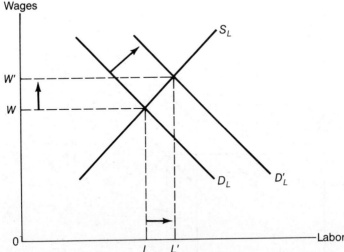

Figure C.2.   The Labor Market for College Graduates. An increase in the demand for college graduates increases the wage rate as well as employment.

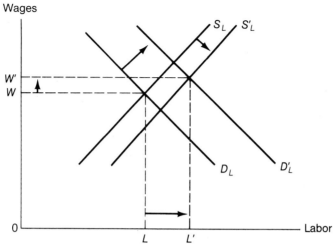

Figure C.3. A Boom Period. An increase in the demand for college graduates outstrips the growth in supply, causing both wages and employment to rise.

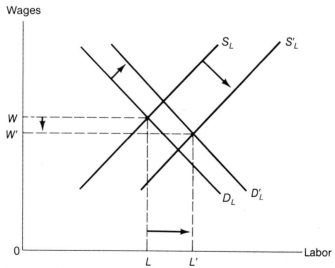

Figure C.4. A Bust Period. An increase in the supply of college graduates outstrips the growth in demand, causing the wage rate to decrease while employment rises.

It appears that the bust period has ended. Since the 1981–1982 recession, the U.S. economy has experienced the longest peacetime expansion in its history. Table C.1 shows the ratio of the earnings of college graduates to the earnings of high school graduates from 1969 to 1986 (see columns 3 and 6). The ratio for males was 1.39 in the 1969–1971 period, which means that the earnings of male college graduates was 39 percent higher than the earnings of males with only a high school degree. This ratio dropped to 1.26 by 1979–1981, which is evidence of the bust period described in this section. Are we currently in a boom period? As Table C.1 indicates, the ratio for male college graduates rebounded to 1.37 by the 1984–1986 period. Table C.1 shows a similar pattern in the ratio for female college graduates. It dropped from 1.44 in 1969–1971 to 1.30 in 1979–1981, and then increased to 1.39 in 1984–1986.

Current Starting Salaries for College Graduates

Labor market conditions for college graduates differ by academic major as well as by type of employment that the student takes after graduation. As we can see in Table C.2, there is a variation in the monthly starting salaries offered bachelor-degree candidates with *different majors.* In September 1988 the top salary offer of $2,894 was made to persons in Pharmacy. The lowest salary offer cited was $1,300 for persons with degrees in Architectural and Environmental Design.

We should note that some of the differences in the "monetary" benefits may be explained by variations in the "nonmonetary" benefits discussed at the beginning of this chapter. For instance, some persons may invest in the humanities, despite the lower potential salary offers, because of higher expected job satisfaction.

Table C.1
Relation of Income and Education, Selected Years, 1969–1986
(Index, income of high school graduates = 1.00)

Years	Males			Females		
	1–3 years high school	1–3 years college	4 years college[1]	1–3 years high school	1–3 years college	4 years college[1]
1969–71	0.89	1.16	1.39	0.84	1.17	1.44
1974–76	.87	1.09	1.28	.82	1.14	1.33
1979–81	.83	1.08	1.26	.82	1.14	1.30
1984–86	.81	1.12	1.37	.78	1.16	1.39

[1] Excludes those with more than 4 years of college.
Note—Data are 3-year averages of indexes of median annual income for year-round, full-time workers, aged 25 and over.
Source: *Economic Report of the President,* January 1988 (Table 5.1).

Table C.2
Average Monthly Salary Offers to Bachelor's Degree
Candidates by Curriculum, September 1988 (Both Sexes)

Business	
Accounting	$2,008
Banking & Finance	1,904
Business Administration	1,813
Human Resources (incl. Labor/Industrial Relations)	1,689
Institutional Management	1,736
Management Information Systems	2,075
Marketing & Distribution	1,795
Humanities & Social Sciences	
Economics	2,035
Letters (incl. English, Lit., etc.)	1,894
Humanities — All Other	1,794
Criminal Justice	1,697
History	2,048
Psychology	1,803
Social Sciences — All Other	1,878
Communications	
Advertising	1,744
Communications	1,733
Journalism	1,573
Technical Writing	2,350
Engineering	
Aerospace & Aeronautical	2,346
Agricultural	2,113
Biomedical & Bioengineering	2,201
Chemical	2,577
Civil (incl. Construction, Sanitary, & Transportation Engrg.)	2,135
Electrical (incl. Computer Engrg.)	2,477
Geological	2,039
Industrial	2,367
Mechanical	2,444
Metallurgical (incl. Metallurgy & Ceramic Engrg.)	2,463
Mining & Mineral	2,370
Nuclear (incl. Engrg. Physics)	2,368
Petroleum	2,638
Engineering Technology	2,293
Sciences	
Agricultural Sciences	1,718

Table C.2   *(Continued)*

Architectural & Environmental Design	1,300
Biological	1,765
Chemistry	2,134
Computer Science	2,290
Mathematics	2,294
Allied Health Professions	2,024
Nursing	2,126
Pharmacy	2,894
Physics	2,347
Other Physical & Earth Sciences	1,699
Renewable Natural Resources	1,698

Source: The College Placement Council, *CPC Salary Survey,* September 1988.

Summary

We identified the costs and benefits of the investment in higher education by students and society. Private costs include earnings forgone by students plus direct, indirect, and psychic costs. The total cost to society is equal to private costs plus institutional costs minus tuition and fees. Students are motivated to attend college because of the immediate consumption benefits they receive while being students as well as the long-run investment benefits received after graduation. The total benefits of higher education to society are equal to these private benefits plus external benefits.

Students will purchase more education as long as the extra benefit they personally expect to receive from the investment exceeds the extra cost. The amount of education provided by the private market will be less than optimal from society's viewpoint since students do not consider the external benefits to other persons when they decide to go to college. If society wants to increase the level of education to the social optimum, it must subsidize households by an amount equal to the value of the external benefits.

We also noted that the market for college graduates has rebounded from the bust period experienced during the 1970s and early 1980s. The increase in the ratio of the earnings of college graduates to the earnings of high school graduates is evidence of the upturn in the college job market.

Key Concepts

total private costs and benefits of higher education
total costs and benefits of higher education to society

immediate consumption and long-run investment benefits to students
external benefits
optimal amount of education
the boom-bust cycle

Discussion Questions

1. What are the costs of your investment in higher education? What are the benefits that you expect to receive after you graduate? How important are the immediate consumption benefits in your decision to attend college?

2. Why will the private market underallocate resources to higher education?

3. Who should pay for higher education? Describe the rationale for public subsidy of higher education.

4. Describe the market conditions for college graduates, tracing the changes from "boom" to "bust" using supply and demand analysis.

Environmental Economics

Objectives

Upon completion of this special topic, you should understand:

1. The various forms of pollution and what causes them.

2. Why the private market fails to allocate resources efficiently when there are external costs.

3. The economic factors that determine the optimal level of pollution control.

4. The basic policy options for reducing pollution.

5. How to evaluate the effectiveness of public policy designed to reduce pollution.

During the past few decades many events called attention to the harm caused by pollution. Some examples include the huge oil spill in Prince William Sound, Alaska; the nuclear accident at Chernobyl; the explosions at the Union Carbide plant in Bhopal, India; the controversy over acid rain; and the hole in the ozone layer of the atmosphere.

Because of such events, the government has taken a more active role in cleaning up the environment. But the issue of how much government intervention is required and which approach to use is very controversial. These problems remain "hot" topics today.

We begin this chapter with a discussion of the nature of environmental problems and why they exist. We then describe how policymakers determine the optimal amount of pollution control. Next, we discuss the various policy options available to deal with pollution. Finally, we present some of the problems associated with the different policy options.

D.1 Different Forms of Pollution

Pollution consists of consumption and production byproducts, such as disposable diapers and the smoke from a coal-fired power plant, that accumulate in the environment. Likewise water has many alternative uses that may not be compatible with each other. One such use of water is waste disposal. If pollutants are dumped into water, the water may be unfit for use for recreation or drinking. Also, industries may require clean water for such uses as diluting chemicals, cooling machinery, and washing equipment.

In many instances pollution is not easily detected, such as lead deposits in the air. Pollution is not limited to the disposal of waste in the air, water, and land, but it also includes noise and visual pollution.

Pollution is not a new problem. Early Roman literature contains references to problems of pollution. But the problems are worse today and more complex. Population growth and the increase in the concentration of economic activity have made it more difficult for the environment to assimilate waste when it is created in massive, concentrated amounts. In addition, because of the increased use of complex chemicals and the problems associated with their disposal, the problem of pollution control is even more difficult to solve.

D.2 Market Failure

The private market mechanism will not allocate resources in a socially efficient manner when resources are collectively consumed (common property resources) and there are external costs.

Common property resources exist when private ownership of the resource is absent, probably due to the difficulties of restricting accessibility to it. In other words, it is difficult to allocate the resource among competing users. Clean air, free-flowing healthy water, wildlife, and the beauty of certain wilderness areas are examples of common property resources. For instance, clean air is no longer abundant in many areas, but people still use air to dispose of trash by burning it. To the polluter, the benefits clearly outweigh the costs, as burning rubbish is a very inexpensive way to get rid of garbage. Most people correctly feel that if they are the *only ones* doing it, burning trash will not affect air quality very much. But because everyone shares the air, they are all free to use as much of it as they like. As a result, because of *overutilization,* air quality deteriorates to the detriment of all. This is an example of society being better off if people did not maximize their own self-satisfaction.

Another example of market failure involves *external costs* (see Chapter 7, Section 7.2). Pollution falls under this category. External costs occur when a consumer or producer undertakes an activity that imposes a cost on third parties in addition to the cost borne by the first and second parties (buyers and sellers). For example, if a chemical firm upstream were to use a river to get rid of its waste, farmers downstream using the water for irrigation would be forced to bear the cost of cleaning up the water or they would face the reduced crop yield that might result from using polluted water.

The existence of the externality has distorted the allocation of resources in this market. By ignoring the externality, too many resources will be devoted to production by the chemical firm, resulting in an *overallocation* of resources because not all costs are considered. See Section 7.2 of Chapter 7 for the graphical analysis of this discussion (Figure 7.1).

We should note that firms which pollute are not as sinister as they may be portrayed. Firms are trying to produce their product as inexpensively as possible. As profit maximizers, they will not include costs that they are not forced to bear. If a firm voluntarily disposed of waste in a manner that did not harm the environment, it would be at a competitive disadvantage. In fact, the firm would be forced out of business if it paid these costs on a voluntary basis. In addition, the firm may not even be aware of the pollution problem it is creating. The government should intervene to correct this situation.

D.3 The Optimal Amount of Pollution Control

We will now develop a model that enables us to determine the optimal level of pollution control.

Determining the Optimal Amount of Pollution Control

Given that government intervention is necessary, policymakers must determine the **optimal amount of pollution control**. How much should the public sector devote to cleaning up the environment? A simple model is presented in Figure D.1. The horizontal axis measures the amount of pollution control. The origin indicates a point where no pollution control is being produced. The farther away from the origin (point 0) on the horizontal axis, the more pollution control produced, and therefore the cleaner the environment. The benefits and costs of pollution control are measured in dollars on the vertical axis.

Demand The demand curve in Figure D.1 indicates society's ability and willingness to pay for each additional unit of pollution control. It is downward sloping because society values later units of pollution control less than earlier ones. For example, as the air is made cleaner and cleaner, the effect on health is less and less (i.e., the first units of clean air produced have the greatest impact on well-being). Therefore, the benefit to society of each additional unit of pollution control, called *marginal social benefit,* decreases as more pollution control is

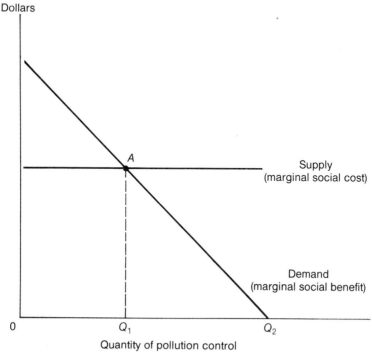

Figure D.1. Determination of the Optimal Level of Pollution Control. The optimal amount of pollution control is produced where the marginal social benefit of the last unit of pollution control produced equals the marginal social cost.

produced. Where the demand curve intersects the horizontal axis (see Q_2), a completely clean environment has been produced.

Supply To simplify the analysis, we assume that it costs society the same amount to produce each additional unit of clean air; i.e., the *marginal social cost* of pollution control is assumed to be constant. Therefore, the supply curve for pollution control is drawn in Figure D.1 as a horizontal line. In fact, it would be more realistic to draw the supply curve as upward sloping to illustrate the fact that the marginal cost of controlling pollution rises as more and more pollution is taken out of the environment.

The Optimal Amount of Pollution Control In Figure D.1, the optimum amount of pollution control produced occurs at Q_1 where the demand curve intersects the supply curve. At point A, the value placed on an additional unit of pollution prevention by society (marginal social benefit or MSB) is exactly equal to the additional cost to society of producing it (marginal social cost or MSC). At any level of production of pollution control to the right of point *A*, too much pollution prevention would be produced, because the additional gain to society *(MSB)* as measured by the demand curve is less than the additional cost to society *(MSC)*. Likewise, at any level of production to the left of point *A*, too little is being produced. The benefit of producing additional units, measured by the demand curve, outweighs the cost of producing these additional units. Therefore, amount Q_1 is the optimal amount of pollution control to be produced.

The Increase in Pollution Control

This model may be used to explain the increased pressures on the government to produce a cleaner environment. It has been shown in numerous studies that as income increases, people buy more and more of the goods they consider desirable. It is natural that their demand for environmental goods will eventually increase. This is due in part to their increased desire to use their leisure time to swim, fish, camp, and engage in many other outdoor activities. They

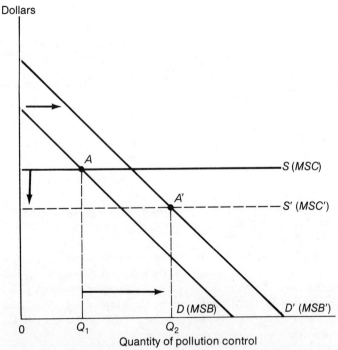

Figure D.2. The Impact of a Simultaneous Increase in Demand and Decrease in the Supply of the Optimal Quantity of Pollution Control. Because of an increase in the demand for a cleaner environment and a reduction in the costs of treating pollution, the optimal amount of pollution control has increased.

also desire to preserve the aesthetic beauty of the world they live in. In addition, people's preferences have changed as their knowledge of the harmful effects of pollution has increased. As a result, the demand curve for pollution control has shifted to the right. This increase in demand has resulted in an increase in the equilibrium quantity of pollution control.

In addition, there have been many technological innovations that have reduced the marginal costs of treating pollution. The overall effect is illustrated in Figure D.2 by the downward shift of the supply curve (due to lower costs) and the rightward shift in the demand curve (due to higher income). The new equilibrium point *(A′)* indicates a greater level of pollution control. The next section examines the various policy tools the government can employ to produce the optimal amount of pollution control.

D.4 Correcting Market Failure

Assume that the government forces the private market to be aware of external costs in order to correct for the overallocation of resources. This will cause the equilibrium level of output to be lower and the equilibrium price to be higher. Various approaches can be used to correct the overallocation of resources caused by external costs: the establishment of property rights, direct regulation, the role of the judicial system, taxes and subsidies, and new methods of pollution control.

The Establishment of Property Rights

In some cases injured parties can attempt to deal with external costs by negotiating directly with the party producing them. Theoretically, one of two situations may occur. Assume that one of two people who are in a room decides to smoke a cigarette and the other person objects. To resolve the conflict, the smoker might compensate the other individual for his or her discomfort. The other possibility is for the nonsmoker to pay the smoker to stop smoking, thus compensating that person for the lost pleasure of smoking. The person who is ultimately compensated is determined by the ownership of *property rights.*

In the real world with large numbers of people involved and the source of the problem not always obvious, property rights may be difficult to establish. In the United States, property rights are established by laws that allow or prohibit the manner in which property is used. For example, laws that do not allow people to smoke in certain areas give ownership of the air in these areas to nonsmokers.

Direct Regulation

Direct regulation involves the setting of specific standards for pollution control by legislative action. For example, standards have been set on emissions from automobiles and coal-burning factories, and on wastes dumped into water. Under emergency periods, direct regulation offers a relatively quick solution. For example, when air pollution is severe, local authorities may close factories and restrict automobile access to the area until conditions improve.

But the application of direct regulation has its problems. Once the standards are set, fines are established to penalize firms who do not meet them. In many instances, these fines are set so low that firms find it cheaper to pay the fine than the cost of cleanup. In addition, enforcement costs tend to be high, which reduces the probability of being caught. Finally, the government agencies set up to monitor or regulate the behavior of firms often end up promoting the interests of the firms themselves. Many of the appointed officials on these regulatory agencies are former officials of the companies the government is regulating.

In setting standards, the principle of equating the additional benefits to society *(MSB)* to the additional cost to society *(MSC)* should be applied. However, given the difficulty of determining costs as well as benefits, the setting of standards is sometimes capricious. Enforcement may also be erratic, dependent not on any type of economic criteria but on public pressure.

The Environmental Protection Agency (EPA) is the primary federal agency responsible for the setting of standards and their enforcement. During the 1970s, the EPA took a stance that was far more aggressive than the one it took in the 1980s under the Reagan administration. The debate over how much pollution control is necessary continues.

The Role of the Judicial System

Injured parties have recourse through the courts. For example, if a factory is emitting a destructive byproduct, people in the neighborhood might ask the courts to prohibit that activity on the grounds that their property rights have been violated. Courts in the past have provided remedies by forcing polluters to properly dispose of waste. To do this, the courts must determine whether a violation has occurred, who is liable for the damage, and how to assess the damage.

The determination of who is liable is often very difficult. For example, it is very difficult to trace air pollution to its source once it gets into the atmosphere. Air pollution may cross over many jurisdictions, possibly international boundaries, making the problem of enforcement even more difficult. For example, in the production of electricity, the Midwest United States uses a grade of coal with a high sulfur content. Because of the large amount of sulfur emitted into the atmosphere, Canada is bearing external costs in the form of acid rain, which is killing life in many of the lakes and forests in the region.

In some cases the effects of environmental damage do not appear for many years. For example, children in schools with ceilings made of asbestos were probably inhaling minute asbestos particles in the classroom. The carcinogen may not have any noticeable effect until these children reach middle age.

Finally, court decisions may not result in an economically efficient solution. It is possible for the courts to force the polluter to employ too much or too little pollution control if it ignores the rule of equating marginal social benefits to marginal social cost.

Taxes and Subsidies

A fourth approach by government is the use of ***taxes and subsidies***. To produce the optimal level of pollution control, the government can force firms to take into account external costs they are generating by taxing them for the pollution they produce, or the government can pay the polluting firm to reduce polluting activity.

Taxation

Taxation can induce buyers and sellers to take their external costs into account, forcing firms to produce at a socially optimal level. If a firm realizes that it may have to pay a tax based on the amount of pollution it emits, the firm will take into consideration the alternative costs of waste disposal. The firm may buy new pollution-control equipment to reduce the cost of this tax. The tax should be set so that marginal social benefits equal marginal social cost. This is the level that will yield the optimal amount of pollution control.

If the firm's pollution treatment costs are less than the tax, the firm will treat the pollution. If the tax is less than the treatment cost, the firm will pay the tax rather than the higher cost of treating the pollutant.

When a tax is applied to many firms in an area, the firms will not produce the same amount of pollution control because of the differences in the costs of reducing waste. Those firms with the greatest costs will pay the tax, while those firms with the lowest costs will find it in their best interest to control pollution as long as the cost of control is less than the tax. As a result, the total cost to society may be less than the costs under a regulatory framework that forces all firms to produce the same amount of pollution control regardless of their costs. The Ruhr Valley in Germany is a heavily industrialized river basin that has successfully used taxes, called *effluent charges,* to make the river basin compatible with recreational, drinking, and industrial uses.

Subsidy

A *subsidy* can be used to reduce pollution. Under this approach, government will pay firms to stop them from polluting. The firm will agree to stop polluting as long as the subsidy is greater than the cost of treating the pollutant. When the cost of treating pollution becomes greater than the subsidy, the firm will stop treating pollution and forfeit the subsidy. If the subsidy is set at the same level as the optimal tax rate, the same amount of pollution prevention will be produced. The difference is that under a system of taxation the firm incurs an additional cost of production which lowers profit. But with a subsidy scheme, the firm will be able to increase its profit if it is able to produce pollution control at a cost less than the subsidy. As a result, this industry will still overproduce, causing the existing overallocation of resources to persist.

Many environmentalists have opposed the subsidy scheme because they feel that those harmed are being taxed to get the dollars needed to stop the firms from polluting, something firms should have been prevented from doing in the first place through direct regulation or taxation. Economists do not consider subsidies a viable solution since they do not result in an efficient or equitable solution.

New Methods of Pollution Control

A number of experimental approaches have been used in the United States by the public sector to deal with the problem of pollution. In one method, the public sector determines how much pollution is allowable and issues the appropriate number of *certificates to pollute*. These certificates give the bearer the right to pollute. A market for these certificates will develop, and through the interaction of buyers and sellers, the price of each unit of pollution will be established. Producers must compare their cost of treating pollution to the price of the certificates in determining whether to purchase certificates or treat pollution. The adoption of this approach will minimize the cost of treating pollution. As we noted in Section 2.4 of Chapter 2, this is called economic efficiency.

A second approach is called the ***bubble concept***. According to this approach, polluting firms are given a standard they must meet. The firm then determines the most cost-effective method of controlling pollution in each of its plants. For example, a steel firm might have five plants. The firm can produce pollution control at different levels in the plants as long as the total pollution emitted meets the standard. Obviously, the firm will want to produce more pollution control at those plants where the costs of treatment are lowest.

D.5 Evaluation of Public Policy

There are a number of problems in implementing appropriate public policy. First, the discussion above assumed that the government has perfect information on the costs facing the firm and the benefits society receives. The more inaccurate the information, the less likely it is that the government will find the point that maximizes social well-being.

A second complication is that resources are valued at different rates over time. If pollution is not treated today, it may become more expensive to treat in the future. For example, industrial chemical wastes that were buried years ago are now plaguing people (e.g., Love Canal, New York). It might have been cheaper to deal with the industrial wastes at the time they were created rather than now. Today the costs involved in removing these wastes are staggering. The "Superfund Act" passed in 1980, and a reauthorization bill passed in 1986, provided over $10 billion to clean up toxic waste sites. This is an example of an intergenerational transfer with current citizens paying for problems created years ago.

Third, it is also important to note that interactions of various programs must be taken into account. A policy that reduces waste disposal in waterways may induce firms to turn to an alternative, less costly way of disposing their waste such as burning it, which would increase air pollution.

Fourth, when the policy imposed is local in origin, it will place the firms in this area at a disadvantage compared to firms in areas that have no pollution controls. These firms would have higher costs than those in areas that lack pollution control. This could possibly force these firms out of business, creating an economic hardship on others in the area. This is a major argument in favor of a broad national policy instead of allowing each locality to set policy. In addition, many environmental problems are worldwide. The United States acting alone will not solve these problems. Unfortunately, international agreements have not proven to be workable.

Finally, nothing has been said of the income distribution effects. Who has gained as a result of the recommended policy? Who is paying the cost? For example, suppose the government uses tax revenue to clean a public beach. There is a redistribution of income if the tax revenue comes from a group different from those benefiting from the clean beach. It may be desirable to compensate the people who paid for the cleanup but who do not enjoy the benefits.

Summary

Pollution can assume many different forms and affect the environment in a variety of ways. For example, pollution alters the air we breathe, the water we drink, and the beauty of our environment. Because of external costs and the overutilization of common property resources, the private market will fail to allocate resources in an efficient manner. If the production of a good results in external costs that are ignored, too much of the good will be produced at too low a price.

In order to determine the optimal level of pollution control, the public sector must compare the marginal social benefit *(MSB)* to the marginal social cost *(MSC)*. Pollution control should be produced up to the point where $MSB = MSC$. Over the past twenty years, increased demand for pollution control and lower costs of producing pollution control have led to a greater amount of pollution control produced.

The public sector has a number of alternative methods to correct market failure. These include direct regulation, the judicial system, taxes and subsidies, and certificates to pollute.

Key Concepts

pollution
common property resources
optimal amount of pollution control
direct regulation
certificates to pollute
bubble concept

Discussion Questions

1. What are the causes of pollution?
2. How are resources misallocated in an industry when there are external costs? Why?
3. How is the optimal level of pollution control determined?
4. Discuss the different approaches for pollution control.

The Farm Problem and Public Policy

Objectives

Upon completion of this special topic, you should understand:

1. The profound changes that occurred in the U.S. agricultural sector during the last thirty years.

2. The causes of the long-term decline in farm income.

3. Why farm income tends to change erratically from one season to the next.

4. Our three federal agricultural programs as well as their costs and benefits.

The U.S. agricultural sector experienced profound changes over the last thirty years. The construction of the interstate highway system and the invention of refrigerator trucks were instrumental in promoting the development of a national market for farm products. The many small regional farm markets that once characterized the United States merged into a national market which has since expanded into an international market for U.S. farm products. In 1987, 36 percent of the U.S. farmland devoted to growing crops was tilled for goods exported to other nations. About 76 percent of wheat, 42 percent of soybeans, 24 percent of corn, and 45 percent of cotton produced in 1987 in the United States were sold abroad.

We begin by surveying major changes in farm production. We then examine major problems confronting farmers and public policies adopted by the federal government to help alleviate these farm problems.

E.1 A Historical Overview

The growth of the agricultural market was accompanied by a sharp decrease in the farm population. While farm families made up about 9 percent of our total population in 1960, they comprised only 2 percent in 1987. About 46 percent of the farms that existed in 1960 had disappeared by 1988.

Most of the 1.8 million farms driven out of business were small. Farming came to be called "agribusiness" because of the growth of big farms. The average size of farms rose from 297 acres in 1960 to 463 acres in 1988. Although the vast majority of farms are still small, they account for an insignificant share of agricultural products produced in the United States. In 1987, 4.5 percent of all farms accounted for 65 percent of net farm income. This is because the bulk of the nation's agricultural land is owned by a relatively small number of farms.

The development of big agribusiness changed both the style of farm management and the methods of production. The production process changed from labor-intensive methods used by the traditional small farms to capital-intensive methods employed by much larger farms. From 1960 to 1986, farm labor decreased 55 percent, while the amount of land in farming decreased 10 percent, and agricultural chemicals increased 341%.

These profound changes in technology worked in conjunction with a phenomenon called *economies of scale*. As we note in Chapter 5, this term refers to the situation where an increase in the size of the production unit (a single farm) results in a decrease in the average cost of production. In other words, the expansion of the agricultural market resulted in a sharp decrease in average production costs for those farms that grew sufficiently large to be able to use the new heavy machinery, equipment, and chemicals developed for agriculture. Those farms that remained small had to continue to employ the old labor-intensive production methods. As a result, small farms became less efficient than large, capital-intensive farms. This disadvantage caused many of the small family-run farms to die in the marketplace. The following discussion examines problems encountered by the farms that did survive.

E.2 The Farm Problem

A persistent problem facing farmers in the U.S. economy is the long-term decline in their income (measured relative to nonfarm income). In addition, farmers have been confronted with fluctuations in farm income from one season to the next. We will explore the causes and consequences of both farm problems.

Long-Term Decline in Farm Income

The causes of the **long-term decline in farm income** can be explained using the supply and demand model. The introduction of capital-intensive methods of production and the ensuing economies of scale led to a significant rise in farm productivity. During the 1960–1986 period, farm productivity (measured in terms of farm output per labor hour) increased 405 percent. The resulting decrease in average production costs caused a tremendous expansion in the supply of farm products.

The demand for farm goods also increased, but it did so by much less than the increase in the supply of farm products. The rise in demand was due primarily to population growth rather than to higher per capita income. Instead of consuming more farm products as their standard of living increased, people used their higher incomes to purchase other goods, such as better housing, more education, and improved health care.

Figure E.1 illustrates these changes in supply and demand conditions. The larger rise in supply resulted in a sharp decrease in price (P_1 to P_2) relative to the increase in the quantity sold (Q_1 to Q_2). Note that farm income is calculated by multiplying price by the quantity sold. Since price had dropped by a larger percentage than the increase in the quantity sold, total farm income fell.

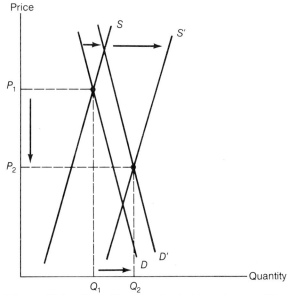

Figure E.1.   Long-Term Decline in Farm Income. The increase in the supply of agricultural products was greater than the increase in demand. Price fell by more than the rise in output, causing farm income to fall.

395

The problem of falling income is a selective one affecting primarily the small, traditional farm. Large farms, which were able to expand output at lower average cost, experienced higher profits while small farms continued to produce low yields at high cost.

Short-Term Instability of Farm Income

A second problem is the ***short-term instability of farm income.*** Farmers often face fluctuations in farm income from one season to the next. Small farmers operating at the brink of poverty and large agribusiness farms investing huge sums of money in machinery and equipment are all vulnerable to sudden drops in farm income. Although business may boom in future years, a sudden decline in current income could be a disaster to the small farms needing to make ends meet as well as the large farms whose managers must meet monthly mortgage payments on expensive equipment.

What causes drastic changes in farm income? Part of the answer lies in the inelastic nature of the demand curve for farm products. The other part of the explanation lies in the erratic changes that occur in supply.

Inelastic Demand As we can see in Figure E.2, the demand curve is highly inelastic (discussed in Chapter 3, *Appendix A*). The supply curve is perfectly inelastic since we are assuming the market period. As we noted in Section 4.1 of Chapter 4, supply is a vertical line in the market period, because the amount produced is fixed and cannot vary with changes in

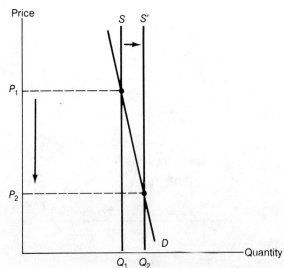

Figure E.2. Short-Term Instability of Farm Income. An increase in supply causes a sharp drop in price and farm income because of inelastic demand.

price. This is a realistic assumption at the end of the harvest season, since farmers are not in a position to increase production if the price of their farm product increases.

The demand for farm products is generally highly *inelastic,* which means that a large percentage change in price causes a relatively smaller percentage change in the quantity demanded. Consumers are generally insensitive to changes in the price of food because food is a necessity. People tend to buy about the same amount of food whether the price is high or low. It is difficult and expensive to store most foods for long periods of time; therefore, households are limited in their ability to stockpile food during a period of low prices.

Changes in Supply Conditions The other part of the explanation for short-term instability of farm income lies primarily in the unpredictable changes in weather (which is a major input in the farm production process) and the effectiveness of methods used to control insects as well as crop and livestock diseases. Changes in weather conditions, for example, will cause erratic shifts in the supply of farm products from one season to the next. Figure E.2 illustrates the impact of an increase in supply from S to S'. Because demand is relatively inelastic, this increase in supply causes a sharp decrease in price (P_1 to P_2) and only a relatively modest rise in the quantity of farm produce sold (Q_1 to Q_2). Farm income falls because the modest increase in the quantity sold is overshadowed by the sharp drop in price.

This fall in income may suddenly be reversed the next year by a decrease in supply. A decrease in supply would cause the price of the farm good to rise by more than the decrease in the quantity sold.

E.3 Public Policy

The federal government currently uses three major programs to help counteract both the long-term decline and the annual fluctuations in farm income. These policies are the price support, crop restriction, and target price programs.

Price Support Program

In the 1930s, the federal government adopted the ***price support program***, which established institutional prices (see Chapter 3, Section 3.6) to stabilize farm prices at levels Congress deemed "fair" to farmers. The primary crops currently affected by this program are wheat, feed grains, soybeans, cotton, rice, peanuts, tobacco, and sugar.

How does the price support program work? For simplicity, suppose that Congress sets the support price $(\overline{P})$ at the initial equilibrium price (P_1) represented in Figure E.3. An increase in supply from S to S' would normally cause the market price to fall from P_1 to P_2. Farm income would fall because the increase in the quantity sold is more than offset by the relatively larger decrease in price. However, under the price support program, the federal government prevents the actual farm prices from falling. How? The government buys up surplus farm produce at the support price $\overline{P}$. We can see that a surplus of Q_1 to Q_2 is initially created by the increase in

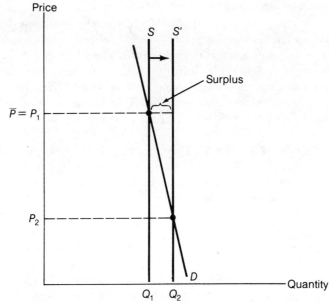

Figure E.3. The Price Support Program and an Increase in Supply. An increase in supply creates a surplus at the support price ($\overline{P}$). This surplus is bought by the government at the support price in order to prevent a drop in farm prices.

supply at the support price $\overline{P}$. By buying up this surplus at the support price, the government prevents the actual price from falling to the equilibrium price of P_2. What are benefits and costs of this program?

Benefits and Costs The price support program is aimed primarily at benefiting farmers by giving them higher and more stable income. The reserve stock of farm produce created also has the benefit of providing a food reserve that would help feed people during a national or international emergency. However, the program does involve certain costs. First, the government is required to store commodities at taxpayer expense. Second, consumers generally end up paying higher prices for less farm output. Third, we are wasting scarce economic resources by paying farmers to produce goods that are not wanted.

An Overview of the Price Support Program There has been a long-term tendency for farm prices to fall. While the price support program's primary aim is to stabilize prices, it also helps to prevent agricultural prices from declining relative to nonfarm prices. To help keep the actual price of farm products from falling, the federal government has had to buy up surplus crops far more often than it has had to sell them. The buildup of large reserves of commodities led the government to develop programs to reduce this farm surplus.

Crop Restriction Program

The government's primary attempt to reduce the increasing surplus of food accumulated under the price support program is the ***crop restriction program***. Under this program, the government compensates farmers for not growing their normal crops, encouraging them to plant instead clover and alfalfa, which put nitrogen back into the earth, making the soil more fertile. Crops currently affected by this program are wheat, cotton, tobacco, and peanuts.

We can see the impact of this program on the market for farm goods in Figure E.4. Under the crop restriction program, the supply of farm produce is reduced, illustrated by a decrease in supply from S to S'. This decrease in supply increases the price of the product from P_1 to P_2, while the amount of the product sold decreases from Q_1 to Q_2. What are the benefits and costs of the crop restriction program?

Benefits and Costs   The crop restriction program benefits farmers by giving them higher income and more fertile soil. It also benefits taxpayers by reducing the expense of crop storage managed by the government. On the other hand, households are affected by the crop restriction program because they are forced to pay a higher price for less output. In addition, taxpayers end up paying higher taxes to compensate farmers for not growing their normal

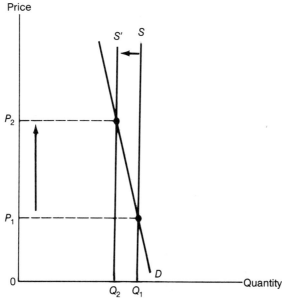

Figure E.4.   Crop Restriction Program. Farmers are paid not to plant. The decrease in supply causes a relatively sharp increase in price (from P_1 to P_2) and only a modest decrease in the quantity sold (from Q_1 to Q_2) because of inelastic demand.

crops. The program also has the potential cost of reduced food reserves that might be needed in a future emergency.

Target Price Program

The **target price program** gives low-income farmers a direct cash transfer payment rather than a way to maintain high farm prices. Figure E.5 illustrates how the target price program operates. Assume that the target price $(\overline{P})$ is set at the initial equilbrium price (P_1). We can see that the increase in supply from S to S' causes the market price to drop from P_1 to the new equilibrium level of P_2, while the quantity of farm produce sold to households increases from Q_1 to Q_2. The government does not prevent these changes in price and quantity from occurring under the target price program, because it does not buy up surplus grain at a support price when market supply increases. Instead, the federal government simply pays farmers a cash subsidy, called a *deficiency payment,* calculated as the difference between the target $(\overline{P})$ and the equilibrium market price (P_2) multiplied by the quantity sold (Q_2). What are the benefits and costs of this program?

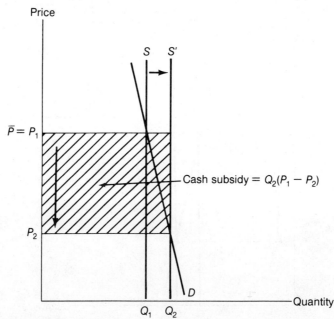

Figure E.5. Target Price Program. Low-income farmers receive a direct-cash subsidy, calculated as the difference between the target price $(\overline{P})$ and the equilibrium price (P_2) multiplied by the quantity sold (Q_2).

Benefits and Costs The target price program has two major benefits. First, farmers receive cash subsidies that increase their income. Second, consumers benefit from this program because they receive more farm produce at a lower price than under the other programs discussed. However, this program also has three major costs. First, taxpayers must pay higher taxes to finance the subsidy. Second, the target price program does not create food reserves that might be needed to support life during a national or an international emergency. Finally, the program supports inefficient farms, keeping them artificially in a business in which they cannot compete. This wastes scarce resources that could be used to produce goods more highly valued by society.

Summary

With the expansion of the agricultural market, farms that were large enough to employ advanced capital-intensive methods of production experienced lower average production costs due to economies of scale. Smaller, labor-intensive farms continued to be high-cost producers, which forced many into bankruptcy.

Why did the income of many farms decline? The supply of farm products increased by more than the increase in demand, which caused the increase in the quantity sold to be more than offset by the drop in farm prices. Fluctuations in farm income are usually caused by erratic shifts in supply, given an inelastic demand for farm products. Unstable farm income is a problem because it creates a great deal of uncertainty and hardship for farmers.

Three programs were instituted to help alleviate these farm problems. First, the price support program attempts to stabilize farm prices and farm income by giving government the authority to buy certain farm products at the support price during a period of surplus, and to sell them at a support price during a shortage. Second, the crop restriction program pays farmers for not growing a portion of their crops. This reduces output, which in turn boosts prices and farm income. The third approach is called the target price program, which directly subsidizes low-income farmers with a cash transfer. This subsidy is equal to the difference between the target price and the equilibrium price multiplied by the quantity of farm goods sold.

Key Concepts

long-term decline in farm income
short-term instability of farm income
price support program
crop restriction program
target price program
benefits and costs of farm programs

Discussion Questions

1. Describe the two farm problems. Using supply and demand analysis, describe the causes of these problems.

2. How do the price support and the target price programs attempt to stabilize farm income?

3. What are the benefits and costs of the three public farm policies?

4. Describe the historic changes in the U.S. agricultural sector over the last thirty years.

Government Regulation

Objectives

Upon completion of this special topic, you should understand:

1. Factors that justify government regulation.

2. The difference between the regulatory approaches of government purchases and production, direct regulation, price regulation, and antitrust regulation.

3. Why government may fail to improve the efficiency of the private market.

4. Stigler's view of regulation.

OSHA, EPA, SEC, FTC, NLRB, CPSA, ICC, FDA, EEOC, NHTSA—no, this isn't a foreign language vocabulary list. These are abbreviations for ten government regulatory agencies. Government regulation affects us every day in a variety of ways. Some regulations are concerned with the lack of competition in the marketplace, insufficient health and safety conditions in factories, and pollution of the environment. Mandatory school attendance, insurance on your savings accounts, the prohibition of smoking in certain areas, and the 55-mph speed limit are other examples of the variety of government regulations.

The impact of regulations has been beneficial, contributing to a cleaner environment, safer workplaces, safer products, and greater competition. But these gains were not free. As noted throughout this book, there are opportunity costs involved whenever we decide to do something. Could the billions spent on complying with the regulations have been better spent on other goods and services? Would society be better off with more or less regulation?

These are very difficult questions to answer. We first examine the reasons for government regulation of market activity. Second, the different types of regulation are discussed. We will also demonstrate that government intervention does not always have the desired effect. Finally, we will examine an alternative approach to regulation advocated by noted economist George Stigler. This special topic assumes that you have understood the material presented in Chapters 3, 4, and 5.

F.1 Why Regulate?

Under pure competition, it is assumed that people will consume and produce that amount and mix of output which makes them best off. In equilibrium, the benefit received from the last unit produced equals the additional cost of producing that unit. In addition, the average cost of production will be minimized. Therefore, pure competition achieves an equilibrium that is efficient. A number of factors cause the actual market to misallocate resources. The **public interest approach** to regulation argues that government should intervene to improve efficiency and equity in order to promote the "public interest."

Factors That Reduce Competition

Whenever a market is imperfectly competitive, each firm possesses some market power. This market power enables the firm to affect price, something the firm is not able to do under pure competition. The firm will set price or quantity at a level that will maximize profit (see Chapter 5, Section 5.1). Through the maximization of profit, imperfectly competitive firms will charge a higher price and produce a lower level of output than if the market were purely competitive. Therefore, imperfect competition leads to an underallocation of resources.

There are a number of factors that reduce competition and thereby justify government intervention to improve efficiency. First, competition may be reduced by *overt collusion* among sellers. Collusion occurs when a group of producers get together and make decisions to maximize their joint profits rather than to compete actively against one another. The most common type of collusion is **price fixing**.

Second, mergers between firms may eliminate competition. Mergers can be **horizontal** (between competing firms), **vertical** (between a firm and its supplier), or **conglomerate** (between unrelated firms). Horizontal mergers frequently reduce competition by reducing the number of independent firms in an industry. Much of the market dominance of such industrial giants as General Motors, General Electric, Kodak, and Dupont can be traced to a series of horizontal mergers in the early part of this century. Vertical and conglomerate mergers are less likely to reduce competition. It is possible that a conglomerate might use profits generated in one division to subsidize price wars designed to eliminate competitors in other areas in which it operates.

Other Factors Justifying Government Intervention

In addition to the reduction of competition, there are three other reasons why government should intervene in the private market. First, as described in Section 7.2 in Chapter 7, when the purely competitive market does not take all the benefits and costs into account, the allocation of resources will be inefficient. This occurs when there are *externalities.* In the presence of external costs, the market supply curve will not reflect the true costs to society, and as a result there will be an overallocation of resources. If there are external benefits, market demand will underestimate the true benefits to society, resulting in an underallocation of resources. In an attempt to improve efficiency, the government may impose regulations on consumers and producers to make them aware of these external costs and external benefits.

The second factor is related to this problem of externalities. The model of pure competition assumes that households and producers make decisions based on the best possible information. But in many instances, producers, and especially households, do not have all the information needed to make the best decision possible. In addition, they may not be able to assimilate or understand the information they obtain. For example, in the health care industry, how does the consumer evaluate the competency of a particular physician? It would require a great deal of education to evaluate the knowledge that each physician possesses. Therefore, in an attempt to assure quality health care, states have required physicians to take competency exams before they are allowed to practice medicine.

Finally, if a monopoly exists, certain groups in society will be able to gain monopoly profit. This affects the distribution of income. Therefore, equity considerations may warrant government intervention to redistribute income.

F.2 Types of Regulation

How does the government regulate? When the government decides to intervene in the private market, it can do so in a number of ways. There are three distinct approaches that involve different degrees of regulation.

Government Purchases and Production

At one extreme, the government may decide to take over production of a firm or group of firms in an industry, called ***nationalism.*** An alternative approach is for the government to purchase large quantities of a good or service instead of allowing the private market to respond to consumer demand. Some examples are the U.S. Postal Service, public schools and colleges, and the Tennessee Valley Authority (a federal dam project to control flooding and to produce electricity in Tennessee). The federal government created the U.S. Postal Service to reduce the cost of delivering mail. Imagine what would happen if there were 100 postal services vying for your dollar. Would mail move as easily from one part of the country to another? The handling of large volumes of mail has reduced the average cost of production because of economies of scale described in Chapter 5 (Section 5.3).

There are different degrees of government production. The government may *nationalize* (take over) an entire industry, creating a public monopoly. An alternative is the yardstick approach. Under the ***yardstick approach***, the government obtains control of one firm in an industry. The government may then use this firm to (1) aggressively compete against others, driving the price down, or (2) obtain information about the costs of production, which can be used to regulate price.

Large-scale government purchases and production have not been as widely adopted in the United States as in other countries. One of the basic tenets of our mixed capitalistic economy is the heavy reliance on the private market for the provision of goods and services. Many feel that government purchases and production weakens this principle. Nevertheless, the *threat* of nationalization can be an effective tool to regulate business behavior. In Western Europe, nationalization is much more common. Some examples are the European passenger railroad system, the postal system, and the telecommunications industry.

Direct Regulation

Direct regulation is a means by which government can allow the private market to operate subject to limitations. First, the government can limit or prohibit production of a good that generates external costs, or alter the manner in which it is produced. For example, the generation of electricity from bituminous coal creates air pollution. The government might close the power plant, specify the type of coal used, or require scrubbers to reduce the amount of pollution emitted into the atmosphere.

See *Special Topic D: Environmental Economics* for a more detailed discussion of this type of regulation.

Second, the government can regulate the prices set by monopolies. As we noted in Chapter 5 (Section 5.1), a price set by a monopoly is higher than the price that would have prevailed if the market had been purely competitive. The goal of regulation would be to force the firm to charge an efficient price.

Figure F.1 illustrates the revenue and cost curves facing a natural monopoly. A *natural monopoly* occurs when there is only one firm in the industry in a given geographic area and this firm experiences significant economies of scale (described in Section 5.3 of Chapter 5). For certain goods it is the most efficient market structure, because the economies of scale give the single large firm a significant cost advantage over smaller firms. In this instance, pure competition is not a desirable market structure. Examples of natural monopolies are electric power production, mass transit, water treatment, waste disposal, and other public utilities.

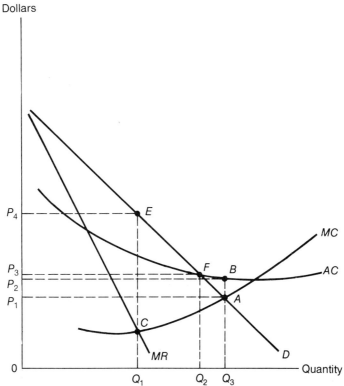

Figure F.1. Pricing Schemes Under Direct Regulation. Policymakers can use (1) price (P_1) equals MC approach or (2) price (P_3) equals AC approach to determine output levels of regulated firms.

Assuming that the natural monopoly is a profit maximizer, it will choose the output at which marginal revenue *(MR)* equals marginal cost *(MC)*. The profit-maximizing level of output will be Q_1, which can be sold at price (P_4). But as stated previously, this is not the most efficient level of output from society's point of view. Since the firm is attempting to maximize profit, it will not voluntarily produce any more than Q_1 since MC would rise above MR causing its profits to diminish. Society desires a level of output equal of Q_3, because at point *A*, demand intersects the *MC* curve and *price equals marginal cost.* This means that the benefit consumers receive from the last unit purchased (measured by price) is identical to the opportunity cost of the resources needed to produce that last unit of output (measured by MC). At any level of output below Q_3, not enough is being produced, since the benefit to consumers (price) exceeds the additional cost of production *(MC)*. For example, output Q_1 is valued at P_4 and MC is equal to C. Clearly, society would benefit by increased production. See Section 5.1 of Chapter 5 for a review of the efficiency criteria.

What can the government do to ensure that this monopoly produces the economically efficient amount? It could use marginal cost pricing. **Marginal cost pricing** forces the firm to produce Q_3 units of output, where price equals MC (where demand intersects the MC curve at point A). Unfortunately, this is not a feasible price. If the firm were forced to produce Q_3 units of output, it would eventually go out of business. At Q_3 units of output the average cost of producing each unit (point B) is greater than the average revenue received by the firm (point A). The firm is taking an economic loss.

As an alternative, the government uses an average cost pricing rule. The **average cost pricing** rule forces the firm to produce at the point where demand intersects the average cost curve. In Figure F.1 this occurs at point F, where the level of output is Q_2 and the price is P_3. At this level of output the firm will break even, making normal profit. This gives the firm the incentive to continue production. Note that this level of output is not the most efficient. Efficiency requires that price equal marginal cost as well as minimum average cost. However, this level of output (Q_2) is as close as the government can get to an optimal solution.

Antitrust Regulation

The least restrictive forms of regulation are antitrust laws. These laws enable various governmental agencies such as the Justice Department and the Federal Trade Commission to use the courts to determine if competition is being impeded. We will review the Sherman Act (1890), the Clayton Act (1914), and three other pieces of legislation that have had the greatest impact in this area of government regulation.

The Sherman Act The **Sherman Act** has just two sections. They are:

1. Every contract, combination in the form of trust or otherwise, or conspiracy, in restraint of trade or commerce among the several states or with foreign nations, is hereby declared illegal.

2. Every person who shall monopolize, or attempt to monopolize, or conspire with any other person or persons, to monopolize any part of the trade or commerce among the several states, or with foreign nations, shall be guilty of a felony.

These two provisions were designed to furnish the courts with the power to deal with any restraint of trade. The breakup of AT&T was the result of a lawsuit filed against AT&T by the Justice Department in 1974. The suit, alleging violation of the second provision of the Sherman Act (i.e., the use of monopoly power), was settled in 1982. The result was that (1) AT&T divested itself of its twenty-two regional phone companies, (2) AT&T was subject to greater competition in the long-distance service area, and (3) AT&T was free to expand into unregulated areas such as computers and telecommunications.

The major problem with the Sherman Act was the general language of the law. The Sherman Act was open to a wide variety of interpretations. For example, in the second section quoted, note the difficulty of proving "the attempt to monopolize." How large a market share is necessary before a monopoly is determined to exist? In Chapter 5 (Section 5.4), we discussed the difficulty of using concentration ratios to measure market power. The Clayton Act was subsequently passed to close loopholes found in the Sherman Act.

The Clayton Act The *Clayton Act* has four major provisions. First, it prohibits interlocking directorates. *Interlocking directorates* occur when a member of the board of directors for one company is also on the board of directors of a competing company. The goal of this provision was to reduce collusion. Second, the Clayton Act prohibits mergers when the purchase of one company's shares by another company lessens competition. Third, the act states that a firm cannot stop a user of its product from buying goods made by its competitors. Finally, the act outlaws price discrimination that restricts competition. *Price discrimination* takes place when a firm sells the same product to two different buyers at different prices, even though the cost of supplying the good to these two buyers is the same.

Other Antitrust Legislation In 1914, the *Federal Trade Commission* (FTC) was created with passage of the *Federal Trade Commission Act.* The FTC was given the general mission of prosecuting unfair methods of competition. The extent to which it fulfills its mandate depends on the level of funding it receives from Congress and the political ideology of the person the president appoints as director. For example, the FTC has attempted to make advertising more useful to consumers by attacking regulations that prohibit advertising. As a result of its work, there are now advertisements for eyeglasses, medical care, and legal services.

In 1936, the *Robinson-Patman Act* was passed, with the intention of toughening the price discrimination provision. Unfortunately, many believe it did just the opposite because its language obscures the issue. Finally, in 1950, the *Celler-Kefauver Anti-Merger Act* was passed. It strengthened the antimerger provision of the Clayton Act by prohibiting the purchase of a firm's assets by another firm if it lessened competition.

The Reagan administration reduced the enforcement of antitrust laws in the belief that mergers did not necessarily reduce competition. As we noted in Chapter 5, there was an increase in the number of mergers of large corporations such as GE, RCA, Gulf, and Chevron. The wave of mergers including "hostile" takeovers which ocurred during the 1980s was so massive it has been termed "merger mania" by many economists.

F.3 Problems in Implementing Government Regulation

We have reviewed the different methods of regulation available to government. As noted in Section 7.5 of Chapter 7, government intervention does not always improve conditions. In fact, sometimes when the government intervenes in the private market, it causes more harm than good. This is called government failure.

A number of problems make it very difficult for the government to determine which markets to regulate and the amount of regulation needed. The first problem is assessing external benefits and costs. When externalities are not correctly measured, a misallocation of resources will result. Second, there is the inability to determine the demand for public goods. Difficulties in measuring individual preferences hamper the government's ability to decide how much of these goods to produce. Majority voting does not always produce efficient results. Finally, X-inefficiency may occur because the government lacks the incentives to reduce costs. Government production is not subject to competitive market forces.

For these reasons deregulation, which began with the Carter administration, has continued into the 1980s. The trucking industry, banks (see Section 11.2 in Chapter 11), airlines, and long-distance telephone companies have seen substantial reductions in the regulations facing them. In addition, the Reagan administration removed many "nuisance" regulations related to the environment and workplace.

F.4 An Alternative to the Public Interest View of Regulation

The previous discussion assumed that regulations are enacted to promote the public interest. Therefore, government regulations that are not in the public interest are considered mistakes due to government failure.

George Stigler, 1982 Nobel prize winner in economics, supports an alternative view of regulation. He believes that some regulations are passed even though they are not necessarily in the public interest, causing some groups to be favored over the rest of society.

Stigler believes that government regulation should be looked at as a good produced for special interest groups operating within the public sector. Under this approach, special interest groups have a real advantage. For example, when there is an issue affecting the environment, the Audubon Society and Sierra Club may rush to mobilize their membership to voice their view. Likewise, a polluting firm may pressure Congress for legislation that permits it to dispose of waste in a manner that damages the environment. People who belong to antipollution groups usually feel very strongly about the issues affecting them. They may be a small group, but they have an advantage over the rest of society since others may not feel very strongly about the issue. Even if the rest of society felt strongly, the costs of transmitting information might be prohibitive, resulting in the larger group's inactivity. Consequently, regulation may be enacted that is not in the best interest of society.

Is the assertion that government failure is worse than market failure correct? Or is the presumption that government intervention improves the allocation of resources more accurate? This dilemma exists because we have an imperfect government trying to control imperfect markets.

Summary

Government regulation affects almost everything we do. Under the public interest approach, the public sector intervenes when the private market misallocates resources. A major factor leading to market failure is the absence of competition. Collusion, price fixing, and mergers increase the market power of firms within an industry. In addition to market power, external benefits and costs, and the lack of perfect information cause an inefficient allocation of resources.

There are three approaches that the government may use to alter the allocation of resources. At one extreme is government purchases and production of goods. Less restrictive is direct regulation. Under direct regulation, the government allows firms to operate in the private market subject to limitations on production and price. Finally, antitrust laws have been passed to enable the government to prosecute firms that restrict competition.

Unfortunately, the government does not always improve the allocation of resources. Because of X-inefficiency and measurement problems, the goverment will find it difficult to determine the optimal level of intervention. George Stigler believes that government regulation is a good produced for special interest groups operating within the public sector.

Key Concepts

public interest approach
price fixing
horizontal, conglomerate, and vertical mergers
government purchases and production
nationalization
yardstick approach
direct regulation
marginal cost pricing
average cost pricing
Sherman Act
Clayton Act

Discussion Questions

1. Discuss factors that reduce competition in the private market. What other factors justify the intervention of the public sector into the private market?

2. Distinguish between the following three types of government intervention:
   a. government purchases and production
   b. direct regulation
   c. antitrust laws

3. Discuss why the government may fail to improve the allocation of resources.

4. George Stigler has proposed an alternative to the public interest approach to regulation. Briefly explain his view of regulation.

Income Distribution and Poverty

Objectives

Upon completion of this special topic, you should understand:

1. How the Lorenz curve measures income inequality.

2. Reasons for differences in personal income.

3. Criticisms of the method used by the federal government to measure poverty.

4. How poverty is perpetuated from one generation to the next.

5. Policy options for reducing poverty.

In 1987, 13.5 percent of U.S. citizens were classified as living in poverty. There is hunger in America. We begin by examining the overall distribution of income among families and the reasons for differences in earnings. Our attention then focuses on the lower end of the income scale. Who are the poor? How does the government measure poverty? In addition to answering these questions, we explore the causes of poverty as well as the various public policies for reducing the number of people living in poverty.

G.1 The Personal Distribution of Income

In 1987, median family income was $30,853, which means that half of the families in the United States had incomes above this level and the other half had lower incomes. How is family income distributed? What causes differences in the amount of income received by families?

Measuring Income Inequality

As we can see in Table G.1, 4.4 percent of all households earned under $5,000 in 1987, and about 22.9 percent earned $50,000 and over. The extent of income inequality in the United States in 1986 is measured by the Lorenz curve presented in Figure G.1. The ***Lorenz curve*** shows the cumulative percentages of total income received by families, where the families are ranked by income bracket from the poorest to the richest (see the horizontal axis of Figure G.1). For example, point *A* indicates that the lowest 40 percent of income recipients received only 15 percent of income. The data for drawing this Lorenz curve are presented in Table G.2, where we can see that the top 5 percent of families received 17 percent of family income in 1987, which is more than the percentage received by the lowest 40 percent of families.

The diagonal line in Figure G.1 is the line of *perfect equality,* which is drawn for the purpose of comparison. It illustrates what the distribution would look like if all persons received the same share of income (e.g., if 20 percent of all families received 20 percent of income, 40 percent of families received 40 percent of income, and so on). Therefore, the more

Table G.1
Percent Distribution of
Income of Households by
Money Income Level, 1987

Income Level	Percent
Under $5,000	4.4
$5,000 – $9,999	7.3
$10,000 – $14,999	9.1
$15,000 – $19,999	9.5
$20,000 – $24,999	9.2
$25,000 – $34,999	17.5
$35,000 – $49,999	20.2
$50,000 and over	22.9

Source: Bureau of the Census, *Statistical Abstract of the United States, 1989* (Washington, D.C.: U.S. Government Printing Office), p. 445, No. 720.

414

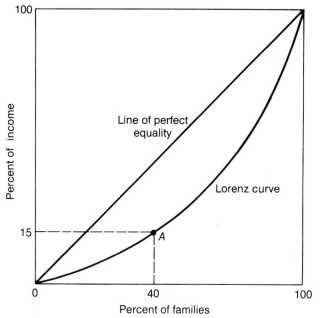

Figure G.1.   The Personal Distribution of Income in the United States in 1987. The Lorenz curve measures the extent of income inequality.

Table G.2
Percent Distribution of
Aggregate Family
Income by Each Fifth
and the Top 5 Percent
of Families, 1987

Family Rank	Percent
Lowest fifth	4.6
Second fifth	10.8
Third fifth	16.9
Fourth fifth	24.1
Highest fifth	43.7
Top 5 percent	16.9

Source: Bureau of the Census, *Statistical Abstract of the United States, 1989* (Washington, D.C.: U.S. Government Printing Office), p. 446, No. 772.

that the actual Lorenz curve bows outward to the right away from this diagonal line, the more unequal is the distribution of income.

Reasons for Differences in Income

People earn unequal amounts of income because of differences in the economic resources they sell in the factor market and the amount of money they are paid for these resources. First, persons with more *education and training* are generally able to receive higher payments for their labor services, as Figure G.2 illustrates. Wages are higher in the market for more educated workers because the supply of these workers tends to be lower relative to demand, compared to the market for less educated workers. Why? The extra cost of obtaining higher education or advanced training limits the supply of workers available in occupations requiring more education and training. In addition, the demand for more educated workers is greater because of the higher productivity of these workers.

> The market for college graduates is discussed in *Special Topic C: The Economics of Higher Education*.

Ability is another factor — some people are born with more ability to do certain things than others. Famous athletes such as Mike Tyson and Herschel Walker earn millions of dollars. Other people earn a lot of money by singing, such as Dolly Parton and Michael Jackson.

The *distribution of opportunities* is also unequal. Women with the responsibility of taking care of young children do not have the same opportunity to work outside the home as persons without such responsibilities. In addition, women and minorities tend to face discrimination in the marketplace, both in terms of job placement and entrance into training programs that lead to advancement. Financial barriers also exist which bar many lower income families from receiving the education and training that will help them find higher paying jobs.

Location can also be a factor because people situated in depressed areas tend to earn less income than those living in areas experiencing rapid economic growth. For example, a garage mechanic working in the Appalachian region of West Virginia tends to earn less than a mechanic doing similar work in Los Angeles.

In addition, workers who are members of powerful unions and who are employed by corporations with a high degree of power in the product market tend to receive higher wages relative to persons working for nonunionized firms in a highly competitive market. For example, unionized custodians working for General Motors tend to make higher income than nonunionized custodians doing the same type of work for a manufacturing firm in a highly competitive market.

Finally, inequality in the *ownership of property* also accounts for differences in income received. We noted in Chapter 6 that the bulk of income earned is through the sale of labor services, with the compensation of employees accounting for 73 percent of national income.

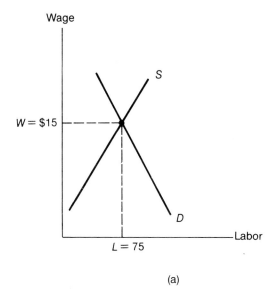

(a)

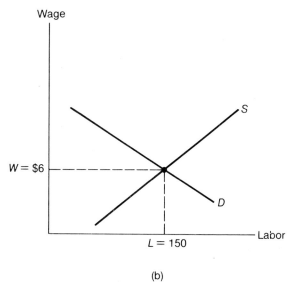

(b)

Figure G.2. The Markets for (a) More Educated Workers and (b) Less Educated Workers. The wage rate is higher for more educated workers since the supply of these workers is lower relative to demand.

The remaining 27 percent is property income earned through the sale of capital and natural resources in the factor market. Much of this property income is received by a relatively small portion of the population. For example, the top 5 percent of all income recipients in the United States receive more than two-thirds of all dividends and about one-half of all property income. Therefore, the highly unequal distribution of wealth in our country contributes to income inequality.

G.2 Measuring the Extent of Poverty

In this section we focus on the lower end of the income scale. We examine the characteristics of persons in poverty, and how the government measures the level at which people are considered "poor."

Who are the Poor?

As Table G.3 indicates, a disproportionate number of the poor are members of minority groups — 32 percent of all blacks and 28 percent of Hispanics were found to be in poverty in 1987, compared to 11 percent of all whites. In addition, over a third of all persons (mostly children) living in a family headed by a female with no husband present were in poverty in 1987 (not shown). The figure was over one-half for families headed by a black female.

Table G.3
Persons Below Poverty Level, 1960–1987

	Year[a]					
	1960	1966	1970	1976	1983	1987
Number (millions)						
All races	39.9	28.5	25.4	25.0	35.3	32.5
White	28.3	20.8	17.5	16.7	24.0	21.4
Black	n.a.	8.9	7.5	7.6	9.9	9.7
Hispanic	n.a.	n.a.	n.a.	2.8	4.6	5.5
Percent of persons						
All races	22.2	14.7	12.6	12.3	15.2	13.5
White	17.8	12.2	9.9	9.7	12.1	10.5
Black	n.a.	n.a.	33.5	31.3	35.7	32.1
Hispanic	n.a.	n.a.	n.a.	26.9	28.0	28.2

[a] n.a., not applicable.
Source: Bureau of the Census, *Statistical Abstract of the United States, 1989* (Washington, D.C.: U.S. Government Printing Office), p. 454, No. 736.

How Does the Government Measure Poverty?

The **official poverty line** for a four-member family was $11,611 in 1987, which means that the federal government classified a family with four persons to be in poverty if its total income fell below this level. How does the government measure this poverty line?

In 1961, the Department of Agriculture estimated the cost of a minimal, emergency diet, called the **economy food plan**, that poor people could live on temporarily. This emergency diet was the basis for constructing the official poverty line, using the following formula:

$$\left(\frac{\text{cost}}{\text{meal}} \times \frac{3 \text{ meals}}{\text{day}} \times \frac{4 \text{ persons}}{\text{family}} \times \frac{365 \text{ days}}{\text{year}} \right) \times 3$$

The cost per meal was multiplied by three meals per day to calculate the cost of feeding one person for one day. This was then multiplied by a factor of 4 to arrive at the daily cost of feeding the entire family, assuming that the family has four persons living in it. The resulting figure was then multiplied by 365 days to calculate a hypothetical food budget that would be needed to feed a family of four for one year on an emergency basis. The official poverty line was then calculated by multiplying this hypothetical food budget by a factor of 3. The factor of 3 was based on a survey taken by the Department of Agriculture, which estimated that low-income families spend about one-third of their total income on food.

Criticisms of the Official Poverty Line

This official measure of poverty has been criticized for a number of reasons. First, critics argue that the *food budget is too low* for adequate nutrition, and therefore it is not a sufficient basis for measuring poverty. The food budget only allowed a person 88 cents per meal in 1987. While the legislation defined the minimal diet as one that people could live on during a temporary emergency situation, many persons in poverty are poor over a prolonged period of time, often stretching over generations. The emergency diet does not allow for adequate nutrition over such a length of time. In addition, the food budget calculated by the government assumed that poor people have the expertise in nutrition to select the most healthy foods for the least amount of money. This certainly is not an accurate assumption for many people, especially those in poverty.

Second, some believe that the formula's multiplication *factor of 3 is too low,* which also causes the official poverty line to underestimate the true extent of poverty. Some studies indicate that low-income families spend about one-fourth or less of their income on food, rather than the one-third estimated by the Department of Agriculture. If the real proportion of income spent on food is one-fourth rather than one-third, the multiplication factor used in the formula should be 4 rather than 3.

Third, the official poverty line measures poverty on an absolute rather than a comparative basis, which means that poor people are counted as being in poverty if their income falls below a certain absolute level. Critics argue that *poverty is relative* and therefore cannot be measured

419

on an absolute basis. For example, if the Joneses buy a new car, the neighbors "feel" poorer even though their absolute income has not changed.

Fourth, the poverty line does not measure the intensity of poverty. Persons just at the poverty line (e.g., $11,611 for a family of four in 1987) are counted as being in the same degree of poverty as a family of four receiving only $2,000 in the same year.

Finally, there are critics who believe that the true dimensions of what it is like to be poor *cannot be measured solely in terms of dollars*. The reality of poverty also includes such nonmonetary costs as the fear of living in a high-crime area where violence, theft, drug abuse, and prostitution are a more frequent part of life. In addition, a disproportionate number of poor people live in congested, polluted areas of the country. The poor suffer more from disease and other health problems, due partly to an inadequate diet and a lack of access to health care facilities.

G.3 The Causes of Poverty and Policy Options

Some inequalities in income are temporary in nature. For example, people tend to be poorer during layoff, illness, or while attending college. What causes poverty of a more permanent nature?

Causes of Poverty

The tendency for persons born into poor families to acquire characteristics that preclude them from getting good jobs as adults has been termed the ***vicious circle of poverty***. First, children raised in an atmosphere of poverty, where "failure" in the job market is the norm rather than the exception, tend to acquire *low expectations* concerning their own ability to raise themselves out of poverty. If George's parents and many of his neighbors have failed, why should he have confidence in his own future? The fatalistic attitude, once a part of the child's psyche, is hard to reverse — causing the child not to realize his or her true potential as an adult.

A *lack of education and training* also hinders people in finding gainful employment. Children raised by poor, uneducated parents may not realize the value of education. In addition, the elementary and secondary school systems in impoverished areas generally have substandard facilities and serve primarily as warehouses for "keeping the kids off the street." Poverty may also force teenagers to leave school early so that they may help support their families.

Two types of discrimination also contribute to poverty: overt and institutional discrimination. *Overt discrimination* refers to the behavior of employers who refuse to hire, train, and promote workers based on personal characteristics not related to the job (e.g., they refuse to hire and train women, minorities, or the elderly). *Institutional discrimination* evolves from our social institutions. For example, housing patterns tend to segregate poor persons, especially those belonging to racial minorities, from access to new job openings. Many of the nation's poor live in the decayed, inner cities of our large urban areas. Over the last several decades, the middle class (primarily whites) as well as firms have fled from the congested inner cities to the suburbs. Since information about job openings is frequently spread by word of mouth through relatives and friends, persons living in the urban ghettos do not find out about job openings in the suburbs. In addition, they often lack adequate means of transportation to commute from the inner city to jobs located in the suburbs.

Two other factors contribute to poverty. Children raised in poor families tend to be hindered by *poor nutrition and health* which makes it difficult for them to learn and to work. Also, the lack of job opportunities in the "legal" job market induces some to commit such crimes as theft, drug selling, and prostitution. *Criminal records* acquired during adolescence can seriously hinder persons from finding decent jobs as adults.

Because of the complicated issues concerning the measurement and causes of poverty, an evaluation of the effectiveness of the programs that have been adopted to reduce poverty is extremely difficult. Consequently, the following discussion will attempt only to survey the policies that have been used. We do not attempt to describe the effectiveness of these programs.

Policies for Reducing Poverty

Two basic approaches are currently being used to help reduce poverty. First, we have *short-term poverty programs*, which are aimed at relieving the *symptoms* of poverty — primarily, the lack of adequate income to buy goods and services. Second, we have *long-term programs*, which are targeted at eliminating the root *causes* of poverty, such as the lack of education and skills.

Short-Term Poverty Programs   An overview of the short-term *income maintenance programs* aimed at relieving the symptoms of poverty is presented in Table G.4. These policies are broken down into two components: (1) cash assistance programs, which give the recipients money to spend as they choose, and (2) in-kind assistance, which provides specific goods and services to the poor.

Let us first examine the *cash assistance* programs listed in Table G.4. The Supplemental Security Income Program (SSI) is designed to aid poor persons who are aged, blind, or permanently disabled. In 1986, 4.4 million persons benefited from this $12.8 billion program. The largest component of the cash assistance program is Aid to Families with Dependent Children (AFDC) because the majority of persons in poverty are children. This program accounted for 54 percent of the overall cash assistance program in 1986, affecting 11 million people. The General Assistance (GA) program is the smallest component of the cash assistance program, affecting 1.3 million persons at a cost of $2.6 billion. This program is operated by state and local governments to assist poor persons who do not technically qualify under the other two major programs.

In-kind assistance, the second income maintenance program, provides poor persons with a specific package of goods and services. As we can see in Table G.4, the food stamp program affected 29.0 million persons in 1986. Food stamps are not free for the majority of recipients

Table G.4

Income Maintenance Programs: Cash and Noncash Benefits for Persons with Limited Income, Total Expenditures by Federal, State, and Local Governments, 1986

	Recipients (millions)	Total Payments (billions)
Cash assistance programs		
Supplemental Security Income	4.4	$ 12.8
Aid to Families with Dependent Children	11.0	17.8
General Assistance	1.3	2.6
Total payments		$ 33.2
In-kind assistance programs		
Food stamps	29.0	$ 13.5
Other food benefits[a]	x	6.6
Medicaid	22.6	25.0
Other medical benefits[b]	x	7.1
Housing benefits	x	13.2
Low-income energy assistance	6.7	1.9
Total payments		$ 67.3
Total payments, all programs		$100.5

[a] Includes school lunch program (free and reduced-price segments); special supplemental food program for women, infants, and children; temporary emergency food assistance; and nutrition program for elderly.

[b] Veterans with nonservice-connected disability, general assistance, Indian health services, maternal and child health services, and community health centers.

Source: Bureau of the Census, *Statistical Abstract of the United States, 1988* (Washington, D.C.: U.S. Government Printing Office), p. 337, No. 557.

and are purchased on a graduated scale, with lower income recipients paying less for them. Other food benefits were provided at a cost of $6.6 billion in 1986 (see footnote to Table G.4). Medicaid accounted for 48 percent of the in-kind assistance program and 29 percent of the overall $100.5 billion income maintenance program in 1986. Under Medicaid, the services of doctors and hospitals are made available to persons who cannot afford such care. The Medicaid program affected 22.6 million persons. An additional $7.1 billion in other medical benefits were provided in 1986 (see footnote to Table G.4). Finally, there are two other policies that currently play a small role in our in-kind assistance programs: housing assistance to help provide shelter, and the low-income energy assistance program to help poor families keep their homes warm when the weather is cold.

Note that the poverty figures described in this special topic represent people counted as being poor after all cash assistance listed in Table G.4 has been considered. There were 32.4 million people still in poverty in 1986 after the $33 billion in cash payments were made. However, if we include the monetary value of in-kind assistance received by the recipients of these programs (excluding institutional expenditures), the 1986 poverty rate for all persons falls from 13.6 percent to 11.6 percent. After this adjustment is made, there still remain 27.6 million poor people in the United States.

Long-Run Poverty Programs The purpose of *long-run programs* is to attempt to get at the root cause of poverty by breaking the vicious circle discussed earlier. First, efforts have been made to increase education and training opportunities, primarily through the Job Training Partnership Act. Each state has a state job training coordinating council which administers the program on a statewide basis. Governmental units of 200,000 persons or more can develop training centers in their areas by forming a private industry council. These councils are community organizations made up of leaders in business, labor unions, and educational agencies. The private industry councils and local government officials petition the state job training coordinating council for funding, and are responsible for running the training program.

In addition, efforts can be made in school to help break the cycle of low expectations, encouraging children to have more self-esteem. This approach has been stressed by the Reverend Jesse Jackson in his campaign to raise pride among blacks.

Another approach taken is to reduce overt discrimination through such legislation as the Equal Pay Act of 1962 and the Equal Rights Act of 1964. The effects of institutional discrimination can also be reduced. For example, attempts to improve the flow of information about jobs have been made by the state employment service, and mass transit systems have been constructed to increase the mobility of the population, especially in urban areas.

Finally, we noted that the food stamp program, the school lunch program, and Medicaid were aimed at relieving the symptoms of poverty. To the extent that they reduce malnutrition and improve the health of poor persons, they can also be considered long-term poverty programs.

Summary

The Lorenz curve is used to illustrate the personal distribution of family income. There are numerous reasons for disparities in income, including differences in education and skills, ability, location, market power, and the ownership of property income. A disproportionate number of those in poverty are women, minorities, and children.

The official poverty line is used to count the number of persons whom the government considers to be poor. Critics argue that this poverty measure is not adequate because the allowance for food is insufficient for adequate nutrition, and that the multiplication factor of 3 is too low. In addition, they claim that the official poverty line fails to measure the true extent of poverty because poverty is relative, and that it cannot be measured solely in terms of dollars.

There appears to be a vicious circle of poverty in which children born into poor families acquire characteristics that preclude them from getting good jobs as adults. They tend to have low expectations about their own ability to succeed, and often they do not get proper education and training. Poor persons also face discrimination, and are hindered by poor nutrition and health. Some of the poor enter the illegal job market in their adolescence, acquiring criminal records that prevent them from getting decent employment as adults.

Short-term poverty programs are aimed at relieving the symptoms of poverty. There are two types of short-term programs: income maintenance and in-kind assistance. Long-term programs attempt to eliminate the causes of poverty. They include efforts to increase education and training opportunities, to raise expectations, to reduce discrimination, and to improve the health and nutrition of poor persons.

Key Concepts

Lorenz curve
official poverty line
economy food plan
vicious circle of poverty
short-term/long-term poverty programs
income maintenance programs
cash assistance/in-kind assistance

Discussion Questions

1. Discuss the reasons for differences in the amount of income earned by families.

2. How does the government measure poverty? Discuss the criticisms of the official poverty line.

3. What is the vicious circle of poverty? Describe the factors that tend to perpetuate poverty.

4. Discuss the various policy options for reducing poverty. Distinguish between short-term and long-term programs.

International Finance

Objectives

Upon completion of this special topic, you should understand:

1. The changes that occurred in the international money market over the last four decades.

2. How a balance-of-payments deficit is eliminated under our present system of exchange.

3. How central banks can modify changes in foreign exchange rates under the dirty float.

Trade between countries is more difficult than trade within a country in part because each nation uses a different currency. For example, if a candy manufacturer located in the United States sells 500 pounds of peanut clusters to a wholesaler located in Canada, the candy manufacturer will want to be paid in U.S. dollars in order to meet payroll, buy supplies, and cover other costs of conducting business in the United States. The wholesaler will be expected to convert its Canadian dollars into U.S. dollars before paying for the peanut clusters. The transaction will take place in a bank that keeps an updated list of the most current exchange rates. Likewise, if you decide to vacation in a foreign country, one of the first things you will do upon arrival is to exchange your country's currency for that of the country you are visiting by going to a bank in the area. This will make your life easier as you venture forth, paying for such goods and services as meals in local restaurants and gifts for people back home. Both the Canadian wholesaler and you have participated in the international money market as buyers of foreign currency and sellers of domestic currency.

Table H.1 shows a listing of foreign exchange rates for 1988. The exchange rates in this table are expressed as the value of foreign currencies in terms of the U.S. dollar. We can see that one U.S. dollar exchanged for .56 British pounds, 1.76 West German marks, 1.46 Switzerland francs, 128.17 Japanese yen, and 1.23 Canadian dollars during this trading period.

What determines the value of one nation's currency in terms of another? In the following

Table H.1
Exchange Rates, Currency Units
Per U.S. Dollar, 1988.

Country/currency	1988
Canada/dollar	1.2306
China, P.R./yuan	3.7314
Denmark/krone	6.7411
Finland/markka	4.1933
France/franc	5.9594
Germany/deutsche mark	1.7569
Greece/drachma	142.00
Hong Kong/dollar	7.8071
India/rupee	13.899
Italy/lire	1302.39
Japan/yen	128.17
Netherlands/guilder	1.9778
Norway/krone	6.5242
Portugal/escudo	144.26
Singapore/dollar	2.0132
South Korea/won	734.51
Spain/peseta	116.52
Sweden/krona	6.1369
Switzerland/franc	1.4642
Taiwan/dollar	28.636
United Kingdom/pound	.5614

Source: Federal Reserve Bulletin, Vol. 75, April 1989 (p. A70, Table 3.28).

pages we will provide an answer to this question by examining a range of possible foreign exchange standards that might be adopted. We will then explore historic changes in the international money market, focusing on the rise and subsequent collapse of the gold standard and the development of a new monetary system called the managed float. Finally, we will turn to the recent concern over volatile changes in the U.S. exchange rate and the U.S. trade balance.

H.1 Foreign Exchange Standards

Countries trade with each other using different currencies. The way in which one currency is converted into another (e.g., U.S. dollars exchanged for British pounds) depends on the foreign exchange standard used. Historically, there have been three foreign exchange standards: (1) the gold standard, (2) the gold exchange standard, and (3) the floating exchange standard.

The Gold Standard and the Gold Exchange Standard

Under the *gold standard*, a country "pegs" (fixes) the value of its currency in terms of gold. To maintain the pegged value, the country's government must be able to buy and sell gold at the officially declared price. The United States was on the gold standard during the 1944–1973 period, and it initially pegged the value of the dollar to gold at $35 per ounce.

Under the *gold exchange standard*, a country fixes the value of its money to another country's currency, which in turn is pegged to gold. For example, when the United States was on the gold standard, Great Britain had pegged its pound to the U.S. dollar at an official rate of 1 pound = $2.80 at a time when the U.S. dollar was pegged to gold at $35 per ounce. This meant that Great Britain was on the gold exchange standard because British citizens could officially exchange 12.5 pounds for the $35 needed to buy 1 ounce of gold.

The Floating Exchange Standard

Under the *floating exchange standard* (also called the *float*), currencies are not fixed in value, either in terms of gold or any other currency. Exchange rates are determined by supply and demand conditions in the international money market. We will now examine the floating exchange standard in detail since it is the standard we are currently using.

For simplicity, assume that there are only two nations: the United States and West Germany. The supply curve for U.S. dollars *(S)* is illustrated in Figure H.1. It represents the willingness of Americans to sell U.S. dollars for marks (in order to buy goods from West Germany) at various exchange rates. For example, suppose that the dollar *depreciates,* falling in value from $1 equals 4 marks to $1 equals 3 marks. Each dollar now buys one less mark, causing West German goods to be more expensive in terms of dollars. As a result, Americans will import fewer goods from West Germany, which in turn causes the quantity of dollars exchanged for marks to fall from Q_s to Q_s'.

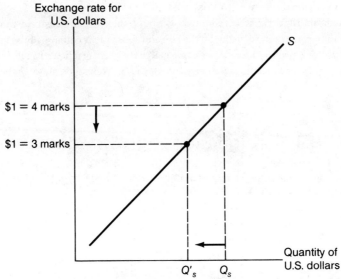

Figure H.1. The Supply of U.S. Dollars. A decrease in the international value of the U.S. dollar will decrease the quantity of dollars supplied on the international money market.

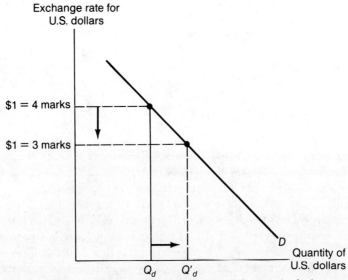

Figure H.2. The Demand for U.S. Dollars. A decrease in the international value of the U.S. dollar will increase the quantity of dollars demanded on the international money market.

Similarly, the demand curve for U.S. dollars shows West Germany's willingness to buy dollars by selling marks (in order to import goods from the United States) at various exchange rates. The demand curve for dollars *(D)* is represented in Figure H.2. For example, suppose again that the dollar depreciates, falling in value from $1 equals 4 marks to $1 equals 3 marks. Before this change, it took 4 marks to buy 1 dollar. Afterward, it takes only 3 marks to buy 1 dollar. Each mark is now worth more in terms of dollars — the mark has *appreciated* (increased) in value. This makes U.S. exports less expensive in terms of marks. As a result, people in West Germany will buy more goods from the United States, which in turn will cause the quantity of dollars exchanged for marks to increase from Q_d to Q'_d.

As we can see in Figure H.3, the equilibrium exchange rate for dollars is established under the floating exchange standard by supply and demand conditions in the international money market. In this example, the equilibrium exchange rate is $1 equals 3 marks. Why is this a stable position? At this exchange rate, our desire to import West German goods is exactly balanced by West Germany's desire to import U.S. goods. Consequently, the money that flows out of each country will exactly equal the amount that flows back in.

Elimination of a Balance-of-Payments Deficit Under the Float

A **balance-of-payments deficit** occurs when the amount of money flowing out of a country exceeds the amount that flows back in. A country cannot sustain a balance-of-payments deficit indefinitely because it will eventually run out of the foreign currency required to buy goods from other nations. The following discussion examines how a balance-of-payments deficit would be eliminated under the floating exchange standard.

Adjustments to trade deficits or surpluses occur automatically under the float through

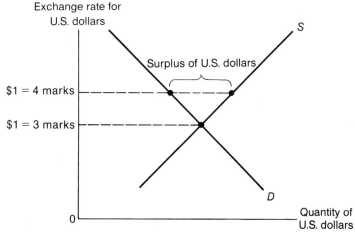

Figure H.3.   The Floating Exchange Standard. If the actual exchange rate ($1 = 4 marks) for U.S. dollars is above the equilibrium level ($1 = 3 marks), a surplus of dollars will develop in the market.

changes in the international price of money (the exchange rates). For example, in Figure H.3 we can see that the dollar is overvalued if the actual exchange rate happens to be $1 equals 4 marks. There is an excess supply of dollars on the international money market because the United States is trying to import relatively more goods from West Germany than West Germany is buying from the United States. The United States has a trade deficit. This surplus of dollars causes the price of the dollar to decline. As the dollar depreciates in value, U.S. exports appear cheaper from the viewpoint of West Germany. This causes foreigners to buy more U.S. exports. Similarly, because the dollar is worth less, it takes more dollars to buy West German goods, which causes the quantity of U.S. imports demanded to decrease. Therefore, as the international value of the dollar falls, U.S. exports increase while U.S. imports decrease. This would continue until the U.S. balance-of-payments deficit is eliminated. In our example, this occurs at the exchange rate of $1 equals 3 marks.

H.2 A Historical Overview of the International Money Market

The international money market experienced a tremendous shock during the early 1970s, which resulted in a major restructuring of the world monetary system. To understand better what happened during the early 1970s, it is necessary to look back to events that occurred forty years ago.

The Adjustable Peg

Trading relations between nations were severely disrupted by World War II. Western allies met in Bretton Woods, New Hampshire, to establish a new monetary system in 1944 (just before the war concluded). The resulting Bretton Woods Agreement set up the *adjustable peg system of exchange*. Under this agreement, the nations basically agreed to adopt either the gold standard or the gold exchange standard discussed earlier. The new monetary system was called the "adjustable peg" because minor adjustments in exchange rates were permitted if nations experienced persistent balance-of-payments deficits.

The United States, which had emerged as an industrial giant after the war, adopted the gold standard. Many other nations did not have a sufficient quantity of gold bullion to be on the gold standard. Instead, they adopted the "dollar standard"—which was the gold exchange standard discussed earlier, with the U.S. dollar being used as the "key" currency.

After a decade had passed, the adjustable peg system began to experience trouble. The United States, which had pegged the value of the dollar to gold at $35 per ounce in 1944, began to experience large balance-of-payments deficits in the early 1950s. Why? These deficits appeared largely as a result of Europe's and Japan's recovery from the massive destruction of World War II. Although the United States experienced significant loss, the devastation of Europe was much worse. Great Britain, France, Germany, Japan, and many other nations suffered direct attacks that destroyed a tremendous number of lives, factories, and homes. The Japanese and West Germans, in particular, rebuilt their steel, automobile, and electronics industries using the most modern technology available. As a result, they experienced a sharp increase in productivity. Other nations began buying more from the Japanese and West Germans and less from the United States, causing our economy to experience severe balance-of-payments deficits.

A New Monetary System: The Managed Float

The U.S. government had maintained that it would buy or sell gold at a fixed exchange rate of $35 per ounce. This exchange rate, however, became unrealistic as other nations came to rival the United States in international trade. By the early 1970s, it was obvious that the U.S. dollar was overvalued, meaning that it was not worth $35 per ounce of gold. Speculators in the international money market began to sell U.S. dollars in exchange for gold, Japanese yen, West German marks, and other strong currencies. The U.S. gold stock quickly became depleted, forcing the U.S. government to go off the gold standard officially in 1973 (after a series of devaluations).

When the U.S. government abandoned the gold standard, it adopted a variation of the floating exchange standard called the **managed float**. The new monetary system is called a "managed" float because the trading nations have agreed to use their central banks to help stabilize sharp fluctuations in exchange rates. Violent changes in exchange rates are undesirable since they create greater uncertainty and risk in financial transactions, which in turn reduces the volume of trade.

To illustrate how the managed float works, suppose that speculators in the international money market expected the value of the dollar to drop in the future. This would cause the supply of U.S. dollars to increase from S to S', which is represented in Figure H.4. Given the

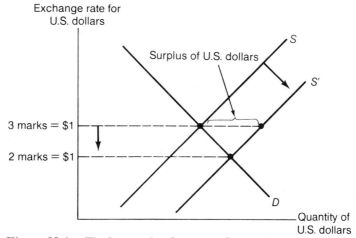

Figure H.4. The Impact of an Increase in Supply. An increase in the supply of U.S. dollars creates a surplus at 3 marks = $1, which would cause the exchange rate to fall to 2 marks = $1 if the rate were not "managed."

431

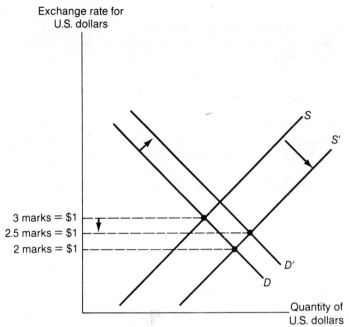

Exchange rate for
U.S. dollars

3 marks = $1

2.5 marks = $1

2 marks = $1

Quantity of
U.S. dollars

Figure H.5.   The Managed Float. To reduce the potential decrease in the exchange rate created by the surplus (see Figure H.5), authorities buy U.S. dollars, causing demand to increase from *D* to *D′*.

new supply curve for U.S. dollars, a surplus of dollars appears at the initial equilibrium exchange rate of 3 marks equals $1. If the countries want to prevent the dollar from falling to the new equilibrium position of 2 marks, they will have their central banks buy dollars. This is illustrated in Figure H.5 by the outward shift in the demand curve for dollars from *D* to *D′*. Note that the authorities have *managed* the exchange rate. They have supported the dollar at an exchange rate of 2.5 marks — preventing the value of the dollar from falling to the rate of 2 marks.

H.3 Recent Developments

Abrupt changes in the U.S. exchange rate and the U.S. trade balance have prompted an increase in pressure for government intervention in the international money market.

Changes in the U.S. Exchange Rate and the U.S. Trade Balance

From late 1980 to early 1985, the real value of the U.S. dollar rose sharply relative to an index of 11 foreign currencies (see Figure H.6). The strong appreciation of the dollar occurred in part because of a net inflow of foreign capital attracted by relatively high real interest rates in

Index, 1973 = 100

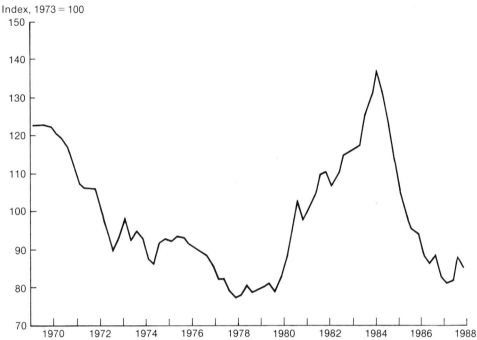

Figure H.6. Real Exchange Rate of the U.S. Dollar Relative to an Index of 11 Foreign Currencies. After appreciating rapidly during the early 1980s, the international value of the U.S. dollar fell abruptly. Source: *Economic Report of the President,* January 1989.

the United States. The appreciation of the dollar was responsible for much of the initial deterioration in the U.S. trade balance of real goods and services by causing U.S. exports to be more expensive and U.S. imports to be less expensive. Figure H.7 shows that during the late 1970s and early 1980s our real net export balance was positive, which means that the United States had a trade surplus during this period (exports exceeded imports). In 1982 there was a real trade surplus of $26 billion.

Beginning in 1983, the real net export balance became negative primarily because of a sharp increase in the U.S. demand for imports. The real value of U.S. imports of goods and services increased 67 percent from 1982 to 1987, while the real value of our exports increased by only 18 percent. Our real trade deficit soared from $20 billion in 1983 to $146 billion by 1986. As Figure H.7 indicates the real trade deficit improved modestly during the 1987–1988 period.

As we would expect, the abrupt drop in the real value of the dollar was in part a market response to these huge trade deficits. Figure H.6 shows the dramatic plunge in the real value of the U.S. dollar since the first quarter of 1985.

Why does the United States continue to incur large real trade deficits in view of the dramatic fall in the value of the dollar? As we noted in Section H.1, depreciation of the dollar

433

Figure H.7. Real U.S. Net Exports (in 1982 dollars). The United States had a trade surplus during the late 1970s and early 1980s. Beginning in 1983, the real net export balance became negative as U.S. imports increased sharply relative to the growth of U.S. exports. Source: *Economic Report of the President,* January 1989.

should decrease the amount of goods imported in the United States at the same time it stimulates our industries producing for export. So far two factors appear to be intervening in the adjustment process. First, foreign producers have reduced the price of goods sold to the United States to compensate for the increased expense of imports caused by a decline in the value of the dollar. These foreign manufacturers have so far been willing to cut their profit margins to avoid losing their share of the U.S. market. Second, U.S. consumers have been willing to pay higher prices for certain foreign-produced goods, either because they are not produced in the United States or because they believe the foreign good to be of better quality than the domestically produced counterpart.

Increased Intervention

In the previous section we described the potential use of a managed float, in which the central banks of leading trading nations could agree to moderate the decline in the value of a currency by buying it. Until 1985 there really wasn't much intervention in the international money market. In that year, U.S. Treasury Secretary James A. Baker met with the finance ministers of France, West Germany, Great Britain, and Japan (called the Group of Five or G-5) to discuss ways of reducing the volatility of exchange rates. Shortly thereafter the Group of Five became the Group of Seven with the inclusion of Canada and Italy as new members. In February 1987, they signed the Louvre Accord in an effort to help stabilize exchange rates among these seven countries.

Summary

Under the gold standard and the gold exchange standard, countries fix the value of their currency to either gold or other foreign currencies. To maintain the peg, they must be able to buy and sell either gold or the key currency at the official price. The United States was on the gold standard from 1944 to 1973, while most other nations were on the "dollar" standard. The adjustable peg exchange system was abandoned when the United States became unable to defend the value of the dollar. Our gold stock became depleted as world trade patterns were changed by the reindustrialization of Europe.

A new monetary system was adopted called the managed float. Based on the floating exchange standard, the managed float permits exchange rates to be determined primarily by supply and demand conditions in the international money market. Changes in the value of currency, however, may be modified by the central banks of the major trading nations. We noted that the U.S. exchange rate and the U.S. trade balance changed abruptly during the 1980s.

Key Concepts

gold standard/gold exchange standard/floating exchange standard
balance-of-payments deficit
adjustable peg system of exchange
managed float

Discussion Questions

1. Describe the gold exchange standards.

2. Describe the adjustable peg system and why it was abandoned.

3. What are the basic features of the floating exchange standard?

4. How do authorities attempt to prevent the value of a currency from falling abruptly under the managed float? Use a graph to illustrate your answer.

5. Describe the changes in the U.S. exchange rate and the U.S. trade balance during the 1980s.

The Labor Movement and Union Objectives

Objectives

Upon completion of this special topic, you should understand:

1. How unions evolved in the United States.

2. The history of public policy in labor-management relations.

3. The objectives sought by unions.

The early period of the American labor movement was characterized by sporadic periods of intense conflict and violence. In 1914, coal mine workers in Ludlow, Colorado, became engaged in a bloody battle with the mine owners in their efforts to organize. The workers, after being fired from their jobs and evicted from their company-owned homes, formed a city of tents in protest against the actions of the firm. The mine owners hired a private army to drive the workers away with machine guns and to set fire to their tents one evening. The next morning several people were found dead from smoke inhalation. The defeat was so decisive that attempts to organize the coal mining industry did not revive for many years.

Another major instance of violence occurred in 1894, when the American Railway Union was destroyed by a brutal strike against the Pullman Sleeping Car Company. The U.S. government, which fully supported management, attached mail cars to the Pullman sleeping cars so that it could send in federal troops to break the strike. It claimed that the union was interfering with the interstate transportation of U.S. mail. The railway union was finally broken by a court injunction which resulted in the imprisonment of union officials.

Workers struggled to organize in the early period of the labor movement. Why did workers seek to form unions under such adverse conditions? We first describe the evolution of unions in the United States as well as the historic development of public policy in labor-management relations. We than examine the objectives that unions try to achieve in their negotiations with management.

I.1 The Evolution of Unions

How did unions evolve in the United States? This section will trace the growth of the U.S. labor movement from the end of the eighteenth century to modern times.

Changes in the Structure of Union Organization

The first labor union in the United States was formed by the cordwainers (shoemakers) in Philadelphia in 1792. You might wonder why the first workers to organize were skilled craftsmen rather than the most poorly paid, unskilled laborers of that era. Part of the answer is that skilled workers had a common identity in their work, giving them a base for organizing. In addition, they had more bargaining power. Why? The threat of a strike by craftsmen had a more severe impact on firms than a similar threat by unskilled workers, since there are fewer substitutes for the services of skilled workers.

During the 1790s, other skilled craftsmen formed *local unions* — including organizations of printers, carpenters, and coopers (barrel makers). These local unions were formed primarily in major cities on the East Coast. A major problem encountered by local unions was that their financial budgets were vulnerable. In periods of prosperity, local unions attempted to build up *strike funds* to be able to financially support their members during a strike. But prolonged strikes and local business depressions frequently wiped out these funds.

Then, in the 1830s, local unions formed *citywide federations* in which different types of craftsmen, such as shoemakers and carpenters, banded together within a given city. The advantage of these federations of local unions was that they broadened the base of their strike funds. When one union went on strike, workers in other unions who remained employed could continue contributing to the strike fund. The citywide federations were not, however, very successful. Shoemakers had difficulty identifying with the needs of carpenters, and vice versa. Also, strikes and local depressions still tended to destroy the funds of these citywide federations. This prompted the craftsmen in different cities to form national unions in the 1850s.

The *national unions* that formed were organizations of craftsmen of the same skill located in different cities (e.g., printers in Boston forming a union with printers in Philadelphia). The even wider economic base gave national unions firmer financial leverage in maintaining their strike funds compared to that of citywide federations. The main problem, however, was that the national unions became involved in jurisdictional disputes when they tried to organize the same group of workers.

A federation of national unions, called the *American Federation of Labor (AFL)*, was established in 1886 primarily to reduce jurisdictional disputes. The success of the AFL stemmed from the strong leadership of its founder, Samuel Gompers, an immigrant cigar maker. Gompers developed a trade union philosophy that was to have a profound influence on the entire U.S. labor movement.

Gompers' Trade Union Philosophy

Gompers' trade union philosophy had three cardinal points. First, he argued that unions should be concerned only with trying to get "more, more, and more — now!" This approach has been termed *business unionism* since it avoids political reform movements in an attempt to get concrete economic gains for its own members.

Second, Gompers felt that the individual national unions, which made up the federation, should be stronger than the AFL. For example, he believed that contract negotiations for higher wages and better working conditions should be conducted solely by the national unions rather than by the AFL. Gompers argued that the AFL should limit its activities to the following three areas: (1) settling jurisdictional disputes between the national unions trying to organize the same workers, (2) communicating the viewpoint of unions to the general public, and (3) lobbying government for pro-labor legislation as well as supporting politicians friendly to AFL causes.

Third, Gompers believed that unions should be formed only among craft lines. He felt that the formation of a union among workers with the same skills would be more successful since they would have a stronger sense of group consciousness than workers with unrelated skills. This was the only tenet of Gompers' philosophy that the U.S. trade union movement eventually rejected.

The AFL-CIO Merger

Prior to the 1930s, most labor organizations were *craft unions*, with the workers organized along craft lines. There were a few *industrial unions*, however, representing all workers in a given industry — skilled and unskilled workers alike. The most important industrial unions at this time were the United Mine Workers, the Clothing Workers, and the Ladies Garment Workers. At the AFL conventions held in 1935 and 1936, the leaders of these industrial unions attempted to persuade the AFL to begin organizing unskilled workers. When they were outvoted, these leaders officially formed a rival federation of national unions in 1938, called the *Congress of Industrial Organizations (CIO)*.

The CIO won its greatest victory in its battle to organize the automobile industry. In 1937, many General Motors plants were struck by workers seeking to form a union. The conflict was especially intense in Flint, Michigan, where the workers occupied the GM factory there in a sit-down strike to prevent management from hiring nonstrikers. GM management demanded that the strikers be forcibly ejected, which caused the National Guard to surround the plant. To avoid an imminent bloodbath and destruction of property, top GM management finally agreed to recognize the union as the representative of its workers in 17 struck plants. The sit-down strike was subsequently declared to be unconstitutional by the Supreme Court.

The CIO's success in organizing GM led to quick unionization of the following industrial giants: Ford, Chrysler, General Electric, Westinghouse, as well as all major companies in the steel, tire, and oil industries.

There was a massive unionization drive from 1936 to 1941, following the passage of the pro-union Wagner Act in 1935 (discussed in Section I.2). Both the AFL and CIO enjoyed an enormous increase in their membership during this brief period.

However, the rivalry between the two federations intensified when the membership drive began to slow down in the early 1950s, following the passage of the Taft-Hartley Act in 1947, which significantly restricted union power (discussed in Section I.2). To end interunion raiding of members and to solidify the labor movement, the American Federation of Labor and the Congress of Industrial Organizations merged in 1955, forming the **AFL-CIO.** Three-fourths of all union members currently belong to the AFL-CIO. The major independent unions not belonging to this federation are the Teamsters and the United Automobile Workers.

Unions Today

Today, about one-half of all union members are located in six states: New York, California, Pennsylvania, Illinois, Ohio, and Michigan. In addition, almost two-thirds of union members work in manufacturing and transportation. The ten largest unions account for almost one-half of all members in the United States.

As Table I.1 indicates, union membership jumped from about 12 percent in 1933 to 36 percent in 1945, leveling off to about 30 percent throughout the 1950–1970 period. The membership drive lost steam after the easiest targets had been organized. The most easily organized employees were the blue-collar workers attached to large firms in the goods-production sector, located primarily in large cities on the East and West Coasts. Those blue-collar workers who remained unorganized tended to be located in small companies in rural areas, where anti-union sentiment ran very high. While the membership drive proceeded in select areas of the service sector (primarily workers in government and large retail sales establishments) during the 1970s, white-collar workers were generally found to be difficult to unionize. Why? Most white-collar workers, particularly those in clerical and sales work, are located in small offices, scattered across the country. It is difficult for these workers to form a sense of group identity. At the higher level of white-collar employment (professional and technical

439

Table I.1
Union Membership, 1880–1987

Year	Thousands	Percent of Nonagricultural Employment
1880	200	2.3
1890	272	2.7
1900	866	4.8
1910	2,141	8.4
1920	5,048	16.3
1930	3,393	8.8
1933	2,857	11.5
1939	8,980	28.9
1945	14,796	35.8
1956	17,490	30.4
1966	17,940	28.1
1970	21,852	30.8
1980	22,811	25.2
1983	17,717	20.1
1987	16,913	17.0

Source: Data through 1945 are from Lloyd Ulman, "American Trade Unionism — Past and Present," in Seymour E. Harris (ed.), *American Economic History* (New York: McGraw-Hill Book Company, 1961), pp. 393, 421. Data from 1956 to 1966 from Bureau of Labor Statistics, *Directory of National and International Labor Unions in the United States,* Bulletin 2079 (Washington, D.C.: U.S. Government Printing Office, 1980). Data for 1970 and 1980 from Bureau of the Census, *Statistical Abstract of the United States, 1984* (Washington, D.C.: U.S. Government Printing Office), p. 440, No. 728. Data for 1983 and 1987 from *Statistical Abstract of the United States, 1989* (Washington, D.C.: U.S. Government Printing Office), p. 416, No. 684.

workers), the employees tend to have a strong identity with management and therefore generally resist attempts at unionization.

The percentage of union membership fell dramatically from 25 percent in 1980 to 17 percent in 1987, partly because of high unemployment and the threat of layoffs during the 1970s and early 1980s. The growth of foreign competition coupled with a series of recessions during this period dealt a severe blow to the labor movement, sapping the bargaining strength of unions across the nation (especially those in the automobile, steel, and coal industries). Anti-union sentiment has also appeared to have increased, led by managerial and government opposition to unions.

I.2 Public Policy in Labor-Management Relations

The evolution of unions described in the preceding section was profoundly affected by public policy. Until 1932 there were no federal or state laws concerning labor-management relations. Lacking any statutory laws legislated by government, the only regulation of union activities was through *common law*, which is the practice of basing current court decisions on past court decisions.

Common Law

Our common law, inherited from England, is based on an aristocratic tradition. Judges, with closer ties to property owners than to laborers, gave preferential treatment to businesses, repressing early attempts of workers to unionize. In general, the courts treated union activity as an illegal criminal conspiracy. Businesses used the courts to break up unions by initiating the criminal prosecution of union activists — charging them with such offenses as trespassing, disturbing the peace, obstructing traffic, and loitering. Civil suits were also levied against unions for disrupting production and reducing the assumed rights of companies to make profit. However, the single most important weapon used against unions was the *court injunction*. Firms were able to easily obtain a restraining order from the courts to stop a strike or to close down a picket line. If the union did not obey the injunction, the leaders were required to pay a heavy fine and/or face possible imprisonment. At the same time, it was standard policy for firms, as a precondition for employment, to require prospective workers to sign a *yellow dog contract*. This was simply a contract requiring workers to agree that they would not join a union.

Statutory Laws Developed During the Great Depression

The first federal law to regulate labor-management relations was the *Norris-LaGuardia Act*, passed in 1932. The purpose of this act was to remove the obstacles that the courts had set up against labor's efforts to organize. As we noted earlier, the courts previously considered unions to be illegal criminal conspiracies, and strikes to be unlawful infringements on the firm's right to make profit. The Norris-LaGuardia Act gave workers the freedom to form unions in order to negotiate the conditions of employment as well as to peacefully strike. In addition, the Norris-LaGuardia Act outlawed yellow dog contracts and eliminated the abusive use of the primary weapon of firms — the court injunction.

Shortly afterward, the *National Labor Relations Act* of 1935 (more commonly called the *Wagner Act*) was passed, giving a strong boost to the labor movement. With the implementation of this act, the federal government went from a position of neutrality (under the Norris-LaGuardia Act) to a position that was distinctly pro-union, strongly encouraging workers to organize. The Wagner Act was revolutionary. When this bill was enacted, the United States was halfway through the worst depression in its history. The Great Depression began in 1929 and did not end until a full decade had passed. The legislature that enacted the Wagner Act assumed that unions could represent the best interests of workers and that workers would choose to join unions if given the opportunity.

The Wagner Act had two important provisions. First, it defined **unfair labor practices on the part of firms**. Employers were forbidden to interfere with the workers' right to organize, to negotiate a contract, and to strike or picket. It was also declared unfair for firms to discriminate against union activitsts. Prior to this law, employers generally refused to hire or promote persons associated with the union movement. Employers had circulated lists identifying "troublemakers." In addition, the Wagner Act required the employer to bargain "in good faith" during negotiations, which meant that there had to be "give and take" in talks between the two parties at the negotiating table.

Second, the Wagner Act set up the **National Labor Relations Board (NLRB)** to implement the policy provisions of this new law. The NLRB has the following two functions: (1) to investigate disputes over unfair labor practice charges, and (2) to conduct election proceedings in an effort to decide whether or not the workers of a particular firm want to form a union.

Post-World War II Legislation

The Great Depression ended as the United States entered World War II in 1941. During this period of crisis, the U.S. economy imposed extensive wage-price controls geared to prevent firms and unions from increasing their wages and prices (discussed in more detail in Chapter 12, Section 12.3). When the war ended in 1945, the wage-price controls were lifted. The wartime period of cooperation between management and unions ended with a number of major strikes across the nation in 1946. Workers in the steel, coal, automobile, and railroad industries struck in an attempt to recover real earnings that had been eroded by inflation during World War II. These strikes alarmed the general public, and the pro-union sentiment of the former decade turned sour.

In 1947, Congress passed the **Labor-Management Relations Act** (more commonly called the **Taft-Hartley Act**), which revealed a distinctly different governmental attitude toward unions than that of the Wagner Act. The Taft-Hartley Act did not assume that workers wanted to join unions or that unions would necessarily represent the best interest of workers. In addition, the legislature passing this act felt that employers had to be protected against abuses by unions.

The Taft-Hartley Act had two major provisions. First, it defined **unfair labor practices on the part of unions**. For example, it outlawed strikes by a union over a dispute with another union trying to organize the same group of workers. Jurisdictional strikes were considered to be unfair since unions hurt firms with which they had no grievance. The act also declared the *closed shop* to be an unfair labor practice on the part of unions in all industries except construction. The closed shop required that new employees become members of the union *before* being hired. This was considered to be unfair since it gave the union rather than the firm control over selection of new employees.

Second, the Taft-Hartley Act contained a ***national emergency clause*** that gave the president of the United States the ability to declare an eighty-day cooling-off period if the strike was deemed dangerous to the health or safety of the general public. During this period, the president is to appoint a special board to resolve the conflict. After eighty days, the parties are permitted to resume the strike unless a special law is passed by Congress to force a settlement of the dispute. This clause has rarely been used since it is difficult for the government to force labor and management to form a contract that both can "live with." A mutually agreed upon contract is vital to the development of a harmonious working relationship.

In 1959, the final major piece of federal legislation was enacted — the ***Labor-Management Reporting and Disclosure Act***, more commonly called the ***Landrum-Griffin Act***. The main goal of this act was *to reduce corruption* in the management of unions as well as to make unions *more democratic*. The Landrum-Griffin Act set up a new agency in the Department of Labor called the ***Bureau of Labor-Management Reports (BLMR)***. The BLMR was given the responsibility of collecting large amounts of internal data from unions concerning the financial dealings of its officers. This was done in an effort to help ensure that union officials were not mishandling union funds. The BLMR also collected information on the constitutions of unions in an effort to make labor organizations better represent the true interests of workers. In addition, this act included a "Bill of Rights" for union members, guaranteeing them the right to vote for candidates for union offices by secret ballot.

1.3 Union Objectives in Collective Bargaining

Unions try to achieve four major objectives in their negotiations with employers. These ***union objectives*** are: (1) to preserve the existence of the union, (2) to ensure job security, (3) to develop a grievance procedure, and (4) to gain other improvements in conditions of employment such as wages and fringe benefits.

Preserving the Union

The first objective of any union is to preserve the right of its organization to exist. During the initial stage of unionization, it is the union's foremost demand. Prior to the passage of the Taft-Hartley Act in 1947, about one-third of all unions had contracts with a clause providing for a ***closed shop***. The closed shop arrangement supported the maintenance of the union since it required workers to join the union *before* being hired by the employer. This gave the union the ablity to choose which workers the firm could hire.

The Taft-Hartley Act outlawed the closed shop in most industries, calling it an unfair labor practice. However, the Taft-Hartley Act did permit the existence of the union shop. Under the ***union shop***, the worker is not required to join the union until a specified time period has passed *after* he or she is hired (e.g., thirty days). This gives the employer, rather than the union, the ability to decide which employees to hire.

Another important negotiating point concerning the preservation of the union is the *automatic checkoff of union dues.* Under this contract provision, the union requires the employer to automatically collect its dues at the payroll office, eliminating the need for union officials to go "hat in hand" to collect money from its members. This saves a tremendous amount of the time and energy that would otherwise be involved in gathering the funds needed to maintain the organization.

Job Security

The second objective of a union is to gain job security for its members. Unions have coped with the problem of job insecurity by using the seniority principle as well as by adopting a variety of strategies to deal with the threat of technological change.

The Seniority Principle
The *seniority principle* is often used to resolve problems of layoff, transfer, promotion, and the allocation of certain fringe benefits, such as the choice of vacation time, parking lot privileges, or use of the newest machine installed in the plant. The seniority principle, which simply gives workers with the most years in the company first choice in such matters, is also widely used in companies that are not unionized. Why? The seniority principle is generally considered to be an equitable (and easy) solution to many of the emotional issues that occur in firms across our nation.

There are, however, problems with implementation of the seniority principle. Management finds it difficult to promote someone based on merit if another person, with fewer qualifications, ranks much higher on the seniority list. The seniority system also reduces labor mobility, causing workers to become attached to their jobs because of the benefits that accrue automatically with the passsage of time. This reduction in labor mobility can cause a misallocation of labor resources by preventing persons from quitting jobs that do not fully use their skills or abilities. Finally, the use of the seniority principle tends to perpetuate the effects of *past* discrimination. Minorities and women who have been recently hired (for positions from which they were previously barred) rank low on the seniority list. Therefore, during a recession, they are the first to be laid off and the last to be recalled to work.

Union Reactions to Technological Change
Another issue affecting job security is the impact of a change in production methods on employment. For example, if an employer introduces a new machine into the shop, the firm may gain higher profit, and consumers may benefit from lower prices, but a number of workers may lose their jos.

Unions have tended to react to technological change in two ways. First, some unions have developed *make-work rules* that are designed to maintain the number of workers a firm must employ. Sometimes a union might require that time-consuming production methods be used. For example, a painters union might require that its members use brushes rather than paint rollers or spray guns. Another union attempt to create work is the requirement that work

444

crews be larger than are really needed to do a job. This has sometimes been a practice of unions in the railroad, airline, trucking, and construction industries.

Second, unions will not be able to block technological change when the expected profit to the firm from innovation is high enough to offset the cost of a possible strike. Instead, unions will try to soften the impact of innovation on their members by letting the displaced workers *share the benefits of the new technology.* The approaches used include pension plans, with an emphasis on early retirement; severance pay for workers laid off permanently; and supplemental unemployment benefits, designed to augment the money received by persons under the state unemployment compensation program. In addition, unions will attempt to give the displaced workers preferential hiring rights in other plants owned by the company.

Development of a Grievance Procedure

Perhaps the most important function of a union is the establishment of a formal procedure for settling grievances between management and labor. Without a formal ***grievance procedure***, workers may be arbitrarily disciplined by management for factors not related to the job (e.g., length of hair). The grievance procedure also provides a basis for interpreting the contract in cases where the provisions are vague or self-contradictory. In addition, the grievance procedure helps to develop a body of "shop law" (akin to common law) in which the decisions on past grievances establish a precedent for future decisions.

Other Objectives

There are a number of other union objectives that form the "bread and butter" issues of negotiations. Unions strive to increase the total compensation (wages plus fringe benefits) that firms pay to their members. The total compensation package has increasingly emphasized such fringe benefits as (1) medical, dental, and life insurance; (2) retirement plans; (3) vacation time; and (4) supplemental unemployment compensation and severance pay. Today, over one-third of total compensation paid unionized workers is in the form of fringe benefits. Why? Workers prefer to receive more supplemental benefits in lieu of higher wages because these benefits are not taxed by government and because companies can buy insurance and other services in bulk at discount rates. Another objective pursued by unions is a reduction in the number of hours worked per week and an increase in the amount of pay for overtime. Unions are also interested in scheduling work hours to fit the pattern preferred by individual members. Finally, unions negotiate to try to improve the health and safety conditions of the plant.

We should note that all the objectives that unions strive to achieve are subject to the give-and-take process of collective bargaining. Any gain by the union in one area involves an opportunity cost because some other objective must be given up. For example, in the early 1980s when Chrysler almost went bankrupt, the workers were willing to take a wage concession in exchange for increased job security.

Summary

Workers formed local unions, citywide federations, national unions, and finally a federation of national unions (the AFL-CIO) to be able to bargain collectively. Public policy had an important impact on the labor movement. Common law attempted to repress early efforts at unionization. The Norris-LaGuardia Act was the first federal law dealing with labor-management relations — it attempted to nullify the repressive effects of previous court decisions. Shortly afterward, the Wagner Act was passed. This act was distinctly pro-union and was partially responsible for the dramatic increase in union membership during the late 1930s and 1940s. After World War II, a number of major strikes in the steel, coal, automobile, and railroad industries alarmed the general public. Subsequently, the Taft-Hartley Act was passed in an attempt to reverse the leverage that the Wagner Act had given to the union movement. The final major piece of union-related federal legislation was the Landrum-Griffin Act, which was designed to make unions more democratic and less corrupt.

The major objectives of unions are to preserve the existence of the organization, increase the job security of its members, and implement a grievance procedure. Other objectives include increased compensation, reduced working hours, better scheduling of working hours, and improved health and safety conditions.

Key Concepts

local unions
strike funds
citywide federations
national unions
American Federation of Labor (AFL)
Gompers' trade union philosophy
craft unions
industrial unions
Congress of Industrial Organizations (CIO)
AFL-CIO
common law
court injunction
yellow dog contract
Norris-LaGuardia Act
National Labor Relations Act (Wagner Act)
unfair labor practices on the part of firms and unions
National Labor Relations Board (NLRB)
Labor-Management Relations Act (Taft-Hartley Act)
national emergency clause

Labor-Management Reporting and Disclosure Act (Landrum-Griffin Act)
Bureau of Labor-Management Reports (BLMR)
union objectives
closed shop
union shop
automatic checkoff of union dues
seniority principle
make-work rules
grievance procedure

Discussion Questions

1. Trace the major changes in the organizational structure of unions from local unions to the formation of the AFL. Why did these changes occur?

2. Explain Gompers' trade union philosophy. Include in your discussion a description of his view of the role of the AFL.

3. Why did the labor movement lose momentum in the early 1950s? Cite reasons why it is more difficult to organize workers today than it was in the mid-1930s and 1940s.

4. Describe the basic provisions of the Wagner Act and the Taft-Hartley Act. What influence did these acts have on the labor movement?

5. What are the overall objectives that unions attempt to achieve in contract negotiations?

Why Study Economics?

Objectives

Upon completion of this special topic, you should understand:

1. How economics compares to other fields of study.

2. The role of economics as a background to different professions.

3. The career opportunities available to economics majors.

Economics provides a general background and an educational base that opens a broad range of professional, educational, and vocational opportunities. Many students who have had an undergraduate major in economics do not go on to pursue careers as professional economists; they go into such fields as law, management, public relations, and labor relations. By helping to develop a student's ability to think and communicate, economics shares in the general liberal arts effort to provide a foundation on which the student can build any one of a large number of possible careers.

First, we will examine how economics complements other fields of study. Second, we will look at how the study of economics may broaden the employment opportunities available to students after they graduate. Finally, we will discuss what career opportunities are available to economics majors.

J.1 Economics as a Complement to Other Fields of Study

Economics is a science of choice: of how choices are made, why choices are made, and what impacts those choices have. Although undergraduate economics courses emphasize choices such as whether to produce steel or aluminum, or whether to raise taxes or lower them, the same principles can apply to choices and decision making in general. The analytical methodology behind a decision to regulate milk prices is quite similar to that behind decisions to eat spaghetti for lunch or to wash the car Saturday morning. All such choices involve comparisons of costs and benefits and a consideration of alternative available opportunities. Efficient decision making involves what economists term *marginal analysis,* which is at the heart of the discipline and is emphasized in almost every course. Economics can be thought of as a method of analysis or a way of thinking that is a valuable adjunct to any field, regardless of subject content. Of course, the content of economics is itself complementary to many other fields. The ties between economics and business are obvious, but ties exist in many other areas as well. As a result, many students combine the study of economics with other academic programs. Students majoring in other areas frequently choose economics as a second major or as a minor. The following are some examples showing how economics complements other fields of study.

Biology

Economists have long been actively involved in environmental and natural resource economics. A basic understanding of economics is useful in examining the problems of air and water pollution, depletable and renewable resources, economic growth, and population growth. Many economics departments offer an entire course in environmental economics.

Geography and Regional Planning

Geography, as a study of patterns of area development, is closely akin to economics. Both disciplines study the use and allocation of human and material resources. Both develop mathematical models for understanding and predicting human behavior in the efficient use of resources. Geography students will find basic economics a valuable introduction to how economists approach these common problems. Courses in urban economics, regional economics, economic development, and environmental economics should also be particularly useful.

Anthropology

Anthropology is a social science that studies the individual in his or her cultural setting, including the economic aspect. Through a knowledge of economics, especially socioeconomic organization, the anthropologist sees more clearly what to observe as a culture is studied. Many economics courses relate to this goal. Among these courses are an introductory course in economics in which the overall organization of our modern economy is developed, as well as courses dealing with specific economies and with cultural change such as the history of economic development.

History

History is another social science that transcends the disciplines. Economic history is often an integral part of many of the topics which historians study. As with the anthropologist, it is useful for the historian to understand the particular point of view from which economists observe society. Since historians deal with economic problems, economic institutions, and economic change and development, it is essential that they understand the basic principles of economics. Therefore, depending on the interests of the historian, most economics courses are of relevance.

Sociology

Sociology (with its study of groups, social psychology, social organization, and social problems) relates closely to economics. Sociologists have been among the most penetrating critics of economics. Almost every problem that economists study is also the focus of sociological study. Thus, a major in sociology may benefit greatly from another perspective. For example, if you are a critic of capitalism, how about broadening your understanding of capitalism by studying comparative systems? Or if urban sociology is your interest, a course in urban economics would be helpful.

Philosophy

Adam Smith was a moral philosopher. Many of the greatest economists since Smith have become social philosophers (e.g., John Stuart Mill, Karl Marx, John Maynard Keynes, Frank H. Knight, J. M. Clark, Kenneth Boulding, John Kenneth Galbraith, Milton Friedman, Walter Heller, and Paul Samuelson). A philsophy major may want to complement his or her study by taking an economics course related to economic philosophy, such as the history of economic thought.

Mathematics

Mathematics majors often seek ways to use their math for understanding and coping with pressing social problems. Of all the social sciences, economics has employed math most

450

extensively. The introductory courses in economics lay down the essential introduction and provide the opportunity to use math in a variety of areas. Courses in econometrics, the economics of corporate decisions, and advanced macro/microeconomic analysis should be of particular interest. A math major plus an economics minor is an excellent undergraduate program leading to many job opportunities and to graduate study in either discipline.

Political Science

Economics and political science are very closely related areas of study. Economics used to be called "political economy." Many of the issues with which political science deals have an economic basis. The political science major must understand the broad outline of economics presented in the introductory course. Such students should also be familiar with the topics of public expenditure and budgeting (e.g., public finance), government intervention in the economy (e.g., the relationship between government and business, and the regulation of industry), and alternative economic systems (e.g., comparative economic systems such as the Soviet, Chinese, and Yugoslavian economies).

Safety Sciences

Concern with consumer and industrial safety has been a major issue in recent years, and economists have developed an extensive literature on the economics of safety and health. In addition to basic economics, the regulation of industry (which covers the Occupational Safety and Health Act and other safety-related regulations) and environmental economics (which covers environmental safety concerns) are just two of a number of courses that should be useful to safety majors.

Economics complements many other disciplines as well, and you can explore these relationships with individual faculty members. Minors in economics are relatively easy to obtain at many schools. Double majors require more coursework, but are accessible to many students and would provide a valuable addition to many undergraduate programs.

J.2 Economics Courses as Background to Professions

Perhaps your concern while in college is to develop the background for later training in a particular profession. The courses you take now may later provide the basis for "differentiating your product"—an economics concept meaning the respects in which you can make yourself different from others who share your professional specialty. Below are illustrations.

Law

If you want to be an antitrust lawyer, you'll find that a necessary background is provided by studying advanced microeconomic analysis, the organization of industry, and the relationship between government and business. Perhaps your interest is labor law; then study labor economics and labor legislation. Maybe money and finance is to be your specialty; then examine advanced macroeconomic analysis and monetary economics. If you want to be knowledgeable about law related to international trade, take courses in international economics.

Politics

With economic problems looming as large as they do, you should become a well-versed generalist in economics. Certainly, an introductory course in economics is the place to begin. Economic history is excellent for breadth. Beyond these courses you may have to narrow your focus according to your interests. You'll find policy-oriented courses of special interest, such as those that examine the regulation of industry and public expenditures.

Business

Much of your life in the business world will be devoted to responding to changes in your economic environment. Many of your actions will be influenced by the economic philosophy to which you adhere. The public expects you to be an expert on economics. The college courses you choose may contribute to how well you fulfill this expected role. Certainly, the study of basic economic principles is essential. Note that humanities and social science majors often acquire the qualities generally considered desirable in a manager — including communication skills, administration capabilities, interpersonal relations, intellectual abilites, and motivation for advancement.

Teaching

Economics is taught from kindergarten through college, sometimes as a special subject but often in the context of social studies. Introductory courses in economics provide the best overview of the subject for your use. Beyond those courses, students should follow their own interests.

Journalism

News of the economy dominates the front sections of every newspaper in the country, yet few journalists have more than a passing acquaintance with the economic principles behind the events they are reporting. Individuals with economic sophistication need to go beyond simple description of events and interpret economic phenomena to the general population. Probably you will be a generalist, making a course in basic economic principles essential to your career, whether your job is in newspapers, periodicals, or television. In addition, courses in areas that interest you and about which you expect to write and speak would be valuable.

J.3 Economics for Those Who Think It Is Useless

Perhaps your major or professional interests are very remote from economics. You may be a research physicist in the making. You may be a theater, vocational education, or social work major. Or you may be in college to master some esoteric language. Nevertheless, with a little imagination on your part you can find uses for a knowledge of economics in your professional specialty or major. You are a citizen and are or will be a wage earner who wants to know about the economy. As a citizen, a worker, a consumer, and a reader of the daily newspaper or a watcher of television, you are part of the economic aspect of our culture.

If nonmajors are to have their eyes really opened to the economic environment in which they live, it will probably be in an introductory course. It is hoped that such a course will help you to understand the modern world and its impact on your own life. You must make many choices in life, and in so doing you should employ economic principles such as opportunity cost and maximization/minimization.

J.4 What Can Economics Majors Do After They Graduate?

Most people working as professional economists have earned advanced graduate degrees, but a wide variety of employment opportunities are available to those with only a bachelor's degree. Most undergraduate economics majors use their economics as an entry to other professions. What can you do with only the bachelor's degree? Here are some possibilities.

Banking and Finance

Banks, stock brokers, small loan agencies, insurance companies, and consumer credit agencies are but a few of the economic institutions hiring economics majors. A knowledge of the economy is indispensable for the successful operation of these institutions. As a result, this knowledge of economics should make you valuable to them.

Economic Journalism

Economists who can write well for the general reader are scarce. With your background in economics, combined with skill in communications, you might become one of the growing body of economic journalists. Consider work as a business writer or editor for a daily newspaper, a free lance writer for popular or trade publications, a local or nationally syndicated columnist, an economic journalist for a national news or business magazine, a television journalist specializing in economic affairs, or even the author of a new popular economics best seller. In the years ahead, as economics becomes more complex, the intermediary between the economic scientist and the public is likely to play an increasingly essential role as both the teacher and economic journalist.

Law

The usual pre-law undergraduate major is in political science, but for many legal specialties, a foundation in economics may be more useful. The law student is certain to develop many important facets of knowledge in law school or subsequent legal practice. But an understanding of economic analysis will almost certainly be developed only through undergraduate study. The study of economics gives an indispensable background for understanding such areas as corporate law, labor law, and government regulation (including antitrust law). Furthermore, the rigor of economic reasoning prepares one for the rigor of legal analysis and reasoning.

The economy provides the setting for many legal issues. Moreover, there has been a vital interplay between economics and law and between economic theory and jurisprudence. An example is the influence of the economic theory of monopoly on legal criteria for restraint of trade. Legal issues of the future (e.g., issues relating to pollution, resource scarcity, pension rights, personal security, and social security) are so largely economic in basis that the lawyer equipped with an economics background is certain to have a real advantage in litigation and in efforts to find better solutions to problems.

Business

Most economics majors who do not pursue graduate study go into business. Economics provides you with an understanding of the broad social setting in which the enterprise operates. Many of the firm's problems and opportunities originate in the economy. Knowledge of the workings of a market economy is essential for an understanding of how a business can succeed and of the social role of business. Much of the content of the business trade journals involves economics. Indeed, to the general public, a business leader is by definition an "authority" on most economic matters. If you are to become an authority, you must prepare yourself to serve this role responsibly.

Government Service

Next to business, some form of government service is the most common nonacademic employment of persons with only a bachelor's degree in economics. You might work in one of the many agencies for which your knowledge of economics is vital, such as the U.S. Department of Commerce (perhaps collecting or assembling statistical data), the U.S. Labor Department, or a state agency concerned with economic development. You might initially be employed in an administrative apprenticeship in which economics is useful for understanding the activities and role of your agency.

Nonuniversity Teaching

The teaching of economics in the secondary schools has been increasing in recent years. To combine the study of economics with that of history or another social science should qualify you for such an occupation. There have been widespread and very successful experiments introducing economic concepts at all grade levels. Increasingly, curricula are designed to provide for the accumulative teaching of economics from kindergarten to college, rather than simply the traditional one-semester or one-year university course. These changes are broadening the market for teachers of economics.

> This special topic is based on the *Economics Undergraduate Handbook* used at Indiana University of Pennsylvania which is an adaptation of the *Handbook for Undergraduate Students in Economics* issued by the Center for Economic Education and Public Policy at the State University of New York at Binghamton. Our thanks to Laurence Leamer for allowing us to freely use his work.

Data Appendix

Table 1
Gross National Product in 1982 Dollars, 1929–1987
(Billions of 1982 Dollars, Except as Noted)

Year	Nominal Gross National Product	Real Gross National Product	Personal Consumption Expenditures				Gross Private Domestic Investment	
			Total	Durable Goods	Non-durable Goods	Services	Total	Change In Business Inventories
1929	103.9	709.6	471.4	40.3	211.4	219.7	139.2	10.8
1933	56.0	498.5	378.7	20.7	181.8	176.2	22.7	−10.7
1939	91.3	716.6	480.5	35.7	248.0	196.7	86.0	3.9
1940	100.4	772.9	502.6	40.6	259.4	202.7	111.8	14.4
1941	125.5	909.4	531.1	46.2	275.6	209.3	138.8	27.8
1942	159.0	1,080.3	527.6	31.3	279.1	217.2	76.7	12.0
1943	192.7	1,276.2	539.9	28.1	284.7	227.2	50.4	.7
1944	211.4	1,380.6	557.1	26.3	297.9	232.9	56.4	−5.2
1945	213.4	1,354.8	592.7	28.7	323.5	240.5	76.5	−8.4
1946	212.4	1,096.9	655.0	47.8	344.2	262.9	178.1	27.9
1947	235.2	1,066.7	666.6	56.5	337.4	272.6	177.9	−1.0
1948	261.6	1,108.7	681.8	61.7	338.7	281.4	208.2	12.3
1949	260.4	1,109.0	695.4	67.8	342.3	285.3	168.8	−9.7
1950	288.3	1,203.7	733.2	80.7	352.8	299.8	234.9	24.2
1951	333.4	1,328.2	748.7	74.7	362.9	311.1	235.2	30.8
1952	351.6	1,380.0	771.4	73.0	376.6	321.9	211.8	10.0
1953	371.6	1,435.3	802.5	80.2	388.2	334.1	216.6	2.8
1954	372.5	1,416.2	822.7	81.5	393.8	347.4	212.6	−4.8
1955	405.9	1,494.9	873.8	96.9	413.2	363.6	259.8	16.3
1956	428.2	1,525.6	899.8	92.8	426.9	380.1	257.8	12.9
1957	451.0	1,551.1	919.7	92.4	434.7	392.6	243.4	3.0
1958	456.8	1,539.2	932.9	86.9	439.9	406.1	221.4	−3.4
1959	495.8	1,629.1	979.4	96.9	455.8	426.7	270.3	16.5

See next page for continuation of table.

456

Table 1 *(continued)*

Year	Net Exports of Goods and Services			Government Purchases of Goods and Services					Percent Change From Preceding Period
					Federal			State and Local	
	Net Exports	Exports	Imports	Total	Total	National Defense	Non-defense		Gross National Product
1929	4.7	42.1	37.4	94.2	18.3			75.9	—
1933	−1.4	22.7	24.2	98.5	27.0			71.5	−2.1
1939	6.1	36.2	30.1	144.1	53.8			90.3	7.9
1940	8.2	40.0	31.7	150.2	63.6			86.6	7.8
1941	3.9	42.0	38.2	235.6	153.0			82.6	17.7
1942	−7.7	29.1	36.9	483.7	407.1			76.7	18.8
1943	−23.0	25.1	48.0	708.9	638.1			70.8	18.1
1944	−23.8	27.3	51.1	790.8	722.5			68.3	8.2
1945	−18.9	35.2	54.1	704.5	634.0			70.5	−1.9
1946	27.0	69.0	42.0	236.9	159.3			77.6	−19.0
1947	42.4	82.3	39.9	179.8	91.9			87.9	−2.8
1948	19.2	66.2	47.1	199.5	106.1			93.4	3.9
1949	18.8	65.0	46.2	226.0	119.5			106.5	.0
1950	4.7	59.2	54.6	230.8	116.7			114.2	8.5
1951	14.6	72.0	57.4	329.7	214.4			115.4	10.3
1952	6.9	70.1	63.3	389.9	272.7			117.3	3.9
1953	−2.7	66.9	69.7	419.0	295.9			123.1	4.0
1954	2.5	70.0	67.5	378.4	245.0			133.4	−1.3
1955	.0	76.9	76.9	361.3	217.9			143.4	5.6
1956	4.3	87.9	83.6	363.7	215.4			148.3	2.1
1957	7.0	94.9	87.9	381.1	224.1			157.0	1.7
1958	−10.3	82.4	92.8	395.3	224.9			170.4	−.8
1959	−18.2	83.7	101.9	397.7	221.5			176.2	5.8

See next page for continuation of table.

457

Table 1 *(continued)*

Year	Nominal Gross National Product	Real Gross National Product	Personal Consumption Expenditures				Gross Private Domestic Investment	
			Total	Durable Goods	Non-durable Goods	Services	Total	Change In Business Inventories
1960	515.3	1,665.3	1,005.1	98.0	463.3	443.9	260.5	7.7
1961	533.8	1,708.7	1,025.2	93.6	470.1	461.4	259.1	7.3
1962	574.6	1,799.4	1,069.0	103.0	484.2	481.8	288.6	16.2
1963	606.9	1,873.3	1,108.4	111.8	494.3	502.3	307.1	16.6
1964	649.8	1,973.3	1,170.6	120.8	517.5	532.3	325.9	15.7
1965	705.1	2,087.6	1,236.4	134.6	543.2	558.5	367.0	25.2
1966	772.0	2,208.3	1,298.9	144.4	569.3	585.3	390.5	36.9
1967	816.4	2,271.4	1,337.7	146.2	579.2	612.3	374.4	28.8
1968	892.7	2,365.6	1,405.9	161.6	602.4	641.8	391.8	21.0
1969	963.9	2,423.3	1,456.7	167.8	617.2	671.7	410.3	25.1
1970	1,015.5	2,416.2	1,492.0	162.5	632.5	697.0	381.5	8.2
1971	1,102.7	2,484.8	1,538.8	178.3	640.3	720.2	419.3	19.6
1972	1,212.8	2,608.5	1,621.9	200.4	665.5	756.0	465.4	21.8
1973	1,359.3	2,744.1	1,689.6	220.3	683.2	786.1	520.8	40.0
1974	1,472.8	2,729.3	1,674.0	204.9	666.1	803.1	481.3	33.3
1975	1,598.4	2,695.0	1,711.9	205.6	676.5	829.8	383.3	−12.8
1976	1,782.8	2,826.7	1,803.9	232.3	708.8	862.8	453.5	22.1
1977	1,990.5	2,958.6	1,883.8	253.9	731.4	898.5	521.3	29.1
1978	2,249.7	3,115.2	1,961.0	267.4	753.7	939.8	576.9	36.8
1979	2,508.2	3,192.4	2,004.4	266.5	766.6	971.2	575.2	15.0
1980	2,732.0	3,187.1	2,000.4	245.9	762.6	991.9	509.3	−6.9
1981	3,052.6	3,248.8	2,024.2	250.8	764.4	1,009.0	545.5	23.9
1982	3,166.0	3,166.0	2,050.7	252.7	771.0	1,027.0	447.3	−24.5
1983	3,405.7	3,279.1	2,146.0	283.1	800.2	1,062.7	504.0	−6.4
1984	3,772.2	3,501.4	2,249.3	323.1	825.9	1,100.3	658.4	62.3
1985	4,014.9	3,618.7	2,354.8	355.1	847.4	1,152.3	637.0	9.1
1986	4,240.3	3,721.7	2,455.2	385.0	879.5	1,190.7	643.5	15.4
1987	4,526.7	3,847.0	2,521.0	390.9	890.5	1,239.5	674.8	34.4

See next page for continuation of table.

458

Table 1 *(continued)*

Year	Net Exports of Goods and Services			Government Purchases of Goods and Services					Percent Change From Preceding Period
				Total	Federal			State and Local	Gross National Product
	Net Exports	Exports	Imports		Total	National Defense	Non-defense		
1960	−4.0	98.4	102.4	403.7	220.6			183.1	2.2
1961	−2.7	100.7	103.3	427.1	232.9			194.2	2.6
1962	−7.5	106.9	114.4	449.4	249.3			200.1	5.3
1963	−1.9	114.7	116.6	459.8	247.8			212.0	4.1
1964	5.9	128.8	122.8	470.8	244.2			226.6	5.3
1965	−2.7	132.0	134.7	487.0	244.4			242.5	5.8
1966	−13.7	138.4	152.1	532.6	273.8			258.8	5.8
1967	−16.9	143.6	160.5	576.2	304.4			271.8	2.9
1968	−29.7	155.7	185.3	597.6	309.6			288.0	4.1
1969	−34.9	165.0	199.9	591.2	295.6			295.6	2.4
1970	−30.0	178.3	208.3	572.6	268.3			304.3	−.3
1971	−39.8	179.2	218.9	566.5	250.6			315.9	2.8
1972	−49.4	195.2	244.6	570.7	246.0	185.3	60.7	324.7	5.0
1973	−31.5	242.3	273.8	565.3	230.0	171.0	59.1	335.3	5.2
1974	.8	269.1	268.4	573.2	226.4	163.3	63.1	346.8	−.5
1975	18.9	259.7	240.8	580.9	226.3	161.1	65.2	354.6	−1.3
1976	−11.0	274.4	285.4	580.3	224.2	157.5	66.8	356.0	4.9
1977	−35.5	281.6	317.1	589.1	231.8	159.2	72.7	357.2	4.7
1978	−26.8	312.6	339.4	604.1	233.7	160.7	73.0	370.4	5.3
1979	3.6	356.8	353.2	609.1	236.2	164.3	71.9	373.0	2.5
1980	57.0	388.9	332.0	620.5	246.9	171.2	75.7	373.6	−.2
1981	49.4	392.7	343.4	629.7	259.6	180.3	79.3	370.1	1.9
1982	26.3	361.9	335.6	641.7	272.7	193.8	78.9	369.0	−2.5
1983	−19.9	348.1	368.1	649.0	275.1	206.9	68.2	373.9	3.6
1984	−84.0	371.8	455.8	677.7	290.8	218.5	72.3	387.0	6.8
1985	−104.3	367.2	471.4	731.2	326.0	237.2	88.8	405.2	3.4
1986	−137.5	378.4	515.9	760.5	333.4	251.4	82.0	427.1	2.8
1987	−128.9	427.8	556.7	780.2	339.0	264.9	74.1	441.2	3.4

Source: Department of Commerce, Bureau of Economic Analysis.

Table 2
Gross Saving, 1929–1987
(Billions of Dollars, Quarterly Data at Seasonally Adjusted
Annual Rates)

	Gross Private Saving				Gross Private Saving		
Year	Total	Personal Saving	Gross Business Saving[1]	Year	Total	Personal Saving	Gross Business Saving[1]
1929	14.9	2.6	12.3	1963	97.9	24.6	73.3
1933	1.9	−1.6	3.6	1964	110.8	31.5	79.3
1939	11.1	1.8	9.3	1965	123.0	34.3	88.7
				1966	131.6	36.0	95.6
1940	14.3	3.0	11.3	1967	143.8	45.1	98.6
1941	22.6	10.0	12.6	1968	145.7	42.5	103.3
1942	42.3	27.0	15.3	1969	148.9	42.2	106.7
1943	50.0	32.7	17.3				
1944	54.9	36.5	18.4	1970	164.5	57.7	106.7
1945	45.4	28.7	16.8	1971	190.6	66.3	124.3
1946	30.3	13.6	16.7	1972	203.4	61.4	142.0
1947	28.1	5.2	23.0	1973	244.0	89.0	155.0
1948	42.4	11.1	31.3	1974	254.3	96.7	157.6
1949	39.9	7.4	32.5	1975	303.6	104.6	198.9
				1976	321.4	95.8	225.6
1950	44.5	12.6	31.8	1977	354.5	90.7	263.8
1951	52.6	16.6	36.0	1978	409.0	110.2	298.9
1952	56.1	17.4	38.7	1979	445.8	118.1	327.7
1953	58.0	18.4	39.6				
1954	58.8	16.4	42.3	1980	478.4	136.9	341.5
1955	65.2	16.0	49.2	1981	550.5	159.4	391.1
1956	72.1	21.3	50.8	1982	557.1	153.9	403.2
1957	76.1	22.7	53.5	1983	592.2	130.6	461.6
1958	77.1	24.3	52.9	1984	673.5	164.1	509.5
1959	82.1	21.8	60.3	1985	665.3	125.4	539.9
				1986	681.6	121.7	560.0
1960	81.1	20.8	60.3	1987	665.3	104.2	561.1
1961	86.8	24.9	62.0				
1962	95.2	25.9	69.3				

[1] Undistributed corporate profits with inventory valuation and capital consumption adjustments, corporate and noncorporate capital consumption allowances with capital consumption adjustment, and private wage accruals less disbursements.

Source: Department of Commerce Bureau of Economic Analysis.

Table 3
Number and Median Income (in 1987 Dollars) of Families and Persons, and Poverty Status, by Race, Selected Years, 1965–1987

| Year | Families[1] | | Below Poverty Level | | | | Persons Below Poverty Level | | Median Income of Persons 15 Years Old and Over with Income[2] | | | |
| | | | Total | | Female Householder | | | | Males | | Females | |
	Number (Millions)	Median Income	Number (Millions)	Rate	Number (Millions)	Rate	Number (Millions)	Rate	All Persons	Year-round Full-time Workers	All Persons	Year-round Full-time Workers
ALL RACES												
1965	48.5	$25,060	6.7	13.9	1.9	38.4	33.2	17.3	$18,093	$23,767	$5,479	$13,748
1966[3]	49.2	26,377	5.8	11.8	1.7	33.1	28.5	14.7	18,582	24,358	5,736	14,098
1967	50.1	27,004	5.7	11.4	1.8	33.3	27.8	14.2	18,902	24,812	6,131	14,290
1968	50.8	28,199	5.0	10.0	1.8	32.3	25.4	12.8	19,535	25,527	6,596	14,923
1969	51.6	29,244	5.0	9.7	1.8	32.7	24.1	12.1	19,931	26,872	6,610	15,740
1970	52.2	28,880	5.3	10.1	2.0	32.5	25.4	12.6	19,523	26,881	6,548	15,922
1971	53.3	28,862	5.3	10.0	2.1	33.9	25.6	12.5	19,372	27,027	6,757	15,999
1972	54.4	30,199	5.1	9.3	2.2	32.7	24.5	11.9	20,239	28,628	7,061	16,444
1973	55.1	30,820	4.8	8.8	2.2	32.2	23.0	11.1	20,603	29,329	7,151	16,593
1974[3]	55.7	29,735	4.9	8.8	2.3	32.1	23.4	11.2	19,479	28,029	7,103	16,534
1975	56.2	28,970	5.5	9.7	2.4	32.5	25.9	12.3	18,695	27,312	7,148	16,300
1976	56.7	29,863	5.3	9.4	2.5	33.0	25.0	11.8	18,819	27,669	7,139	16,595
1977	57.2	30,025	5.3	9.3	2.6	31.7	24.7	11.6	18,986	28,263	7,391	16,531
1978	57.8	30,730	5.3	9.1	2.7	31.4	24.5	11.4	19,050	27,981	7,087	16,795
1979[4]	59.6	30,669	5.5	9.2	2.6	30.4	26.1	11.7	18,443	27,368	6,814	16,489
1980	60.3	28,996	6.2	10.3	3.0	32.7	29.3	13.0	17,282	26,444	6,786	15,987
1981	61.0	27,977	6.9	11.2	3.3	34.6	31.8	14.0	16,836	25,858	6,820	15,567
1982	61.4	27,591	7.5	12.2	3.4	36.3	34.4	15.0	16,425	25,498	6,932	16,087
1983[3]	62.0	28,147	7.6	12.3	3.6	36.0	35.3	15.2	16,725	25,674	7,307	16,528
1984	62.7	28,923	7.3	11.6	3.5	34.5	33.7	14.4	17,069	26,265	7,515	16,875
1985	63.6	29,302	7.2	11.4	3.5	34.0	33.1	14.0	17,232	26,411	7,625	17,170
1986	64.5	30,534	7.0	10.9	3.6	34.6	32.4	13.6	17,739	26,840	7,888	17,458
1987	65.1	30,853	7.1	10.8	3.6	34.3	32.5	13.5	17,752	26,722	8,101	17,504

See next page for continuation of table

Table 3 (continued)

Year	Families¹ Number (Millions)	Families¹ Median Income	Below Poverty Level Total Number (Millions)	Below Poverty Level Total Rate	Below Poverty Level Female Householder Number (Millions)	Below Poverty Level Female Householder Rate	Persons Below Poverty Level Number (Millions)	Persons Below Poverty Level Rate	Median Income — Males All Persons	Median Income — Males Year-round Full-time Workers	Median Income — Females All Persons	Median Income — Females Year-round Full-time Workers
WHITE												
1970	46.5	29,960	3.7	8.0	1.1	25.0	17.5	9.9	20,521	27,651	6,632	16,203
1971	47.6	29,948	3.8	7.9	1.2	26.5	17.8	9.9	20,309	27,788	6,870	16,184
1972	48.5	31,375	3.4	7.1	1.1	24.3	16.2	9.0	21,228	29,661	7,107	16,767
1973	48.9	32,211	3.2	6.6	1.2	24.5	15.1	8.4	21,618	30,178	7,220	16,874
1974[3]	49.4	30,901	3.4	6.8	1.3	24.8	15.7	8.6	20,406	28,575	7,184	16,675
1975	49.9	30,129	3.8	7.7	1.4	25.9	17.8	9.7	19,638	27,944	7,222	16,338
1976	50.1	31,019	3.6	7.1	1.4	25.2	16.7	9.1	19,839	28,493	7,199	16,723
1977	50.5	31,396	3.5	7.0	1.4	24.0	16.4	8.9	19,886	28,841	7,504	16,635
1978	50.9	31,998	3.5	6.9	1.4	23.5	16.3	8.7	19,952	28,501	7,172	16,954
1979[4]	52.2	32,003	3.6	6.9	1.4	22.3	17.2	9.0	19,267	28,159	6,878	16,633
1980	52.7	30,211	4.2	8.0	1.6	25.7	19.7	10.2	18,383	27,199	6,823	16,141
1981	53.3	29,388	4.7	8.8	1.8	27.4	21.6	11.1	17,865	26,465	6,897	15,827
1982	53.4	28,969	5.1	9.6	1.8	27.9	23.5	12.0	17,365	26,177	7,026	16,304
1983[3]	53.9	29,474	5.2	9.7	1.9	28.3	24.0	12.1	17,595	26,359	7,434	16,748
1984	54.4	30,294	4.9	9.1	1.9	27.1	23.0	11.5	18,018	27,165	7,603	17,042
1985	55.0	30,799	5.0	9.1	2.0	27.4	22.9	11.4	18,078	27,144	7,773	17,413
1986	55.7	31,935	4.8	8.6	2.0	28.2	22.2	11.0	18,720	27,590	8,044	17,726
1987	56.0	32,274	4.6	8.2	1.9	26.7	21.4	10.5	18,854	27,468	8,279	17,775

BLACK												
1970	4.9	18,378	1.5	29.5	.8	54.3	7.5	33.5	12,167	18,835	6,038	13,276
1971	5.2	18,072	1.5	28.8	.9	53.5	7.4	32.5	12,112	19,001	6,019	14,290
1972	5.3	18,647	1.5	29.0	1.0	53.3	7.7	33.3	12,858	20,030	6,640	14,344
1973	5.4	18,590	1.5	28.1	1.0	52.7	7.4	31.4	13,076	20,340	6,516	14,309
1974[3]	5.5	18,451	1.5	26.9	1.0	52.2	7.2	30.3	12,376	20,062	6,467	14,683
1975	5.6	18,538	1.6	27.1	1.0	50.1	7.5	31.3	11,741	20,796	6,561	15,609
1976	5.8	18,451	1.6	27.9	1.1	52.2	7.6	31.1	11,945	20,408	6,784	15,634
1977	5.8	17,935	1.6	28.2	1.2	51.0	7.7	31.3	11,801	19,884	6,480	15,548
1978	5.9	18,952	1.6	27.5	1.2	50.6	7.6	30.6	11,952	21,829	6,458	15,714
1979[4]	6.2	18,122	1.7	27.8	1.2	49.4	8.1	31.0	11,927	20,294	6,260	15,241
1980	6.3	17,481	1.8	28.9	1.3	49.4	8.6	32.5	11,046	19,138	6,317	15,055
1981	6.4	16,578	2.0	30.8	1.4	52.9	9.2	34.2	10,623	18,724	6,127	14,293
1982	6.5	16,011	2.2	33.0	1.5	56.2	9.7	35.6	10,406	18,591	6,197	14,572
1983[3]	6.7	16,610	2.2	32.3	1.5	53.7	9.9	35.7	10,229	18,794	6,323	14,867
1984	6.8	16,884	2.1	30.9	1.5	51.7	9.5	33.8	10,338	18,539	6,745	15,358
1985	6.9	17,734	2.0	28.7	1.5	50.5	8.9	31.3	11,376	18,986	6,632	15,414
1986	7.1	18,247	2.0	28.0	1.5	50.1	9.0	31.1	11,217	19,452	6,806	15,510
1987	7.2	18,098	2.1	29.9	1.6	51.8	9.7	33.1	11,101	19,385	6,796	16,211

[1] The term *family* refers to a group of two or more persons related by blood, marriage, or adoption and residing together; all such persons are considered members of the same family. Beginning 1979, based on householder concept and restricted to primary families.

[2] Prior to 1979, data are for persons 14 years and over.

[3] Based on revised methodology; comparable with succeeding years.

[4] Based on 1980 census population controls; comparable with succeeding years.

Note — The poverty level is based on the poverty index adopted by a federal interagency committee in 1969. That index reflected different consumption requirements for families based on size and composition, sex and age of family householder, and farm–nonfarm residence. Minor revisions implemented in 1981 eliminated variations in the poverty thresholds based on two of these variables, farm–nonfarm residence and sex of householder. The poverty thresholds are updated every year to reflect changes in the consumer price index. For further details, see *Current Population Reports*, Series P-60, No. 160.

Source: Department of Commerce, Bureau of the Census.

Table 4
Unemployment Rate, 1948–1987 (Percent)

Year	Unemployment Rate, All Workers[1]	Unemployment rate, civilian workers[2]												
		All Civilian Workers	Males			Females			Both Sexes 16–19 Years	White	Black and Other	Black	Experienced Wage and Salary Workers	Married Men, Spouse Present[3]	Women Who Maintain Families
			Total	16–19 Years	20 Years and Over	Total	16–19 Years	20 Years and Over							
1948	—	3.8	3.6	9.8	3.2	4.1	8.3	3.6	9.2	3.5	5.9		4.3	—	
1949	—	5.9	5.9	14.3	5.4	6.0	12.3	5.3	13.4	5.6	8.9		6.8	3.5	
1950	5.2	5.3	5.1	12.7	4.7	5.7	11.4	5.1	12.2	4.9	9.0		6.0	4.6	
1951	3.2	3.3	2.8	8.1	2.5	4.4	8.3	4.0	8.2	3.1	5.3		3.7	1.5	
1952	2.9	3.0	2.8	8.9	2.4	3.6	8.0	3.2	8.5	2.8	5.4		3.4	1.4	
1953	2.8	2.9	2.8	7.9	2.5	3.3	7.2	2.9	7.6	2.7	4.5		3.2	1.7	
1954	5.4	5.5	5.3	13.5	4.9	6.0	11.4	5.5	12.6	5.0	9.9		6.2	4.0	
1955	4.3	4.4	4.2	11.6	3.8	4.9	10.2	4.4	11.0	3.9	8.7		4.8	2.6	
1956	4.0	4.1	3.8	11.1	3.4	4.8	11.2	4.2	11.1	3.6	8.3		4.4	2.3	
1957	4.2	4.3	4.1	12.4	3.6	4.7	10.6	4.1	11.6	3.8	7.9		4.6	2.8	
1958	6.6	6.8	6.8	17.1	6.2	6.8	14.3	6.1	15.9	6.1	12.6		7.3	5.1	
1959	5.3	5.5	5.2	15.3	4.7	5.9	13.5	5.2	14.6	4.8	10.7		5.7	3.6	
1960	5.4	5.5	5.4	15.3	4.7	5.9	13.9	5.1	14.7	5.0	10.2		5.7	3.7	
1961	6.5	6.7	6.4	17.1	5.7	7.2	16.3	6.3	16.8	6.0	12.4		6.8	4.6	
1962	5.4	5.5	5.2	14.7	4.6	6.2	14.6	5.4	14.7	4.9	10.9		5.6	3.6	
1963	5.5	5.7	5.2	17.2	4.5	6.5	17.2	5.4	17.2	5.0	10.8		5.6	3.4	

Year															
1964	5.0	5.2	4.6	15.8	3.9	6.2	16.6	5.2	16.2	4.6	9.6		5.0	2.8	
1965	4.4	4.5	4.0	14.1	3.2	5.5	15.7	4.5	14.8	4.1	8.1		4.3	2.4	
1966	3.7	3.8	3.2	11.7	2.5	4.8	14.1	3.8	12.8	3.4	7.3		3.5	1.9	
1967	3.7	3.8	3.1	12.3	2.3	5.2	13.5	4.2	12.9	3.4	7.4		3.6	1.8	4.9
1968	3.5	3.6	2.9	11.6	2.2	4.8	14.0	3.8	12.7	3.2	6.7		3.4	1.6	4.4
1969	3.4	3.5	2.8	11.4	2.1	4.7	13.3	3.7	12.2	3.1	6.4		3.3	1.5	4.4
1970	4.8	4.9	4.4	15.0	3.5	5.9	15.6	4.8	15.3	4.5	8.2		4.8	2.6	5.4
1971	5.8	5.9	5.3	16.6	4.4	6.9	17.2	5.7	16.9	5.4	9.9		5.7	3.2	7.3
1972	5.5	5.6	5.0	15.9	4.0	6.6	16.7	5.4	16.2	5.1	10.0	10.4	5.3	2.8	7.2
1973	4.8	4.9	4.2	13.9	3.3	6.0	15.3	4.9	14.5	4.3	9.0	9.4	4.5	2.3	7.1
1974	5.5	5.6	4.9	15.6	3.8	6.7	16.6	5.5	16.0	5.0	9.9	10.5	5.3	2.7	7.0
1975	8.3	8.5	7.9	20.1	6.8	9.3	19.7	8.0	19.9	7.8	13.8	14.8	8.2	5.1	10.0
1976	7.6	7.7	7.1	19.2	5.9	8.6	18.7	7.4	19.0	7.0	13.1	14.0	7.3	4.2	10.1
1977	6.9	7.1	6.3	17.3	5.2	8.2	18.3	7.0	17.8	6.2	13.1	14.0	6.6	3.6	9.4
1978	6.0	6.1	5.3	15.8	4.3	7.2	17.1	6.0	16.4	5.2	11.9	12.8	5.6	2.8	8.5
1979	5.8	5.8	5.1	15.9	4.2	6.8	16.4	5.7	16.1	5.1	11.3	12.3	5.5	2.8	8.3
1980	7.0	7.1	6.9	18.3	5.9	7.4	17.2	6.4	17.8	6.3	13.1	14.3	6.9	4.2	9.2
1981	7.5	7.6	7.4	20.1	6.3	7.9	19.0	6.8	19.6	6.7	14.2	15.6	7.3	4.3	10.4
1982	9.5	9.7	9.9	24.4	8.8	9.4	21.9	8.3	23.2	8.6	17.3	18.9	9.3	6.5	11.7
1983	9.5	9.6	9.9	23.3	8.9	9.2	21.3	8.1	22.4	8.4	17.8	19.5	9.2	6.5	12.2
1984	7.4	7.5	7.4	19.6	6.6	7.6	18.0	6.8	18.9	6.5	14.4	15.9	7.1	4.6	10.3
1985	7.1	7.2	7.0	19.5	6.2	7.4	17.6	6.6	18.6	6.2	13.7	15.1	6.8	4.3	10.4
1986	6.9	7.0	6.9	19.0	6.1	7.1	17.6	6.2	18.3	6.0	13.1	14.5	6.6	4.4	9.8
1987	6.1	6.2	6.2	17.8	5.4	6.2	15.9	5.4	16.9	5.3	11.6	13.0	5.8	3.9	9.2

[1] Unemployed as percent of labor force including resident armed forces.
[2] Unemployed as percent of civilian labor force in group specified.
[3] Data for 1949 and 1951–1954 are for April; 1950, for March.

Note.— Data relate to persons 16 years of age and over.

Source: Department of Labor, Bureau of Labor Statistics.

Table 5
Consumer Price Indexes, Major Expenditure Classes, 1946–1987
(1982 to 1984 = 100)

Year	All Items	Food and Beverages		Housing				Apparel and Upkeep	Transportation	Medical Care	Entertainment	Other Goods and Services	Energy
		Total¹	Food	Total	Shelter	Fuel and Other Utilities	Household Furnishings and Operation						
1946	19.5		19.8					34.4	16.7	12.5			
1947	22.3		24.1					39.9	18.5	13.5			
1948	24.1		26.1					42.5	20.6	14.4			
1949	23.8		25.0					40.8	22.1	14.8			
1950	24.1		25.4					40.3	22.7	15.1			
1951	26.0		28.2					43.9	24.1	15.9			
1952	26.5		28.7					43.5	25.7	16.7			
1953	26.7		28.3		22.0	22.5		43.1	26.5	17.3			
1954	26.9		28.2		22.5	22.6		43.1	26.1	17.8			
1955	26.8		27.8		22.7	23.0		42.9	25.8	18.2			
1956	27.2		28.0		23.1	23.6		43.7	26.2	18.9			
1957	28.1		28.9		24.0	24.3		44.5	27.7	19.7			21.5
1958	28.9		30.2		24.5	24.8		44.6	28.6	20.6			21.5
1959	29.1		29.7		24.7	25.4		45.0	29.8	21.5			21.9
1960	29.6		30.0		25.2	26.0		45.7	29.8	22.3			22.4
1961	29.9		30.4		25.4	26.3		46.1	30.1	22.9			22.5
1962	30.2		30.6		25.8	26.3		46.3	30.8	23.5			22.6

Year													
1963	30.6	35.0	31.1	30.8	26.1	26.6	42.0	46.9	30.9	24.1	40.7	35.1	22.6
1964	31.0	36.2	31.5	32.0	26.5	26.6	43.6	47.3	31.4	24.6	43.0	36.9	22.5
1965	31.5	38.1	32.2	34.0	27.0	26.6	45.2	47.8	31.9	25.2	45.2	38.7	22.9
1966	32.4		33.8		27.8	26.7		49.0	32.3	26.3			23.3
1967	33.4		34.1	36.4	28.8	27.1	46.8	51.0	33.3	28.2	47.5	40.9	23.8
1968	34.8		35.3	38.0	30.1	27.4	48.6	53.7	34.3	29.9	50.0	42.9	24.2
1969	36.7		37.1	39.4	32.6	28.0	49.7	56.8	35.7	31.9	51.5	44.7	24.8
1970	38.8	40.1	39.2	41.2	35.5	29.1	51.1	59.2	37.5	34.0	52.9	46.4	25.5
1971	40.5	41.4	40.4	45.8	37.0	31.1	56.8	61.1	39.5	36.1	56.9	49.8	26.5
1972	41.8	43.1	42.1	50.7	38.7	32.5	63.4	62.3	39.9	37.3	62.0	53.9	27.2
1973	44.4	48.8	48.2	53.8	40.5	34.3	67.3	64.6	41.2	38.8	65.1	57.0	29.4
1974	49.3	55.5	55.1	57.4	44.4	40.7	70.4	69.4	45.8	42.4	68.3	60.4	38.1
1975	53.8	60.2	59.8	62.4	48.8	45.4	74.7	72.5	50.1	47.5	71.9	64.3	42.1
1976	56.9	62.1	61.6	70.1	51.5	49.4	79.9	75.2	55.1	52.0	76.7	68.9	45.1
1977	60.6	65.8	65.5		54.9	54.7		78.6	59.0	57.0			49.4
1978	65.2	72.2	72.0		60.5	58.5		81.4	61.7	61.8			52.5
1979	72.6	79.9	79.9		68.9	64.8		84.9	70.5	67.5			65.7
1980	82.4	86.7	86.8	81.1	81.0	75.4	86.3	90.9	83.1	74.9	83.6	75.2	86.0
1981	90.9	93.5	93.6	90.4	90.5	86.4	93.0	95.3	93.2	82.9	90.1	82.6	97.7
1982	96.5	97.3	97.4	96.9	96.9	94.9	98.0	97.8	97.0	92.5	96.0	91.1	99.2
1983	99.6	99.5	99.4	99.5	99.1	100.2	100.2	100.2	99.3	100.6	100.1	101.1	99.9
1984	103.9	103.2	103.2	103.6	104.0	104.8	101.9	102.1	103.7	106.8	103.8	107.9	100.9
1985	107.6	105.6	105.6	107.7	109.8	106.5	103.8	105.0	106.4	113.5	107.9	114.5	101.6
1986	109.6	109.1	109.0	110.9	115.8	104.1	105.2	105.9	102.3	122.0	111.6	121.4	88.2
1987	113.6	113.5	113.5	114.2	121.3	103.0	107.1	110.6	105.4	130.1	115.3	128.5	88.6

[1] Includes alcoholic beverages, not shown separately.

Note— Data beginning 1978 are for all urban consumers; earlier data are for urban wage earners and clerical workers. Data beginning 1983 incorporate a rental equivalence measure for homeowners' costs and therefore are not strictly comparable with earlier figures.

Source: Department of Labor, Bureau of Labor Statistics.

Table 6
Changes in Consumer Price Indexes, Commodities, and Services, 1929–1987 (Percent Change)

Year	All Items Year to Year	Commodities			Services		Energy[1] Year to Year
		Total Year to Year	Food Year to Year	Commodities Less Food Year to Year	Total Year to Year	Medical Care Services Year to Year	
1929	0		1.2				
1933	−5.1		−2.8				
1939	−1.4	−2.0	−2.5	−1.6	0	1.2	
1940	.7	.7	1.7	.5	.8	0	
1941	5.0	6.7	9.2	5.4	.8	0	
1942	10.9	14.5	17.6	10.8	3.1	3.5	
1943	6.1	9.3	11.0	4.6	2.3	4.5	
1944	1.7	1.0	−1.2	5.3	2.2	4.3	
1945	2.3	3.0	2.4	4.2	1.5	3.1	
1946	8.3	10.6	14.5	6.0	1.4	5.1	
1947	14.4	20.5	21.7	12.9	4.3	8.7	
1948	8.1	7.2	8.3	7.4	6.1	7.1	
1949	−1.2	−2.7	−4.2	−1.3	5.1	3.3	
1950	1.3	.7	1.6	−.3	3.0	2.4	
1951	7.9	9.0	11.0	7.6	5.3	4.7	
1952	1.9	1.3	1.8	.9	4.5	6.7	
1953	.8	−.3	−1.4	.3	4.3	3.5	
1954	.7	−.9	−.4	−1.2	3.1	3.4	
1955	−.4	−.9	−1.4	−.6	2.0	2.6	
1956	1.5	1.0	.7	.9	2.5	3.8	
1957	3.3	3.2	3.2	2.9	4.3	4.3	
1958	2.8	2.1	4.5	1.1	3.7	5.3	0
1959	.7	0	−1.7	1.4	3.1	4.5	1.9

468

Year							
1960	1.7	.9	1.0	.6	3.4	4.3	2.3
1961	1.0	.6	1.3	.3	1.7	3.6	.4
1962	1.0	.9	.7	.6	2.0	3.5	.4
1963	1.3	.9	1.6	.8	2.0	2.9	0
1964	1.3	1.2	1.3	.8	2.0	2.3	−.4
1965	1.6	1.1	2.2	.8	2.3	3.2	1.8
1966	2.9	2.6	5.0	1.3	3.8	5.3	1.7
1967	3.1	1.9	.9	2.4	4.3	8.8	2.1
1968	4.2	3.5	3.5	3.6	5.2	7.3	1.7
1969	5.5	4.7	5.1	4.3	6.9	8.2	2.5
1970	5.7	4.5	5.7	4.1	8.0	7.0	2.8
1971	4.4	3.6	3.1	3.9	5.7	7.4	3.9
1972	3.2	3.0	4.2	2.2	3.8	3.5	2.6
1973	6.2	7.4	14.5	3.5	4.4	4.5	8.1
1974	11.0	11.9	14.3	10.7	9.2	10.4	29.6
1975	9.1	8.8	8.5	9.1	9.6	12.6	10.5
1976	5.8	4.3	3.0	5.0	8.3	10.1	7.1
1977	6.5	5.8	6.3	5.5	7.7	9.9	9.5
1978	7.6	7.2	9.9	5.8	8.6	8.5	6.3
1979	11.3	11.3	11.0	11.6	11.0	9.8	25.1
1980	13.5	12.3	8.6	13.8	15.4	11.3	30.9
1981	10.3	8.4	7.8	8.6	13.1	10.7	13.6
1982	6.2	4.1	4.1	4.1	9.0	11.8	1.5
1983	3.2	2.9	2.1	3.2	3.5	8.7	.7
1984	4.3	3.4	3.8	3.1	5.2	6.0	1.0
1985	3.6	2.1	2.3	2.0	5.1	6.1	.7
1986	1.9	−.9	3.2	−3.3	5.0	7.7	−13.2
1987	3.6	3.2	4.1	2.6	4.2	6.6	.5

¹ Household fuels — gas (piped) electricity, fuel oil, etc., — and motor fuel. Motor oil, coolant, etc. also included through 1982.

Note— Data beginning 1978 are for all urban consumers; earlier data are for urban wage earners and clerical workers.

Source: Department of Labor, Bureau of Labor Statistics.

Table 7
Money Stock and Liquid Assets, 1959–1987

Year and Month	M1	M2	M3	L
	Sum of Currency, Demand Deposits, Travelers Checks, and Other Checkable Deposits (OCDs)	M1 Plus Overnight RPs and Eurodollars, MMMF Balances (General Purpose and Broker/ Dealer), MMDAs, and Savings and Small Time Deposits	M2 Plus Large Time Deposits, Term RPs, Term Eurodollars, and Institution-only MMMF Balances	M3 Plus Other Liquid Assets
December:				
1959	140.0	297.8	299.8	388.7
1960	140.7	312.4	315.3	403.7
1961	145.2	335.5	341.1	430.8
1962	147.9	362.7	371.5	466.1
1963	153.4	393.3	406.1	503.8
1964	160.4	424.8	442.5	540.4
1965	167.9	459.4	482.3	584.5
1966	172.1	480.0	505.1	614.8
1967	183.3	524.4	557.1	666.6
1968	197.5	566.4	606.3	729.0
1969	204.0	589.6	615.1	763.6
1970	214.5	628.1	677.4	816.2
1971	228.4	712.7	776.2	903.1
1972	249.4	805.3	886.1	1,023.1
1973	263.0	861.0	985.1	1,142.6
1974	274.4	908.5	1,070.4	1,250.3
1975	287.6	1,023.2	1,172.2	1,367.0
1976	306.5	1,163.7	1,311.9	1,516.7
1977	331.4	1,286.7	1,472.8	1,705.4
1978	358.7	1,389.0	1,646.9	1,911.0
1979	386.1	1,500.2	1806.6	2,119.5
1980	412.2	1,633.1	1,990.8	2,327.6
1981	439.1	1,795.5	2,236.5	2,599.0
1982	476.4	1,954.0	2,443.2	2,852.9
1983	522.1	2,185.2	2,693.2	3,154.4
1984	551.9	2,363.6	2,978.3	3,519.4
1985	620.1	2,562.6	3,196.4	3,825.9
1986	725.4	2,807.7	3,490.8	4,134.3
1987	750.8	2,901.0	3,664.1	4,328.9

Note—The nontransactions portion of M2 is seasonally adjusted as a whole to reduce distortions caused by substantial portfolio shifts arising from regulatory and financial changes in recent years, especially shifts to MMDAs in 1983. A similar procedure is used to seasonally adjust the remaining nontransactions balances in M3.

Source: Board of Governors of the Federal Reserve System.

Table 8
Prime Rate Charged by Banks, 1929–1988

Year	Prime Rate Charged By Banks[1]	Year	Prime Rate Charged By Banks[1]	Year	Prime Rate Charged By Banks[1]
1929	5.50–6.00	1960	4.82	1980	15.27
1933	1.50–4.00	1961	4.50	1981	18.87
1939	1.50	1962	4.50	1982	14.86
		1963	4.50	1983	10.79
1940	1.50	1964	4.50	1984	12.04
1941	1.50	1965	4.54	1985	9.93
1942	1.50	1966	5.63	1986	8.33
1943	1.50	1967	5.61	1987	8.22
1944	1.50	1968	6.30	1988[p]	9.32
1945	1.50	1969	7.96		
1946	1.50				
1947	1.50–1.75	1970	7.91		
1948	1.75–2.00	1971	5.72		
1949	2.00	1972	5.25		
		1973	8.03		
1950	2.07	1974	10.81		
1951	2.56	1975	7.86		
1952	3.00	1976	6.84		
1953	3.17	1977	6.83		
1954	3.05	1978	9.06		
1955	3.16	1979	12.67		
1956	3.77				
1957	4.20				
1958	3.83				
1959	4.48				

[1]Prime rate for 1929–1933 and 1947–1948 are ranges of the rate in effect during the period.
p = preliminary.

Sources: Department of the Treasury, Board of Governors of the Federal Reserve System, Federal Home Loan Bank Board (FHLBB), Moody's Investors Service, and Standard & Poor's Corporation.

Table 9
Federal Receipts, Outlays, Surplus or Deficit, and
Debt, Selected Fiscal Years, 1929–1990
(Billions of Dollars; fiscal years)

Fiscal Year or Period	Total			Gross Federal Debt (End of Period) Total
	Receipts	Outlays	Surplus or Deficit (—)	
1929	3.9	3.1	0.7	16.9[1]
1933	2.0	4.6	−2.6	22.5[1]
1939	6.3	9.1	−2.8	48.2
1940	6.5	9.5	−2.9	50.7
1941	8.7	13.7	−4.9	57.5
1942	14.6	35.1	−20.5	79.2
1943	24.0	78.6	−54.6	142.6
1944	43.7	91.3	−47.6	204.1
1945	45.2	92.7	−47.6	260.1
1946	39.3	55.2	−15.9	271.0
1947	38.5	34.5	4.0	257.1
1948	41.6	29.8	11.8	252.0
1949	39.4	38.8	.6	252.6
1950	39.4	42.6	−3.1	256.9
1951	51.6	45.5	6.1	255.3
1952	66.2	67.7	−1.5	259.1
1953	69.6	76.1	−6.5	266.0
1954	69.7	70.9	−1.2	270.8
1955	65.5	68.4	−3.0	274.4
1956	74.6	70.6	3.9	272.7
1957	80.0	76.6	3.4	272.3
1958	79.6	82.4	−2.8	279.7
1959	79.2	92.1	−12.8	287.5
1960	92.5	92.2	.3	290.5
1961	94.4	97.7	−3.3	292.6
1962	99.7	106.8	−7.1	302.9
1963	106.6	111.3	−4.8	310.3
1964	112.6	118.5	−5.9	316.1
1965	116.8	118.2	−1.4	322.3
1966	130.8	134.5	−3.7	328.5
1967	148.8	157.5	−8.6	340.4
1968	153.0	178.1	−25.2	368.7

See next page for continuation of table.

Table 9 *(continued)*

Fiscal Year or Period	Total			Gross Federal Debt (End of Period) Total
	Receipts	Outlays	Surplus or Deficit (—)	
1969	186.9	183.6	3.2	365.8
1970	192.8	195.6	−2.8	380.9
1971	187.1	210.2	−23.0	408.2
1972	207.3	230.7	−23.4	435.9
1973	230.8	245.7	−14.9	466.3
1974	263.2	269.4	−6.1	483.9
1975	279.1	332.3	−53.2	541.9
1976	298.1	371.8	−73.7	629.0
Transition quarter	81.2	96.0	−14.7	643.6
1977	355.6	409.2	−53.6	706.4
1978	399.6	458.7	−59.2	776.6
1979	463.3	503.5	−40.2	828.9
1980	517.1	590.9	−73.8	908.5
1981	599.3	678.2	−78.9	994.3
1982	617.8	745.7	−127.9	1,136.8
1983	600.6	808.3	−207.8	1,371.2
1984	666.5	851.8	−185.3	1,564.1
1985	734.1	946.3	−212.3	1,817.0
1986	769.1	990.3	−221.2	2,120.1
1987	854.1	1,003.8	−149.7	2,345.6
1988	909.0	1,064.0	−155.1	2,600.8
1989[2]	975.5	1,137.0	−161.5	2,868.8
1990[2]	1,059.3	1,151.8	−92.5	3,107.2

[1] Not strictly comparable with later data.
[2] Estimates.

Note—Through fiscal year 1976, the fiscal year was on a July 1 – June 30 basis; beginning October 1976 (fiscal year 1977), the fiscal year is on an October 1 – September 30 basis. The 3-month period from July 1, 1976 through September 30, 1976 is a separate fiscal period known as the transition quarter. Refunds of receipts are excluded from receipts and outlays. See *Budget of the United States Government, Fiscal Year 1990* for additional information.

Sources: Department of Commerce (Bureau of Economic Analysis), Department of the Treasury, and Office of Management and Budget.

473

Table 10
Federal and State and Local Goverment Receipts and Expenditures, National Income and Product Accounts, 1929–1987
(Billions of Dollars)

Year	Total Government			Federal Government			State and Local Government		
	Receipts	Expendi-tures	Surplus or Deficit (−), National Income and Product Accounts	Receipts	Expendi-tures	Surplus or Deficit (−), National Income and Product Accounts	Receipts	Expendi-tures	Surplus or Deficit (−), National Income and Product Accounts
1929	11.3	10.3	1.0	3.8	2.7	1.2	7.6	7.8	−0.2
1933	9.4	10.7	−1.4	2.7	4.0	−1.3	7.2	7.2	−.1
1939	15.4	17.6	−2.2	6.8	9.0	−2.2	9.6	9.6	.0
1940	17.8	18.5	−.7	8.7	10.0	−1.3	10.0	9.3	.6
1941	25.0	28.8	−3.8	15.5	20.5	−5.1	10.4	9.1	1.3
1942	32.7	64.1	−31.4	23.0	56.1	−33.1	10.6	8.8	1.8
1943	49.2	93.4	−44.2	39.3	85.9	−46.6	10.9	8.4	2.4
1944	51.2	103.1	−51.8	41.1	95.6	−54.5	11.1	8.5	2.7
1945	53.4	92.9	−39.5	42.7	84.7	−42.1	11.6	9.0	2.6
1946	52.6	47.2	5.4	40.7	37.2	3.5	13.0	11.1	1.9
1947	57.8	43.4	14.4	44.1	30.8	13.4	15.4	14.4	1.0
1948	59.6	51.1	8.4	43.9	35.5	8.3	17.7	17.6	.1
1949	56.6	60.0	−3.4	39.4	42.0	−2.6	19.5	20.2	−.7
1950	69.4	61.4	8.0	50.4	41.2	9.2	21.3	22.5	−1.2
1951	85.6	79.5	6.1	64.6	58.1	6.5	23.4	23.9	−.4
1952	90.5	94.3	−3.8	67.7	71.4	−3.7	25.4	25.5	−.0
1953	95.0	102.0	−7.0	70.4	77.6	−7.1	27.4	27.3	.1
1954	90.4	97.5	−7.1	64.2	70.3	−6.0	29.0	30.2	−1.1
1955	101.6	98.5	3.1	73.1	68.6	4.4	31.7	32.9	−1.3
1956	110.2	105.0	5.2	78.5	72.5	6.1	35.0	35.9	−.9
1957	116.7	115.8	.9	82.5	80.2	2.3	38.5	39.8	−1.4
1958	115.7	128.3	−12.6	79.3	89.6	−10.3	42.0	44.4	−2.4
1959	130.3	131.9	−1.6	90.6	91.7	−1.1	46.6	47.0	−.4
1960	140.4	137.3	3.1	96.9	93.9	3.0	50.0	49.9	.1
1961	145.9	150.1	−4.3	99.0	102.9	−3.9	54.1	54.5	−.4
1962	157.9	161.6	−3.8	107.2	111.4	−4.2	58.6	58.2	.5
1963	169.8	169.1	.7	115.6	115.3	.3	63.4	62.9	.5
1964	175.6	177.8	−2.3	116.2	119.5	−3.3	69.8	68.8	1.0

See next page for continuation of table

Table 10 (continued)

Year	Total Government Receipts	Expendi-tures	Surplus or Deficit (−), National Income and Product Accounts	Federal Government Receipts	Expendi-tures	Surplus or Deficit (−), National Income and Product Accounts	State and Local Government Receipts	Expendi-tures	Surplus or Deficit (−), National Income and Product Accounts
1965	190.2	189.6	.5	125.8	125.3	.5	75.5	75.5	−.0
1966	214.4	215.6	−1.3	143.5	145.3	−1.8	85.2	84.7	.5
1967	230.8	245.0	−14.2	152.6	165.8	−13.2	94.1	95.2	−1.1
1968	266.2	272.2	−6.0	176.9	182.9	−6.0	107.9	107.8	.1
1969	300.1	290.2	9.9	199.7	191.3	8.4	120.8	119.3	1.5
1970	306.8	317.4	−10.6	195.4	207.8	−12.4	135.8	134.0	1.8
1971	327.3	346.8	−19.5	202.7	224.8	−22.0	153.6	151.0	2.6
1972	374.0	377.3	−3.4	232.2	249.0	−16.8	179.3	165.8	13.5
1973	419.6	411.7	7.9	263.7	269.3	−5.6	196.4	182.9	13.5
1974	463.1	467.4	−4.3	293.9	305.5	−11.6	213.1	205.9	7.2
1975	480.0	544.9	−64.9	294.9	364.2	−69.4	239.6	235.2	4.5
1976	549.1	587.5	−38.4	340.1	393.7	−53.5	270.1	254.9	15.2
1977	616.6	635.7	−19.1	384.1	430.1	−46.0	300.1	273.2	26.9
1978	694.4	694.8	−.4	441.4	470.7	−29.3	330.3	301.3	28.9
1979	779.8	768.3	11.5	505.0	521.1	−16.1	355.3	327.7	27.6
1980	855.1	889.6	−34.5	553.8	615.1	−61.3	390.0	363.2	26.8
1981	977.2	1,006.9	−29.7	639.5	703.3	−63.8	425.6	391.4	34.1
1982	1,000.8	1,111.6	−110.8	635.3	781.2	−145.9	449.4	414.3	35.1
1983	1,061.3	1,189.9	−128.6	659.9	835.9	−176.0	487.7	440.2	47.5
1984	1,172.9	1,277.9	−105.0	726.0	895.6	−169.6	540.5	475.9	64.6
1985	1,270.8	1,402.6	−131.8	788.7	985.6	−196.9	581.8	516.7	65.1
1986	1,344.6	1,489.0	−144.4	828.3	1,033.9	−205.6	623.0	561.9	61.2
1987	1,469.5	1,574.4	−104.9	916.5	1,074.2	−157.8	655.7	602.8	52.9

Note—Federal grants-in-aid to state and local governments are reflected in federal expenditures and state and local receipts. Total government receipts and expenditures have been adjusted to eliminate this duplication.

Source: Department of Commerce, Bureau of Economic Analysis.

475

Table 11
State and Local Government Revenues and Expenditures, Selected Fiscal Years, 1927 – 1987
(Millions of Dollars)

Fiscal Year[1]	General Revenues by Source[2]							General Expenditures by Function[2]				
	Total	Property Taxes	Sales and Gross Receipts Taxes	Individual Income Taxes	Corporation Net Income Taxes	Revenue from Federal Government	All Other[3]	Total	Education	Highways	Public Welfare	All Other[4]
1927	7,271	4,730	470	70	92	116	1,793	7,210	2,235	1,809	151	3,015
1932	7,267	4,487	752	74	79	232	1,643	7,765	2,311	1,741	444	3,269
1934	7,678	4,076	1,008	80	49	1,016	1,449	7,181	1,831	1,509	889	2,952
1936	8,395	4,093	1,484	153	113	948	1,604	7,644	2,177	1,425	827	3,215
1938	9,228	4,440	1,794	218	165	800	1,811	8,757	2,491	1,650	1,069	3,547
1940	9,609	4,430	1,982	224	156	945	1,872	9,229	2,638	1,573	1,156	3,862
1942	10,418	4,537	2,351	276	272	858	2,123	9,190	2,586	1,490	1,225	3,889
1944	10,908	4,604	2,289	342	451	954	2,269	8,863	2,793	1,200	1,133	3,737
1946	12,356	4,986	2,986	422	447	855	2,661	11,028	3,356	1,672	1,409	4,591
1948	17,250	6,126	4,442	543	592	1,861	3,685	17,684	5,379	3,036	2,099	7,170
1950	20,911	7,349	5,154	788	593	2,486	4,541	22,787	7,177	3,803	2,940	8,867
1952	25,181	8,652	6,357	998	846	2,566	5,763	26,098	8,318	4,650	2,788	10,342
1953	27,307	9,375	6,927	1,065	817	2,870	6,252	27,910	9,390	4,987	2,914	10,619
1954	29,012	9,967	7,276	1,127	778	2,966	6,897	30,701	10,557	5,527	3,060	11,557
1955	31,073	10,735	7,643	1,237	744	3,131	7,584	33,724	11,907	6,452	3,168	12,197
1956	34,667	11,749	8,691	1,538	890	3,335	8,465	36,711	13,220	6,953	3,139	13,399
1957	38,164	12,864	9,467	1,754	984	3,843	9,252	40,375	14,134	7,816	3,485	14,940
1958	41,219	14,047	9,829	1,759	1,018	4,865	9,699	44,851	15,919	8,567	3,818	16,547
1959	45,306	14,983	10,437	1,994	1,001	6,377	10,516	48,887	17,283	9,592	4,136	17,876
1960	50,505	16,405	11,849	2,463	1,180	6,974	11,634	51,876	18,719	9,428	4,404	19,325
1961	54,037	18,002	12,463	2,613	1,266	7,131	12,563	56,201	20,574	9,844	4,720	21,063
1962	58,252	19,054	13,494	3,037	1,308	7,871	13,489	60,206	22,216	10,357	5,084	22,549
1963	62,890	20,089	14,456	3,269	1,505	8,722	14,850	64,816	23,776	11,136	5,481	24,423
1962–63	62,269	19,833	14,446	3,267	1,505	8,663	14,556	63,977	23,729	11,150	5,420	23,678
1963–64	68,443	21,241	15,762	3,791	1,695	10,002	15,951	69,302	26,286	11,664	5,766	25,586
1964–65	74,000	22,583	17,118	4,090	1,929	11,029	17,250	74,678	28,563	12,221	6,315	27,579

476

Fiscal year												
1965–66	83,036	24,670	19,085	4,760	2,038	13,214	19,269	82,843	33,287	12,770	6,757	30,029
1966–67	91,197	26,047	20,530	5,825	2,227	15,370	21,197	93,350	37,919	13,932	8,218	33,281
1967–68	101,264	27,747	22,911	7,308	2,518	17,181	23,598	102,411	41,158	14,481	9,857	36,915
1968–69	114,550	30,673	26,519	8,908	3,180	19,153	26,118	116,728	47,238	15,417	12,110	41,963
1969–70	130,756	34,054	30,322	10,812	3,738	21,857	29,971	131,332	52,718	16,427	14,679	47,508
1970–71	144,927	37,852	33,233	11,900	3,424	26,146	32,374	150,674	59,413	18,095	18,226	54,940
1971–72	167,541	42,877	37,518	15,227	4,416	31,342	36,162	168,549	65,814	19,021	21,117	62,597
1972–73	190,214	45,283	42,047	17,994	5,425	39,256	40,210	181,357	69,714	18,615	23,582	69,446
1973–74	207,670	47,705	46,098	19,491	6,015	41,820	46,541	198,959	75,833	19,946	25,085	78,096
1974–75	228,171	51,491	49,815	21,454	6,642	47,034	51,735	230,721	87,858	22,528	28,155	92,180
1975–76	256,176	57,001	54,547	24,575	7,273	55,589	57,191	256,731	97,216	23,907	32,604	103,004
1976–77	285,157	62,527	60,641	29,246	9,174	62,444	61,124	274,215	102,780	23,058	35,906	112,472
1977–78	315,960	66,422	67,596	33,176	10,738	69,592	68,436	296,983	110,758	24,609	39,140	122,476
1978–79	343,278	64,944	74,247	36,932	12,128	75,164	79,864	327,517	119,448	28,440	41,898	137,731
1979–80	382,322	68,499	79,927	42,080	13,321	83,029	95,466	369,086	133,211	33,311	47,288	155,277
1980–81	423,404	74,969	85,971	46,426	14,143	90,294	111,599	407,449	145,784	34,603	54,121	172,941
1981–82	457,654	82,067	93,613	50,738	15,028	87,282	128,926	436,896	154,282	34,520	57,996	190,098
1982–83	486,753	89,105	100,247	55,129	14,258	90,007	138,008	466,516	163,876	36,655	60,906	205,079
1983–84	542,730	96,457	114,097	64,529	17,141	96,935	153,570	505,008	176,108	39,419	66,414	223,068
1984–85	598,121	103,757	126,376	70,361	19,152	106,158	172,317	553,899	192,686	44,989	71,479	244,745
1985–86	641,457	111,710	135,001	74,354	19,982	113,099	187,312	605,594	210,819	49,368	75,868	269,540
1986–87	686,164	121,227	144,293	83,681	22,672	114,996	199,296	656,064	226,658	52,199	82,520	294,687

[1] Fiscal years not the same for all governments. See Note.

[2] Excludes revenues or expenditures of publicly owned utilities and liquor stores, and of insurance-trust activities. Intergovernmental receipts and payments between state and local governments are also excluded.

[3] Includes other taxes and charges and miscellaneous revenues.

[4] Includes expenditures for libraries, hospitals, health, employment security administration, veterans' services, air transportation, water transport and terminals, parking facilities, and transit subsidies, police protection, fire protection, correction, protective inspection and regulation, sewerage, natural resources, parks and recreation, housing and community development, sanitation other than sewerage, financial administration, judicial and legal, general public buildings, other governmental administration, interest on general debt, and general expenditures, n.e.c.

Note—Data for fiscal years listed from 1962–1963 to 1986–1987 are the aggregations of data for government fiscal years that ended in the 12-month period from July 1 to June 30 of those years. Data for 1963 and earlier years include data for government fiscal years ending during that particular calendar year. Data are not available for intervening years.

Source: Department of Commerce, Bureau of the Census.

Table 12
Common Stock Prices,
1949–1988

Year	Common Stock Prices[1] Dow Jones Industrial Average
1949	179.48
1950	216.31
1951	257.64
1952	270.76
1953	275.97
1954	333.94
1955	442.72
1956	493.01
1957	475.71
1958	491.66
1959	632.12
1960	618.04
1961	691.55
1962	639.76
1963	714.81
1964	834.05
1965	910.88
1966	873.60
1967	879.12
1968	906.00
1969	876.72
1970	753.19
1971	884.76
1972	950.71
1973	923.88
1974	759.37
1975	802.49
1976	974.92
1977	894.63
1978	820.23
1979	844.40
1980	891.41
1981	932.92
1982	884.36
1983	1,190.34
1984	1,178.48
1985	1,328.23
1986	1,792.76
1987	2,275.99
1988[p]	2,060.82

[1] Includes 30 stocks.
[p] = preliminary.

Note —All data relate to stocks listed on the New York Stock Exchange.

Sources: New York Stock Exchange, and Dow Jones & Co., Inc.

478

Glossary

Ability-to-pay principle: The belief that persons with higher incomes should pay out a higher percentage of their incomes in taxes to ensure an equal sacrifice among the different income groups.

Absolute advantage: A country has an absolute advantage if it can produce more of any good relative to another country.

Actual investment: The sum of planned investment and unplanned investment (unintended change in inventories).

Adjustable peg: See *Bretton Woods Agreement.*

Administrative lag: The amount of time it takes to choose the appropriate policy and to get the legislation approved by Congress and the executive branch.

AFL-CIO: The American Federation of Labor and the Congress of Industrial Organizations. The merger of these two federations of national unions in 1955 served to end the interunion raiding of members and to solidify the labor movement.

Aggregate demand: The amount of total spending in all markets of the economy by consumers, business, and government.

Aggregate supply: All goods and services produced in the economy.

Allocative efficiency: The production of goods in that combination that maximizes the total satisfaction of consumers.

American Federation of Labor: A federation of national unions established in 1886 by Samuel Gompers to reduce jurisdictional disputes, to communicate the viewpoint of unions, and to lobby government for pro-labor legislation.

Annually balanced budget: The budget position created when the government annually equates expenditures to the level of taxes collected.

Antitrust laws: Laws that enable various branches of government such as the Justice Department and the Federal Trade Commission (FTC) to establish criteria for determining whether or not competition is being impeded and to use the courts to enforce their rulings.

Automatic checkoff of union dues: A labor contract provision whereby the employer collects the union's dues at the time the employees are paid.

Automatic stabilizers: Expenditure and tax items incorporated in the federal budget that help to smooth the business cycle by reducing changes in aggregate demand without an act of Congress, such as the personal income tax and unemployment compensation.

Autonomous expenditures: Consumption, investment, and government spending levels that are determined by variables *other* than income. For example, consumption and investment may be affected by changes in the interest rate.

Autonomous savings: Savings by households that is influenced by variables *other* than income. For example, savings can be affected by households' expectations about inflation.

Average cost of labor: The firm's cost per worker, calculated by dividing the total cost of labor by the total number of workers employed.

Average cost of production: The firm's cost per unit of output, calculated by dividing the total cost of production by the number of units produced.

Average cost pricing: A pricing rule used by government in regulating the rates of public utilities. The utility is required to charge a price equal to the average cost of production.

Average revenue: Revenue per unit of output, calculated by dividing total revenue by the number of units produced.

Balance-of-payments deficit: The amount by which money flowing out of the country exceeds the money flowing into the country.

Barriers to entry: Obstacles that prevent or inhibit the entrance of firms into the market in the long run, creating an oligopoly or a monopoly.

Barter economies: Economies in which money is not used to conduct transactions; instead, goods and services are traded directly for other goods and services.

Base year: The year against which all prices are compared.

Benefit-cost analysis: A method of analysis used to choose among alternative courses of action when a common measure of inputs (generating costs) and outputs (generating benefits) exists.

Benefit-received principle: The belief that people should pay taxes in proportion to the benefits received from government.

Board of Governors: The seven-member board of the Federal Reserve that makes monetary policy decisions and coordinates the actions of the Federal Reserve district bands.

Bottlenecks: A critical shortage of key resources.

Breakeven point: The point where average revenue and average cost are equal.

Bretton Woods Agreement: The monetary system agreed to by the Western allies that met in Bretton Woods, New Hampshire, in 1944 (just before World War II concluded). This set up the adjustable-peg system of exchange. The nations basically agreed to adopt either the gold standard or the gold exchange standard. The new monetary system was called the "adjustable peg" since minor adjustments in exchange rates were permitted if nations experienced persistent balance-of-payments deficits.

Bubble concept: A regulatory approach that allows a multiplant firm to meet pollution standards by using the most cost-effective methods for controlling pollution among each of its plants.

Business cycle: The course of business activity that has tended to occur in a cyclical fashion, with expansion followed by a contraction, followed by expansion, and so on.

Capital: Human-made inputs, also called *intermediate* goods since they do not satisfy wants directly. Instead, they are created to produce more of other goods in the future (both consumer and capital goods). There are three types of capital: (1) construction (or buildings), (2) machinery and equipment, and (3) inventories (unsold goods).

Capital-intensive technology: A technology in which the amount of capital used per unit of output produced is relatively higher than the amount of other inputs used per unit of output.

Cartel: A group of firms that reaches an agreement permitting it to control price.

Ceiling price: An institutional price set below the equilibrium position. It is called a ceiling price because the actual market price bumps against this upper limit as it attempts to move up to the equilibrium position.

Celler-Kefauver Antimerger Act: Passed in 1950, this act strengthened the antimerger provision of the Clayton Act by prohibiting the purchase of a firm's assets by another firm if it lessened competition.

Central business district: The center of business activity in a city.

Central plan: The overall master plan for running a command economy. In the Soviet economy, the central plan is initially established for a five-year period and is revised each year to adjust for previous failures and successes in production.

Central planning: A system in which most economic decisions are made through the government, which devises an overall master plan for running the economy. In the Soviet Union, state planning substitutes for the profit motive in guiding resources in production.

Certificates to pollute: Permits that give the holder the right to pollute. The public sector determines how much pollution is allowable and issues the requisite number of certificates. A market for these certificates determines their price.

Circular flow diagram: A model showing how households and firms interact in the product and factor markets. Households receive income payments from firms through the sale of inputs; firms, in turn, receive income from households through the sale of goods.

Citywide federations: Associations formed by local unions of craftsmen within a number of cities in the 1830s to broaden the base of their strike funds.

Classical model: A theory that argued that there is a tendency for the economy to stabilize automatically at full employment.

Clayton Act: An act passed in 1914 consisting of four provisions: (1) the prohibition of interlocking directorates, (2) the prevention of mergers when competition is lessened, (3) the disallowing of a firm from stopping a user of its product from selling or using competitor's goods, and (4) the outlawing of price discrimination.

Closed shop: A union arrangement that requires new employees to become members of the union before being hired.

Coincidence of wants: To reach a barter agreement, it is necessary to locate an individual who wants the good or service you desire to exchange for the good or service that they possess.

Coincident indicators: Measures of economic activity that reflect current activity in the economy.

Coinsurance: The portion of health expenses that an insurance company pays.

Collective interest: The interest of society at large.

Collusion: See *Overt collusion.*

Command economy: An economy that tries to solve its economic problems through government decree.

Common law: The practice of basing current court decisions on previous court decisions.

Common property resources: Property characterized by collective ownership, probably due to the difficulties of allocating it or restricting accessibility to it (e.g., air, large lakes, and oceans).

Complementary good: A product that we tend to buy along with the purchase of another good.

Complex relationship: A relationship between two variables which is both direct and inverse.

Concentration ratio: A ratio that measures the percentage of total sales in the market produced by the largest firms (usually the top four) in an industry. In general, higher concentration ratios indicate lower degrees of competition.

Conglomerate mergers: Combinations of unrelated firms producing different products, for example, a merger between a publishing firm and a car rental company.

Congress of Industrial Organizations: An industrial federation of national unions formed in 1938 that eventually merged with the American Federation of Labor in 1955.

Consumer goods: Goods that satisfy the final wants of households, also called final goods.

Consumption: Household spending for consumer goods.

Consumer price index: A measure of changes in the prices of goods and services purchased by consumers.

Constant GNP: See *Real GNP.*

Contestable markets: The competition of firms between industries. For example, the airline industry competes with the automobile, bus, and train industries in selling transportation service.

Contract: An agreement between two or more parties that is enforceable in a court of law.

Contraction: The phase of the business cycle in which output is decreasing because of a fall in total spending.

Cost-push inflation: Inflation caused by increases in input costs.

Council of Ministers: A governmental unit in the Soviet Union that sets the overall targets concerning what to produce and in what quantity.

Craft union: Workers organized along craft lines, such as coopers and shoemakers.

Crop restriction program: An attempt to reduce farm surplus as well as to raise farm income. The government compensates farmers for not growing their normal crops.

Crowding out: The belief that an increase in government spending leads to an increased demand for loanable funds, forcing interest rates up, which in turn leads to a decrease in private investment.

Currency: That portion of the money supply made up of coins and paper money.

Current GNP: The money value of goods and services sold at current prices (also called nominal GNP).

Cyclical unemployment: Unemployment that occurs when overall business activity declines due to decreases in aggregate demand below full-employment supply.

Cyclically balanced budget: The budget position created when the government equates expenditures to tax revenue over the course of the business cycle.

Deductive reasoning: A method of reasoning that begins with a general theory of the relationship between variables to make specific predictions. The reasoning sequence is from the general to the particular.

Deficit budget: The budget position created when the government spends more than the tax revenue it receives.

Deflation: A fall in the level of prices of goods and services.

Demand curve: The curve showing the quantity that buyers are willing and able to purchase at various prices in a given time period, given all other influences.

Demand deposits: Checking accounts.

Demand for loanable funds: Firms borrow money to invest in machinery and other capital goods. Their willingness to borrow and invest depends on whether the return from investing covers the cost of obtaining funds (the interest rate). As the rate of interest falls, the quantity of loanable funds demanded by firms will increase.

Demand-pull inflation: Inflation that occurs when aggregate demand is greater than full-employment output. Excess aggregate demand pulls up the general level of prices because no new output can be produced to meet this increased demand.

Demand schedule: The table showing the quantity that buyers are willing and able to purchase at various prices in a given time period, given all other influences.

Depository Institutions Deregulation and Monetary Control Act of 1980: Legislation that has increased competition in the banking industry and increased the power of the Federal Reverse System by forcing all banks with demand deposits to keep reserves on deposit at the Federal Reserve banks.

Depression: A contraction in the business cycle which is more severe then a recession in terms of unemployment and excess plant capacity.

Derived demand: The demand for labor in the labor market is derived from the demand for goods by households in the product market.

Descriptive statistics: The process of collecting, classifying, summarizing, and presenting data to describe economic relationships.

Direct regulation: A means by which the government can allow the private market to operate subject to limitations when the private market fails to allocate resources efficiently. For example, the government can impose controls on the disposal of industrial waste by firms if it believes that the pollution is dangerous to society.

Direct relationship: A relationship between two variables such that an increase in one variable is associated with an increase in the other variable, shown as an upward sloping curve.

Discounting: The process that enables the decisionmaker to compare benefits received and costs incurred in different time periods.

Discount rate: The interest rate charged by the Federal Reserve System for loans that it makes to banks.

Discretionary fiscal policy: The management of aggregate demand through changes in purchases, taxes, and transfers by the federal government to stabilize the business cycle.

Diseconomies of scale: If a plant becomes too large, further increases in plant size results in higher average costs of production.

Disposable income: The amount of income that people have at their discretion to spend. It is calculated by deducting personal taxes (i.e., income, property, and inheritance taxes) from personal income.

Dissaving: The amount by which household spending exceeds current earnings. This forces households to draw upon past savings.

Double counting: An accounting error whereby expenditures on the same item are counted more than once, which would lead to an overstated GNP.

Durable goods: Goods that have an expected life of more than one year (e.g., cars, refrigerators).

Economic efficiency: The adoption of the technology that minimizes the total cost of production.

Economic loss: The amount by which total revenue falls short of total cost.

Economic models: A method of reasoning used by economists to simplify the real world into a pattern that is easier to understand.

Economic profit: The amount by which total revenue exceeds the total cost of production (including the opportunity cost of the owners' own resources). Therefore, economic profit is above-normal profit. In a competitive market, economic profit serves the vital function of enticing rival firms into the market.

Economic resources: The labor, capital, and natural resources used to produce goods and services.

Economics: A social science that studies the principles governing the allocation of scarce resources among alternative uses to maximize the satisfaction of unlimited wants.

Economies of scale: The average cost of production decreases as a firm increases the size (scale) of its plant.

Efficiency: See *Economic efficiency, Technical efficiency,* and *Allocative efficiency.*

Effluent charges: Government taxes on a firm's pollution. These taxes are intended to induce the firm to take its external costs into account, forcing it to produce the socially desired level.

Elastic supply or demand: The percentage change in the quantity demanded or the quantity supplied is greater than the percentage change in price. As a result, the elasticity coefficient is greater than 1.

Elasticity coefficient: A measure of the degree of elasticity, calculated by dividing the percentage change in the quantity supplied or demanded by the percentage change in price. The coefficient is greater than 1 when supply or demand is elastic, less than 1 when supply or demand is inelastic, and equal to 1 when there is unitary elasticity.

Entrepreneurship: The action of a person who takes the risk of initiating a business venture that may fail.

Equation of exchange: An identity relationship between the total spending (MV) and the value of total supply (PQ), which is expressed as follows: $MV = PQ$, where M is the money supply, V is the velocity of money, P is the general price level, and Q is real output.

Equilibrium condition: The condition that brings about equilibrium.

Equilibrium GNP: The only level of income that the economy will be able to sustain. Market conditions will force actual GNP toward the equilibrium level.

Equilibrium price: A position of stability toward which the actual price (the current price) moves. It occurs when the quantity demanded equals the quantity supplied.

Equity: The economic goal of fairness.

Excess reserves: Bank reserves that are available to be lent out, calculated as total reserves minus required reserves.

Exclusion principle: When a person does not pay for a good, he or she is excluded from consuming the good.

Expansion: The phase of the business cycle in which output is growing because of an increase in total spending.

Expenditure approach: A method of measuring GNP by summing all current expenditures on final goods and services.

Explicit costs: Expenditures for resources that are not owned by the owner of the business, such as the cost of hired labor.

Exports: Goods produced in the United States and sold in foreign countries.

External benefits: The case when a consumer engages in an action that yields a benefit to third parties (persons outside the market). By ignoring this externality, too few resources will be devoted to the production of a good resulting in an underallocation of resources because not all benefits are being considered.

External benefits of education: Educational benefits for all members of society, including technological progress, cultural development, the solutions to complex social problems, and continued economic growth—all of which depend heavily on the knowledge and creative abilities fostered by experiences gained in college.

External costs: The case when a consumer or producer engages in an action that generates an outcome that imposes a cost on third parties (persons outside the market) in addition to the cost borne by the original buyer and seller. This results in an overallocation of resources because not all costs are being considered.

Factor market: The market for economic resources (also called factors of production).

Factors of production: See *Economic resources.*

Fallacy of composition: The incorrect supposition that what is true for the individual is necessarily true for everyone.

Federal Open Market Committee: The twelve-member committee of the Federal Reserve that is responsible for open market policy.

Federal Reserve Bank: The central bank of the United States, which has responsibility for controlling the money supply.

Federal Trade Commission: The government agency that was given the general mission of prosecuting firms suspected of practicing unfair methods of competition.

Federation of national unions: An organization of national unions.

Fee for service: Payment for a service performed, not success of performance (which is the real measure of output). This is the primary payment mechanism used in the health care industry.

Final goods and services: Goods and services that satisfy the final wants of households.

Financial capital: The means of financing the purchase of real capital (human-made inputs) by borrowing from banks and by selling stocks and bonds.

Firm: A production unit that makes such decisions as what goods to produce and how many workers to employ.

Firm's demand for labor: The quantity of labor a firm plans to employ at various wages. Since a firm will hire additional workers because of their contribution to the firm's total revenue, the marginal revenue product of labor is the firm's demand for labor.

Fiscal policy: The attempt to stabilize the business cycle by managing aggregate demand through changes in government purchases, taxes, and transfers.

Fixed inputs: Factors of production that cannot be increased or decreased to adjust output in the given time period. Inputs that are fixed in the short run include buildings, machinery and equipment, and land since it takes firms more time to acquire or to sell these assets than is available in this time period.

Floating exchange standard: Currencies are not fixed in value, either in terms of gold or any currency. Exchange rates are determined by supply and demand conditions in the international money market.

Floor price: See *Price support.*

Free riders: Individuals who cannot be excluded from consuming a good once it is purchased by someone else. For example, when someone beautifies the property around his or her house, those in the neighborhood who enjoy the benefits of a more attractive home in the area are free riders.

Frictional unemployment: Unemployed individuals who are temporarily between jobs (such as the individual going into a better job) and people who have entered the labor force for the first time (such as high school and college graduates).

Full employment: The employment of all persons 16 years of age or older who are able and willing to work in the labor market, excluding those who are frictionally or structurally unemployed.

Full-employment GNP: The level of aggregate supply that could be produced if economic resources are fully employed.

Functional distribution of income: The income earned in the overall economy (national income) broken into components according to the source of income. These components are (1) compensation paid to employees (wages, salaries, and fringe benefits), (2) proprietors' income (the income earned by small businesses), (3) corporate profits, (4) rental income (payments made to persons providing the services of natural resources), and (5) net interest (payments made to the owners of financial capital).

Functional finance: The belief that the government should use the budget to achieve noninflationary full employment.

Gold exchange standard: The practice by which a country fixes the value of its money to another country's currency, which in turn is pegged to gold.

Gold standard: The international monetary system in which a country fixes the value of its currency in terms of gold. To maintain this value, the country's government must be able to buy and sell gold at the officially declared price.

Goldsmith banks: Early banks where people paid to leave their gold in safe surroundings in exchange for a receipt that could be traded for merchandise or exchanged for the gold deposited.

Gompers' trade union philosophy: The trade union philosophy that Gompers developed. It had three cardinal points: (1) unions should avoid political reform movements and only attempt to get concrete economic gains for its own members; (2) individual national unions, which make up the federation, should be stronger than the AFL; and (3) unions should be formed only along craft lines.

Gosbank: The state banking system of the Soviet Union, which monitors the failures and successes of the annual plan as it is being implemented.

Gosplan: The state planning agency of the Soviet Union, which sets production quotas for each specific industry in order to carry out the overall targets of the Council of Ministers. These quotas are set in terms of the central plan.

Government purchases and production: The government may decide to take over production of a firm or group of firms in an industry or purchase large quantities of a good or service in the presence of market failure.

Government expenditures: The sum of government purchases and transfers.

Government failure: Government intervention that does not improve the well-being of society because of the problems associated with X-inefficiency and majority voting.

Government purchases: Purchases of goods and services by government; such as, defense, health, education, and highways.

Government transfers: The redistribution of funds from one group to another through programs such as Social Security, welfare, and unemployment compensation.

Grievance procedure: A clause in a union contract that provides a formal procedure for settling disagreements between management and labor.

Gross national product: The market value of final goods and services produced in the economy in a given period.

Gross private domestic investment: The national income account measure of investment by firms within the United States before the deduction of depreciation.

Health insurance: Insurance that covers a person for potential health problems. Normally, the insurer agrees to pay a portion of an individual's medical bill.

Health maintenance organizations: A health care service for which individuals pay a fixed fee per year regardless of the number of visits made to the HMO. This program attempts to deal with the problem of increasing costs in the health care industry by placing the incentive on the physician to keep the individual well and away from the doctor's office.

Horizontal mergers: Combinations of competing firms producing similar products; for example, a merger between two producers of beer.

Household: The family unit, which makes such decisons as where to work and what goods and services to buy.

Human resources: An economic resource consisting partly of the ability of workers to perform physical tasks. It also contains human capital, which refers to the skills and knowledge that people acquire during their lifetimes as well as the entrepreneurial ability of the owners of businesses.

Immediate consumption benefits of education: The increased satisfaction that a person enjoys while "being a student."

Imperfect substitution of inputs: The case in which the production of different goods requires a different combination of inputs. For example, the production of automobiles requires more capital and less labor relative to the amount of capital and labor needed to produce hand-crafted pottery.

Implicit costs: The opportunity costs of the resources owned by the owners of the firm, calculated as the value of the next best alternative use of these resources. For example, a major implicit cost is the opportunity cost of the owner's time spent in the business, estimated by the highest annual salary that the owner could have earned by working for another firm.

Imports: Goods produced in foreign countries and sold in the United States.

Income approach: A method of measuring GNP by summing all incomes earned by different factors of production owned by households (e.g., wage, rent, interest, profit).

Income gap: The difference between equilibrium GNP and full-employment GNP.

Income multiplier: GNP changes by a multiple of an initial change in autonomous spending. When people spend a part of their income, it creates income for others involved in the production of the goods purchased. They, in turn, spend a part of their income, setting off another round of income creation.

Income policies: An attempt by government to restrain inflationary wage and price increases through wage-price controls. The government tries to reduce the effects of the inflationary psychology by preserving the existing relative shares of income between the various groups that make up our economy.

Inconvertible money standard: A monetary standard which states that money cannot freely be converted into gold or silver through government.

Independent good: A good that is neither a substitute nor a complementary good. If the price of an independent good changes (e.g., pencils), it will not affect the demand for other independent goods (e.g., housing).

Indexing: Changes in salaries, wages, interest rates, and other components of income are tied to the inflation rate.

Induced consumption: The positive relationship between consumer spending and income. For example, when income increases, it induces households to spend more.

Induction: A method of reasoning from many specific cases to a general conclusion.

Industrial union: An organization of skilled and unskilled workers in a given industry.

Inelastic supply or demand: The case where the change in quantity is not very responsive to a change in price. More specifically, the percentage change in the quantity demanded or the quantity supplied is less than the percentage change in price. As a result, the elasticity coefficient is less than 1.

Inferior good: An increase in income causes a decrease in the demand for this type of good.

Inflation: A general rise in the prices of goods and services.

Inflationary gap: The amount by which aggregate demand exceeds full-employment supply.

Inflationary psychology: The expectation of continued high inflation in the future.

Innovation: A change in technology.

Inputs: See *Economic resources.*

Institutional prices: Prices established by government.

Intercepts: Points that fall on the horizontal and vertical axes of a graph. They account for all influences other than the independent variable.

Interest rate: The percentage of return to persons who provide financial capital.

Interlocking directorates: The situation where a member of the board of directors of one company is also on the board of directors of a competing company.

Inventories: The stock of produced goods not yet sold by the firm.

Inverse relationship: A relationship between two variables such that an increase in one variable is associated with a decrease in the other.

Investment: An increase in the stock of capital goods.

Jurisdictional disputes: A disagreement between unions trying to organize the same group of workers.

Keynesian model: A macroeconomic model that examines how changes in aggregate demand (or total spending) create the business cycle.

Labor market imbalances: A factor contributing to the Phillips curve trade-off. As total spending for goods increases in the overall economy, the demand for more educated workers with skills rises. This pushes their wage rates up, contributing to inflation. At the same time, the demand remains low for less educated people without skills, causing persistent unemployment.

Labor productivity: The measure of the amount of output produced per hour of labor.

Labor-intensive technology: A technology in which the amount of labor used per unit of output produced is relatively higher than the amount of other inputs used per unit of output.

Labor-Management Relations Act: See the *Taft-Hartley Act.*

Labor-Management Reporting and Disclosure Act: See the *Landrum-Griffin Act.*

Lagging indicators: Measures of economic activity that reflect changes after the economy has turned up or down. They are used to confirm whatever signal the leading indicators gave.

Land-intensive technology: A technology in which the amount of land used per unit of output produced is relatively higher than the amount of other inputs used per unit of output.

Landrum-Griffin Act: An act passed in 1959 to reduce corruption in the management of unions as well as to make unions more democratic. The law has two basic provisions: (1) it established the Bureau of Labor-Management Reports (BLMR) to collect information from the unions concerning their constitutions and the financial dealings of its officers, and (2) it included a "Bill of Rights" for union members, guaranteeing them a right to vote for candidates for union offices by secret ballot.

Law of demand: Households are willing and able to buy less of a good as the price of that good increases in a specific time period, assuming all other influences do not change.

Law of diminishing returns: As more units of a variable input (such as labor) are combined with a fixed input (such as land or capital), eventually the extra output per additional variable input will fall.

Law of increasing costs: To produce more and more of one good, society must give up an increasing amount of other goods.

Law of supply: Competitive firms will increase the amount they offer for sale as the price of their product increases in a given time period, given all other influences.

Leading indicators: Measures of economic activity that reflect upswings and downswings in the economy before current GNP shows the change.

Leakage-injection equality: One of the equilibrium conditions for GNP in the Keynesian model which states that income that is not spent is equal to spending injected into the economy. Without government, the condition is met when savings equal planned investment. With government, the condition is met when net taxes plus savings equals government purchases plus planned investment.

Local unions: The first labor unions, organized in major cities across the East Coast by skilled craftspersons (e.g., printers, carpenters).

Long run: (1) In the *product market,* the time period long enough for firms to make any adjustment in production. All inputs are variable, and there is sufficient time for firms to enter or to exit the market. (2) In the *labor market,* households have enough time to migrate, to find new occupations, and to acquire more education and new skills.

Long-run average costs for an industry: The cost of production per unit of output for all firms in the market in the long run. The long-run average cost curve for an industry may be constant, decreasing, or increasing.

Long-run investment benefits of higher education: Benefits that a student receives over his or her lifetime after graduation, which include both monetary and nonmonetary components.

Long-run supply: The same as a competitive industry's long-run average cost curve since price is eventually driven to the average cost of roduction by the entry and exiting of firms.

Long-term poverty programs: Public policies geared to eliminate the root causes of poverty such as inadequate education and training.

Lorenz curve: A curve used to illustrate the distribution of income and wealth. It shows the accumulative percentages of total income received by families, where the families are ranked by income bracket from the poorest to the richest.

Loss: The amount by which total revenue falls short of total cost.

Lump-sum tax: A tax that is autonomous (independent of income).

Lump-sum transfer: A transfer that is autonomous (independent of income).

Macroeconomics: The study of aggregate economic behavior. Macroeconomics examines the business cycle, focusing on the causes of unemployment and inflation.

Majority voting: A method of decision making frequently used to make choices in the public sector in which the majority of voters determine public policy for everyone.

Make-work rules: Union rules designed to maintain the number of workers that a firm must employ (e.g., requiring time-consuming production methods or excessively large work crews).

Managed float: A variation of the floating exchange standard under which trading nations have agreed to use their central banks to help stabilize sharp fluctuations in their exchange rates.

Marginal analysis: The process by which a decision maker balances the additional cost against the additional benefit in taking a given course of action. For example, a firm will increase output as long as the extra revenue exceeds the extra cost of production.

Marginal cost of labor: The cost of hiring an

additional worker, calculated as the change in total labor costs divided by the change in labor.

Marginal cost of production: The cost of producing one additional unit of output, calculated by dividing the change in total cost by the change in output.

Marginal cost pricing: Pricing by the $MR = MC$ rule.

Marginal physical product of labor: The contribution that each additional worker makes to production, measured as the change in total output divided by the change in labor.

Marginal profit: The change in total profit per additional unit of output, which is calculated by subtracting the marginal cost of production from the marginal revenue.

Marginal propensity to consume: The fraction of additional income that households plan to spend.

Marginal propensity to save: The fraction of additional income that households plan to save.

Marginal revenue: Revenue received from selling one additional unit of output, calculated by dividing the change in total revenue by the change in output.

Marginal revenue product of labor: The contribution that an additional worker makes to the firms's total revenue, calculated as the change in total revenue divided by the change in the number of workers employed.

Marginal social benefit: The benefit to society of each additional unit of a good produced, such as education.

Marginal social cost: The additional cost to society of each unit of a good produced.

Market: A place where buyers and sellers interact, establishing the price and the quantity sold during a given period of time. There are two types: the product market and the factor market.

Market demand curve: See *Demand curve.*

Market demand schedule: See *Demand schedule.*

Market failure: The failure of the market to allocate resources efficiently; this occurs because some firms possess market power and some activities produce externalities.

Market period: The time period in which a given amount of output has been produced and is ready to be sold on the market. There is not sufficient time for firms to increase production.

Market supply curve: See *Supply curve.*

Market supply schedule: See *Supply schedule.*

Medium of exchange: The role of money when it is used to purchase or sell an item.

Microeconomics: The study of the behavior and the interaction of firms and households in markets.

Mixed economy: An economy in which there is a private enterprise system plus a role for government. While individuals act out of self-interest, government attempts to act in the collective interest of all members of society.

Monetarism: A philosophy that emphasizes the steady growth in the money supply in stabilizing the economy. Monetarists believe that by allowing the money supply to grow at a rate equal to the increase in productivity each year, the economy will experience long-term noninflationary growth.

Monetary policy: The attempt to stabilize the business cycle by controlling the money supply.

Money: Anything that is commonly accepted in exchange for goods and services.

Money GNP: The measure of GNP that takes into account current prices (also called nominal or current GNP).

Money multiplier: The potential amount by which the banking system can expand its loans and therefore the money supply, given an increase in excess reserves. It equals the reciprocal of the reserve requirement.

Money supply: Assets that can be used directly as a medium of exchange, a standard unit of value, and as a store of value.

Monopolistic competition: The market structure in which there are: (1) many buyers and sellers and acting independently, (2) product differentiation which gives each firm slight control over price, and (3) free entry in the long run.

Monopoly profit: Above-normal profit that results from the control that monopolies and oligopolies exert over supply. By restricting production, given significant barriers to entry, firms with market power can raise the price at which they sell their product above the level that would have prevailed in a competitive market.

MR = MC rule: The rule that states that to maximize total profit, the firm should produce that level of output at which marginal revenue *(MR)* equals marginal cost *(MC)*.

$MRP_L = MC_L$ rule: The rule that states that the profit-maximizing level of employment for any firm is always that level of employment where the marginal revenue product of labor *(MRP_L)* equals the marginal cost of labor *(MC_L)*. As long as the marginal revenue product of labor exceeds the marginal cost of labor, the firm will have the incentive to hire more workers since total profit will increase as additional workers are hired.

Mutual interdependency in pricing: The pricing practice in which each of the dominant firms in an oligopoly considers the effects of its pricing decision on its rivals and the possible reactions of these rivals to its price change. Because the number of dominant sellers is small enough for the pricing activities of a single seller to affect the pricing activities of other firms, mutual interdependency in pricing will likely lead to price-leadership behavior and, occasionally, overt collusion.

National debt: The debt of the federal government, which is created when the government borrows money from households, financial institutions, and other sources.

National health insurance: A public program that would allow all citizens to get medical care when they need it.

National income: A measure of total income earned. It is equal to net national product minus indirect business taxes.

National income accounting: The federal government's collection and dissemination of data describing production, employment, prices, and international trade.

National Labor Relations Act: See the *Wagner Act.*

National Labor Relations Board: A federal agency that implements the policy provisions of the National Labor Relations Act (the Wagner Act). The NLRB has the following two functions: (1) to investigate disputes over unfair labor practice charges and (2) to conduct election proceedings in an effort to decide whether or not the workers of a particular firm want to form a union.

National unions: Organizations of craftspersons of the same skill located in different cities (e.g., printers in Boston forming a union with printers in Philadelphia).

Natural monopoly: A monopoly that has arisen because of economies of scale.

Natural resources: Economic resources that exist in nature (not made by humans) such as land, water, air, and the deposits of minerals.

Near-money: Assets that, while not directly spendable, can be easily converted for transactions. These assets are less liquid than demand deposits, which means that they are not as easy to convert into currency.

Net exports: Exports minus imports.

Net national product: The total output available for use, calculated by deducting depreciation from GNP.

Net taxes: Taxes minus transfers.

Nominal GNP: The money value of goods and services sold at current prices (also called current or money GNP).

Nondurable goods: Goods that have an expected life of one year or less (e.g., milk, beef).

Nonprice determinants of demand: Factors other than the current price of the product that affect how much we plan to buy. They are also called demand-shift factors because a change in any of them will shift the demand curve (a change in demand). This is to be distinguished from a movement along the curve caused by a change in the current price of the product (a change in the quantity demanded).

Nonprice determinants of supply: Factors other than the current price of the product that affect the production decisions of firms. These factors are also called shift factors since a change in any one of them will shift the supply curve (a change in supply). This is to be distinguished from a movement along the curve caused by a change in the current price of the product (a change in the quantity supplied).

Nonrival consumption: For a given amount of production, the consumption of a good by one person does not reduce the amount of the good available for others to consume.

Nonwage determinants of the demand for labor: Factors that, when changed, will shift the demand for labor (also called shift factors).

Nonwage determinants of the supply of labor: Factors that, when changed, will shift the supply of labor (also called shift factors).

Normal goods: Goods for which demand increases as income increases.

Normal profit: The return necessary to cover the opportunity cost of the resources possessed by the persons who own the firm, including the time spent in the business, the market value of their buildings, and land. In addition, normal profit is partially a measure of the opportunity cost of the risk that they take when they commit resources to business ventures that may fail. It is also a payment for entrepreneurial ability, referring to the special skills that are involved in the management of a business.

Normative economics: Value judgments concerning what ought to be.

Norris-LaGuardia Act: The first federal law in labor-management relations, passed in 1932. The purpose of this act was to remove the obstacles that the courts had set up against the efforts of labor to organize. It gave workers the freedom to form unions as well as to strike peacefully. In addition, the act outlawed yellow-dog contracts and eliminated the primary weapon of firms — abusive use of the court injunction.

Official poverty line: The income measure used by the federal government to count the number of poor persons in the United States.

Oligopoly: An industry dominated by several large firms, with mutual interdependency in pricing and significant barriers to entry. There are two types of oligopolies: (1) differentiated oligopolies, in which firms produce products that are good substitutes for each other but are in some way different (e.g., automobiles), and (2) pure oligopolies, in which firms produce identical products (e.g., aluminum).

Open market operations: The buying and selling of U.S. government bonds by the Federal Reserve Open Market Committee. Through open market operations, the Federal Reserve can tighten or loosen bank reserves and thereby change the money supply.

Operational lag: The time it takes for public policy to have the desired effect once a program is implemented.

Optimal amount of pollution control: The socially desirable amount of pollution control produced that occurs where the value placed on an additional unit of pollution prevention by society (marginal social benefit) is exactly equal to the additional cost to society of producing it (marginal social cost).

Overt collusion: Collusion that occurs if the dominant producers in an oligopoly formally agree upon what prices to charge for their products. Collusive contracts are not enforceable by the courts and are illegal.

Peak: The top of the business cycle, occurring where actual output is highest.

Perfectly inelastic supply: The condition in which the quantity supplied is not affected by changes in price since firms cannot produce any more of the product; the supply curve is a vertical line. See *Market period.*

Personal consumption expenditures: The expenditures on goods and services by households.

Personal income: A measure of income received. It is equal to national income minus Social Security contributions minus retained earnings minus corporate taxes plus transfers.

Phillips curve trade-off: An increase in demand will reduce unemployment at the expense of a higher rate of inflation given the Phillips curve. Conversely, a reduction in demand will achieve lower inflation, but at the cost of higher unemployment.

Planned investment: The intended expenditure by firms to construct new plants and equipment and to build up inventories.

Pollution: Consumption and production by-products that accumulate in the environment.

Positive economics: Statements of fact that are empirically verifiable using the scientific method. It involves what was, what is, and what will be.

Post hoc fallacy: An erroneous cause-effect conclusion that implies that because B follows A, B was caused by A.

Premature inflation: An increase in total spending within the intermediate range of the *AS* curve which causes inflation to occur before full-employment is reached.

Price controls: Government action that forces firms to rescind price increases that exceed the price targets established by law (unless the price increases can be justified on the basis of higher production costs).

Price discrimination: The practice of a firm selling the same product to two different groups of buyers at different prices even though the cost of supplying the good to these two groups of buyers is the same.

Price-fixing: Collusion which occurs when firms jointly set prices.

Price leadership: A process through which firms in an oligopolistic market reach an agreed-upon price. In the case of three firms, if firm X decides to increase its price, firms Y and Z simply agree to follow suit. Price leadership is not an illegal practice since it does not involve overt collusion to restrain trade.

Price-price spiral: Inflation caused by firms which increase the price of their products in anticipation of inflation.

Price support: An institutional price that is set above the market equilibrium price. It is also called a floor price, since it prevents the actual market price from falling to the equilibrium position (i.e., the actual price hits the "floor" and stops).

Price support program: Establishes an institutional price to stabilize farm prices at levels Congress deemed "fair" to farmers. To prevent the actual price from falling, the federal government buys surplus farm produce at the support price.

Price taker: A firm that has no control over the market price. It must accept the price which is determined by the supply and demand conditions of the purely competitive market.

Principle of comparative advantage: Each nation can gain through trade by specializing in the production of those goods that it can make relatively more efficiently.

Private market system: The market system based on private property (the ownership of assets by individuals) and the concept of self-interest motivation.

Private property: Ownership of assets such as land and buildings by individuals (rather than by government).

Procyclical: A policy that pushes the economy farther into a recession or increases inflationary pressures.

Product differentiation: Differences in the products produced in a particular industry. The quality difference might be *real* in the sense that it performs better or *imagined* if we simply believe it is a better product because of successful advertising.

Product market: The market for goods and services produced such as houses, cars, and medical services.

Production possibilities model: All possible combinations of two goods that an economy can produce given the following assumptions: (1) only two types of goods and services are produced, (2) all inputs are limited in amount and are fully employed, and (3) the state of technology is not changing, the substitution of inputs is imperfect, and the most efficient technologies available are used.

Profit: See *Normal profit, Economic profit,* and *Monopoly profit.*

Profit-push inflation: Inflation caused by an increase in prices by firms in anticipation of inflation. Their attempt to protect their real profits reduces aggregate supply, which causes inflation.

Progressive tax: A tax in which persons with higher income pay out a larger percentage of their income in taxes compared with persons with lower income.

Prohibitive tariff: A tariff which raises the international price of a good to the level which would have prevailed in that country without trade, which eliminates imports of that good.

Property rights: Rights that result from laws that allow or prohibit the manner in which property is used.

Proportional tax: A tax in which persons with higher income pay out the same percentage of their income in taxes as persons with lower income.

Public debt: See *National debt*.

Public interest approach: The theory of regulation that proposes that the government should improve the allocation of resources when there is market failure.

Public property: Assets owned by society through government such as roads, forest preserves, and military bases.

Public utility: A firm which is given the right to be the sole producer by government because the firm is a natural monopoly. In exchange for this right, government has the authority to regulate the price which the firm charges the public.

Pure competition: A model used to describe how buyers and sellers would interact in the market under perfect conditions. The purely competitive market model is based on the following assumptions: (1) there are many households and many small firms in the market acting independently of each other, (2) each firm in a given industry produces an identical product, and (3) there is free entry and exiting of firms in the long run. The result of these assumptions is that the individual firm or household has no control over price.

Pure monopoly: A model in which there is only one firm selling a unique product, which means that there are no close substitutes for the good.

The monopolist can remain as the only seller due to barriers that prevent rival firms from entering the market.

Pure private good: A good subject to the exclusion principle and rival consumption.

Pure public good: A good which is not subject to the exclusion principle and rival consumption.

Rational expectations theory: The belief that countercyclical policy will have little or no impact on real output because people are able to anticipate policy changes correctly over time and make the adjustments necessary to protect their relative shares of income.

Real capital: See *Capital*.

Real GNP: The market value of current production, measured in constant prices.

Real income: The purchasing power of money income (i.e., the value of the goods that can be purchased with the dollars earned after these dollars are adjusted for inflation). If money income grows at a slower rate than inflation, then real income will fall.

Recession: An economic downturn in the economy in which real GNP declines for two consecutive quarters or more.

Recessionary gap: The amount by which total demand is less than full-employment supply. A recessionary gap results in unemployment.

Recognition lag: The time it takes policymakers to realize that the economy is (1) heading downward into a recession, (2) reaching full employment, or (3) approaching an inflationary period.

Regressive tax: A tax in which persons with lower income pay out a larger percentage of their income in taxes compared with persons with higher income.

Rent: Income paid to the owners of natural resources, such as land and minerals.

Required reserves: The dollar amount kept on deposit at a Federal Reserve bank calculated by multiplying total deposits by the reserve requirement.

Reserve requirement: The percentage of their deposits that banks must keep at a Federal Reserve bank or other financial institution.

Rival consumption: The benefits of a good which only satisfies the person who consumes the good.

Robinson-Patman Act: An act passed in 1936 with the intention of toughening the price discrimination provision of the Clayton Act.

Role of economic loss: If firms in the market begin experiencing economic loss, they will cut back production in the short run by laying off workers and reducing their employment of other variable inputs. In the long-run period, when there is sufficient time for firms to sell their plant facilities, land, and other inputs that were previously fixed in the short run, firms will go out of business.

Role of economic profit: If economic profit appears in the market, existing firms will be motivated to produce more output in the short run by employing more workers and other variable inputs. In the long-run period, when there is sufficient time for entry, new firms will appear in the market in search of this above-normal (economic) profit.

Role of prices: (1) In the case of a shortage in the product market, households bid the price of the good up, which signals the need for increased production while some households are rationed out of the market. (2) In the case of a surplus in the product market, firms bid the price of the good down, which signals the need for decreased production while some households are rationed into the market.

Role of wages: (1) In the case of a shortage in the labor market, firms bid the wage up, which signals the need for increased labor services from households while some firms are rationed out of the market. (2) In the case of a surplus in the labor market, households bid the wage down, which signals the need for decreased labor services while some firms are rationed into the market.

Savings: Income received by households that is not spent.

Savings-investment equality: The GNP equilibrium condition in the absence of government in which planned investment equals savings.

Say's law: A basic assumption of the classical economists, which states that production creates a level of income sufficient to purchase the goods produced. Supply creates its own demand.

Scarcity: Due to limited resources, it is not possible to produce enough goods and services to satisfy our unlimited wants.

Scientific method: The formulation of questions about the relationships between different possibilities (called variables). It involves a systematic procedure for seeking the truth.

Seasonal unemployment: Individuals who are periodically laid off because of changes in the seasons. For example, farm workers are temporarily unemployed during the winter.

Self-interest: The motivation of individuals to behave in a manner that benefits themselves.

Semipublic goods: The many goods and services that are characterized by degrees of privateness or publicness. People can be excluded from consuming them and they have external benefits.

Seniority principle: A procedure that gives workers with the most years in the company the first opportunity to be considered in such matters as promotion, choice of vacation time, and parking lot privileges.

Sherman Act: An act passed in 1890 designed to furnish the courts with the power to deal with restraints of trade. It suffered from general language, opening it to a wide variety of interpretations.

Shortage: (1) In the product market, households are seeking to buy more of a particular good than firms have to sell at the current price. (2) In the factor market, firms are seeking to employ more of a particular input than households plan to sell at the current price.

Short run: (1) In the *product market,* a time period in which there are (a) both variable and fixed inputs and (b) no entry or exiting of firms. This time period is longer than the market period since firms have some ability to adjust production to changes in market conditions. (2) In the *labor market,* there is not sufficient time for households to migrate from one area of the country to another or to move from one occupation to another. In addition, workers do not have enough time to acquire more education or new skills.

Short-term poverty programs: Income maintenance policies aimed at relieving the symptoms of poverty. These programs are broken down into two components: (1) cash assistance programs, which give the recipients a transfer of money to spend as they choose, and (2) assistance in kind, which provides specific goods and services to the poor.

Slope: A measure of the steepness of a curve, calculated as the change in variable Y (measured on the vertical axis) divided by the change in X (measured on the horizontal axis).

Social costs: Costs to society, made up of private costs and external costs.

Stabilization policy: The federal government's attempt to smooth the business cycle by increasing or decreasing total demand.

Stagflation: The coexistence of unemployment and inflation, with *stag* referring to stagnation (i.e., unemployment) and *flation* referring to inflation.

Standard unit of value: The role of money when it is used to express the prices of goods.

State ownership of capital: In a command economy, the government owns and operates factories, machinery and equipment, and other forms of capital (e.g., the Soviet economy).

Store of value: The role of money when it is saved so it can be spent in the future.

Strike: Members of a labor union agree not to work for a specific employer until certain conditions are met.

Strike funds: A portion of union dues is held to support the income of workers during a strike.

Structural unemployment: Unemployment resulting from a mismatch in the composition of supply and demand conditions in the labor market because of the lack of education and skills, people located in the wrong geographic locations, and discrimination.

Subsidies: A cash transfer from one group to another. An example is a payment to a family in poverty under the welfare program.

Substitute good: A good that we may use easily instead of another product. An increase in the price of a substitute good (e.g., butter) will increase the demand for the other good (e.g., margarine).

Suburbanization: The growth of areas surrounding cities.

Supply curve: The curve showing the quantity that sellers are willing and able to sell at various prices in a given time period, given all other influences.

Supply of loanable funds: The quantity of loanable funds supplied is positively related to the interest rate. As the interest rate rises, households will be induced to put more of their money into the loanable funds market (via savings accounts and the purchase of private bonds) rather than spending it.

Supply schedule: The table showing the quantity that sellers are willing and able to sell at various prices in a given time period, given all other influences.

Surplus: (1) In the product market, households are seeking to buy less of a particular good than firms plan to sell at the current price. (2) In the factor market, firms are seeking to employ less of a particular input than households plan to sell at the current price.

Surplus budget: The budget position that exists when tax revenues exceed government spending.

Taft-Hartley Act: An act passed in 1947 that has two major provisions: (1) it defines unfair labor practices on the part of unions, and (2) it contains a national emergency clause that gives the president of the United States the ability to declare an 80-day cooling-off period if the strike is deemed dangerous to the health or safety of the general public.

Target price program: The federal government directly subsidizes individual farmers with low income. The federal government pays farmers a cash subsidy (called a "deficiency payment") in the amount of the difference between the target price and the equilibrium market price multiplied by the quantity sold.

Tariff: A tax that government places on imports.

Technical efficiency: An engineering concept that entails producing an output with the least amount of inputs.

Technology: A method of production.

Third parties: Persons outside a market transaction between buyers and sellers (the first and second parties).

Third-party payers: Institutions such as insurance companies and government who pay some portion of a patient's health care costs.

Three basic economic problems: The way in which an economy produces and distributes goods depends on its solution to the three basic economic problems: (1) what to produce and in what quantity, (2) how to produce, and (3) for whom to produce.

Time periods: See the three time periods—*Market period, Short run,* and *Long run.*

Total costs of production: The overall cost of producing goods, made up of explicit costs and implicit costs.

Total reserve: The total amount of currency held by commercial banks.

Total revenue: Total sales receipts (income) received by the firm, calculated by multiplying price (or average revenue) by the quantity sold.

Transfers: Government programs that involve the redistribution of funds from one group to another through such programs as Social Security, welfare, and unemployment compensation.

Trough: The bottom of the business cycle; the lowest point of business activity relative to how much could be produced at full employment.

Turnover costs: The expenditures that firms make in attempting to hire and train new employees after their former workers quit.

Uncertainty: Less than perfect information.

Unemployment rate: The percentage of people in the labor market who are willing and able to work but cannot find jobs.

Unintended change in inventories: See *Unplanned investment.*

Union shop: The worker is not required to join the union until a specified time period has passed after he or she is hired (e.g., 30 days).

Unitary elasticity of supply or demand: The percentage change in the quantity demanded or the quantity supplied is equal to the percentage change in price. As a result, the elasticity coefficient is equal to 1.

Unplanned investment: A change in inventories above or below the planned level.

Variable inputs: Factors of production that can be increased or decreased by firms in the given time period.

Velocity: The average number of times each unit of money is used in transactions per year.

Vertical merger: Combination between a firm and its supplier, for example, a merger between a book publisher and a paper mill.

Vicious circle of poverty: The tendency for individuals born into poor families to acquire characteristics that preclude them from getting jobs that pay enough to raise them out of poverty when they become adults.

Wage controls: A federal law which prevents workers from receiving wage increases in excess of a certain percentage prescribed by the federal government (unless the wage hike can be justified in terms of advances in labor productivity).

Wage-price spiral: Inflation caused by workers which demand an increase in their wages in anticipation of inflation.

Wage-push inflation: Inflation that results when the expectation of continued high inflation causes unions to make wage demands in excess of productivity to maintain the purchasing power of the money income. Their attempt to protect real wages reduces aggregate supply, which causes inflation.

Wagner Act: A revolutionary law passed in 1935 with two important provisions: (1) it defined unfair labor practices on the part of firms, and (2) it set up the National Labor Relations

Board (NLRB) to implement the policy provisions of this new law.

X-inefficiency: The less than optimal use of resources within the firm. It can occur because of poor management, poor organizational structure, or poor performance of employees due to a lack of the profit motive.

Yardstick approach: The policy under which the government obtains control of one firm in an industry so that they may then use this firm to (1) compete aggressively against others, driving the price down, or (2) to obtain information about the costs of production, which can be used to regulate price.

Index